Comparative Corporate Governance

Comparative Corporate Governance

– Essays and Materials –

Edited by

Klaus J. Hopt

Director of the Max-Planck-Institute
for Foreign Private and Private International Law,
Hamburg, Germany

Eddy Wymeersch

Professor at the University of Ghent, Belgium
Director of the Seminar of Commercial and Enterprise Law

W DE G

1997

Walter de Gruyter · Berlin · New York

Library of Congress Cataloging-in-Publication Data

Comparative corporate governance : essays and materials / edited by Klaus J. Hopt and Eddy Wymeersch.
XIV, 356 p. 15,5 × 23,0 cm.
"This book has grown out of a conference entitled 'Comparative Corporate Governance, an International Conference, United States – Japan – Western Europe' which was held in Brussels on 14 June 1995" – Pref.
English with some contributions in French and German.
ISBN 3-11-015765-9
1. Corporate governance – Congresses. 2. Comparative management – Congresses. 3. Corporate governance – Law and legislation – Congresses. 4. Comparative law – Congresses. I. Hopt, Klaus J., 1940– . II. Wymeersch, E.
HD2741.C6247 1997
658.4–dc21 97-27485
CIP

Die Deutsche Bibliothek – CIP-Einheitsaufnahme

Comparative corporate governance : essays and materials / ed. by Klaus J. Hopt and Eddy Wymeersch. – Berlin ; New York : de Gruyter, 1997
ISBN 3-11-015765-9

Printing: WB-Druck, D-87669 Rieden am Forggensee
Binding: Lüderitz & Bauer GmbH, D-10963 Berlin
Printed in Germany.

Preface

Corporate governance has become an important issue in all industrial economies. Corporate governance relates to the internal organization and power structure of the firm, the functioning of the board of directors both in the one-tier and the two-tier system, the ownership structure of the firm, and the interrelationships among management, board, shareholders and possibly stakeholders, in particular the workforce of the enterprise and the creditors. These interrelationships include monitoring of the management by the board and external supervisors, and shareholder activism.

Most large companies around the world are facing governance issues, either at the level of the board's composition, role and behavior, or with respect to the company's relationship with shareholders - particularly large shareholders and institutional investors - as well as other stakeholders. These governance issues come up in governance systems that are quite varied. They differ widely from country to country. The Anglo-Saxon scheme and the German-Dutch model are perhaps the most prominent systems. The former is a more market oriented system, while the latter is more oriented towards enterprise organization and bank influence. The differences in governance may be related to substantial differences in financial structures, in particular the prevalence of securities financing in the Anglo-Saxon countries (with the far-reaching separation of credit banks and investment banks imposed by law in the United States) versus the predominant role of the banking system, especially of the universal banking system, in Germanic countries. Other governance systems such as the Japanese keiretsu system lead to different outcomes. The path dependency of these systems is patent, while the evaluation of this dependency is highly complex.

This book has grown out of a conference entitled "Comparative Corporate Governance, An International Conference, United States - Japan - Western Europe" which was held in Brussels on 14 June 1995. It was organized by the Financial Law Institute of the University of Ghent, and the Study Center on Groups of Enterprises in Brussels under the scientific direction of Eddy Wymeersch. The book contains the contributions by the speakers in an enlarged and updated form together with source material and references. The Business Roundtable on Corporate Governance in Belgium was chaired by Professor J.L. Duplat, chairman of the Commission bancaire et financière, Brussels. Although it attracted much attention at the conference, it did not present itself to being printed. Instead we have collected a selection of 18 documents on corporate governance from 7 countries (United Kingdom, USA, Canada, France, Germany, the Netherlands and Belgium). By far the most are in English language with a very few left in their original French and German version. These documents date from the 1990s, most of them from 1995 and

1996, and are to be made available more easily to business and academia in other countries than the one in which they have been elaborated. They offer a wealth of data, insights, self-regulatory experiences and legislative proposals which show that, despite all the national deep-rooted differences, the core problems are very similar indeed.

The book is the first of a series of publications which is to be edited by both of us in collaboration with colleages from the United States and Japan. The next publication will collect contributions on the field with an interdisciplinary and international focus as arising from the Symposion on "Comparative Corporate Governance - The State of the Art and Emerging Research" held from 15 to 17 May 1997 at the Max Planck Institute for Foreign Private and Private International Law at Hamburg.

We thank the sponsors, the contributors and the numerous participants in the Brussels Conference who by their enthusiastic response to the topic made us plan this publication, to the many persons and organizations who kindly contributed the documents and to our assistants and secretaries, in particular Mrs. Stahl at the Max-Planck-Institute who unremittingly and with technical expertise converted the manuscripts and documents into a print ready format.

Hamburg and Brussels, April 1997

Klaus J. Hopt *Eddy Wymeersch*

Table of Contents

Part One: Essays

Part Two: Materials

IV. France

V. Germany

VI. The Netherlands

VII. Belgium

The Contributors

Erik Berglöf

Associate Professor, Director, Stockholm Institute of Transition Economics and East European Economies (SITE), Stockholm School of Economics 1996; Assistant Professor ECARE Université Libre de Bruxelles 1991-1996; Expert for different EC-related panels and teams, i.a.: Invited Expert, Academic Panel for evaluation of the effects of the internal market, Team Leader, EC team to provide advice for the Russian Government; Center for Economic Policy Research (CEPR) Fellow.

Author of: Corporate Control and Capital Structure - Essay on Property Rights and Financial Contracting (1991) IIB; Ownership and Control in the Firm - A Comparative Study of Six Financial Systems (1988) SOU; Corporate Governance Reform - Redirecting the European Agenda, (1997) Economic Policy; Short-term vs. Long-term Interests - Capital Structure with Multiple Investors, Quarterly J. of Economics (1994) (with E.-L. von Thadden); Corporate Governance Structure of the Japanese Financial Keitretsu, 36 J. Fin. Econ. (1994) (with E. Perotti); A Control Theory of Venture Capital, (1994) J. of Law, Economics and Organization; Corporate Governance, Financial Systems and the Transition of Capitalism - Towards a Conceptual Framework, (1977) Property Rights, Incentives and Welfare.

Paul L. Davis

Fellow and Tutor in Law, Balliol College, Oxford and Professor of Law of the Enterprise in the University of Oxford; born 1944; BA, Oxford, 1966; MA (Oxon); LL.M., London, 1968; LL.M., Yale, 1969; Lecturer in Law, University of Warwick, 1969-73; visiting Assistant Professor, Yale Law School, 1975; Leverhulme Fellow, Centre de Droit Comparé du Travail et de la Sécurité Sociale, Université de Bordeaux, 1980; Research Consultant to the Committee of Inquiry on Industrial Democracy, 1976; Expert appointed by the Commission of the EC on the revision of the Transfers Directive.

Author of: Labour Law: Text and Materials (1st and 2nd editions, with M.R. Freedland); Kahn-Freund's Labour and the Law (3rd edition, 1983, with M.R. Freedland); (with others) Palmer's Company Law (23rd, 24th and 25th editions); Take-overs and Mergers (1976); Editor, Gower's Principles of Modern Company Law, 6th ed., 1997; Labour Law and Public Policy (1993); Various articles in professional journals on employment law, company law and securities regulation.

Klaus J. HOPT

Professor of commercial and business law and director at the Max-Planck-Institute for Foreign Private and Private International Law in Hamburg. Dr. iur. h.c. (ULB, Brussels 1997), Dr. iur. h.c. (UCL, Louvain 1997); Professor of Law in Tübingen, Florence, Bern and Munich (1974-1995); Judge, Court of Appeals of Stuttgart (1981-85); Member of International Fcaulty; Visiting professor in Brussels ULB, Paris I, Geneva, Univ. of Tokyo, Univ. of Kyoto, Univ. of Pennsylvania and Univ. of Chicago.

Author of: Kapitalanlegerschutz im Recht der Banken (1975); Legal Harmonization and the Business Enterprise (1988, with Buxbaum); Kommentar zum Handelsgesetzbuch (Baumbach-Duden, 29th ed. 1995); Ed.: Groups of companies in European Law (1982); Corporate Governance and Directors' Liabilities (with Teubner, 1985); European Business Law (with Buxbaum et al., 1991); European Insider Dealing (1991), European Takeovers (1992), and European Company and Financial Law, 2nd ed. 1994 (all with Wymeersch); Institutional Investors and Corporate Governance (1994, with Baums, Buxbaum); European Business and Enterprise Law (with Buxbaum et al., 1996); Börsenreform (with Rudolph et al., 1997).

Hideki KANDA

Hideki Kanda is Professor of Law at the University of Tokyo. Mr. Kanda was born in 1953 and received an LL.B. from the University of Tokyo. His main areas of specialization include commercial law, corporate law, securities regulation and banking regulation. Mr. Kanda served as Visiting Professor of Law at the University of Chicago Law School in 1989, 1991 and 1993, and at Harvard Law School in 1996.

Author of several English language articles on corporate and securities law: Debtholders and Equityholders, 21 Journal of Legal Studies (1992) 431; Explaining Creditor Priorities, 80 Virginia L. Rev. (1994) 2103 (with S. Levmore); Politics, Formalism and the Elusive Goal of Investor Protection: Regulation of Structured Investment Funds in Japan, 12 U.Pa.J.Int'l.Bus.L. (1991) 569; Taxes, Agency Costs, and the Price of Incorporation, 77 Virg. L. Rev. (1991) 211 (with S. Levmore); The Stock Exchange as a Firm: The Emergence of Close Substitutes for the New York and Tokyo Stock Exchanges, 75 Cornell L. Rev. (1990) 1007 (with J. Macey).

Steven N. KAPLAN

Professor of Finance at the Graduate School of Business of the University of Chicago. He has been a member of the faculty since 1988. Professor Kaplan earned his Ph.D. in Business Economics from Harvard University. He received his A.B., summa cum lauda, in Applied Mathematics and Economics from Harvard College. Prior to completing his Ph.D. studies, Professor Kaplan held positions with Kidder, Peabody & Co. and Booz, Allen & Hamilton.

Professor Kaplan's research, teaching, and consulting focus on issues in corporate restructuring, corporate governance and corporate finance. He has published papers in the Journal of Finance, The Journal of Financial Economics, The Journal of Political Economy, The Quarterly Journal of Economics, The Journal of Applied Corporate Finance, and the Journal of Law, Economics and Organizations. Professor Kaplan and his work are cited regularly in the popular press on corporate restructuring and governance issues. Currently, Professor Kaplan serves on the editorial board of The Journal of Finance and Quantitative Analysis, and European Financial Management. He is also a Faculty Research Fellow at the National Bureau of Economic Research.

Professor Kaplan teaches an advanced M.B.A. course financial management. Professor Kaplan was named one of the top 12 business school teachers in the United States in Business Week's 1994 Survey of M.B.A. programs.

Mark. J. ROE

Professor of Law at Columbia Law School.

Author of: Strong Managers, Weak Owners, The political Roots of American Corporate Finance (Princeton U. Press, 1994); The Modern Corporation and Private Pensions, 41 UCLA L. Rev. (1993) 75; Political and Legal Constraints of Ownership and Control of Public Companies, 27 J. Fin. Econ. (1990) 7; A Political Theory of Amercan Corporate Finance, 91 Columbia. L. Rev. (1991) 10; Political Elements in the Creation of a Mutual Fund Industry, 24 Securities L. Rev. (1992) 599; Some Differences in Corporate Structure in Germany, Japan and the United States, 102 Yale L.J. (1993) 1927; (with R. Gilson) Understanding the Japanese Keiretsu: Overlaps Between Corporate Governance and Industrial Organization, 102 Yale L.J. (1993) 871.

Jack C. SHAW

Sir John C. Shaw, CBE, (64) has been a Deputy Governor of Bank of Scotland since 1991. He is Chairman of the Scottish Higher Education Funding Council, a member of the Scottish Economic Council and holds a number of other public appointments. He is Chairman of two Investment Trusts and a director of a number of other publicly listed companies. He is Deputy Chairman of the Edinburgh Festival Society. Sir John practised as a Chartered Accountant for over 25 years and was President of the Institute of Chartered Accountants of Scotland 1983/84 and a member of the Financial Reporting Council until May

1996. He held the Johnstone Smith Chair of Accountancy at the University of Glasgow for 6 years until December 1982 and is now a Visiting Professor there. He was the first Executive Director of Scottish Financial Enterprise until June 1990 and was elected non executive chairman in 1995. Sir John is Chairman of the David Hume Institute and a member of the Steering Committee of its (1990/91) study "Corporate Takeovers and the Public Interest", and became Chairman of the Advanced Management Programme in Scotland Limited on its formation in 1995.

François VINCKE

Secretary General, Legal Department, Petrofina S.A.; Law Degree, Catholic University of Leuven; Diploma of European Integration, University of Amsterdam (European Institute); Assistant, University of Antwerp; joined Petrofina in 1974, where he has worked principally in the areas of international negotiations in finance and in exploration and production; several titles of distinction at Petrofina (Managing Director to Norske Fina A/S, President of Fina Exporation in Norway, and Board member of several Petrofina affiliates); President of the Commission "Bribery and Extortion" of the I.C.C. Paris (1994); President of the Legal Commission of the 'Federation of Belgian Enterprises' (VBO-FEB).

Eddy WYMEERSCH

Professor for Commercial Law, University of Ghent, Belgium; Regent, National Bank of Belgium; has published on subjects of securites regulation, company law, expecially on groups of companies and on legal issues of accounting; acting as consultant to the EC Commission, to the World Bank and IFC and to regulators of securites markets in several European states.

Author: Supervision of the Securities Markets (EC Commission, 3 vol.); Groups of Companies in the EEC, 1993, Berlin; Further perspectives in Financial Integration, 1994, Berlin, 281 p.; with K.J. Hopt: European insider dealing (1991, Butterworths); European Takeovers, Law and Practice (1992, Butterworths); European Company and Financial Law, 2nd edition (1994, Berlin). On Corporate Governance: Institutional Investors and Corporate Governance, (Th. Baums, R.M. Buxbaum and K.J. Hopt, ed.) 1994; Aspects of corporate governance in Belgium, in Prenctice D.D. en Holland, P.J.R. (Ed.), Contemporary Issues in Corporate Governance, Oxford, 219 p.; De regulering van overnamebiedingen in een rechtsvergelijkend perspektief, Kluwer 1994, 66 p.; Elements of Comparative corporate governance in Western Europe, in Aspects of Corporate Governance, Mats Isaksson and Rolf Skog (ed.), Stockholm, Juristförlaget, 1994.

Part One: Essays

The German Two-Tier Board (Aufsichtsrat) A German View on Corporate Governance

Klaus J. Hopt

Contents*

I. The German Aufsichtsrat and Its Roots

1. The mandatory two-tier system

In German corporations the board is divided as a matter of law into the management board (Vorstand) and the supervisory board (Aufsichtsrat). The

---

* Lecture given in Brussels, 14 June 1995. The text has been kept, footnotes have been added.

management board manages the company according to its own business judgment and represents the company in its business dealings and in litigation. The supervisory board oversees the management. Members of one board cannot sit as members of the other board.

The supervisory board consists of at least three members and at most 21 members, depending on the stated capital of the corporation. In the case of corporations having at least 500 workers, one third of the supervisory board members must be from the workforce of the corporation.

If the corporation normally employs more than 2,000 workers, half the supervisory board members represent the workforce and some of these must be representatives of the unions. In the case of such corporations the size of the supervisory board varies according to the number of workers employed. If normally there are more than 20,000 workers, the supervisory board consists of 20 members, 10 representing the shareholders, seven the workforce of the corporation and three representing the trade unions. In a case of deadlock the chairman of the supervisory board, who is elected by the shareholders, has two votes, giving slightly greater voting strength to the shareholders. In 1989 the German Supreme Court considered this a crucial consideration when it upheld this provision under the requirements of the German Constitution.[1] However since this landmark decision the bench has changed completely and the Court might reconsider its view if the occasion were to arise.

2. *Appointment and dismissal*

The supervisory board appoints the members of the managing board for a term of up to five years. Reappointment is permissible and usual. The supervisory board may designate one member to serve as chairman of the managing board. Members of the managing board may be dismissed only for compelling reasons such as, in particular, gross breach of duty, inability to conduct the corporation's business properly, or a vote of no-confidence carried at a shareholders general meeting, provided it is not based on clearly arbitrary grounds. This gives management a certain degree of security and independence in office for a number of years, which is what the legislator intended and which seems to meet with widespread approval.

The double vote of the chairman can also be used when members of the managing board are nominated or removed; however this calls for a long and complicated procedure, clearly intended to deter the shareholders from using it.

1 Codetermination Act of 4 May 1976 (German Federal Gazette I 1153); German Supreme Court, BVerfGE 60, 290 = NJW 1979, 699. The legal regime of the supervisory board is described by M. LUTTER and G. KRIEGER, Rechte und Pflichten des Aufsichtsrats, 3d ed. (1993).

In fact, the second vote is rarely used: forcing through important decisions in this way would worsen relations with labor within and beyond the supervisory board.

Remuneration for managing board members is fixed by the supervisory board. Stock participations may be granted, but are not nearly as common as for example in the USA. Accordingly excessively generous payments to managers are very rare in Germany and board remuneration is a much less controversial topic than it is in the USA.

The shareholders elect their representatives on the supervisory board, while the employee representatives are elected by the workers of the corporation or appointed by the trade unions. The members of the supervisory board are elected for a term which results to be between four and five years.[2] Shareholder representatives may be dismissed earlier by a resolution requiring three fourths of the votes cast or by the court if there is a compelling reason. This is one of the many difficulties impeding hostile takeovers.[3] Remuneration for the supervisory board is fixed by the general meeting of shareholders. The usual pay is rather modest (if the job is taken seriously).[4] The chairman of the supervisory board in particular is usually underpaid.

3. *The tasks of the supervisory board*

According to the law, the supervisory board has two main tasks: first, as already mentioned, to appoint and if need be to dismiss members of the managing board, and secondly, to supervise the management of the company.

---

2 I.e. not beyond the end of the shareholders meeting in the fourth year following the beginning of the term of office.

3 The reasons for the rarity of takeover bids in Germany are complex, cf. K.J. HOPT, European Takeover Regulation: Barriers to and Problems of Harmonizing Takeover Law in the European Community, in: K.J. HOPT and E. WYMEERSCH (eds.), European Takeovers, Law and Practice (1992) 165 at 167 et seq. As to the controversies concerning the Draft 13th EU Directive of 1996 and the voluntary German Takeover Code of 1995 see SAME, Europäisches und deutsches Übernahmerecht, ZHR 161 (1997) issue 3 (in print).

4 The average remuneration of the management board members in 1992 was DM 420,000 (DM 94,000 in 1960), the average remuneration of supervisory board members was DM 16,900 in 1992 (DM 13,100 in 1960). See M. HOFFMANN-BECKING, Rechtliche Möglichkeiten und Grenzen einer Verbesserung der Arbeit des Aufsichtsrats, Festschrift für H. Havermann (1995) 230 at 245. According to F.A. SCHMID, Zeitschrift für Betriebswirtschaft 67 (1997) 67, board member remuneration ranges from DM 3,000 to DM 107,300 with an average of DM 34,400 per annum (sample of 1991). He finds that supervisory board remuneration is positively related with performance as well as with company size. Cf. also L. KNOLL, J. KNOESEL and U. PROBST, Zeitschrift für betriebswirtschaftliche Forschung 49 (1997) 236.

There are a number of additional, more specific tasks such as to call shareholders meetings, to examine the annual financial statements and provide a written report on the result of the audit for the shareholders meeting and to represent the company in its dealings with members of the management board. If the articles of incorporation so provide or the supervisory board so decides, specific types of transactions need to be approved by the supervisory board. However it is made clear in the Act that the supervisory board is not directly involved in management decisions. Indeed the law does not allow managerial functions to be delegated to the supervisory board. This is very different from the one-tier board model.

In order to make supervision possible, the management board must inform the supervisory board of its policies for the future conduct of business, the profitability and in general the business of the corporation. Furthermore the chairman of the supervisory board must be notified of any other important event. The supervisory board may at any time ask the managing board for any other information about the corporation if it considers this necessary.

4. *Historical development*[5]

The German two-tier board system dates back to the beginning of modern German corporation law. The Reform Act of 1870 provided for an obligatory supervisory board. It was meant to be a substitute for the state charter and the continuous state control which were abolished. This is the historical reason why the Aufsichtsrat is an outside board, i.e. it links people other than the owners with the enterprise. It performs functions not unlike those historically intended for the disclosure requirements in Britain. Very soon it became clear that the supervisory board did not live up to these expectations. Yet in 1884 and in later years when stock corporation law reform acts were enacted, the legislator adhered to the two-tier board system, hoping to improve its functioning by special reforms, which divided the functions and responsibilities of both organs more clearly, improved the information to be given to the supervisory board and increased the legal duties and liabilities of board members. To this day supervisory board reform has remained a major subject in the debate about legislative reform.

---

5 K.J. HOPT, Zur Funktion des Aufsichtsrats im Verhältnis von Industrie und Bankensystem, and N. HORN, Aktienrechtliche Unternehmensorganisation in der Hochindustrialisierung (1860-1920), in: N. HORN and J. KOCKA (eds.), Law and the Formation of the Big Enterprises in the 19th and Early 20th Centuries (1979) 227 et seq. and 123 at 144 et seq. Cf. also G. LANDWEHR, Die Verfassung der Aktiengesellschaften, Rechtsverhältnisse in Preußen vom Anfang des 19. Jahrhunderts bis zum Jahre 1870, Zeitschrift der Savigny-Stiftung für Rechtsgeschichte, Germanistische Abteilung (ZRG GA) 99 (1982).

5. *Stock corporations and other forms of companies*

The two-tier structure is obligatory for all stock corporations irrespective of their size and workforce. Yet most German enterprises are not stock corporations. There are some 600,000 limited liability companies (GmbH) as compared with about 3,600 stock corporations, of which only about 700 are listed on the stock exchange.[6]

A limited liability company may have a supervisory board and in fact many GmbHs choose to have one or to have an informal advisory board. Limited liability companies are subject to the same regime of labor co-determination as stock corporations which means that there must be a supervisory board if a limited liability company normally employs at least 500 workers. This is provided for by the Works Constitution Act 1952. However, the range of tasks carried out by these supervisory boards is narrower than that of their counterparts in stock corporations. In particular the appointment and dismissal of managers is the responsibility of the partners of the company. However, in companies with more than 2,000 workers the supervisory boards have the same rights and duties as to appointment and dismissal as do the supervisory boards of stock corporations. This is laid down in the Co-determination Act of 1976 and other co-determination acts.

By the end of 1989, 522 enterprises were covered by the Co-determination Act of 1976: 303 stock corporations, 200 GmbHs, 6 partnerships limited by shares (KGaA), 9 limited liability partnerships (GmbH & Co) and 4 co-operative societies.[7] In Germany stock corporations account for 21.1. per cent of total turnover, limited liability companies for 25.5 per cent (figures for 1986).[8] The break-down of the turnover of the limited liability companies according to their workforce is not known. However it is estimated that German firms which have supervisory boards account for no more than around 30 per cent of total turnover.[9]

---

6 H. HANSEN, AG 1995, R 272. The latest figures on stock corporations and stock exchanges in Germany and other countries can be found in K.J. HOPT, B. RUDOLPH and H. BAUM (eds.), Börsenreform, Eine ökonomische, rechtsvergleichende und rechtspolitische Untersuchung (1997) 289 et seq.; Deutsches Aktieninstitut, DAI-Factbook 1996; Deutsche Börse, Fact Book 1996.

7 WSI-Mitteilungen 1990, 468; G. HUECK, Gesellschaftsrecht, 19th ed. (1991) § 24 II 2 a. The latest figures are: 740 enterprises including 406 stock corporations and 329 GmbHs, W. TEGTMEIER, Die Mitbestimmung 10/1996, 28.

8 According to HANSEN, AG 1995, R 228, the AGs and the GmbHs (Kapitalgesellschaften) accounted for 50.7 per cent of the total turnover (as measured by the turnover tax statistics 1992) as compared to only 33.4 per cent in 1962.

9 J. EDWARDS and K. FISCHER, Banks, finance and investment in Germany (1994) 75, 94.

II. The Functioning of the German Two-Tier Board System in the Real World

The subject of the present study is the Aufsichtsrat, the equivalent of the two-tier board system from a comparative law perspective. Neither labor co-determination nor the influence of the German banks on stock corporations can be dealt with in any detail. Data on the subject of labor co-determination are scarce and their evaluation is difficult;[10] the influence which universal banks may have on German stock corporations goes far beyond the Aufsichtsrat.[11]

1. Data on the constitution of the Aufsichtsrat

A representative interview study was conducted by the micro-economist Bleicher, University of St. Gall, in 1985/86.[12] According to this study the average size of the Aufsichtsrat was then 11 or 12 members.

In only about 75 per cent of the corporations, committees of the Aufsichtsrat had been formed. In these corporations an average of 2 committees were formed (1.5 as to the total). There were personnel committees (58 per cent), chairman s committees (29 per cent), finance committees (24 per cent), investment committees (18 per cent), audit committees (7 per cent) and committees for social affairs, for co-determination and for ad hoc matters (4 per cent each). In order of importance these committees were ranked as follows: finance committee, investment committee, chairman s committee, personnel committee and audit committee (only in fifth place). While in general audit committees

---

10 Infra II 4.

11 Infra IV 6. This is also true for the discussion on the networks between large German enterprises, banks, investment funds and insurance companies. The supervisory board is only one of the tools for maintaining these networks. Cf. Monopolkommission, Wettbewerbspolitik in Zeiten des Umbruchs. Elftes Hauptgutachten der Monopolkommission 1994/95, 1996; A. PFANNSCHMIDT, Personelle Verflechtungen über Aufsichtsräte. Mehrfachmandate in deutschen Unternehmen, 1993; P. WINDOLF and J. BEYER, Kölner Zeitschrift für Soziologie und Sozialpsychologie 47 (1995) 1; J. BEYER, Zeitschrift für Betriebswirtschaft, Ergänzungsheft 3/1996, 79; C. LEIMKÜHLER, Wirtschaftsprüfung 49 (1996) 305; T.J. ANDRÉ, Tulane L. Rev 70 (1996) 1819.

12 K. BLEICHER, Der Aufsichtsrat im Wandel, 1987. A short survey of other empirical research concerning particularly the information flow from the managing board to the supervisory board is given by M. THEISEN, Grundsätze ordnungsmäßiger Information des Aufsichtsrats, 2d ed. (1996) 19 et seq. Further data as to II 1 - 5 can be found in E. BREMEIER, J.B. MÜLDER and F. SCHILLING, Praxis der Aufsichtsratstätigkeit in Deutschland - Chancen zur Professionalisierung, 1994; Deutsche Schutzvereinigung für Wertpapierbesitz (ed.), Aufsichtsräte in Deutschland, 1995; KORN/FERRY INTERNATIONAL, Board Meeting in Session. European Boards of Directors Study, 1996; C. LEIMKÜHLER, Wirtschaftsprüfung 49 (1996) 305.

were considered less important, the representatives of the workers held audit committees and personnel committees to be more important.

Informal advisory boards in addition to supervisory boards are rare.

2. *Data on the members of the Aufsichtsrat*

44 per cent of all the members sat only on one supervisory board. 10 per cent held seats on the supervisory boards of more than 6 corporations. The average number of seats held was 2.85. Around a third of boardroom mandates were held in groups of companies, namely in subsidiaries. The larger the Aufsichtsrat, the stronger the feeling of members that they were not being given enough information. There was no similar correlation between the wish for more information and the number of seats held by the particular member. Nevertheless 34 per cent of all board members interviewed thought that the number of seats to be held by one person should be further limited by law to around 5 or 6 mandates. Yet it is worthwhile to note that such a limitation would affect only 10 per cent of the board members interviewed.

Only 7.3 per cent of the chairmen of the Aufsichtsrat work full time. Only 20 per cent of the board members interviewed think the chairmen should be full-time, while 77 per cent are opposed, perhaps because they consider a full-time chairmanship not useful or because they fear that it would create too close an affiliation of the chairman with the corporation.

3. *Data on the day-to-day working of the Aufsichtsrat*

German supervisory boards meet on average about 3.8 times a year. About half meet 4 times and another quarter meet 3 times. The meetings lasted an average of 3.74 hours. This means that 14 hours 13 minutes per year on average were spent in sessions.

Chairman's committees meet most often, namely 3.5 times a year, finance committees 3.12 times and audit committees 3.07 times. The longest sessions were those of the audit committee which lasted more than 3 hours. Interestingly the board members interviewed did not think that the audit committee should meet more often; they even considered that meetings should last well under 3 hours.

Contact between the Aufsichtsrat and the Vorstand seems to occur a little more frequently than 4 times a year. When asked whether the supervisory board should play a more consultative role in its relationship with the Vorstand, the opinions of those interviewed were evenly divided. It was the opinion of 90 per cent that the Aufsichtsrat has a great deal of influence or at least a good deal of influence with the Vorstand. Contrary to what one might expect, the possible role of the Aufsichtsrat in helping to establish and maintain external relationships for the corporation is not very often stressed. The representation of the shareholders and the workers in the Aufsichtsrat is considered important; surprisingly the representation of banks is clearly considered less important.

4. *The German system of labor co-determination by means of representation on corporate boards*

The traditional one third labor co-determination on corporate boards is not a topic of discussion in Germany. This is different for the quasi-parity co-determination. In the 1970s this far-reaching form of co-determination on corporate boards was highly controversial. In the meantime public controversy has very much died down. It is only in the most recent reform debate that some commentators have criticized boardroom co-determination for weakening effective supervision by the Aufsichtsrat, while others have rejected this criticism on the basis of their boardroom experience.[13] On the whole it is fair to say that, in the last two decades, German business and banks have learned to live with co-determination. Their experience was that it helped to build a consensus between capital and labor and, more recently, that it has also been a formidable weapon against hostile takeovers.[14] True enough, co-determination has its price. It tends to slow the decision-making process, presents dangers for confidentiality and influences decisions to hire and fire. On the other hand, co-determination functions as an early warning system for social conflicts and as an instrument of collective crisis management. The overall economic and social pros and cons are very difficult to evaluate.[15]

5. *The role of the German universal banks*

A few introductory remarks should be made about the role of the banks in German corporate governance - a matter which raises many very difficult

---

13 Infra IV 3 b.

14 Supra note 2.

15 K.J. HOPT, Labor Representation on Corporate Boards: Impacts and Problems for Corporate Governance and Economic Integration in Europe, International Review of Law and Economics 14 (1994) 203; a more complete version in German language can be found in: K.J. HOPT, Arbeitnehmervertretung im Aufsichtsrat, Festschrift für U. Everling (1995) 475. See also the discussion on this report in: R.M. BUXBAUM, G. HERTIG, A. HIRSCH and K.J. HOPT (eds.), European Economic and Business Law (1996) 261-281. Cf. also W. KOLVENBACH, Die weitere Entwicklung der Betriebsverfassung und Unternehmensmitbestimmung in den Mitgliedstaaten der Europäischen Union, Festschrift für U. Everling (1995) 669.

issues. Detailed figures were given by the German Monopolies Commission in 1978.[16] According to its enquiry the representation of banks on the supervisory boards of the largest 100 stock corporations in 1974 was impressive. The banks representatives were chairmen in 31 stock corporations and deputy chairmen in 35 (the figures for the three big banks were 21 and 19 respectively). Bank representatives held 113 simple board memberships, 62 of these being held by the big three. In toto the banks held 179 seats.

However if one looks at the total number of board memberships, the picture changes substantially. According to a study of supervisory boards of stock corporations with more than 2,000 employees (i.e. where quasi-parity co-determination was obligatory),[17] 39.7 per cent of the shareholder seats (employee seats not being counted) were held by domestic non-banks, 13.2 by governments, 5.7 by private shareholders and only 16.4 by domestic banks.

The most recent study dates from 1995.[18] It shows that of 1,561 boardroom seats available in the largest 100 enterprises, 760 seats were held by labor (trade unions held 211 of these), 427 were held by representatives of other enterprises, 99 by representatives of private banks and 67 by politicians and bureaucrats. Thus the overall boardroom representation of the private banks was 6 per cent of all seats or 12 per cent of the shareholder seats. This is much less than one would have expected even though these figures are merely averages and are not representative of particular groups of co-determined enterprises (e.g. the 10 largest or enterprises in a specific sector) or of private bank representatives (in particular those belonging to the big Three or Five).

However, the influence of the German universal banks on stock corporations must be seen in the wider context, not just that of supervisory board seats. Representation in the boardroom is only part of the picture. The real influence and, according to some, the economic power of the banks stem from the combination of supervisory board seats, stock participations (blocks of shares), bank proxy votes and the banks credit and underwriting business. This is very difficult to evaluate[19] and should not been judged on the basis of ideological premises.[20] In any case, it goes well beyond the German Aufsichtsrat.

16 Monopolkommission, Hauptgutachten II: Fortschreitende Konzentration bei Großunternehmen (1978) 300 et seq. See also the figures given by EDWARDS and FISCHER (supra note 9) 124, 136.

17 E. GERUM, H. STEINMANN and W. FEES, Der mitbestimmte Aufsichtsrat - eine empirische Untersuchung (1988) 54.

18 Bundesverband Deutscher Banken e.V. (Cologne 1995).

19 Cf. EDWARDS and FISCHER (supra note 9) p. 129 et seq.; K.J. HOPT, Corporate Governance und deutsche Universalbanken, in: D. FEDDERSEN, P. HOMMELHOFF and U.H. SCHNEIDER (eds.), Corporate Governance (1996) 243.

20 Infra IV 6.

III. Path Dependence[21] and the One-Tier v. the Two-Tier Board Model

1. *Countries with a one-tier board such as the USA and the UK*

The movement which led, first in the USA and then in Great Britain, to the appointment of outside directors for listed corporations is well known. For the purposes of this paper it is sufficient to realize that there is a clear trend to add outside or independent directors to one-tier boards.[22] While this is certainly helpful in dealing with the problems of adequate remuneration, conflicts of interests and, more generally, control of management and the CEO, it is not necessarily sufficient to solve these problems completely. After all, outside non-executive directors are the very basis of the German Aufsichtsrat, and their introduction has certainly not eliminated these very same problems in Germany. The important point in the context of this paper is that a certain convergence of the two types of board is occurring which is only in part imposed by the legislator and stems in part from the needs and the chosen practice of large enterprises.

2. *Countries which allow a choice between the two models such as France*

It is only in a few countries that corporations are allowed to choose between the one-tier and the two-tier board model. This has been possible in France since the basic company law reform of 1966. Yet most corporations, whether old or newly established, continue to adhere to the traditional one-tier system: the CEO (PDG) is elected by the shareholders and combines the roles of chief executive and chairman of the board (conseil d'administration). By 1990 only 7.6 per cent of French stock corporations had chosen the new system which divides the directoire and the conseil de surveillance.[23] In 1995 the one-tier model was used by 155,000 companies out of a total of 158,000 and the two-

21 Cf. P.A. DAVID, Clio and the Economics of QWERTY, Am. Ec. Rev. Vol. 75 No. 2, 332; M. ROE, Chaos and Evolution in Law and Economics, 109 Harv. L. Rev. 64 et seq. (1996).

22 As to the USA cf. American Law Institute, Principles of Corporate Governance: Analysis and Recommendations, Vol. 1 (1994) § 3A.01 Composition of the Board in Publicly Held Corporations; as to the UK cf. The Cadbury Committee Report: Financial Aspects of Corporate Governance, 1992: The Code of Best Practice concerning Non-Executive Directors (Annex I/1). Cf. also for Switzerland P. BÖCKLI, Verwaltungsrat oder Aufsichtsrat? Konvergenz der Systeme in der Spitzenverfassung der Aktiongesellschaft, in: A. REIST and G. RAU (eds.), Durchblick, 39 Persönlichkeiten zu Unternehmung und Gesellschaft, Festschrift für Walter Reist (1992) 3.

23 J. CHARKHAM, Keeping good company, A study of corporate governance in five countries (1994) 135.

tier model only by the remaining 3,000.[24] Some of these 3,000 are highly successful companies. Some corporations have changed back and forth between the two systems, each of which has advantages and disadvantages. The fact that such an overwhelming majority of enterprises adheres to the old system may be due mainly to tradition and to many decades of legal and practical experience with the one-tier system.[25]

3. *Countries with a two-tier board such as Germany*

In Germany the two-tier board system is mandatory for stock corporations, but not for other types of companies, so that very many German companies do not have two-tier boards.

The main reason other than tradition for not allowing all companies to choose freely between the one- and the two-tier models is clearly Germany's system of labor co-determination. The trade unions treat labor co-determination in corporate boards as sacrosanct. The only minor concession made in 1994 in the Stock Corporation Law Simplification Act was to allow companies with fewer than 500 workers to do without such co-determination even if they are not family-owned, but this concession was withheld from stock corporations already in existence. It was surprising that the trade unions made even such a small concession; the relevant provision of the Act may have passed only because the time chosen and the circumstances prevailing in German politics were particularly favorable at the time.

In this political environment it is obvious that giving the companies the choice between the two board systems would be relevant only for stock corporations with fewer than 500 workers. The shareholders of companies with more than 500 workers would not opt for the one-tier board, for that would mean having the labor representatives involved in all management decisions.

Apart from this it is interesting to note that the above-mentioned empirical study (supra II 5) has shown that a full 25 per cent of the board members interviewed were clearly against the strict division of the tasks of management and control between two boards.[26] This view is favored particularly by members of supervisory boards who sit on more than three boards. The reason given is that the German supervisory board cannot really control management and that the

---

24 ERNST & YOUNG, La simplification de la réglementation sur le fonctionnement des sociétés anonymes dans l'Union Européenne, Rapport définitif, Décembre 1995.

25 This was mentioned by Swiss practitioners as being a major reason for preferring the stock corporation form and not choosing the limited liability company form which is available in Switzerland. Choosing an unusual company form could lead to unpleasant surprises in court and in other situations.

26 BLEICHER (supra note 12) 50 et seq.

American unitary board is considered preferable. Those board members who were generally satisfied with the two-tier board system liked the clear separation between management and control and thought the supervisory board a good forum for control by and advice from major shareholders, outside directors from other companies, bankers and representatives of the workforce. Nevertheless, they believed strongly that the functioning of the two-tier board system could be greatly improved.

4. Implications for harmonisation within the EU

The consequences for the 5th EU Directive are relatively straightforward. There is no compelling reason for adopting and prescribing one single board system for all member states, be it the two-tier or the one-tier system. While in theory the two-tier system may have some advantages, these advantages can be obtained in countries with a one-tier system by rules on outside directors. Furthermore experience in the UK shows that, at least in circumstances similar to those in this country, such rules need not be part of the law, but may be prescribed by bodies such as the stock exchanges as part of their requirements for admission. Even without such rules there is a tendency amongst large enterprises to add outside directors to their boards.

If the EC Commission chooses to harmonize the structure of the corporation and particularly the board systems (a controversial subject which cannot be analysed here in greater detail[27]), the directive cannot but allow the member states to opt between the two systems, as has indeed been envisaged in all the drafts so far presented. Recently it was proposed that the member states be required to pass on the option to the enterprises in conformity with the French system. Indeed this could be a step forward for the economic benefit of choosing one system or the other is best evaluated by the individual enterprise at the market. Even so, this would probably not lead to major changes in the corporate reality of the member states.

---

27 Cf. the controversial concept of competition between the legislators: R. ROMANO, The State Competition Debate in Corporate Law, Cardozo L. Rev. 8 (1987) 709; L. BEBCHUK, Federalism and the Corporation: The Desirable Limits on State Competition in Corporate Law, 105 Harv. L. Rev. 1437 (1992); F. KÜBLER, KritV 1994, 79; H. MERKT, RabelsZ 59 (1995) 545; SCHÖN, ZHR 160 (1996) 221; K.J. HOPT, ZHR 161 (1997) issue 3 sub II 1, 2.

IV. Present-Day Debate concerning Reform of the German Aufsichtsrat[28]

1. *No fundamental reforms of the Aufsichtsrat*

As mentioned before fundamental reform of the Aufsichtsrat is not being considered or even seriously debated in Germany. Legal theory and practice overwhelmingly support the two-tier system. It is said that steps which are intended to change the Aufsichtsrat into a kind of supermanagement are going in an entirely wrong direction.[29] Even the German trade unions, for political or economic reasons, have refrained from advocating the introduction of the one-tier board. Instead the reform discussion is concerned with concrete ways and means of improving the functioning of the supervisory board. Labor co-determination is more or less accepted in theory and practice, and for a political party to touch the fine-tuned balance between shareholder and labor interests, would be a recipe for disaster.

2. *Technical reforms as to size and membership*

a) The number of supervisory board members is generally considered to be too high for efficient work. In large corporations there may be up to 20 supervisory board members and in addition 6 management board members together with a number of collaborators and the auditors. This easily amounts to 30 persons or more. According to some critics, the size of the supervisory board should be limited to 10, but this might create problems for co-determination, in particular for the representation of the trade unions.[30] According to others, the maximum number should be 15. Indeed, according to group interaction theory and experience, the number probably should not exceed 10 or 15 at the very outside. However, the determination of the most suitable size, particularly from the point of view of labor co-determination, is best made by the individual enterprise. The legislator should set only minimum and maximum limits.

28 The literature is very extensive. Cf. e.g. E. NIEDERLEITHINGER, ZIP 1995, 597 (601 et seq.) and U. SEIBERT, ZBB 1994, 349 (both from the Federal Ministry of Justice); M. LUTTER, AG 1994, 176 and ZHR 159 (1995) 287; BAUMS, ZIP 1995, 11; W. BERNHARDT, ZHR 159 (1995) 310; P. HOMMELHOFF, Ist das bestehende Aktiengesetz im Sinne von Corporate Governance voll genutzt?, in: PICOT (ed.), Unternehmensüberwachung auf dem Prüfstand - Corporate Governance (1995) 1. See now also the very moderate recommendations of the 61th Deutscher Juristentag, Karlsruhe 1996, section Business Law. As to the two controversial draft acts of the Government and the Opposition Party see infra notes 49 and 52.

29 E.g. E.R. SCHNEIDER-LENNÉ, member of the board of the Deutsche Bank, Gesetzesinitiativen auf dem Gebiet des Aktienrechts, Vortrag vor dem Beraterkreis der Deutsche Bank AG am 30.3.1995.

30 The Government draft 1996 (infra note 52) provides for such a reduction, but this has met with resistance by the Ministry of Labor and the trade unions.

b) At present a member of a supervisory board may be not on the boards of more than 10 corporations. A management board member of a parent company may hold an additional five seats on the supervisory boards of the subsidiaries (so-called group clause). This restriction was introduced by the so-called lex Abs. Formerly one person could belong to many more boards. The maximum number known was 40, held by a private banker from Cologne at the turn of the century. The number of seats held by one person is very likely to be reduced to 5 and a chairmanship will count as two.[31] The group clause will remain untouched because representation of the parent company on the board of the subsidiary serves different purposes and may be needed for steering the group.[32]

What may be more important is the effort to reduce conflicts of interests. A member of a supervisory board should not, at the same time, be allowed to be a member of either of the boards of a competing company.[33] Representatives of business and particularly of the banking sector, while not rejecting this suggestion outright, have pointed out that it might be too difficult in particular cases to determine whether a company is a "competing company".[34] However, this difficulty should not be treated as an insurmountable obstacle.

c) According to some commentators, the chairmanship of the supervisory board should be a full-time position if the supervisory board is to be a match for the management,[35] but whether it should be prescribed by law may well be doubtful.[36]

Furthermore, the practice of the chairman of a management board on retirement becoming chairman of the supervisory board of the same corporation has been questioned. Indeed, how could such a chairman correct decisions which he himself made when he still belonged to the management board? On the other

---

31 Cf. for example E. SCHEFFLER (business economist), AG 1995, 207 (209), who pleads for a maximum of 6 to 7 seats and for counting the role of chairman as double or triple; a further reduction may be necessary in crisis situations.

32 As to the supervisory board in groups of corporations see M. HOFFMANN-BECKING, ZHR 159 (1995) 325; K.-P. MARTENS, ZHR 159 (1995) 567.

33 According to some authors this is forbidden already de lege lata, cf. M. LUTTER, Die Unwirksamkeit von Mehrfachmandaten in den Aufsichtsraten von Konkurrenzunternehmen, Festschrift für K. Beusch (1993) 509; according to others the legislator should intervene, cf. J. REICHERT/E.R. SCHLITT, AG 1995, 241.

34 SCHNEIDER-LENNÉ (supra note 29).

35 H. FRANZ (chairman of the supervisory board of Siemens) at the Adolf Weber Foundation Forum "Reform of self-regulation within the corporation" at the Dresdner Bank on 7 April 1995 in Frankfurt; M. LUTTER, NJW 1995, 1133; T.M.J. MÖLLERS, ZIP 1995, 1725.

36 According to M. LUTTER, loc. cit, the legislator should even make it obligatory for the stock corporation to provide the chairman of the supervisory board with an office and with adequate secretarial help.

hand the experience of the former chairman of the management board may be invaluable. This is said to be particularly true of the contribution he could make to the work of the credit committees of the supervisory board of banks. Similar, though less acute, problems would arise if the retired chairman or another member of the management board were to join the supervisory board of the same company as an ordinary member.

3. Internal control, better information and audit committees

a) There is widespread agreement that the key to successful reform is better internal control. Traditional internal control within corporations often fails to live up to modern requirements and possibilities.[37] This has been particularly apparent in the case of banks as a consequence of the derivatives movement. The banks themselves, the national bank supervisory agencies and supranational bodies like the Basle Committee and the EC Commission have already done a great deal of work to bring about improvements. Similar needs exist in the case of non-banks. However, this goes beyond the scope of this paper.

b) As far as the Aufsichtsrat is concerned, the key is information. A body which as a general rule meets less frequently than 4 times a year cannot be expected to control effectively the management of a large corporation. The supervisory board should meet 6 to 8 times a year at least and should receive more and better information than hitherto. Monthly reports by the chairman of the management board should be a standard requirement and a general policy report on the stock corporation and its business is indispensable.[38] Most importantly the chairman of the supervisory board should become more involved in his task. At least in certain cases he should be expected to work full-time instead of only part-time.

Furthermore, the supervisory board should make better use of the information supplied by the auditor of the corporation. Members of the supervisory board should receive the auditor's report well before their meeting. Widespread board practice at present is to let them have the report only at the meeting itself. The reason for this is said to be co-determination which, according to some observers, leads to occasional breaches of confidentiality by the labor representatives.

---

37 Cf. for example H. GÖTZ, AG 1995, 337. Business economists such as M. THEISEN and E. SCHEFFLER plead for the development of (non-legal) principles of orderly control of the management by the supervisory board. Cf. M. THEISEN, Grundsätze einer ordnungsmäßigen Information des Aufsichtsrats, 2d ed., 1995; SAME, AG 1995, 193; E. SCHEFFLER, AG 1995, 207.

38 E. SCHEFFLER, AG 1995, 207 (210 et seq.).

The supervisory board could also broaden the kind and scope of the transactions which are subject to its mandatory consent. However, it must be remembered that when labor co-determination was introduced by law in the 1970s, a number of stock corporations reduced the range of transactions for which the consent of the Aufsichtsrat was required.

c) Most of this is difficult to prescribe by law. What could be prescribed at least for large or listed companies is audit committees. In other countries this is done by the stock exchanges. Indeed, there is widespread agreement that more committee work is essential, if the performance of the unwieldy German supervisory boards is to be improved. However many companies already have audit committees. It is doubtful whether the legislator should force the establishment of this or indeed of any other committee upon all stock corporations regardless of size, listing and other features of the particular case. A significant shift of the functions of the full Aufsichtsrat to committees is bound to give rise to a difficult legal and political issue: should the composition of these committees fully reflect the principles of co-determination?[39]

4. *Responsibility of the members of the Aufsichtsrat*

Members of supervisory boards are jointly and severally liable for mere negligence in the performance of their functions and they even bear the burden of proving that they acted with due care.[40] In practice however suits against members of supervisory boards are very rare. Management boards are reluctant to sue supervisory board members for lack of control over the management board. A suit must be brought if the general meeting of the shareholders so decides or if a minority of shareholders representing at least ten per cent of the stated capital so requires. To reach this quorum in large public companies is rarely possible. In addition there is the risk of having to reimburse the corporation for its litigation costs if the suit fails.

It has been proposed that this threshold be lowered, according to some commentators to five per cent or alternatively to an amount well under 1 million DM.[41] Others suggest allowing derivative suits of single shareholders, possibly under the control of the court.[42] However it is questionable whether this would be a major improvement. Oppressive suits are well-known in

39 C. JAEGER, ZIP 1995, 1735.

40 K.J. HOPT, Die Haftung von Vorstand und Aufsichtsrat - Zugleich ein Beitrag zur corporate governance-Debatte -, Festschrift für E.-J. Mestmäcker (1996) 909.

41 HOMMELHOFF (supra note 28).

42 M. LUTTER, ZHR 159 (1995) 287 (305 et seq.); H. WIEDEMANN, Organverwaltung und Gesellschafterklage in der Aktiengesellschaft (1989) 47 et seq.; similarly TRESCHNER, DB 1995, 661.

German corporations. It may be that other methods would be more effective than retroactive legal liability. Other incentives could be better pay for the board members[43] and a requirement that the chairman of the supervisory board answer questions addressed to him at general meetings.[44]

5. *The auditors*

The forthcoming reform of the supervisory board may well comprise reform measures concerning the auditors. After a number of spectacular failures of corporations the auditing profession has been the subject of much critical debate. Auditors, acting fraudulently or at least with considerable negligence, had granted unlimited certification for the financial statements of these corporations not long before they collapsed. The role of auditors as such is not questioned, but the scope of their work, their duties and their responsibilities are being debated critically. One measure would be particularly far-reaching. A draft Act pending in Parliament would fix a non-renewable term of 5 years for auditing firms. This is meant to make auditing firms less dependent upon major clients. Experts in the field oppose this reform arguing that such a measure would be counterproductive, since an auditor needs one or more years of working with a firm in order to know it really well.[45]

Other proposals[46] include changing the auditing team, but not necessarily the auditing firm, after 5 years,[47] requiring the auditor to "blow the whistle" (as prescribed already for auditors of banks and insurance companies who have to inform the supervisory agencies in case of major problems) and reforming the relationship between the auditor, the supervisory board and the general assembly of shareholders. Occasionally one hears criticism of the close contact between the auditor and the management board which usually precedes the actual writing of the report and its submission to the supervisory board.[48] Yet even though this practice leads to interference by management, it is clear that the auditor cannot prepare his report without the cooperation of the management, in particular the information provided by it. It may be expected that some of these proposals will be taken up by the legislator.

---

43 J. SEMLER, Unternehmensüberwachung durch den Kapitalmarkt, in: PICOT (supra note 28) 77 et seq.
44 HOMMELHOFF (supra note 28).
45 A. MOXTER, Den Wirtschaftsprüfer nicht zum Sündenbock machen, FAZ 27.3.1995, p. 18.
46 See the survey by M. THEISEN, WPK-Mitt. 1995, 185.
47 Cf. SCHNEIDER-LENNÉ (supra note 29).
48 HOMMELHOFF (supra note 28).

6. *The German universal banks*

There is a strong body of opinion which considers that the private banks have too much economic power. Some proposals encourage far-reaching reforms. A draft Act pending in Parliament[49] would cut down the equity participation held by banks, change their depository vote system dramatically and would, indirectly, but considerably, diminish their board room representation. Much of this is based more on populism and ideology than on hard legal and economic facts. The economic interaction of the universal banking system with market structures and with traditional institutions such as the stock exchanges raise very serious and highly complicated questions. These questions and the behavior patterns of enterprises and financial intermediaries have never been sufficiently analyzed.[50] Until these problems are better understood, it is best to prefer limited reforms[51] to the kind of drastic measures of which the German draft Act is an example. That Act has little chance of being adopted which is not a cause for concern or regret. Further study is needed to elucidate these problems. Most recently another draft Act has been introduced which is more moderate and has good chances to be adopted in 1997.[52]

---

49 This draft Act was introduced by the SPD parliamentary group. One of the advisers for this draft Act was M. ADAMS; cf. his contributions in ZBB 1994, 77 and AG 1994, 148.

50 Most recently this is improving, cf. f. ex. EDWARDS and FISCHER (supra note 9); E. WYMEERSCH, AG 1995, 299 with a good collection of empirical data on corporate governance in Western Europe; see also the contributions to the Parliamentary Hearing on the Power of the Banks, ZBB 1994, 69 et seq., and FEDDERSEN, HOMMELHOFF and SCHNEIDER (supra note 19).

51 M. LUTTER, NJW 1995, 2766.

52 Entwurf eines Gesetzes zur Kontrolle und Transparenz im Unternehmensbereich (KonTraG), see SEIBERT, WM 1997, 1.

The Cadbury Report, Two Years Later

John C. Shaw

Contents

I. Introduction

I am flattered by the invitation to contribute to this international conference and congratulate the organisers on their initiative in bringing us all together today.

1. What is a non-executive director?

Perhaps someone coming from a Bank which has conducted the same business, under the same name, and in the same legal entity over 300 years can try to offer a long-term perspective on some questions of corporate governance. The first point to emphasise is that the British structure of corporate governance reflects its legal, economic and cultural history. As Professor Hopt has pointed out, the corporate legal framework in the United Kingdom depends primarily on accountability as the means of securing relationships between the corporation and its proprietors (shareholders who enjoy limited liability) and between the corporation and the state.

In any comparative discussion it is also essential to distinguish sharply between two quite different elements of what is loosely called the "German model". The origins, structure, and functions of the Aufsichtsrat should not be confused with arrangements for co-determination. Size criteria brings them both into play in the most prominent German companies, and they do interact (for example, in deterring hostile takeover bids) but the "Supervisory Board" is really the Aufsichtsrat - and it is the reform of that body which is currently being debated in Germany. I note the point because of a view that the Cadbury Report is likely to drive institutional convergence between Britain and Germany as far as corporate governance is concerned. The report's identification, within the so-called "Unitary Board" of a specific type of director - the non-executive director or independent director - and the attribution to him of specific and special duties, creates a de-facto type of 'Aufsichtsrat' - or Supervisory Board. But we are not quite there yet!

I would like to ask you to close your eyes and think please of this mental picture.

The occupants of a hot air balloon were being swept along before strong winds and looked down to see a deep ravine.

Stretched across the ravine was a tightrope and balanced on this tightrope was a middle aged, perhaps one might even say elderly man, wearing a kilt, apparently oblivious to the depth of the ravine and the threat of instant death were he to fall.

On the ground a number of people watched, scratching their heads in bemusement while at the far end of the tightrope stood a man proffering the tightrope walker a £1 note.

"What's going on?" the balloonists asked those on the ground. "Well", came the reply, "that's the appointment of a new Scottish Non-Executive Director".

"How do you know?" the balloonists enquired. "Easy" they said, "The people watching don't know what he's up to, the man himself has no idea what it's about and isn't aware of the risks, and the guy at the far end is trying to get him to do it for next to nothing!"

This is probably an extreme picture of the state of corporate governance two years after the introduction of the Cadbury Code, but it is a light hearted view offered by the Chairman of Scottish Power PLC, Mr. Murray Stuart.

2. *Why Cadbury?*

Let me now turn to considering the success or otherwise of the Cadbury Report two years on. A study group set up under the auspices of the Cadbury Committee has just published the results of its review of compliance with the Cadbury Code since its publication in December 1992 (see attached appendices showing the key results of their findings). They have found encouraging evidence of widespread compliance by most of the listed companies to which the Code is addressed. I shall refer to that review briefly later, but am really much more concerned by the substance of corporate governance than by the form of compliance with the Cadbury Code.

But before we go any further we should remind ourselves how the Code came to existence and why the Cadbury Committee was set up.

The Committee chaired by Sir Adrian Cadbury which reported at the very end of 1992 had terms of reference restricted to the financial aspects of corporate governance. Its work focused on the structures and practices of boards of large UK companies. It was set up in May 1991 by a triumvirate of private sector interests: the Financial Reporting Council, the London Stock Exchange and the Accountancy profession. During the winter of 1990/91 there emerged in Britain a perceived lack of confidence in financial reporting and in the exercise of effective supervision of executive management by company boards. There had been a number of high profile corporate collapses such as "Polly Peck", "Exco" and "Coloroll".

Subsequent events elsewhere have demonstrated that corporate collapse and scandal are not unique to the U.K.! We should also remember that the very early years of this decade marked the low-water mark of economic recession in Britain. The buoyancy of economic boom creates cover for corporate mistakes and misjudgements and allows the adverse consequences of such errors to be rapidly recovered. The difficult trading conditions of recession are unforgiving and the speed of transition from "boom" to "bust" exposes incompetence or dishonesty unequivocally at precisely the moment when businesses under pressure will be trying to create camouflage or at least manufacture excuses.

Ironically, as the report was being finalised further high profile corporate collapses provided dramatic evidence of the problem - e.g. the Maxwell saga, and the failure of BCCI. There was therefore substantial public interest in the work of the Committee and in its report. Cadbury was, in essence, a political response to public disquiet in the U.K. about the conduct and effectiveness of corporate governance. Recognition of that political dimension is important to what I shall say later.

3. *The Cadbury Code*

The 'Cadbury Code ' of December 1992 is intended to improve the way UK companies are run. Its concern is with the whole area of corporate governance "the system by which organisations are directed and controlled" - and puts an emphasis on systems, processes and controls over accountability and decision-making which lie at the heart of every organisation. (It is, interestingly, a very

British characteristic to attribute bad behaviour to weak systems rather than to individual failure to uphold personal standards of conduct. But of course structures and codes *can* influence personal conduct.)

The four primary principles underlying the "Cadbury" approach to improved corporate behaviour and incorporated within its Code of Best Practice are:

1) A clear division of responsibilities at the head of a company to ensure a balance of power and authority, such that no one individual has unfettered powers of decision. (Combining the roles of Chairman and Chief Executive is not prohibited - but certainly discouraged.)
2) Every Board should include *non-executive* directors of sufficient calibre and number for their views to carry significant weight in decisions. (It should be explained that the typical British company "promotes" to its Board as Directors those who have been successful functional executives. There is generally inadequate help given to these people to achieve the transformation from "management" to "governance". A recent Coopers & Lybrand survey found only 7% of companies have formal arrangements in place for training would-be directors.)
3) Institutional investors should take a *positive* interest in the composition of boards of directors, with particular reference to avoiding unrestrained concentration of decision making. They should secure the appointment of a core of non-executive directors of the necessary calibre, experience and independence. In other words, institutional shareholders have a particular responsibility to be active in corporate democracy - not passive. A nominating committee will help to identify potential Board appointees and reduce the risk of chairmen appointing "place men". A Remuneration Committee will help the Board as a whole to determine appropriate rewards for Board members - always a sensitive issue!
4) The Board structure should clearly recognise the importance and significance of the finance function. An Audit Committee will help to secure that recognition .

   It is, of course, expected that these three special committees - nominating, remuneration and audit - will comprise a majority of non executives. The objective of the Cadbury Code is to focus on three fundamental pillars of good corporate governance:- Openness, Integrity and Accountability. Buttressing these pillars by observation of the Code will help organisations to improve standards of management and to enhance levels of accountability to the organisation's proprietors, who provide the assets and resources of the business .

Although I shall suggest that progress towards meeting these Cadbury goals has been limited, do not misunderstand me as a critic of the Code per se. Jean Christian Sibelius, the Finish composer said "Pay no attention what the critics say. A statue has never been erected in honour of a critic!" I believe the Cadbury Code should be looked upon as the first rung of a ladder which as we all know was never meant to be where we finish, but holds a man's foot long enough to enable him to put the other higher, towards achieving his ultimate objective.

II. Cadbury: two years on: a success?

Perhaps there is nobody better to answer the question than the people who are doing the job. Let me provide some information from a 1994 survey of Scottish non-executive directors.

KPMG, the international Chartered Accountancy firm and the Scottish Business Insider magazine teamed up for research in Scotland to identify the role and remit of non-executive directors in business. 160 respondents of their questionnaire gave a range of very honest, outspoken and enlightening comments on the issues which most effected them in their execution of their duties. (This was a high response rate from their survey population, and respondents seem to have been the most active appointees - as measured by the number of appointments.)

1. "The existing non-executive force is spread too thin"

Cadbury advocated that every Board should include non-executive directors of sufficient *calibre* and *number* for their weight to carry significant weight in decisions.

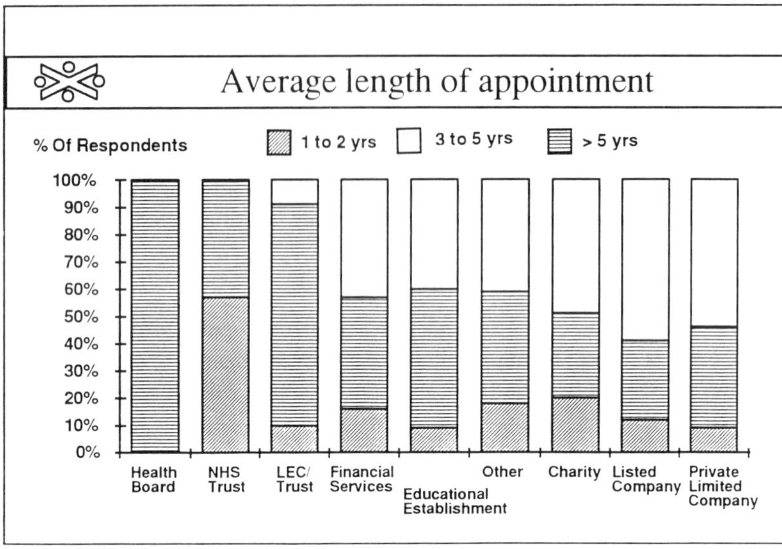

The 159 questionnaires returned by the deadline covered 423 positions as non-executive directors which gives us an average of 2.7 positions per person! And as the data shows there's not a lot of turnover - once appointed, we hold on!

a. Numbers and calibre

The numbers of non-executive appointments implied by the universal adoption of the Cadbury Code throughout all significant British companies (not just those on the Stock Exchange) is very large. On the other hand the supply of appropriate candidates appears to be limited and there is an obvious need to restrict the number of appointments which any one person can expect to fill effectively.

b. Calibre

Hitherto, senior professionals - lawyers, accountants, administrators etc. - have been a common source of non-executive directors and they are likely to continue to be useful in the context of public interest responsibilities. But they may not be the best qualified or the most effective in providing supervision and vigorous challenge to managerial decisions.

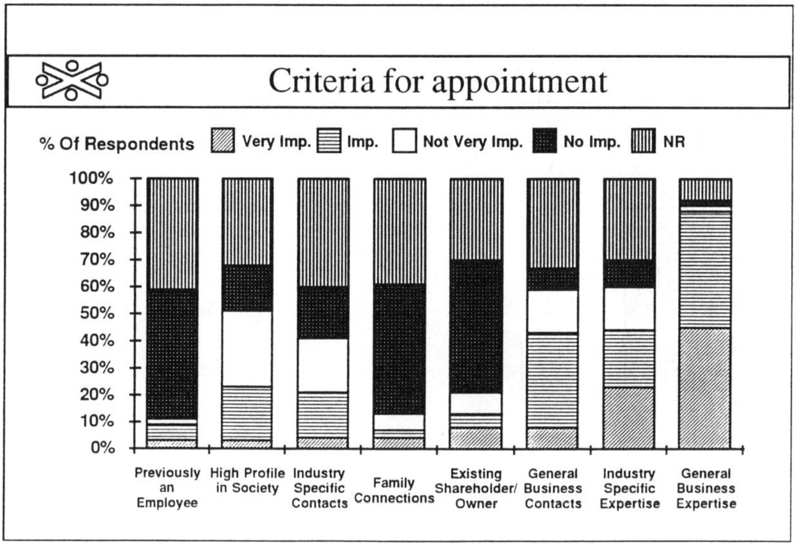

Business failure is neither necessarily, nor even often, the result of a failure of technical competence. Indeed, it seems that in general, the practical systems of corporate *management* operate reasonably well to provide adequate development of competence in technical areas, whether in production, distribution, marketing, finance, industrial relations, administration, design, and so on. But when the individual is required to meet additional responsibility as a director and in that role contribute to corporate policy and corporate governance, mere technical competence is obviously not enough.

We need better education to ensure that individuals can be adequately prepared to understand and discharge their duties as directors!

2. *The selection and appointment process is quite inadequate*

At present the way in which NEDs are selected tends to be rather haphazard. Rather than having a situation where an appointment is made through a formal selection process involving the whole board and using the nomination committee to carry out the selection process and to make proposals to the Board as suggested by Cadbury, we have a situation where invitations by the Chairman to a particular high profile NED is the norm.

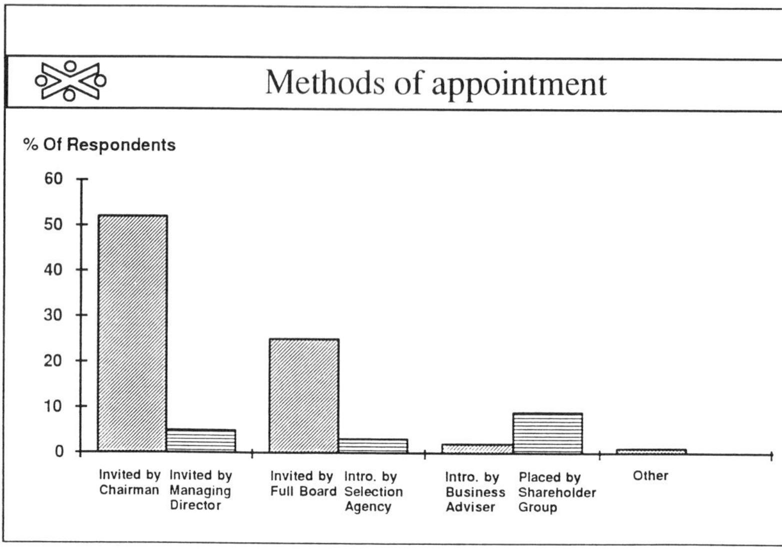

Invitation by the Chairman was clearly the most frequent method of appointment for 50% of respondents. The whole board were responsible for the approach in only 25 % of all appointments.

A related issue in this selection process is that question of the special responsibilities of institutional investors. Cadbury advocated that they should communicate directly with boards of directors on matters of concern. Thus non-executive directors can be used as "sounding posts" or communication channels. This is preferred to the alternative of institutional investors communicating their displeasure at board decisions or company results by offloading their shares. As it has been put elsewhere, rather than dash for the "exit" to avoid a problem, investors should use their "voice" to correct and avoid errors.

But Cadbury ignores an important issue here: the non-executive directors have responsibilities to the company as an entity and to all shareholders as well as to fellow directors. That duty may be in conflict with the particular interests of an investor or be misaligned with his specific goals. I suggest that the institutional investor should be looked on simply as one of all the shareholders - albeit a very important one! Like other shareholders, he will have individual responsibilities and goals. No director can expect to satisfy them all universally and all the time. The director's primary duty is to the company.

By their combined actions, the constantly changing constituency of shareholders places the directors into a pivotal position and by implication, they authorise the directors to decide where the best interests of the company lie. To that extent directors become proxy proprietors. I do not think that an individual representative of one investing institution can be expected to act as the regulator of the board or as the custodian of the interests of *all* shareholders.

3. We are not using NEDs to full advantage

There is certainly some ambivalence about the significance of the contribution directors make. But they do think they could more with some help!

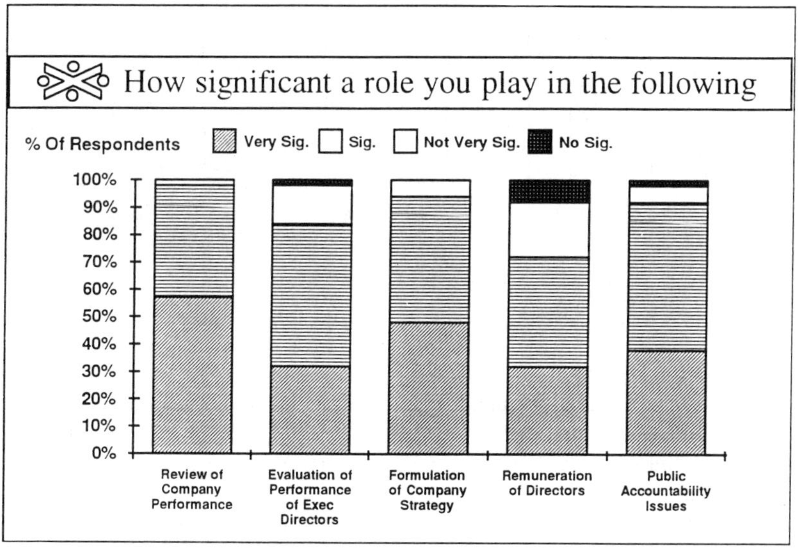

Non-executive directors must be provided with the necessary tools to equip them for the tasks they are required to undertake! This could include a formal induction process for new non-executives which could include, as a core element, an explanation by the people who run the organisation on a daily basis, of how the business operates and what are the key economic and market factors influencing its performance. The KPMG survey found that the elements most frequently listed as likely to affect the non-executives' ability to discharge their responsibilities include the inadequacy of management information. Over one-third of respondents felt management information was the primary problem either in terms of relevance, quality or detail!

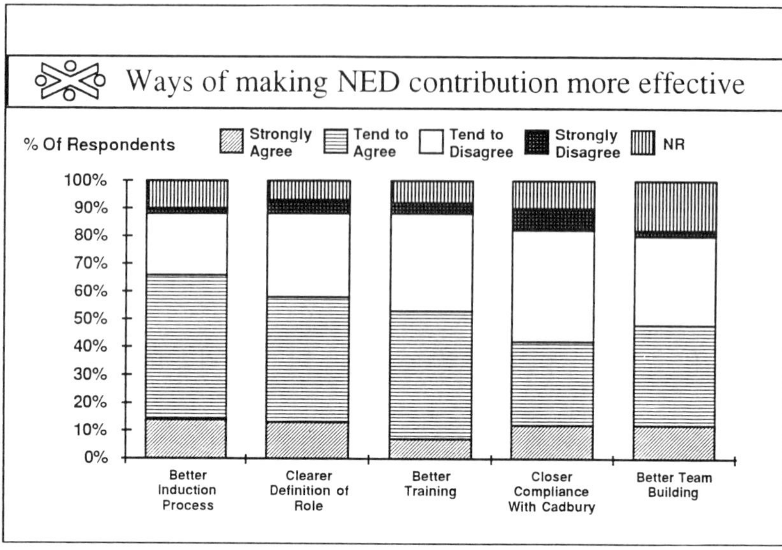

The response to this question suggests that the following must be considered essential.

1. Better induction
2. Proper training and understanding of the business and people
3. Timely information
4. Definition of matters to which board attention is given
5. Informal contacts and relationships between executives and non-executives that builds mutual confidence and respect, on which depends where the balance is struck between challenge and support, between openness and confidentiality.

4. The expectations, responsibilities and rewards do matter

Putting it simply, unless the rewards for the non-executive director match the responsibilities of the roles (or the punishment fits the crime!) they will not come forward in the desired quality and quantity. Fees paid to non-executives should represent the responsibilities which they carry!

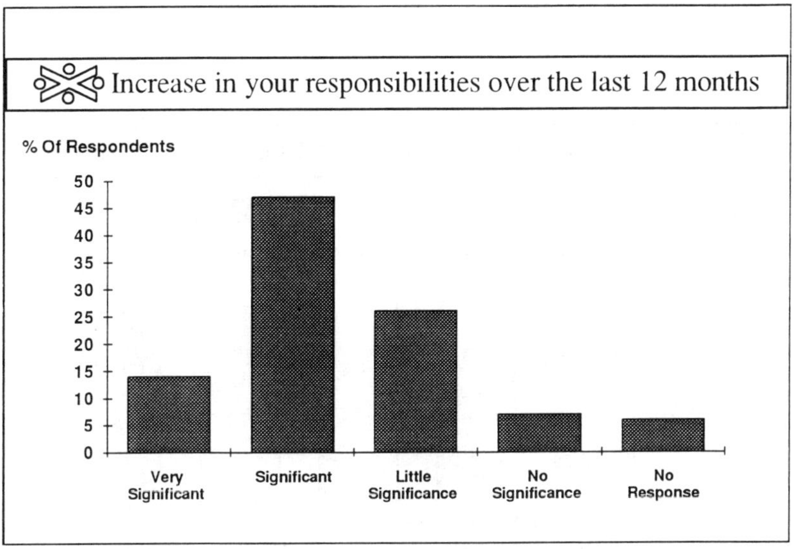

The KPMG survey showed that nearly two-thirds of all respondents felt that their responsibilities had increased "significantly" or "very significantly" over the last twelve months. The most frequent source of feeling increased responsibilities was the importance attached to the Audit Committee and Remuneration Committee. Over 40% of respondents who indicated that they felt their new responsibilities were burdensome, gave that reason. The frequency and detailed agendas of meetings of these committees were also given as a source for increased responsibility.

In light of the ratio of risk/reward it cannot be surprising for some non-executives to think twice about accepting such appointments!

Putting all those points together suggests the following steps to enhance the performance and value of non-executives.

At least you can see what they thought in the following table.

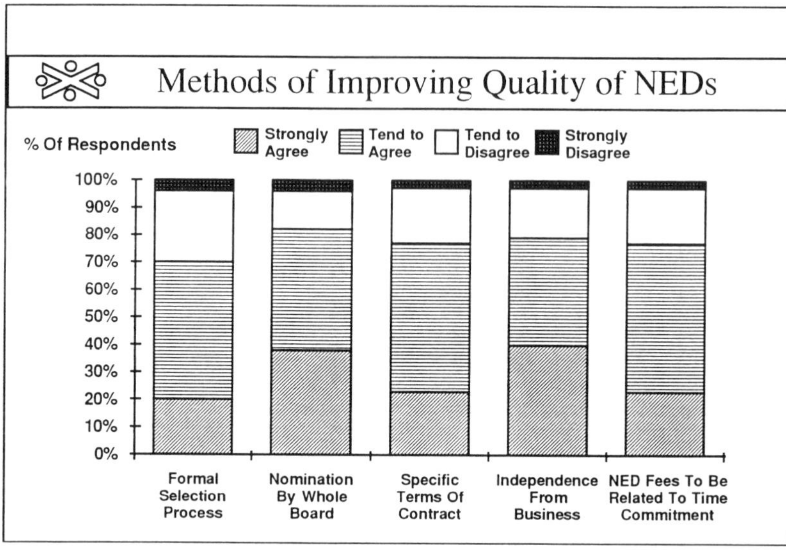

5. The finance function

The Cadbury Committee contended that the Board structure should clearly recognise the importance and significance of the financial function. Some have contended that we have increased in the U.K. the already impressive "regulatory overload" or excessive detail in accounting standards to ensure compliance. History always repeats itself. Every recession catches out the reckless individuals, such as Maxwell, who get away with it in boom times.

These are failure by individuals, not systems. Regrettably, instances of audit failure still abound despite the suggestions put forward by Cadbury.

Like Cadbury, I agree that these so-called audit failures are failures of executive management and of corporate boards who have failed to exercise effective managerial control. In other words, I agree with the diagnosis but not the proposed cure! Regulation does not itself secure good conduct.

What is required is appropriate action by responsible individuals.

Company directors should exercise effective management control over their finance function, and the auditing profession should recapture ground it has lost in terms of its independent authority by showing to the wider public in the U.K. that auditors will not modify their view in response to client pressure by signing accounts as "true and fair", when they are patently neither! What we need are a few heroes who will occupy the moral and professional high ground!

6. *What next?*

As noted above, the report of the review of compliance with the Code was published at the end of May 1995. The Financial Times (of 25th May 1995) reported the result as follows:

"The Cadbury Code which was designed to improve the way U.K. companies are run, has met with a high degree of compliance, particularly among the largest companies, (the Report's) authors said yesterday "we have been heartened by the response of listed companies to our Code" .

The authors of the Code indicated that an important factor encouraging compliance with the Code was a London Stock Exchange rule requiring listed companies to disclose in their annual report the extent to which they complied or to explain in what respects and why they did not.

The real question, of course, is - are you behaving better? Are you supervising effectively? Evidence for that it harder to find.

These broad statements of substantial compliance with the Code do not, of themselves, mean the Committee' s job is done. But publication of the Cadbury Code has contributed importantly to bringing the whole topic of corporate governance into very much sharper focus.

This has become evident over the past two years in a number of different ways.

1) The public sector has adopted "corporate governance". The U.K. Treasury has a model code for members of public boards and of the boards of "non departmental public bodies" (or "Quangos"). There seems, therefore, to be in government circles, evidence of desire to marry the rigorous but narrow practices of parliamentary accountability to the more flexible patterns of governance of the private corporate sector.
2) The exercise by investment fund managers and executives of institutional investors of their Cadbury-defined responsibilities is raising again different questions of institutional democracy. These managers participate in corporate democracy in a very undemocratic way; they do not consult with the savers, policy-holders, investors or pensioners whose interests they have to serve. Are the managers of institutional funds any more entitled to claim unquestioned authority in defining the best interests of these individual savers and pensioners than the executive directors are in claiming an unchallenged right to identify the best interests of shareholders?

3) Public concern in Britain is now focused on levels of senior executive remuneration and the sometimes complex ways of transferring wealth from the corporation to individual directors (in a tax-efficient way). Work done by the David Hume Institute[1] suggests that remuneration committees have not yet been totally effective in striking the right balance between personal gain and corporate performance. At a time when economic pressures secure tight constraints on wage levels, large increases in the total rewards of a few individual senior executive seem anomalous. Apparent personal greed is seen to be inconsistent with public declarations of "corporate responsibility". The issue has again become political.
So we have yet another private-sector group - the Greenbury Committee - established earlier this year to review corporate remuneration practices. This seems yet another example of the British assumption that people are blameless but systems are flawed! While greed is as unpleasant to behold as it is universally evident through time and place, the British response to this latest manifestation seems unduly fastidious. We await the results of the Greenbury Committee's deliberations with some interest but with limited expectations.

7. *The future - Cadbury mark II?*

Following the work of the Review Group which has already reported its view of the level of compliance achieved with the Cadbury Code, there will now be further consideration of its terms and of the companies to which it should be applied. We have already noted the important impact in these early days of the requirements of the London Stock Exchange, but these relate to only a small numerical minority of U.K. companies, albeit including most of the largest ones. In the midst of conflicting views about the desirability of extending the scope of the Code, and whether to tighten its detailed requirements or relax them, four points seem to be emerging.

1. It should be made easier for shareholders to present resolutions for consideration at Annual General Meetings. Regulations for the securities industry in the U.S.A. have recently achieved this. But this liberalisation must not be abused. If access to the forum of a company's Annual Meeting can be obtained by "activists" who need make only a minute investment, they will find too easily a platform for their political ends which may be totally irrelevant to the business

1 B.G. Main and J. Johnston, The Remuneration Committee as an instrument of Corporate Governance, Hume occasional Paper No. 35.

interests of the company. Corporate Accountability and Corporate Democracy must not be corrupted by zealots who put special interests such as "environmentalism" or "animal rights" above the legitimate business, economic and social goals of the company.

2. Consideration should be given as to how smaller companies can be encouraged to comply with the Cadbury Code. Small companies need external, independent advice and challenge even more than large companies, but such small companies have even less ready access to that non-executive support than do those already trying to comply with the Code.
3. There is a widely recognised need to encourage continuing improvement in the quality of professionalism and personal self-regulation among the non-executive director cohort. Preparation and training for those capable of becoming candidates for such appointments needs to be much more widely available and accessible.
4. Those responsible for managing the investments of the institutional investors, now so important to the British economy, have to work out how they are to discharge the special responsibilities in Corporate Governance which the Cadbury Committee identified for them. Various organisations to which those institutions belong - such as the National Association of Pension Funds, the Association of British Insurers - or which seek to advise them - for example the Pensions Investment Research Consultants - also have a contribution to make in defining how that role should be perceived and how it should be discharged .

As the Cadbury Review Group stated "There is still some way to go!".

Appendices

The following data is drawn from the results of the Monitoring Sub-Committee which was formed to assess how far complaince with the Code had progressed and whether the Code needed updating in line with emerging issues.
The source: The financial aspects of corporate governance compliance with the code of best practice 24 may 1995, Gee Publishing Ltd.

Table 1 - Percentage of Reports Examined for period 1993/94

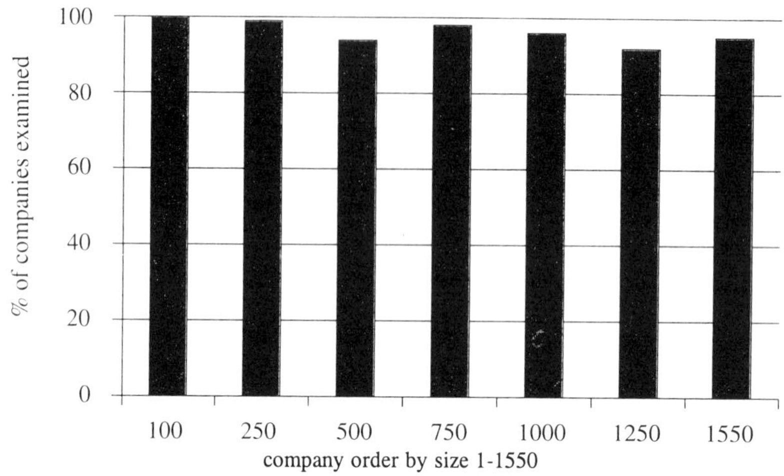

Table 1 shows the percentages of companies in the sample whose report and accounts were examined. The lowest percentage recorded is 92% for company order 1001 - 1250, rising to 100% for the top 100.

Table 2 - Companies Issuing Compliance Statements for period 1993/1994

The Committee has maintained that statements of full and limited compliance are equally acceptable; the main principle being that of disclosure, although compliance would generally be indicative of a higher standard of corporate governance.

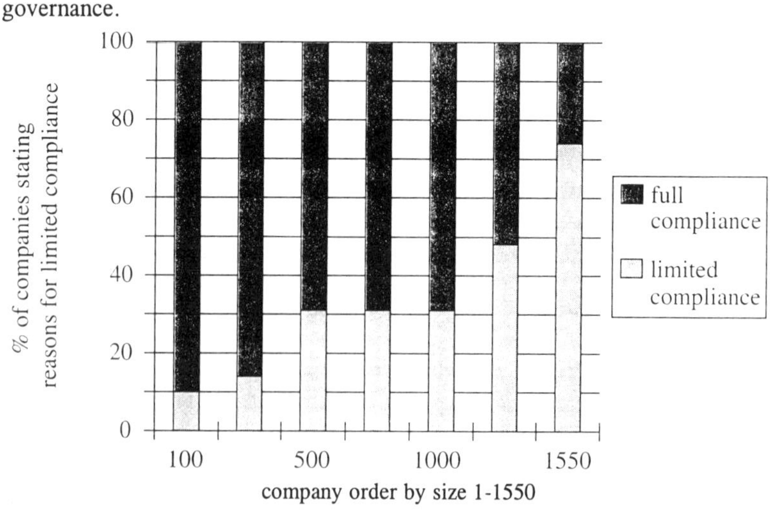

This table displays the percentages of companies who made statements of full compliance and limited compliance in their annual reports and accounts.

Table 3 - Chairman/Chief Executive Combined for period 1993/1994

The Code of Best Practice does not require that companies should split the roles of Chairman and Chief Executive, although it does recommend that where the roles are assumed by one person, there should be a strong and independent element on the board, with a recognised senior member.

% of companies with role of Chairman/Chief Executive:

co order by size	(a) separate	(b) combined *with* independent element of NEDs	(c) combined *without* independent element of NEDs
1 — 100	82	15	3
101 — 250	83	15	2
251 — 500	82	11	7
501 — 750	73	17	10
751 — 1000	81	13	6
1001 — 1250	74	15	11
1251 — 1550	72	5	23

In the majority of all groups sampled, the roles of Chairman and Chief Executive were split. The above figures also show the number of companies in which the roles were combined both with and without there being an independent element of non-executive directors. In the majority of groups, where the roles of Chairman and Chief Executive are combined, there is likely to be an independent element of NEDs. Where an independent element exists, it is most likely to comprise three or more non-executive directors, and in all but three of the companies within the sample there was an easily identifiable senior member. However, there were a small number of companies within the sample where there were two non-executives.

Table 4 - Number of NEDs on the Board

The Code of Best Practice recommends that company boards should have a minimum of three non-executive directors.

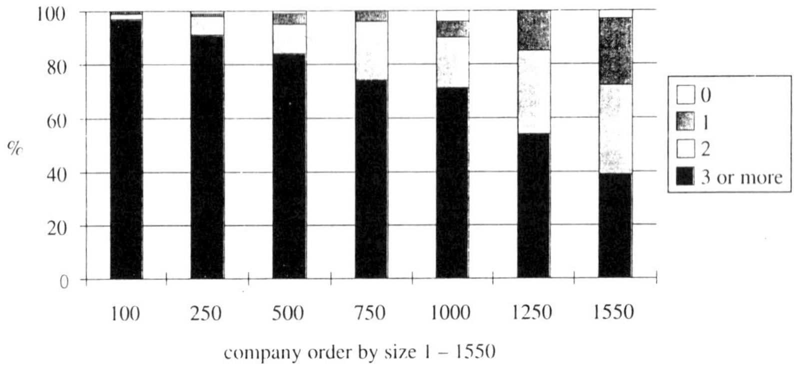

This table shows that there exists a clear relationship between company size and the number of non-executive directors - as a company increases in size, so it becomes more likely that it will have three or more non-executive directors.

Table 5 - Composition of Audit Committee

The establishment of an Audit Committee of at least three non-executive directors is a requirement of the Code of Best Practice.

(A) Three or more NEDs

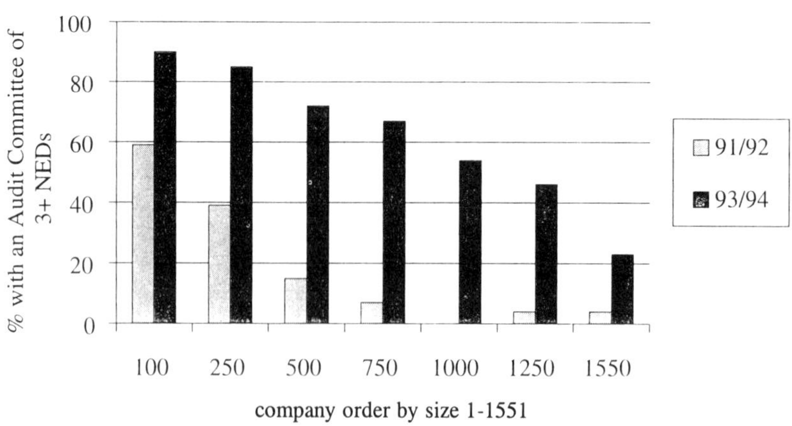

(B) Two NEDs

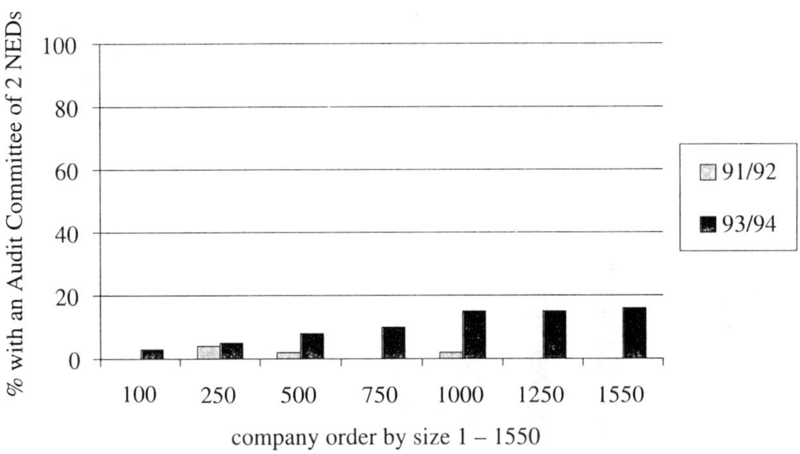

These tables show that the majority of all companies in the top 500 reporting in 1993/94 state that they comply with the requirement to have an Audit Committee comprising three non-executive directors, although disclosed compliance decreases in relation to the size of the company. What is most noticeable is the great increase in disclosure of the existence of Audit Committees comprising three NEDs since the introduction of the Code.

Companies outside the top 500 also show an increased disclosure of Audit Committees comprising two non-executive directors. The number of such committees disclosed in the 1991/92 accounts was very small indeed.

Table 6- Nomination Committee

The Committee's Report states that the setting up of a Nomination Committee is 'one approach to making board appointments, which makes clear how these appointments are made and assists boards in making them...'. It is not part of the Code of Best Practice.

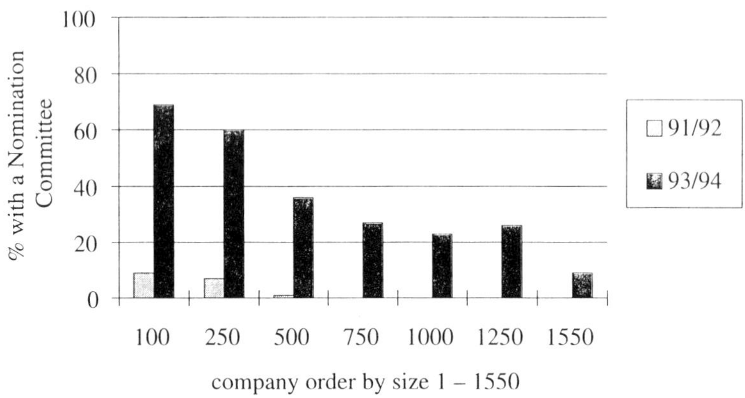

The above table shows that there has been a significant increase in companies of all sizes disclosing the existence of a Nomination Committee. For example, within the sample, no company outside the top 500 disclosed the existence of a Nomination Committee in its 1991/92 report and accounts.

Table 7 - Remuneration Committee

The Code of Best Practice advises that executive directors' pay should be subject to the recommendations of a Remuneration Committee made up wholly or mainly of non-executive directors. In the light of the subsequent public debate on the role of the Remuneration Committee, it is relevant to point out that other than defining its membership, the Committee did not in the Report or Code set out any further guidance, for example, by providing Specimen Terms of Reference.

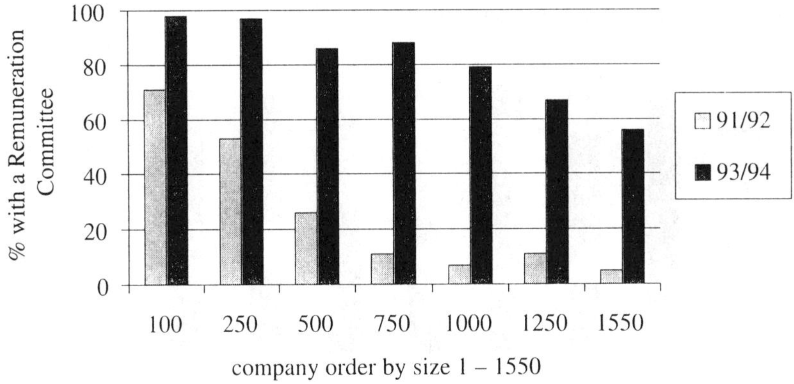

This table shows the great increase in the disclosure of the existence of Remuneration Committees in all sizes of companies between 1991/92 and 1993/94. The change in the top 250 companies was considerable, with percentages rising from over 50% to nearly 100%. However, the greatest relative change has taken place amongst companies outside the top 500 (i.e. with a market capitalisation of less than £120 million) where there was a rise from an average of 4% of the sample to over 70%.

Table 8 - All or Majority of NEDs Independent

The Code of Best Practice states that the majority of non-executive directors on a board should be 'independent of management and free from any business or other relationship which could materially interfere with the exercise of their independent judgement...'.

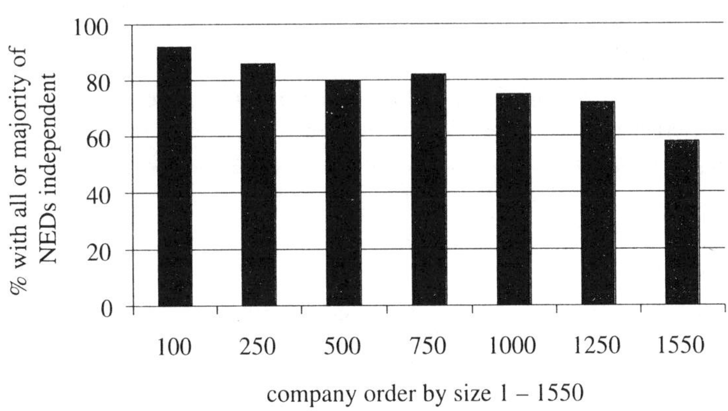

Table 9 - Number of Independent NEDs on the Board

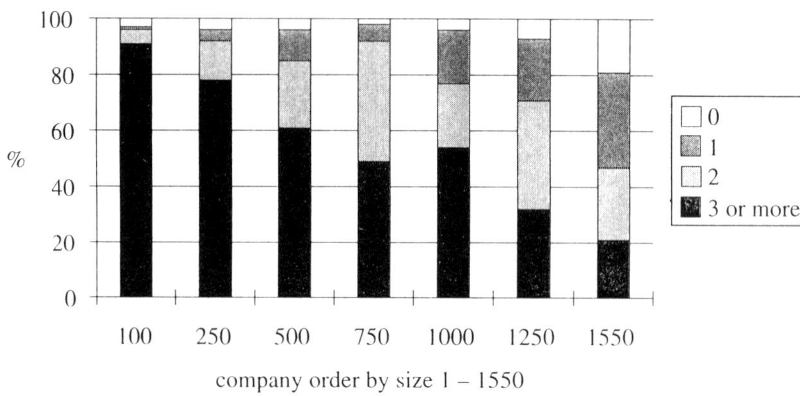

In compiling the above tables, information has been gained from companies' reports and accounts, and also from direct contact with companies in many cases. The independence of non-executives is a subjective judgement, and relies on the integrity of such directors in disclosing to the board any facts which could have a bearing on the exercise of their independent judgement. When undertaking this research the existence of independence has been assumed unless there has been any evidence to suggest that the definition in the Code (quoted above) could not be complied with. For example, if the non-executive director is a close relative of an executive director; if he has had a connection with the company exceeding 20 years; if he was formerly an executive director; or if he is an employee of the company. This view of independence may, in certain cases, run contrary to the expressed view of the board and its auditors.

Table 10- NEDs' Formal Terms

It is recommended in the Code of Best Practice that non-executives should have formal terms of appointment, covering their duties, term of office, remuneration, and its review.

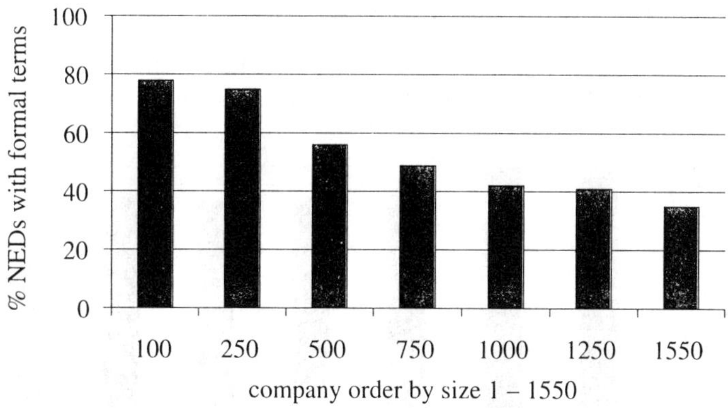

This table shows that while the majority of companies in the top 500 have disclosed compliance with this point in the Code, companies outside the top 500 are less likely to disclose compliance, the smaller they are.

Table 11 - Schedule of Matters Reserved to the Board

The Code of Best Practice states that the board should have a formal schedule of matters specifically reserved to it for decision to ensure that the direction and control of the company is firmly in its hands.

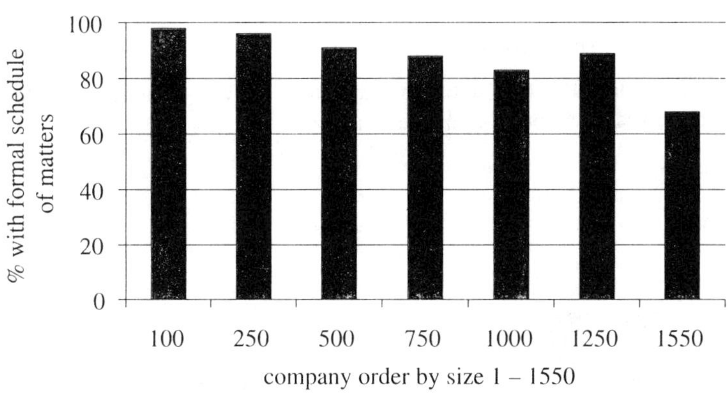

The above table shows that a significant majority of companies of all sizes have disclosed their compliance with this requirement, with compliance ranging from 98% of the top 100 to 71% of companies in the order 1251-1550.

Table 12 - Agreed Procedure for Independent Advice

The Code of Best Practice says that there should be an agreed procedure for directors to take independent professional advice in the furtherance of their duties.

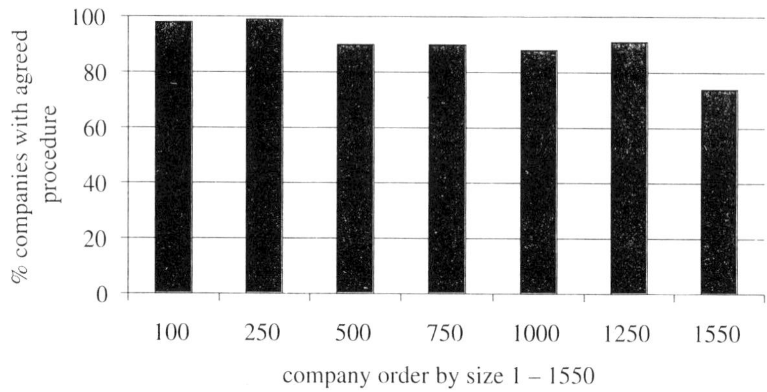

This table shows that a .significant majority of companies of all sizes have disclosed their compliance with the requirement in the Code. There was least disclosure of compliance with this requirement of the Code amongst the very smallest companies, whilst 94% of the top 500 companies complied with this provision.

Table 13 - Executive Contracts

The Code of Best Practice states that directors' service contracts should not exceed three years without shareholders' approval.

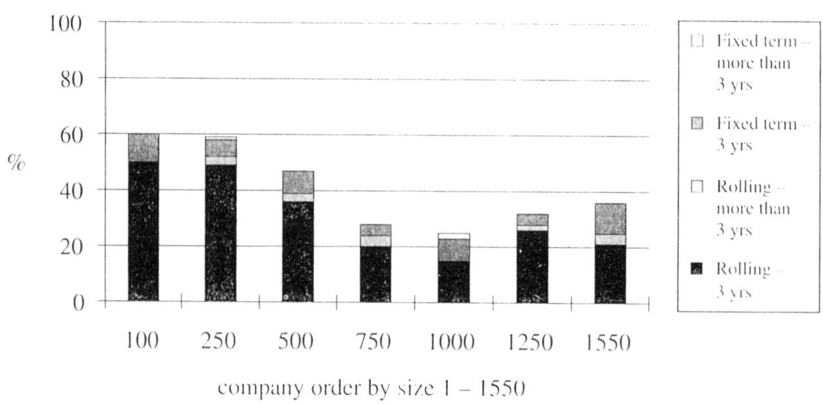

The above table shows the percentage of companies disclosing three-year contracts, and those of more than three years. The percentages for rolling contracts and fixed-term contracts have been shown separately. The balance of the percentages is accounted for by companies whose directors were on contracts of less than three years.

Institutional Investors as Corporate Monitors in the UK

Paul L. Davies

Contents

I. Introduction

The purpose of this paper is to explain the role played by institutional investors in monitoring corporate management in the UK. By institutional investors I mean primarily pension funds and insurance companies and, which is very important in this context, the fund managers which manage funds on behalf of institutional investors. What role do they play vis-a-vis the managements of the companies in which they invest? Do they, at the one extreme, simply sell the shares of portfolio companies with whose management they are dissatisfied or, at the other end of the spectrum, do they routinely involve themselves in the strategic decision-making which is central task of the top management of the modern corporation?

First, however, let me try to explain why this is an important issue in the UK. The formal system of corporate governance in the UK is still a very traditional one. At least in terms of its legal structure it has changed very little since its main outlines were set down when the modern form of the registered company was devised by Parliament in the middle of the nineteenth century. At its centre remain the shareholders. It is the shareholders as a whole who traditionally constitute 'the company'. In the legal terminology the shareholders are the 'members' of the company. It is the interests of the company i.e. of the shareholders as a whole, which the directors must promote when they exercise the discretionary decision-making powers which are invested in them by the constitution of the company. That at least is the traditional view.

Unlike some other European systems of company law, English law has not developed a notion of the company which embraces all the 'stakeholders' in the company i.e. all those who may be affected by its decisions, still less a notion of the company as a thing in itself independent of the stakeholders. Some such ideas were floated in the UK in the 1970s in connection with worker representation on the board, but they did not take root.[1] All that eventuated was a minor amendment to the company's legislation requiring directors to take into account the interests of the employees, along with those of the shareholders, but that change seems to have had a minimal impact upon UK company law and practice.[2]

Consequently, the formal structure of UK company law today is still one which puts the shareholders in the dominant position; it is they, normally, who elect the whole of the board of directors and certainly there is no requirement for worker representation on the board; and the unitary board has direct responsibility for the conduct of the business of the company i.e. there is no management board interposed between the supervisory board on which the shareholders are represented and the executive management of the company. So the whole orientation of UK company law is towards managerial promotion of the utility of the shareholders, a utility measured normally in terms of maximising the profitability of the company.

This paper is not concerned with the question of whether a corporate governance system which takes shareholder utility as its motto is a good system - though that is an enormously controversial question - but rather with the question of whether, taken on its own terms, it actually works in the way the above description of the formal mechanisms would lead one to expect. In order to answer that question one needs to understand the structure of shareholdings in large UK companies. Very few large companies in the UK are controlled by families (though there are notable exceptions, especially in the retailing field); instead, the shareholdings are usually widely dispersed and quoted on a public exchange, which provides a liquid market for those who wish to trade in such securities. So in 1990 in only 16% of quoted UK companies did a single shareholder have more than 25% of the shares, whereas in Germany that situation obtained for as many as 85% of quoted companies. Also in 1990 there were 2500 companies quoted on the London Stock Exchange and the Unlisted

---

1 For an analysis of this episode see P.L. DAVIES and M. FREEDLAND, Labour Legislation and Public Policy (1993) 396-404.

2 The change was introduced by the Companies Act 1980 and is now contained in s 309 of the Companies Act 1985. In part the lack of impact can be attributed to the fact that the duty laid upon the directors is a subjective one (i.e. they must take into account what they, not the court, perceive to be the interests of the employees) and because no easy mechanism has been made available for the enforcement of the duty by the employees or their representatives. So the change remains largely cosmetic.

Securities Market, compared with only 680 in France and 450 in Germany. And the top 100 quoted companies represented 52% of GDP.[3]

The comparison with Germany demonstrates the dominance in the UK of equity financing via the Stock Market as opposed to debt financing via the banks. Again, controversy rages over the merits of different forms of financing, but the point of significance for this paper are the implications of wide-spread shareholdings for the shareholder-dominated corporate governance system of the UK. As long ago as 1932 two American law professors pointed out, in what is probably the most famous book written in English on company law, that where shareholdings in a large company were widely dispersed, it was no longer to be expected that shareholders would display the degree of activism in relation to their company which the traditional model of company law seemed to require.[4] Given the collective action problems which are unavoidable in a dispersed shareholder body, any individual shareholder with only a small shareholding would become rationally apathetic as far as the corporate governance machinery was concerned. Activism ('voice') would be unlikely to provide the size of pay-off on a relatively small shareholding which would outweigh the costs of intervention, whilst the liquid public market offered an attractive (because low-cost) alternative way of remedying (through exit) an unfavourable situation.

The impact of this argument, which became orthodoxy on both sides of the Atlantic, on the UK theory of corporate governance was dramatic. If the shareholders could not be relied upon to police management, then UK company law provided no other candidates for that monitoring role and the conclusion must be that managerial discretion was largely uncontrolled as far as company law was concerned. Of course, the product market or the market for corporate finance would impose their own disciplines, no doubt, but for those who believed that the system of corporate governance was important, such responses were of little comfort.

In the post-war period one can detect three types of response to the Berle and Means problem. In the 1940s and 1950s the trend, at least on the left, was to say that the problem would be solved by nationalisation of private-sector companies, which would substitute monitoring by state bureaucracies for monitoring by shareholders. That is hardly a solution today, if ever it was one, since the nationalised sector of industry has virtually been eliminated and there is no immediate or even medium-term prospect of the reversal of that situation. Then followed a period in which the threat of the takeover bid was put forward

3 See for a general consideration of this area FRANKS and MEYER, Capital Markets and Corporate Control: A Study of France, Germany and the UK, 10 Economic Policy 191 (1990).

4 A.A. BERLE and G.C. MEANS, The Modern Corporation and Private Property (Rev'd ed. 1967).

as the main instrument which would align management and shareholder aspirations. The system of regulation of takeovers in the UK is favourable to the hostile bid i.e. one made over the heads of the incumbent management to the shareholders of the target company.[5] It was argued that the threat of such a bid would keep the management on its toes in terms of putting the shareholders' interests at the forefront of its concerns. I think there is no doubt that the threat of the takeover bid does have some impact in this direction, but equally few people now think that this threat can be regarded as the sole answer to the hole at the centre of UK corporate governance. The costs of a successful bid are high so that only egregious cases of corporate incompetence or self-seeking are likely by themselves to trigger a bid. A bidder will need to pay a hefty premium to the market price of the target to induce the shareholders to accept, as well as incur substantial professional fees. As a routine, across-the-board device for monitoring management behaviour the takeover bid clearly leaves a lot to be desired.[6]

So we arrive at last at the subject matter of this paper. Is it possible that six decades after Berle and Means wrote their book that the traditional system of corporate governance can be put back into effect in the UK because the dispersal of shareholdings, which was the basis of their thesis, has now been sufficiently reversed as a result of the aggregation in recent decades of shareholdings in the hands of the institutional shareholders? The situation today in the UK is clearly still not one in which a single shareholder often dominates a large company. The question rather is whether the re-concentration of shareholdings in the hands of institutional investors has proceeded so far that the number of shareholders, who need to co-ordinate their actions in order effectively to influence the management, has been reduced to the point where the collective action problems can be overcome, at least in a significant number of cases. This paper will examine some statistics, based on research carried out in Oxford, which bear upon the answer to this question, but let me first state what the overall conclusion will be. It is that activism on the part of institutional shareholders has become a significant part of the corporate governance system in the UK and in particular that the institutions have become a powerful lobbying force in relation to the regulation of companies, especially the regulation of listed companies. As far as intervention in the affairs of individual companies is concerned, however, whilst such intervention is again a significant part of the scene, it has not reached, and is unlikely to reach, the

5 P.L. DAVIES, Defensive Measures: the Anglo-American Approach, in: K.J. HOPT and E. WYMEERSCH (eds.), European Takeovers: Law and Practice (1992) 195.

6 For an extended critique of the takeover as a tool for disciplining management see J.C. COFFEE, Regulating the Market for Corporate Control: A Critical Assessment of the Tender Offer's Role in Corporate Governance, 84 Colum. L. Rev. 1145 (1984), especially at Part III.

level of routine involvement. Such intervention, at least at any level beyond the giving of information, tends to be crisis driven and linked to the absence of alternative strategies for dealing with the problem, notably sale in the market or to a takeover bidder. Having examined the facts, the paper will try to analyse the determinants and constraints of institutional shareholder activism.

II. The Rise of Institutional Shareholders

Table I: Ownership of UK Equities

Sector of beneficial owner

	1963	1969	1975	1981	1991	1994
Individuals	54.0	47.4	37.5	28.2	19.9	20.3
Other personal sector	2.1	2.1	2.3	2.2	2.4	1.3
Public sector	1.5	2.6	3.6	3.0	1.3	0.8
Banks	1.3	1.7	0.7	0.3	0.2	0.4
Insurance companies	10.0	12.2	15.9	20.5	20.8	21.9
Pension funds	6.4	9.0	16.8	26.7	31.3	27.8
Unit trusts	1.3	2.9	4.1	3.6	5.7	6.8
Other financial Institutions	11.3	10.1	10.5	6.8	2.3	3.3
Industrial & commercial companies	5.1	5.4	3.0	5.1	3.3	1.1
Overseas	7.0	6.6	5.6	3.6	12.8	16.3
Total	100.	100.	100.	100.	100.	100.

Note: 'Other financial institutions' includes investment trusts.

Source: Central Statistical Office, Share Ownerhsip: A Report on the Ownership of Shares at 31 December 1994 (London, 1995) p 8.

Table I gives the data concerning the changes which occurred during the period 1963 and 1994 in the beneficial ownership[7] of equity shares issued by companies listed on the International Stock Exchange, London. As can be seen, the percentage of the total held directly by individuals[8] has fallen from 54% in

7 The picture which emerges if analysis is confined to the registered owners of the shares is, of course, wholly misleading because of the widespread use of nominee names for the holding of shares. On the other hand, bearer shares, although permitted by English law, are not widely used.

8 This figure refers to the *direct* holdings by individuals in companies (including, rather unfortunately for present purposes, their holdings in investment trusts, which are companies) but not their indirect holdings via unit trusts, which are shown separately, or in other ways: Central Statistical Office, Share Ownership: A Report on the Ownership of Shares at 31 December 1994, HMSO (1995) para. 3.6. To the

1963 to 20.3% in 1994. Interestingly, that percentage has declined steadily over the period until the late eighties, and the most that the numerous privatisation issues made by the British government since 1979 seem to have achieved has been the stabilisation of the situation in the most recent period. These issues may have increased substantially the number of individual shareholders but they have not had the same effect on the percentage of total UK listed equities held by this category of investor. Overall, almost two-thirds of the shares held by individuals were in holdings of £100,000 or less, and over one fifth were in holdings of £5,000 or less.[9] Thus, the picture of individuals' holdings which emerges from the survey corresponds very much to the Berle and Means stereotype of a large number shareholders with a small, or even very small, number of shares overall and, a fortiori, in any one company.

By contrast, the percentage of shares held by the institutions (meaning here the insurance companies, pension funds, unit trusts and 'other financial institutions'[10]) has grown, collectively, from 29.0% in 1963 to 59.8% in 1994. There was particularly rapid growth up to 1981, though since then the overall growth in institutional shareholding has been modest.[11] However, within the overall category of institutional shareholding, there have been significant differences in the rate, and even the direction, of the changes. The most dramatic increase has been in the percentage of listed equities held by pension funds i.e. from 6.4% in 1963 to 27.8% in 1994, a more than four-fold increase.[12] Insurance companies merely doubled their holdings in the period and so lost their position as the largest category of institutional shareholder. Nevertheless, these two categories of institution held between them very nearly 50% of the equities of listed companies in 1994.

What these figures suggest is much more than a simple shift by individuals out of direct holdings of shares into collective investment schemes. That has been happening, no doubt, but if that were the predominant trend in the period, it would have led to a much higher figure for unit trusts than their 6.8% market share in 1994 and, presumably, the figure for 'other financial institutions' (i.e. mainly investment trusts) would not have shown a decline. The remarkable growth of the percentage of listed equities held by pension funds suggests that the main drive behind the figures has been the development of long-term

---

extent that holdings in investment trusts are included in this figure individuals' direct holdings in operational companies are overstated.

9 Ibid.

10 To which investment trusts constituted two-thirds of the 1994 figure.

11 This is probably due to a slowing down in the rate of expansion of pension funds which, after a rapid growth in the 1960s and 1970s, now seem to have reached something of a plateau, probably both because pensionable employment has reached an, at least temporary, ceiling and because individual funds are coming to maturity.

12 There was a similar increase in the percentage held by unit trusts but from a very small base.

savings by employees and employers in order to provide a satisfactory income in retirement. These savings have been funnelled traditionally into occupational pension schemes i.e. a form of private, but collectivised, saving, tied to particular employments, and leading to the creation of a pension fund out of which the pensions promised by the employer could be paid. The same factors would also help to explain the (lesser) growth of insurance company holdings, since the purchase of life insurance policies is a popular way, especially for small occupational pension schemes and the self-employed, to build up lump sums for the purchase of annuities upon retirement.

The climate in the UK in the post-war period has been favourable to the development of occupational pension schemes as the preferred way of providing an income in retirement. On the one hand, there has been a steady growth in the levels of personal disposable income among those in work, which has generated a social demand for greater protection against poverty in old-age. On the other hand, the state pension scheme, established on a pay-as-you-go basis, was envisaged in the Beveridge Report of 1942 as no more than a flat-rate minimum provision. By the time the state got around to contemplating more generous arrangements in the 1960s, the occupational pension schemes were too well established to be displaced from their central role in pension provision.[13] Had the state scheme, with its pay-as-you-go funding basis, occupied from an early date a more prominent position in the UK scheme of things, then there would have been less scope for private, funded schemes with their need to find an investment home for the steady stream of contributions by and in respect of those still at work.

Of course, there is no rule of natural law to the effect that the employer's pension promises to its employees must be backed by the creation of a separate pension fund. For example, pension monies might be reinvested in the employing company without any separate legal institution being created to take charge of the investments. However, the tax rules in the UK encouraged employers to set up pension funds as trusts external to the employing enterprise, and this tended to put a severe brake on the sort of self-investment of pension monies, by way of liability reserves, which is common in Germany.[14] Again, even if there has to be an external fund which invests

---

13 L. HANNAH, Inventing Retirement (1986) ch. 4 and P.L. DAVIES, Institutional Investors in the United Kingdom, in: D.D. PRENTICE and P.R.J. HOLLAND (eds.), Contemporary Issues in Corporate Governance (1993) at 70-73. More recently, the state has resiled even from the limited extensions which were made to the state scheme at this time. See the state's promotion of personal pensions as a substitute for its own State Earnings Related Pensions Scheme (SERPS), described in P.L. DAVIES and M.R. FREEDLAND (supra note 1) 571-3.

14 On the impact of the tax rules in the UK see the Report of the Pension Law Review Committee (Chairman: Professor Roy Goode), Cm 2341-1, (1993) 59-60. On Germany see M. HAUCK, The Equity Market in Germany and its Dependency on

outside the employing company, pension fund trustees could choose from a range of investment instruments of which equities constitute only one example. However, in an inflationary economy, which is what the UK had been in most of the post-war period, fixed-interest securities had only limited attraction, and property (or art-works or whatever else investment fashion dictated from time to time) did not carry the high levels of liquidity which are characteristic of investments on well-established stock exchanges. Consequently, it has been a feature of pension fund investment policy that a high proportion of the contributions has been invested in equities.[15]

III. General Intervention by Institutional Shareholders

The growth in the overall share of the equity market owned by the institutions has naturally led to them becoming more influential in the debates about the proper regulation of large companies, whether those debates are initiated by government, the Stock Exchange or other City interests. Such intervention by the institutions may be referred to a 'general-level' monitoring by which is meant the adoption and attempted enforcement by the institutions, or some group of them, of a policy which applies to all companies or to a particular category of company, for example, the proposition that companies should not issue non-voting equity shares. General intervention is to be contrasted with 'particular' intervention, by which is meant the devotion of institutional effort to solving a problem which is confined to an individual company or group of companies (typically a problem of how to define or implement its business policy), though, of course, the experience gained in solving one company's problems may be useful vis-a-vis another. Particular intervention will be

---

the System of Old Age Provision, in: T. BAUMS, R.M. BUXBAUM and K.J. HOPT (eds.), Institutional Investors and Corporate Governance (1993) at 555. In 1990 the pension fund obligations of German companies amounted to DM 345 billion, but only DM 82.5 billion was funded through external pension funds: ibid p. 558. In the United Kingdom, on the other hand, self-investment of pension monies by companies is regarded as a suspect activity and has been the subject of legislative restriction: Social Security Act 1990, Sch. 4, para. 3 and the Occupational Pension Schemes (Investment of Schemes Resources) Regulations SI 1992 No 246, which restrict the level of self-investment to 5% of the fund. See further R. NOBLES, Pensions, Employment and the Law (1993) 179-180, 183-4 and 194.

15 The percentage of total pension fund assets invested in UK equities hovers around the 55% mark. It has been expected for some time that the arrival of more pension funds at a stage of maturity and the introduction of a 'minimum solvency requirement', as proposed by the Goode Report and now contained in the Pensions Act 1995, would cause funds to look more favourably on fixed-interest securities because they need to bring about a closer matching of assets and liabilities. However, there is not much evidence as yet of such a development.

discussed below after we have analysed the position of fund managers. Here, we will confine ourselves to general intervention.

Intervention by the institutions on matters of general company policy is both longer-established and more widespread than intervention in the affairs of particular portfolio companies. It is perhaps not difficult to see why this should be so. The development of a general policy involves a lesser input of resources than producing a solution to the management problems of a particular company. Moreover, a general policy, once agreed, can be applied over a range of companies at relatively little cost, whereas the solution to a particular company's management problems may have few generalisable features. Of course, a general policy is not much use unless it is implemented in relation to particular companies, but, whereas the implementation of a particular policy will often involve the institutions' convincing or replacing the failing management which has thrown up the problem, general policies may be capable of being implemented through existing regulatory structures, for example, the Listing Rules of the London Stock Exchange. General intervention is co-ordinated by the industry associations to which the institutional investors themselves belong: the National Association of Pension Funds, the Association of British Insurers and the Institutional Shareholders' Committee being the most prominent.

It is not possible to provide in the space available a comprehensive account of institutional intervention on grounds of general policy, but the following account give some flavour of both the scope and the history of such intervention. It concentrates on institutional intervention to protect shareholder rights, to establish structures of corporate governance and to control abusive executive compensation schemes.

(a) Shareholder Rights. The purpose of intervention here is to maintain the potential for institutional influence over management by safeguarding the shareholders' basic rights. Thus, the institutions have long run a campaign against non-voting shares. In spite of a legislative refusal to take steps to prohibit such issues, the campaign has had considerable success. Weinberg reports that 'a number of proposals to make capitalization issues to ordinary shareholders in non-voting shares have been dropped following institutional objections' and, perhaps more important, 'there are no instances in recent years of a company seeking a listing for any class of non-voting equity capital.'[16] Opposition to 'the creation of equity shares which do not carry full voting rights' still appears as the third point in the Institutional Shareholders'

16 WEINBERG and BLANK on Take-overs and Mergers (1989) para. 3-805. During 1993 a number of prominent listed UK companies with dual-class share structures announced enfranchisement programmes for their restricted-voting shares.

Committee's recent statement of good practice on the responsibilities of institutional shareholders,[17] and the Institutional Fund Managers' Association has carried the same message, though without obvious immediate success, to continental stock exchanges as well.[18]

An equally long-running saga has been institutional insistence on pre-emption rights for existing shareholders when a company makes an equity issue for cash. Here, institutional pressure did achieve a legislative result, though one primarily due to the UK's obligation to implement the Second Community Directive.[19] But the institutions continue to insist with some success on more restrictive rules than the statute imposes. Consequently, whereas the statute allows the shareholders to disapply the pre-emption requirement for periods of up to five years at a time, the International Stock Exchange's rules, under institutional shareholder influence, limit the period, in effect, to that between the annual general meetings,[20] whilst the National Association of Pension Funds and the Association of British Insurers have imposed, seemingly effectively, an even more rigorous policy. This policy, embodied in informal guidelines issued by the Stock Exchange, commits the institutions to voting for disapplication, even on an annual basis, only where the company in question undertakes to limit any non-rights issue to 5% of the issued capital of the company in any one year and to 7.5% in any rolling period of three years.[21] Interestingly, these guidelines, unlike the statute, cover vendor placings, which, technically, do not involve the issue of shares for cash, but which in economic terms achieve a similar result.[22] Thus, the institutions, operating through the mechanism of the Stock Exchange, have been able to achieve, though not without controversy, a distinctly tougher regime for listed companies than general company law requires, and this is a measure of their influence.[23]

---

17 ISC, The Responsibilities of Institutional Shareholders in the UK (1991) 5 (hereafter 'institutional shareholders' code'). Earlier in the same year the ISC published a Statement of Best Practice on the Role and Duties of Directors (hereafter 'directors' code').

18 "Investors seek more European rights", Financial Times, 15 July 1992.

19 Directive 77/91/EEC. See now Companies Act 1985 ss 89-95.

20 London Stock Exchange, The Listing Rules para. 9.20.

21 Pre-emption Rights, 27 Bank of England Quarterly Bulletin 545 (1987).

22 In a vendor placing the issuer allots the shares to the vendor of the asset the issuer wishes to acquire and the vendor immediately places the shares with investors in exchange for cash.

23 A somewhat similar picture emerges in relation to repurchases of shares by companies, where the Stock Exchange and the Association of British Insurers impose tougher requirements than the statute. See Share Repurchases by Quoted Companies, 28 Bank of England Quarterly Bulletin 382, 385 (1988) and the Listing Rules (supra note 20) ch. 15, especially para. 15.7 relating to purchases of more than 15% of the equity shares.

A policy of opposing the issue of non-voting shares helps to preserve the shareholders' position of ultimate control and insistence on pre-emption rights does both this and protects the shareholders' equity interest from dilution. Both policies also make it indirectly more difficult for management to take pre-bid defensive measures against take-over bids.

(b) Structure and composition of the board. A more recent, but certainly not new, concern of the institutional shareholders has been the structure and composition of boards of directors of portfolio companies. The ISC's institutional investors' code of practice, whilst not specifically calling for a split in the roles of the chairman of the board and the chief executive of the company, nevertheless refers to the need to avoid 'concentrations of decision-making power not formally constrained by checks and balances appropriate to the particular company.' It also calls for the appointment of a 'core' of appropriately qualified non-executive directors.[24] These precepts clearly had a strong influence on the report of the Cadbury Committee, where these suggestions appear in a somewhat stronger form, but coupled with an express endorsement of the ISC code.[25] And the institutions have played an increasingly public role in securing the implementation of the changes recommended by Cadbury.[26] Research suggests that pressure from the institutions, both directly and via the Cadbury Committee, has had its effect upon companies. In 1993 77% of quoted companies split the role of chairman and chief executive officer, but approximately one third of those companies had introduced that change in the period between 1988 and 1993. The same research showed that the proportion of non-executive directors on the boards of quoted companies (as a percentage of total board membership) increased from 36% in 1988 to 41% in 1993, though it is not clear whether all these non-executive directors met the Committee's definition of independence.[27]

(c) Executive Remuneration. Institutional concern at the potential conflicts of interest involved in the setting of executive remuneration is, again, not new. The temptation for executive directors who set their own reward packages to act, consciously or unconsciously, in their own, rather than the shareholders' interests, is obviously a strong one, and it provides a classic illustration of the

---

24 ISC (supra note 17) 5.

25 Report para. 6.11.

26 Two institutional investors with a combined total of more than £100bn under management have written to the UK's largest public companies setting out corporate governance policies to which they expect them to adhere: Financial Times, 17 February 1996.

27 M.J. CONYON, Corporate Governance Changes in UK Companies Between 1988 and 1993, 2 International Review of Corporate Governance (1994) 97.

agency problems which shareholders face vis-a-vis executive management.[28] Most recently, that concern has focused on three issues: the rate and level of growth of executive salaries and their lack of relationship to the performance of their companies;[29] the operation of executive share option schemes;[30] and the size of the pay-offs received by some departing chiefs of companies whose businesses have been run with a conspicuous lack of success.[31] These concerns again find expression in the statement in the ISC institutional investors' code that 'institutional investors encourage the disclosure of the principles upon which directors' emoluments are determined.' More important, perhaps, the ISC directors' code recommended that companies establish compensation committees, made up of non-executive directors, in order to implement the principle that 'executive directors should not play any part in deciding their own compensation packages'

Again, the influence of these views upon the Cadbury Committee and, more recently, the Greenbury Committee[32] does not need stressing. The Cadbury Committee recommending that remuneration committees should consist 'wholly or mainly of non-executive directors and [be] chaired by a non-executive director'.[33] Research suggests that nearly all quoted companies now have

---

28 S. GROSSMAN and O. HART, An analysis of the principal agent problem, 51 Econometrica 7 (1983).

29 See "Research adds fuel to top pay row", Financial Times, 6 March 1994, and P. GREGG et al., The disappearing relationship between directors pay and corporate performance, 31 British Journal of Industrial Relations 361 (1993).

30 See the recent document produced by the National Association of Pension Funds and the Association of British Insurers, Share Scheme Guidance (1993) attempting to ensure that executive share option schemes 'should be subject to some realistic measure of management performance'. However, whilst the industry associations try to impose standards on the managements of portfolio companies, the executives of fund managers themselves are not immune from these temptations: see "M and G faces criticism of executive option scheme", Financial Times, 22 January 1994 and the reply by the managing director of M and G repudiating the guidelines: Financial Times, 4 February 1994.

31 "The history of handshakes", Financial Times, 1 November 1991, quoting as examples the Burton Group, Berisford, Ferranti and British Aerospace. See also "Shareholders wage war", Financial Times, 6 November 1991. To some degree, the payments to departing executives can be justified as compensation for breach of (often rolling) fixed-term contracts (see no. 24 above), and in one of its few proposals for changes in the law the Cadbury Committee recommended that s 319 of the Companies Act 1985 be amended so as to reduce from 5 to 3 years the maximum length for which directors' service contracts can be fixed without shareholder approval: op. cit. para. 4.41. The ISC directors' code had previously made the same recommendation.

32 Directors' Remuneration: Report of a Study Group chaired by Sir Richard Greenbury (1995). Both the National Association of Pension Funds and the Association of British Insurers had nominess on this eleven-man (as indeed it was) committee.

33 Cadbury Committee Report, para. 4.42 and see generally paras. 4.40 to 4.46.

remuneration committees, as opposed to only half in 1988, but that the ISC recommendation that such committees be composed entirely of non-executives is followed much less frequently, for 41% of committees had the principal executive director as a member.[34] It can still be asked, therefore, whether remuneration committees function so as to resolve the agency problems to which compensation issues give rise or whether they simply disguise them.

The Greenbury committee explicitly saw itself as taking forward guidance which had previously been issued in this area inter alia by the Association of British Insurers and the National Association of Pension Funds, and in continuing the trends towards more independent remuneration committees and greater disclosure of information about remuneration to shareholders. These two bodies are playing a full part in the implementation of the Greenbury recommendations, especially the controversial suggestions about the disclosure of the value of the pension entitlements of directors.[35]

Interesting though these examples of institutional shareholder-inspired regulation are, they do not take us to the heart of the matter, which is how within particular companies the corporate governance structures actually operate. Clearly, the institutions have been influential in designing those structures, but have they been influential qua shareholders in individual companies in putting the control mechanisms into practice? This question can be answered sensibly only after we have analysed who exercises the votes attached to the shares owned by the institutions, i.e. after we have examined the role of the fund managers.

IV. Funds and Fund Managers

Despite the dominance by pension funds of the equity markets (over one third of listed equities in 1992) press accounts of interventions by institutional shareholders in the affairs of particular companies only relatively infrequently refer to pension funds as among those active in the intervention. The most frequently-named interveners are insurance companies and the investment-management arms of financial conglomerates, usually based around merchant or, less often, clearing banks. The explanation for this situation requires us to make a distinction between the pension funds and the trustees of those funds, on the one hand, and those who manage the investment of the fund's assets, on the other. Of course, the trustees may directly employ investment managers, but it is estimated that only half by value of pension assets are managed in-house. For the rest, the investment management function is, in effect, delegated to external

34 CONYON (supra note 27) 104-107.
35 Financial Times, 16 February 1996, p. 8.

fund managers. Insurance companies, on the other hand, are much more likely to manage their funds in-house (usually through an investment management subsidiary). Moreover, these subsidiaries often offer investment management services to outside funds, including pension funds.[36] Since the investment management function normally carries with it the right to vote the shares beneficially owned by the pension fund, but registered with a nominee chosen by the manager, one can see how in cases of intervention the insurance companies and the pension funds seem to have an importance which is the reverse of what one would expect from a simple analysis of the percentage of equities owned by these two categories of institution.

Table II: Fund Managers Holding > 1% of UK Equities, 1991

Manager	Market value of UK equities managed from the UK at end-1991 (£ million)	As proportion of market value of total quoted UK equities at end-1991 (%)
Mercury Asset Management plc	20,403	3.81
Prudential Portfolio Managers Ltd	19,063	3.56
PosTel Investment Management Ltd	11,400*	2.13
The Standard Life Assurance Company	11,326	2.11
Barclays de Zoete Wedd Investment Management Ltd	10,501	1.96
Phillip & Drew Fund Management Ltd	9,561	1.78
Robert Fleming Asset Management Ltd	9,015	1.68
Schroder Investment Management Ltd	8,870	1.66
Scottish Widows Investment Management Ltd	7,395	1.38
Legal & General Investment Management Ltd	7,267	1.36
CIN Management Ltd	7,102**	1.33
Norwich Union Fund Managers Ltd	7,066	1.32
Commercial Union Asset Management Ltd	6,890	1.29
AMP Asset Management plc	6,100	1.14
M&G Investment Management Ltd	5,700	1.06
County NatWest Investment Management Ltd	5,577	1.04
Baring Asset Management Ltd	5,387	1.01
Hill Samuel Investment Management Group Ltd	5,377	1.00

* as at March 31, 1992.
** a hybrid figure combining the value of UK equities managed for British Coal Staff Superannuation Scheme as at April 5 1992 and for the Mineworkers' Pension Scheme as at September 30, 1992.

Sources: Calculations from information in Hymans Robertson, Pension Fund Investment Manager Survey: Manager Analysis (1992); London Stock Exchange, Stock Exchange Quarterly (Winter 1991); information supplied to G P Stapledon by Postel Investment

36 Thus, 20% of the total assets under management by Prudential Portfolio Managers Ltd, the investment management subsidiary of Prudential Assurance, at the end of 1991 consisted of external, segregated pension fund monies.

Management Ltd, Commercial Union Asset Management Ltd, AMP Asset Management plc, annual reports of British Coal Staff Superannuation Scheme and the Mineworkers' Pension Scheme (the bulk of the assets of which are managed by CIN Management Ltd).

Some of these points are illustrated by Table II.[37] This lists those fund managers which controlled 1% or more of the UK equity market in 1991. Of the 18 managers there listed only 2 are pension funds,[38] whereas there are 6 insurance companies listed[39] and the largest category consists of the 9 investment management arms of financial conglomerates.[40]

Table III: Fund Managers' Stakes in FT-SE 100 Companies, 1991-92

Institution	No of FT-SE 100 companies in which a notifiable interest held, 1991-92 (with breakdown by interest size)					
	3% ≤x≤4%	4% ≤x≤5%	5% ≤x≤6%	6% ≤x≤7%	7% ≤x≤8%	8% ≤x≤34%	Total
PPM	28	16	3	6	3	1	57
Schroder	13	5	2	-	-	-	20
Fleming	9	2	1	2	-	-	14
BZWIM	11	1	-	-	-	-	12
Scot Widows	9	2	1	-	-	-	12
MAM	-	-	4	1	-	2	7
PDFM	2	3	1	1	-	-	7
Norwich Un	1	2	-	-	-	1	4
Morgan Gren	2	1	1	-	-	-	4
Prov Mutual	3	1	-	-	-	-	4
Abu Dhabi	1	-	-	1	2	-	4
Gartmore	3	-	-	-	-	-	3
Sun Life	3	-	-	-	-	-	-
Total	86	35	14	12	5	4	156

Sources: Annual reports and accounts of the companies which made up the FT-SE 100 index at December 31, 1991. The annual reports were in respect of financial years ending between July 1 1991 and June 30, 1992.

37 Tables II and III reflect research carried out in Oxford by *Geof Stapledon* under the supervision of the writer, which research will shortly be published in full.

38 PosTel Investment Management Ltd. (the investment management subsidiary of the pension fund for the Post Office and the telecommunications industry) and CIN Management Ltd (the investment management arm of the coal industry pension fund).

39 Prudential, Standard Life, Scottish Widows, Legal and General, Norwich Union, Commercial Union.

40 MandG Investment Management Ltd is a specialist fund manager rather than a financial conglomerate.

['PPM': Prudential Portfolio Fund Managers Ltd; 'Schroder': Schroder Investment Management Ltd; 'Fleming': Robert Fleming Asset Management Ltd; 'BZWIM': Barclays de Zoete Wedd Investment Management Ltd; 'Scot Widows': Scottish Widows Investment Management Ltd; 'MAM': Mercury Asset Management plc; 'PDFM': Phillips & Drew Fund Management Ltd; 'GRE': GRE Asset Management Ltd; 'Norwich Un': Norwich Union Fund Managers Ltd; 'Morgan Gren': Morgan Grenfell Asset Management Ltd; 'Prov Mutual': Provident Mutual Life Assurance Association; 'Abu Dhabi': Abu Dhabi Investment Authority; 'Gartmore': Gartmore Investment Ltd; 'Sun Life': Sun Life Investment Management Services Ltd.]

However, in terms of likely intervention into the affairs of portfolio companies, the more relevant statistics relate, not to the percentage of the overall market held by a particular institution, but rather to the size of an institution's holding in the company in question. Table III gives some information on that question, showing the size of blocks of shares controlled by fund managers in the FT-SE 100 companies (i.e. the largest quoted companies) where these blocks exceeded the (then operative) 3% notification level.[41] Two points emerge from this Table. First, although institutions still dominate the picture,[42] it is not precisely the same institutions which appear in this table as appeared in Table II, and those which do appear are not listed in the same rank order. This suggests that different institutions, although all holding more than 1% of the total market, follow somewhat different policies in relation to the size of the stakes they are prepared to hold in individual companies, i.e. that they follow somewhat

41 Table III is ultimately based on data which Part VI of the Companies Act 1985 requires those having interests in 3% or more of a company's voting capital to provide to that company and which must be recorded by the company in a public register. At the time the Table was compiled the relevant legal regime (The Public Companies (Disclosure of Interests in Shares)(Investment Management Exclusion) Regulations, SI 1988 No 706) provided that interests of fund managers in listed shares were to be disregarded in computing the 3% figure if the manager was not the registered holder of the shares and its only interest consisted in a power to dispose of the shares. As noted in the text, most fund-management agreements give the manager the right to vote the shares in question and in such cases the manager would not be able to benefit from the exemption in the regulations. However, the standard fund-management agreement of one of the largest managers, Mercury Asset Management (MAM), does not give it the right to vote the shares in which its clients are beneficially interested (which is not to say that the client might not be heavily influenced by MAM's advice on voting matters). So MAM, unusually, would fall within the exemption, and to this extent Table III understates the importance of MAM. As a result of the amendment made to s 199 of the 1985 Act by the Disclosure of Interests in Shares (Amendment) Regulations, SI 1993 No 1819, implementing Directive 88/627/EEC, the distinction between fund managers with, and those without, the right to vote the shares under management becomes irrelevant to the obligation to disclose. However, the disclosure threshold for all fund managers is raised to 10%, so that the information contained in Table III will be more difficult to compile in the future.

42 Abu Dahbi is not, of course, an institutional shareholder in the sense in which the term is used in this paper.

different policies as to the spreading of risk. Alternatively or in addition, they may follow somewhat different policies in respect of the balance of their portfolios as between the FT-SE 100 companies and smaller companies.

Second, Table III indicates that the presence of very large institutional stakes in the FT-SE 100 companies is a rarity: 121 of the 156 notifiable interests recorded in this table are in the range of 5% or less. The significance of this fact, which may not obtain for the smaller quoted companies, is discussed below in relation to the need for institutional shareholders, which wish to intervene effectively in these large companies, to do so by means of coalitions with other institutions.[43]

V. Company-specific Monitoring by Institutional Shareholders

We have now identified the agents who are most likely to be the exercisers of the institutions' voting potential, i.e. the fund managers, and we have a statistical portrait of the holdings of the fund managers in at least the largest companies. However, knowing how often that potential for intervention is actually translated into action is no easy task, because the intervention does not typically take the form of the casting of votes at a shareholders' meeting. Although the ultimate threat which dissident shareholders can make against management is the calling of an extraordinary shareholders' meeting and the removal of the existing board - hence the institutions' desire to maintain their voting rights - in practice the institutions regard it as an indication of their lack of success and of management intransigence if matters have to be taken that far. In most instances the institutions bring their influence to bear through private meetings with incumbent management, at which the threat of action at the shareholders' meeting is implicit. Both institutions and management have a strong incentive to compose their differences in this way and without a public battle. It therefore follows that measuring institutional influence is a difficult task for the researcher, and that concentration on published accounts of intervention means one is analysing only the tip of the iceberg.

Nevertheless, some systematic work on the incidence of private intervention by institutional shareholders has now been undertaken[44] and that, coupled with an analysis of the public information, has given us the broad outlines of the

---

43 Only four double-digit institutional holdings in large quoted companies were found in this period: Standard Life Assurance's 33% holding in the Bank of Scotland; Mercury Asset Management's 18% holding in Blue Circle Industries; Cooperative Insurance Society's 17% holding in MEPC Ltd; and Kuwait Investment Office's 10% holding in Midland Bank.

44 By Professors BLACK and COFFEE in New York, see ID., 'Hail Britannia? Institutional Investor Behaviour Under Limited Regulation', 92 Mich. L. Rev. 1997 (1994), and by G.P. STAPLEDON in Oxford (see supra note 37).

picture. In the words of Professors Black and Coffee, the overall picture of interaction between institutional shareholders and their portfolio companies is one of 'frequent dialogue, occasional informal intervention when a firm is in trouble and a very infrequent formal intervention.'[45] Thus, although keeping in touch is a routine part of institutional shareholder relations with portfolio companies, action on the former's behalf to secure a change in business policy is not. Intervention to change policy, which may or may not involve changing management as well, is essentially crisis-driven, i.e. it occurs when the portfolio company is in trouble. Even then, the extent and the timing of the intervention is likely to be influenced by the availability to the shareholders of alternative solutions to their problem (for example, the likelihood of a takeover bid materialising); the size of the institution's stake in the company;[46] and the amenability of incumbent management to the suggested changes (for example, a company needing access to the facilities of the capital markets is likely to be more open to shareholder pressure at that time).[47]

The reasons for the traditionally low level of institutional intervention in the business policy of portfolio companies are now relatively well understood. For a variety of liquidity and prudential reasons the institutions have spread their investments widely so that a typical institution has acquired a range of portfolio companies which far exceeds its ability to engage in effective monitoring, especially given the modest size of in-house staff.[48] Some of the costs of intervention, which in the case of business policy are potentially quite high, can be spread through collective institutional action, which is probably in any event necessary in order to bring enough pressure to bear upon management. However, fund managers (other than in-house managers) are normally in competition with one another for management business, and generating effective collective action among potential competitors is not always easy, for the competitive pressures operate against collective solidarity. There is always the temptation for individual institutions to free-ride and refuse to join a proposed coalition or to abandon an intervening group after it has been formed.

45 Op. cit.

46 In the largest quoted companies, as Table III above shows, a coalition of shareholders will need to be put together to exercise effective pressure on management, but in smaller companies a single institution may have a large enough stake to make individual action feasible - and even necessary, given the difficulty of disposing of a large stake without depressing the price. See supra note 30.

47 See "The institutions get militant", Financial Times, 11 June 1991, citing the examples of Asda, Granada, and B. Walker "Tougher at the top", Financial Times, 28 September 1991, adding the case of British Aerospace.

48 E. MORGAN and A. MORGAN, Investment Managers and Takeovers: Information and Attitudes, Hume Occasional Paper 25 (David Hume Institute, Edinburgh, 1990), ch. 2.

Competition among fund managers for institutional business is intense, and so coalitions put together for the purposes of intervention are subject to a certain inherent tension, whilst managers need to keep a careful eye on the costs of intervention, because it does not automatically follow that these can be passed on to the institutions whose portfolios an intervening manager has charge of. A further consequence of the fact that responsibility for action rests with the managers is that conflicts of interest are a potential problem, especially for managers which are members of financial conglomerates. Although the institutional investors themselves, especially the pension funds, usually have an uncomplicated investment relationship with portfolio companies, at the fund management level, by contrast, it may be that other parts of the financial conglomerates act, for example, in a corporate finance role vis-a-vis the company into whose affairs the investment management arm is contemplating an intervention. The issue is not simply one of confidentiality or insider dealing, but whether there is a disincentive for the management arm to be an active intervener if that will damage the group's overall relations with the company.[49]

Finally, it would be wise not to under-estimate the skill and effort which incumbent management is likely to devote to maintaining its position and to exploiting any potential divisions among the coalition of institutional investors with perhaps rather diverse interests and views as to the merits and de-merits of the incumbents.[50] It is not usual for incumbent management to give up without a fight, and victory for the interveners is by no means a foregone conclusion.

These factors are all matters which fund managers need to weigh in the balance whenever it is suggested to them that the value of their holding in a particular company would be increased by a successful piece of firm-specific intervention. They are all arguments which suggest that the intervention might be more costly or less successful than would be necessary to make intervention by the fund manager a rational decision. However, underlying the whole basis of this calculation by the fund manager on behalf of the institution is an understanding that the relationship between institution and company is

---

49 The fund management subsidiaries of insurance companies also face, to varying degrees, a disincentive to being active interveners because of the potential for that intervention to cause damage to the insurance-providing sides of their businesses. Large composite insurers, in particular, not only have large equity holdings as a result of their life businesses, but also compete vigorously for lucrative commercial insurance on the general insurance sides of their businesses.

50 Cf. "A coalition versus a dictator", Financial Times, 27 May 1992. The story of institutional intervention in the affairs of the Savage Group is interesting from this point of view. The institutions maintained solidarity over the removal of the incumbent management but lost it over the issue of whom to install instead, allowing the non-executive directors to take control: "When men in grey suits choose to apply Savage pressure", Financial Times, 20 December 1990.

generated by the former's need to maximise its investment return within the appropriate time-frame. Institutions do not contemplate intervention in the affairs of portfolio companies because they think it is in the public interest to do so. They intervene (and perhaps only should intervene), if they intervene at all, because it is in the interests of those whose investments they manage to do so.

In this context one must not loose sight of the structure of the relationship between the institution and the company and its limited nature. It is only an investment relationship and, even in these days when relational investing has become a buzz phrase, there are limits to the involvement even a long-term shareholder can rationally contemplate. The point was put well some years ago by the Group Investment Manager of the Prudential when he said, drawing an implicit contrast with Germany:

> My guess is that any conceivable increase in [monitoring] activity will not amount to a major new element of accountability in our system matching that of bank-based economies, since share ownership unaccompanied by the additional involvement in providing finance and other services will never provide the depth of knowledge and commitment that arises with the combination of banking and proprietary interests.[51]

So I think one must conclude that institutional shareholder activism is not going to fill the hole at the heart of the UK shareholder-based system of corporate governance. The question of whether corporate management is appropriately accountable for its actions remains even after the institutions have done all that can and ought to be reasonably expected of them. Action by the institutions may be a very important part of the overall structure of accountability within which the management of large companies operate, but it is not and cannot be the whole of the answer to the problem.

51 NATIONAL ASSOCIATION OF PENSION FUNDS, Creative Tension? (1990) 14.

Holding Companies in Belgium

Eddy Wymeersch

Contents

I. General Overview

The Belgian enterprise scene is characterised by the presence of relatively numerous and powerful groups of business firms. These groups are headed by the so-called "holding" companies, many of which are stock exchange listed[1]. There are two types of holding companies, that play a substantially different role: these are often referred to as "industrial" v. "financial" holding companies. Both are structured as pyramidal groups of companies, parent companies holding shares in numerous subsidiaries.

Under Belgian law, holding companies are formally identified as being subject to a specific form of supervision, organised by the Royal Decree (RD) no. 64 of 10 November 1967. This supervision mainly aims at ensuring the disclosure i.a. of intragroup relations, under the supervision of the Banking and Finance Commission (BFC).

For the purposes of the present analysis, the definition of the holding company as defined in the RD no. 64 will be followed. The legislator having

---

1 The Société Générale de Belgique mentions that the number of companies included in its consolidated accounts for 1994 (1993) were as follows: 199 (316) fully consolidated, 6 (36) cases of proportional consolidation while 721 (648) were dealt with under the equity method. In addition, the company also held substantial investments in shares that did not meet the criteria for consolidation (e.g. a 1,36% stake in Elf Aquitaine). Furthermore, a substantial trading portfolio was reported.

used formal legal criteria to define the holding company, no distinction was made between the financial and the industrial holding companies. Is a "holding company" in the legal sense, a company the shares of which are listed on a stock exchange or its total portfolio in listed companies exceeding 0.5 billion BEF[2].

As of 30 June 1995 there were 105 holding companies registered with the BFC, 103 of which were stock exchange listed (97 were listed on the Brussels spot market). Also, about 80% of the market capitalisation of the Belgian stock exchanges is represented by shares issued by these 103 holding companies, the remaining 20% being shares issued by another 55 smaller companies.

1. Industrial groups

Most business firms are organised as parent and subsidiary companies, many of these being located abroad. This applies both to privately held companies and to stock exchange listed companies. For many firms the creation of subsidiaries merely constitutes a form of organisation: the subsidiaries are whether fully owned, or are joint ventures, partly owned with other groups. Minority shares at the level of the subsidiary are rare, and parents would make efforts to convince minority shareholders whether to sell their shares or exchange these for shares of the parent[3]. This type of group is managed on an integrated basis, mainly by appointing directors directly accountable to the parent's management and by establishing integrated group budgets and reporting rules. At the level of the subsidiary, directors are whether parent company directors or employees of the parent. Most of the time, there is no real divergence of interests between the group 's interests and the subsidiary's interests. Minority shares therefore usually are found at the level of the parent only. It is also at this level that governance issues are encountered more frequently. This type of company corresponds more or less to the pattern frequently found in the US and in the UK.

There is however one important difference: at the level of the parent company, shares usually are not widely held, but one or a few large shareholders exercise effective control. These controlling shareholders are whether stock exchange listed "financial holding" companies, or companies owned by important families or by other entities relating to individual interests. Therefore stock exchange listed companies most of the time are dominated by other listed holding companies, which on their turn are dominated by further - Belgian or foreign - companies. This pyramidal structure therefore continues on

2 For the full definition, see art. 1, RD no. 64 of 10 November 1967.
3 The Companies Act, art. 190 quinquies provides for freezing-out 5% minorities.

an almost endless number of layers. It will be further studied in the next section.

Along with these influential shareholders, other investors are whether individuals, smaller holding companies, or institutional investors. Institutionals, especially also foreign institutionals have increased their holdings in the Belgian companies, with some effect on governance techniques. However, most Belgian institutionals would not be willing to openly oppose management, while others would not be able to act very freely as they also belong to the same control network[4].

The enterprise type that has just been described is often is referred to as the "industrial group", as it engages in one specific type of industrial activities (e.g. banking, oil and gas, insurance, etc.). It also is a "holding company" as it uses the subsidiary technique not as an instrument to take part in diversified range of activities but as an organisational form for specific purposes within the general framework of the overall industrial business activity.

2. *Financial Holding Companies*

The other type of holding company, that is quite frequently found in Belgium, and presents specific characteristics is the so-called "financial holding" company. This type of business firm does not itself engage in an industrial or commercial activity, but mainly holds shares in a widely diversified range of businesses. The holding company itself is mostly stock exchange listed, and dominated by larger shareholders which are also stock exchange listed companies. In many cases these dominant shareholders are foreign companies, especially French, and less frequently UK or German[5]. Shareholders often belong to one group, although the larger entities are based on the joint participation of several groups. This pyramidal structure continues up to the final owners of the control, often detained by members of the founding families, wealthy individuals or successful entrepreneurs. Foreign shareholders also very often constitute the ultimate unit in the chain. Therefore, there will be a certain tendency to identify these groups with their ultimate controlling shareholders, although, in equity terms, their share often is quite limited.

The economic and social factors underpinning the development of this shareholder structure of Belgian enterprises into these widely diversified, non-industrial entities would call for extensive historical research. One could

4 Management of portfolios is often being undertaken by subsidiaries of the same holding companies, or by bank subsidiaries, the bank being more or less under control (see infra 26) of the holding company.

5 See H. DAEMS and P. VAN DE WEYER, Buitenlandse invloed in België (1993) about the influence of foreign heads of groups.

however mention a few factors. In the nineteen century, at the beginning of the industrial revolution, the Société Générale stood as a model for industrial entrepreneurship. With the support of the Dutch King, Belgian capitalists planned to invest in a diversified industrial portfolio thereby reducing their risk. The formula proved highly successful, up to the first World War, when Belgium's industrial base was destroyed. During the later years, this structure was further developed and pursued, especially in the southern part of Belgium. In the Flemish region, enterprises starting in the early years of the 20th century were based on entrepreneurial initiatives and control was - and often still is - more strongly kept in the hand of their founding families. The small size of the country may also explain the tendency for business to expand by diversification, rather by expansion of their main lines of business for which the local market was too small anyway. Therefore, financiers preferred to invest in existing enterprises, rather than start up new ones.

Different from the industrial groups, financial holding companies are confronted with minority issues at several levels of the group. This feature explains the traditionally keen interest in Belgium in issues of minority protection within a group of companies. Originally matters of disclosure and financial reporting - hence the considerable theoretical developments on the subject of consolidation of accounts[6] - called attention, from 1967 on embodied in the organisation of state supervision on "holding companies" and more recently to repeated legislative interventions[7].

II. Data

The following data aims at giving a better insight into the structure of the companies that are listed on Belgian stock exchanges (First market). The data is based on the public disclosure of significant shareholdings to which holders of shares in listed companies are subject, pursuant to a 1989 law, implementing the 1988 EEC directive on disclosure of major shareholdings[8]. Due however to

---

6 Which was the angle under which the Study center for the groups of enterprises started its activities at the 1980 Conference; the proceedings of this conference have been published under the title: Aspects juridiques des comptes consolidés - Juridische aspecten van geconsolideerde jaarrekeningen (1980).

7 For an interesting analysis of this type of supervision, see H. BIRON, Le régime belge des sociétés à portefeuille, prémices d'un droit des groupes? in: C.D.V.A., Modes de rapprochement structurel des entreprises (1988) 175. Much of the administrative case law as developed by the Banking and Finance Commission has been embodied in the Companies Act or in the rules on take-overs.

8 Council Directive of 12 December 1988 on the information to be published when a major holding in a listed company is acquired or disposed of (88/627/EEC), OJ L 348, 17.12.1988, 62-65. For an analysis of this regime in Belgium, C. VAN

the somewhat hermetic nature of some of the notifications, this information should be read with caution.

All stock exchange listed companies have been classified according to the density of control. In most cases, a clear percentage of shares had been notified, identifying the principal shareholder. In a few cases, shareholders acting in concert have been dealt with as one single party; sometimes the two principal shareholders have been mentioned, if these hold a substantial percentage, yielding de facto joint control. In other cases, the principal shareholder as reported has been indicated.

As short overview indicates that more than 65.69% of listed companies are in firm hand. For practical purposes one could state that this applies to 70.07%, as according to Belgian law, the board of a 45% held company can increase the shares with 10% in case of danger. In the last category, i.e. those with a less than 30% shareholder, one will identify some of the largest Belgian companies (Petrofina, BBL, GIB, Solvay). Here an additional qualification is necessary: Petrofina is jointly controlled by two partners, holding together more than 40%. A similar, but more complex situation exists in the BBL-bank. Solvay has protective rules in its articles of incorporation subjecting the admission of legal persons to the board's authorization.

Table 1

	companies	%
over 50%	90	65,69
45%-50%	6	4,38
40%-45%	13	9,49
30%-40%	12	8,76
under 30%	16	11,68
total[9]	137	100,00

The list of Belgian stock exchange listed companies has been divided in 5 classes. Each time the principal shareholder(s) or group has been mentioned with the blocks of shares officially reported. For some companies, no information was available. With respect to most companies the list contains the most recent data as published in their annual reports[10].

ACKER, Commentary of the Act of 2 March 1989, in: Overzicht Handels en Economisch Recht (1995) (looseleaf).

9 As of 30 June 1996, there were 137 stock exchange listed companies.

10 As attached.

III. Analysis

In the following paragraphs an analysis of the functioning of the Belgian holding companies will be attempted, both with respect to the functioning of the board and the influence exercised by the major shareholders. These subjects have not been investigated in an empirical manner. Therefore, some evidence of the functioning of the board will be based on externally available information, while other will be based on press reports.

More detailed research as was undertaken in the U.S. by Lorsch and McIver would be highly welcome[11].

1. Board Composition

Technically, the Belgian companies are functioning under a unitary board system. Except in the banking field, the law does not provide for a two tier board[12]. It only allows delegation of powers to some of its members or to an "executive committee", composed, in whole or in part of board members. The Companies Act, although allowing this delegation of powers, does not offer a legal framework for the organisation of this committee.

In practice in most companies actual management is delegated to a "comité de direction" ("executive committee"). Sixty-four, out of 132 listed companies[13] had management committees, the remaining companies having delegated powers to one or more directors.

In the majority of cases, these executive committees are composed of directors, while only in a minority officers outnumbered directors. Often the chairman of the board is also member of the management committee, the number of cases in which he only serves as chairman being about 1 out of four. The chairman of the board often is also chairman or board member of the company's controlling shareholder.

The executive committee's president, the CEO, usually would be member of the board and often acting as its sole vice-president. It is not an uncommon situation - in fact 9 out of 64 cases have been found as far as listed companies are concerned[14] - that the chairman of the board would also chair the executive committee.

In addition, one often finds informal committees within the group structure. These are composed e.g. of the chairman of the board, the CEO, and the

11 See J.R. LORSCH and E. MACIVER, Pawns or Potentates, The reality of America's Corporate Boards, Harvard Business School (1989).

12 See art. 26 of the Act of 22 March 1993.

13 See note 19 in fine.

14 The Société Générale de Belgique being an exception, its board chairman also taking part in the executive committee.

leaders of the main subsidiaries, the latter corresponding to the main production lines. Decisions are rendered operational throughout the group by having these group committees agreeing upon common guidelines. Some companies have several of these committees, the competencies of which are difficult to establish on the basis of the published information[15].

Some of the smaller stock exchange listed companies have maintained the structure which is usually followed in smaller businesses, i.e. the board delegates two or several of its members with the power to represent the company. These "executive directors" ("administrateur délégué - gedelegeerd bestuurder") have wide powers to represent the company, but normally would act in closer liaison with the board of directors than would be the case if an "executive committee " has been constituted.

Although no formal separation between the board and the executive committee has been introduced in the Belgian legal system, the board would mainly exercise a supervisory function, and decide on general policy issues. It would delegate actual management decisions to the "executive committee" or to the executive directors. Business transactions would not be submitted to the board except if strategic choices are involved, for matters of great importance, or upon crossing certain thresholds. Often the board is called upon to ratify decisions previously adopted by the executive committee. By and large, one could state that in large Belgian companies, boards de facto act as supervisory boards. The law does not formally recognise this separation of functions. Although the legal situation is rather imprecise, no court cases have been reported where this status has resulted in difficulties or liabilities.

In the banking sector, a formal separation between board of directors and executive committee has been rendered obligatory, resulting in a legally structured two-tier board. Based on prudential considerations, the actual running of the bank is the committee's prerogative, while the board is entitled to decide on the general policy issues and on those matters the Companies Act expressly reserves to the board's decision[16].

---

15 E.g. Société Générale has a) a board of directors; b) a comité exécutif; c) a comité de groupe; d) a comité de direction. In addition, an "audit committee" has been formed within the board.

16 See art. 26 Act of 22 March 1993; also no director of the holding company except one can be director of the bank. This regime has been organized to avoid the holding company intervening in the credit decisions of the bank. See for the text of the protocol: Commission bancaire, Annual report, 1973-1974, 242 and for the latest version: 1990-1991, 32 et seq. Also see A. BRUYNEEL, La Commission bancaire belge, Banque (Fr) 1972, no. 303, 12 et seq., no. 304, 125 et seq.; no. 305, 247 et seq.; PH. DEMAIN, L'autonomie de la fonction bancaire en Belgique: Réflets et perspectives (1976) 3 et seq.; R. HENRION, La concertation et l'autonomie bancaire, Journal des Tribunaux (1972) 293; R. WTTERWULGHE and D. PHILIPPE, Le protocole bancaire, un code de comportement: Reflets et perspectives (1978) 354.

The members of the board of directors are elected by the general meeting, usually the annual general meeting. If during the year a board seat becomes vacant, the board may designate, by co-optation, a new member, subject to confirmation by the general meeting. In practise, co-optation is the usual technique for selecting board members.

There is no limit on the number of board seats one single member can hold. Most boards are composed of a quite substantial number of members, usually between ten to twenty members, sometimes up to 30. On average holding companies have boards with almost double as many members as other listed companies. The press publishes from time to time a list of memberships, indicating that especially directors of holding companies hold numerous seats in other companies, including controlled companies.

As a consequence, board membership essentially consists of supervising the company's activities and results and does not include the actual management of the company. Most board members exercise effective management functions in only one or two group companies, usually the top holding company in which the said directors serve as CEO, or members of the "executive committees". This discrepancy between the legal and the "de facto" situation, according to which the board actually manages the company[17], is sometimes criticized, but in practise does not seem to create special difficulties.

The following tables gives an overview of the number of board members in the Belgian listed companies. The table refers to all listed companies, separately mentioning the holding companies.

Table 2

Board membership in Belgian listed companies[18]	Portfolio holding	%	Other companies	%	Total	%
3-10 members	59	63	34	89	93	70
11-16 members	21	22	1	3	22	17
more than 16	14	15	3	8	17	13
Total[19]	94	100	38	100	132	100
average	10,44		6,84		9,4	

17 Art. 53, Companies Act.

18 1994 annual reports.

19 Portfolio holding companies as defined in Royal Decree no. 64 of 10 November 1967. In addition, 6 companies were in liquidation, and have not been included in the calculation. Moreover, the Central Bank being a listed company, is subject to specific rules on board composition. As of 31 December 1995, there were 139 stock exchange listed companies.

Table 3

	Board of Directors		Executive Committee Committee		Board Members in Committee		Non Board Members in	
	1994	1995	1994	1995	1994	1995	1994	1995
	a	b	c	d	e	f	c-e	d-f
A. Holding Companies								
Ackermans & van Haaren	7	7	6	5	4	3	2	2
Almanij	21	21	None	None				
Bernheim-Comofi	13	11	9	9	6	6	3	3
Brederode	5	5	N/A	N/A				
CNP / NPM	16	17	8	9	6	8	2	1
Cobepa	26	26	9	11	2	3	7	8
Electrafina	8	8	None	None				
Finoutremer	7	7	None	None				
Floridienne	6	6	2	2	2	2	0	0
GBL	20	20	10	10	10	10	0	0
Gevaert	32	35	9	8	9	8	0	0
Immobel	13	12	10	10	3	4	7	6
Powerfin	15	12	4	4	3	4	1	0
Société Générale de Belg.	20	20	7	7	2	2	5	5
Sofina	12	12	6	6	6	6	0	0
Average	14,73	14,6	7,27*	7,36*				
Average all holding companies	10,48	6,71*						
B. Large Banks								
BBL	27	28	6	6	6	6	0	0
General Bank	26	26	7	7	7	7	0	0
Kredietbank	17	19	5	6	5	6	0	0
Average	23,33	24,33	6,00	6,33				
C. Other Companies								
Belgolaise	10	10	5	5	5	5	0	0
Fimeuse	6	6	None	None				
Campine	6	6	None	None				
Average	7,33	7,33						
Average all listed cie.	5,54		5*					

* if one is installed

Some companies have boards that largely exceed the 10 seat average. The ten listed companies with the largest boards are the following[20].

Table 4

	1994	1995
Gevaert*	32	35
Bank BBL	27	28
General Bank	26	26
Cobepa*	26	25
Tractebel*	25	24
Electrabel	24	23
Almanij*	21	21
GBL*	20	20
Société Générale*	20	20
Royale Belge	20	20
Petrofina	20	19

In comparison to the American practise the average figures seem to indicate no major differences: the average number of directors was reported to be 12-13. The larger Belgian companies however tend to substantially exceed the said average.

However, 83% of the U.S. boards were reported to have a majority of outside directors as early as 1979. On an average U.S. board, 9 (out of 13, or 69%) were outside directors, being strictly defined as non management personnel with no other contact with the company. Here the Belgian situation evidently is quite different for the reasons explained above.

Selection of board members will normally depend on the structure of the ownership of the shares. In practice, the composition of the board of directors therefore takes into account the relative position of the different important shareholders. Composition of key board representation will often be the subject of agreements between shareholders. The latter would also apply to companies in which two or more large partners hold significant amounts of shares: power will usually be divided between these shareholders along the lines of their relative shareholdings. This may lead to delicate balances of power, sometimes maintained through the existence of similar but reverse situations in other group entities. In addition, outside members will be selected to the board mainly from the leading Belgian or foreign business circles.

20 The * refers to financial holding companies.

Boards are however not exclusively composed of trusted representatives of the controlling shareholders. In order to avoid the board to be the expression of a single, major shareholder; most groups prefer to compose their boards in a more balanced way. As a consequence, even in companies that are majority owned by one group, the board will not necessarily consist of representatives of that single shareholder: The latter pattern is more likely to be found in the industrial subsidiaries of the holding companies, although even there outside directors often are called upon[21].

In financial holding companies, the presence of a clear majority shareholder seems to offer the possibility to call on a wide range of outside interests, whether directors of the companies in which the holding company takes a substantial interest, or of other groups with whom the holding company wants to maintain a relationship of good neighbourhood, and possibly develop future business ties. Therefore most boards will include outside members, leading business men, former politicians or diplomats, and so on. These directors are sometimes referred to as "outside directors". However, Belgian practice does not formally recognise the presence of "independent directors" in the meaning and with the assignment of their American or British counterparts.

Formally board members are elected by the general meeting. In fact appointment takes place as a consequence of a co-optation mechanism in which the CEO plays a substantial if not decisive role. Most of the time, CEO's or leading businessmen from other firms will be called to the board. The intertwining of business relationships and personal ties between board members results in the same persons being present in a large number of boards[22].

The selection procedures do not provide for specific requirements. Hence although some companies orally inform the general meeting about the curriculum and background of candidates, no such information is available in the documentation circulated in connection with the general meeting nor in the annual reports. Only guesswork and speculation can one identify which directors belong to the dominant groups of shareholders, and which could be identified as "outside" directors.

There is little empirical evidence about the number of meetings held by Belgian boards of directors, but from anecdotal evidence, it would seem that,

---

21 E.g. Recticel is an example in which 4 out of a total of 14 directors are outside directors.

22 See G. ELEWAUT, Holdingbazen kontroleren ekonomisch België, FET, 30.6.1994. According to this press comment, one of the leading businessmen held 25 major board memberships, standing for assets of 260 billion BEF managed ($ 8 billion), another 28 for 211 billion BEF. Other research revealed that holding company directors on average held 4 or board memberships, pointing to a strong concentration in the largest enterprises. (Trends, April 1991, and F. VANDENBROECKE, Netwerkanalyse van de Belgische economische elite, Thesis Ufsia, 1992).

except in extraordinary circumstances, four to six meetings a year would constitute the prevalent practise. Also the internal functioning of the board is poorly documented.

The functioning of the boards would seem to correspond to the main lines Lorsch and McIver have found in their US survey of the functioning of US board.

One could find a majority of Belgian directors subscribing some of the following ideas:

— board decisions should not be taken by a majority vote: in fact votes are very seldom taken and often constitute the announcement of fundamental differences of opinion;
— board members own loyalty firstly to the shareholders[23], but this notion may have a different meaning in companies with dominant shareholders;
— the previous statement does not prevent that directors will consider it appropriate that as part of the company's long term future, broader societal interests may be taken into account[24]. In Europe, the balance would probably more oriented towards the longer term;
— the CEO's power is mainly based on his knowledge of the affairs of the company, and least on the selection of board members[25];
— In the US the selection of the CEO is rated the highest source of the directors' power; this would probably be considered less important than the company's capital structure.

With respect to the actual functioning of the board's meeting, e.g. as far as information, minutes of the meeting, confidentiality etc. are concerned, interesting comparisons could further be made.

A subject which has repeatedly been dealt with in the Belgian press is the issue of remuneration of board members. The absence of full scale empirical analysis is mainly due to the - somewhat confused - state of information and disclosure.

Companies usually pay their directors by way of a fixed sum and by way of part of the company profits (so-called "tantièmes"). The former are part of the company 's expenses and paid before taxes, the latter are part of the distributable profits, and hence distributed after taxes. Sometimes they also provide for the reimbursement of expenses, or allocate options that entitle to shares.

---

23 LORSCH and MACIVER (supra note 11) table 3-1, p. 38.
24 LORSCH and MACIVER (supra note 11) table 3-1, p. 38.
25 LORSCH and MACIVER (supra note 11) table 5.3, p. 81. The sources of director's influence may be valued differently.

Annual accounts provide information on both items. However, this formation is disclosed in aggregate form including - the understandably higher - salaries of the managing directors (members of the "executive committee") and the remuneration of the members of the board. Moreover, information often relates to the parent company only, and does not include salaries paid at the level of subsidiaries. Technically, consolidated accounts should include the same information on a consolidated basis, but disclosed information obviously has a tendency to consider this information less material.

Emoluments are regularly determined whether by the general meeting or by the articles of incorporation. The articles often contain detailed rules about profit distribution, e.g. which part of the profits will be reserved, allocated for remuneration of directors, or attributed to general interest patronage.

According to press reports, directors received in 1993 an average remuneration of about 1,94 million BEF ($ 60000)[26]. The overall amount of directors remuneration is quite different: some companies reportedly had to earmark quite substantial sums (Gevaert: 100 million BEF [$ 3,3 mill.]) for the remuneration of their numerous directors (in this case: 32). Remuneration paid to a director as part of his representation of the parent company would normally go to the parent. With respect to a board membership which the director exercises in his personal name, the remuneration would be paid to him personally.

The overall charge of managing Belgian holding companies is quite substantial. Although this subject has to be investigated in more detail, the following figures gives some insight in the relationship between income, profits and charges.

Table 5: Holding Companies' management charges (in 000)

Ackermans en van Haaren		1992	1993	1994	1995	Average
a	Profits	359606	180742	253492	873970	
b	dividends received	459628	171280	424167	405453	
c	taxes	2111	4788	0	941	
d	directors	0	0			
e	dir's part of profits	2100	2100	2100	2100	
f	personnel	39113	43052	48565	48218	
g	total c, d, e, f	43324	49940	50665	51259	
i=g%a		12,05	27,63	19,99	5,87	5,13
j=g%b		9,43	29,16	11,94	12,64	4,85

26 See E. WYMEERSCH, Corporate governance after the Investment Services Directive, European Financial Services Law (1996) 130-141.

Almanij		1991-92	1992-93 18 months	1994	1995	
a	Profits	1710013	2606552	2219521	2574389	
b	dividends received	1987551	2763232	2351171	2526511	
c	taxes	0	781	357	39383	
d	directors*					
e	dir's part of profits	56650	87524	61967	63661	
f	personnel	22740	64707	34006	43190	
g	total c, d, e, f	79390	153012	96330	146234	
i=g%a		4,64	5,87	4,34	5,68	5,13
j=g%b		3,99	5,54	4,10	5,79	4,85

*: exempted from disclosing data

Brederode		1992	1993	1994	1995	
a	Profits	1652083	747875	558534	657210	
b	dividends received	197184	231804	352160	349216	
c	taxes	9448	169	574	2400	
d	directors	8184	8255	8125	8159	
e	dir's part of profits	0	0	0	0	
f	personnel	11543	11824	12115	10956	
g	total c, d, e, f	29175	20248	20814	21515	
i=g%a		1,77	2,71	3,73	3,27	2,87
j=g%b		14,80	8,73	5,91	6,16	8,90

Cobepa		1992	1993	1994	1995	
a	Profits	2513498	2524902	3591012	2810866	
b	dividends received	1970548	2180867	2303072	2234416	
c	taxes	601	811	500	550	
d	directors *	24552	24552	20318	20927	
e	dir's part of profits	0	0	0	0	
f	personnel	75242	80081	83663	85356	
g	total c, d, e, f	100395	105444	104481	106833	
i= %a		3,99	4,18	2,91	3,80	3,72
j= %b		5,09	4,83	4,54	4,78	4,81

*: consolidated results

Finoutremere		1992	1993	1994	1995
a	Profits	378812	449649	466622	272766
b	dividends received	172649	204850	237111	268788
c	taxes	168	28464	385	2754
d	directors	16963		25862	9262
e	dir's part of profits	9084	9420	8762	8885
f	personnel	32395	33294	38576	12753

g total c, d, e, f	58610	71178	73585	33654	
i=g%a	15,47	15,83	15,77	12,34	14,85
j=g%b	33,95	34,75	31,03	12,52	28,06

Floridienne	1992	1993	1994	1995	
a Profits	37653	-241908	-38275	35910	
b dividends received*	66422*	12876	53879	43060	
c taxes	0	0	0	0	
d directors					
e dir's part of profits	0	0	0	1425	
f personnel	15813	22608	26788	341	
g total c, d, e, f	15813	22608	26788	1766	
i=g%a	42,00			4,92	23,46
j=g%b	23,81	175,58	49,72	4,10	63,30

*: interests included

Gevaert	1992	1993	1994	1995	
a Profits*	2082583	7078642	2003061	2103369	
b dividends received**	1725264	1821624	1837140	2000454	
c taxes	36	18003	16900	30640	
d directors	x	97900	92300	x	
e dir's part of profits	90455	97946	92306	92312	
f personnel	8157	8281	8154	8430	
g total c, d, e, f	98648	222130	209660	131382	
i=g%a	4,74	3,14	10,47	6,25	6,15
j=g%b	5,72	12,19	11,41	6,57	8,97

**: interests included (1992-1993)
*:1993: included intra-group transactions

Groupe Bruxelles Lambert	1992	1993	1994	1995	
a Profits	5568005	4944386	18999376	6148759	
b dividends received	3243007	2988163	3242004	5303840	
c taxes	0	8020	0	10471	
d directors	83316	65158	58400	80900	
e dir's part of profits	0	0	0	0	
f personnel	193373	158362	129169	139755	
g total c, d, e, f	276689	231540	187569	231126	
g=g%a	4,97	4,68	0,99	3,76	3,60
h=g%b	8,53	7,75	5,79	4,36	6,61

Immobel		1992	1993	1994	1995	
a	Profits		544441	501898	-118359	
b	dividends received			125000	133000	
c	taxes		5613	75755	5852	
d	directors			2156	5894	
e	dir's part of profits		31928	29099	0	
f	personnel		114044	82864	66917	
g	total c, d, e, f		151585	189874	78663	
i=g%a			27,84	37,83		32,84
j=g%b				151,90	59,15	105,52

Mecaniver		1992	1993	1994	1995	
a	Profits	651608	472718	473559	489140	
b	dividends received	54795	275777	264190	102948	
c	taxes	444952	158476	128187	62840	
d	directors	7700	7700	7700	7700	
e	dir's part of profits	0	0	0	0	
f	personnel	10701	8741	7700	7700	
g	total c, d, e, f	463353	174917	143587	78240	
i=g%a		71,11	37,00	30,32	16,00	38,61
j=g%b		845,61	63,43	54,35	76,00	259,85

NMP		1992	1993	1994	1995	
a	Profits	1313748	2277397	2114782	2393518	
b	dividends received	933425	1575217	1576153	2163936	
c	taxes	26717	66795	15986	29020	
d	directors *	12480	13335	19739	19985	
e	dir's part of profits	0	0	0	0	
f	personnel	40686	41406	45053	38432	
g	total c, d, e, f	79883	121536	80778	87437	
i=g%a		6,08	5,34	3,82	3,65	4,72
j=g%b		8,56	7,72	5,13	4,04	6,36

*: 1995 consolidated

Powerfin		1992	1993	1994	1995
a	Profits	9409124	11028185	6132596	6633987
b	dividends and interests received	5537247	5766346	6447811	6947790
c	taxes	0	16200	0	2033
d	directors*				

e	dir's part of profits	16613	17610	16357	16612	
f	personnel	3150	1750	0	0	
g	total c, d, e, f	19763	35560	16357	18645	
i=g%a		0,21	0,32	0,27	0,28	0,27
j=g%b		0,36	0,62	0,25	0,27	0,37

*: no data in annual report

Sidro			1992	1993	1994	1995
a	Profits	193878	195955	213492	231130	
b	dividends received	127057*	95114	150593	158015	
c	taxes	17460	682	1429	13088	
d	directors	4208	4808		5005	
e	dir's part of profits	4810	4810	4810	4810	
f	personnel	9340	15120	13769	11672	
g	total c, d, e, f	35818	25420	20008	34575	
i=g%a		18,47	12,97	9,37	14,96	13,94
j=g%b		28,19	26,73	13,29	21,81	22,52

Societe generale de belgique		1992	1993	1994	1995	
a	Profits	5108725	23424947	7064033	7330234	
b	dividends received	5445768	6290017	5398506	6754143	
c	taxes	20000	21030	20000	15860	
d	directors	42811	39160	62884	56432	
e	dir's part of profits	43315	48877	44494	45120	
	Patronage	20348	20355	23298	23298	
f	personnel	368423	338187	387802	375436	
g	total c, d, e, f	494897	467609	538478	516146	
g=g%a		9,69	2,00	7,62	7,04	6,59
h=g%b		9,09	7,43	9,97	7,64	8,53

Sofina		1992	1993	1994	1995	
a	Profits	1367651	2100328	1342333	1477658	
b	dividends received	834213	715148	825629	813157	
c	taxes	50000	60000	30000	0	
d	directors	9380		11849	13440	
e	dir's part of profits	30035	31359	30324	30763	
f	personnel	64607	88832	82919	78928	
g	total c, d, e, f	154022	180191	155092	123131	
i=g%a		11,26	8,58	11,55	8,33	9,93
j=g%b		18,46	25,20	18,78	15,14	19,40

Stock exchange listed companies have not frequently reported on the functioning of board committees. According to published information, only a few have organised committees, such as audit committees[27] and remuneration committees. In practice it would seem that these committees often function in an informal way. More frequently annual reports mention committees dealing with specific issues of group liaison: these are in fact group-wide executive committees and cannot therefore be compared to the audit, or other internal committees.

2. *The Shareholders*

Most Belgian stock exchange listed companies have issued only one class of shares. Several have also issued convertible bonds and warrants, whether attached to bonds or not, and these securities may be used for the purpose of securing control. Therefore, control percentages should take into account full exercise of these rights to acquire additional voting stock.

According to the law, voting rights are proportional to the capital subscribed. Hence one does not find double voting rights, nor disproportional voting rights. Moreover, the use of voting caps, e.g. stipulating in the articles of incorporation that no shareholder may exercise more than a stated percentage of the total votes attached to the shares, has only been allowed by a change of the law in 1995[28].

As a consequence, under Belgian law, control is mainly if not exclusively secured by ownership of a majority or a large minority of the voting stock. At a difference from other legal systems, Belgian company law does not recognize control without ownership. This characteristic may help to explain the prevalence of controlling shareholders, their power often being based on holding companies, organized in a pyramidal structure.

It is characteristic of the Belgian share market that most companies have only part of their securities listed on the stock exchange. The shares that have not been listed could therefore not be traded on the exchange, although these might be transferred in a private transaction. Transfer of shares often is restricted due to agreements among shareholders. There is no information available with respect to the latter agreements.

27 E.g. Kredietbank, Société Générale de Belgique.
28 See art. 76, Companies Act, as amended by Act of 13 April 1995.

Traditionally Belgian companies issue both bearer and nominative shares[29]. The latter often represent the shares held by the controlling shareholders. With respect to nominative shares parties could more easily exercise control over transfers as these have to be reported to the board before being entered into the register.

Information about the holders of shares in Belgian stock exchange listed companies has increased substantially as a consequence of the L. March 2, 1989, obliging all 5% or more shareholders, whether individually or acting in concert, to disclose their holdings. The articles of incorporation may reduce this percentage, but only one major company seems to have availed itself of this flexibility, obliging all 3% holders to disclose. Although there is some doubt whether all holders of shares crossing the 5% thresholds have disclosed, substantially all of these can be identified. In some cases the BFC has granted exemptions i.a. for motives of personal security[30].

In companies other than listed companies, minority shares are usually held in larger blocks. Only rarely would one find public investors in these privately held companies.

Holders of shares in Belgian companies could be classified in controlling shareholders, reference shareholders and public shareholders.

Control is legally defined as the power to determine the appointment of the majority of the members of the board and to determine the company's policies. It can be whether full legal control, or de facto control. The latter type of control is presumed if the shareholder has cast the majority of the votes that were effectively cast at the last and the penultimate general meeting. Therefore, even a relatively large minority holding could lead to control.

Frequently one will find a certain number of shareholders joining forces to control the company. These control agreements (based on voting agreements and preferential rights upon share acquisition) have been declared legally binding in 1991, in a move to better protect Belgian companies against foreign take-overs. Often even smaller shareholders will joint these "shareholder syndicates" triggering the obligation to disclose as acting in concert with a party that is subject to the disclosure rules.

In addition, the law recognises, e.g. for accounting purposes the presence of "significant shareholders", who are often represented on the board, and who's opinion often will be taken into account with respect to important decisions.

---

29 The Act of 7 April 1995 has introduced a further class of shares: "dematerialized" shares for which no certificates are issued nor mention made in the company's books. For an analysis, see M. TISON, De uitgifte van gedematerialiseerde vennootschapseffecten. Bemerkingen bij de wet van 7 april 1995, in: H. BRAECKMANS and E. WYMEERSCH (eds.), Het gewijzigde vennootschapsrecht 1995 (1996).

30 See BFC annual report, 1990-1991, 108.

The ownership of a "significant percentage" often established at 20% or more, allows its owner to account for its stake under the equity method of accounting. Finally, the 10% or more shareholder is recognised as holding a "participating interest", meaning an interest that forges a permanent and specific link enabling its holder to influence the investee policies[31].

The significant shareholder often will be considered a "reference shareholder", a notion that is not recognized in the legal system. It is the shareholder which without exercising control, should normally be consulted before important decisions are taken.

As mentioned above, many stock exchange listed companies are not exposed to the threat of an aggressive take-over bid, the majority of their shares being held by one shareholder or group of shareholders. In the remaining cases in which a take-over risk still subsists, one should further take into account protective techniques which these companies have put in place. Some of these have been adopted by the legislature itself and could therefore should be mentioned here:

— the board of directors of a company may decide to acquire its own shares in case of a grave and imminent danger. The threat of a take-over would be considered the be "a grave danger"[32].
— the board may be empowered by the articles of incorporation to issue and additional 10% of shares, in favour of one single party, provided this is done at the take-over price; as a consequence, the majority in terms of voting rights is de facto reduced from 50+% to 45+% (being 1/2 of 110 = 55% - 10%)[33].
— autocontrol mechanisms are severely restricted. Cross shareholdings - whether between parent and subsidiary companies, or between independent companies, may not be voted[34], in the last case provided they exceed a 10% threshold. However, a generous grand fathering clause has exempted all holdings between a stock exchange listed companies and their indirect subsidiaries[35] and all cross holdings between independent companies, provided these had been reported to the Banking and Finance Commission before the beginning of 1996[36].

---

31 See definition of "participating interest" - "participation" "deelneming" in the annex to the RD of 8 October 1976.
32 Art. 52 bis, § 1, al. 3, Companies Act.
33 Art. 33 bis, § 3, Companies Act, as modified by Act of 13 April 1995.
34 Art. 52 sexies § 1, as amended by Act of 13 April 1995 provided that the voting rights attached to these shares would be suspended. However, an amendement on this article is proposed in Parliamentary Documents, Chamber of Representatives, Session 1995-1996, no. 570/1.
35 A different regime if applicable to cross holding between the parent and its direct subsidiaries, and the parent and the subsidiaries.
36 See art. 217, § 4, Companies Act.

In addition companies have developed other protective devices, such as restricting the transfer of the shares to physical persons. Legal persons would first have to be admitted by the board.

As a consequence it is fair to assume that only very few Belgian companies could be taken over against the will of its present controlling shareholder, and - as a consequence - of the incumbent board.

Among the other shareholders, institutional investors still play a relatively minor role. One can estimate that Belgian institutionals - including investment companies, insurance companies, pension funds, and banks - do not hold more than 20% of the overall amount of shares issued on the market. In practice this percentage is even less as some majority stakes in listed banks are included[37].

A substantial amount of controlling shares is being held by insurance companies, who have greater liberty to invest in shares than e.g. banks. Hence one regularly finds insurance companies among the shareholders subject to disclosure. Several insurance companies hold substantial blocks of shares in banks, one being even the single shareholder of a bank[38].

The 1993 change of the banking law, allowing banks to hold shares in companies, whether for investment or for trading purposes, does not seem to have significantly changed the banks' previous reluctance to invest in shares of other companies, unrelated to their banking business. Recent annual reports indicate that banks do not hold shares in their banking books,other than in subsidiaries engaged in or closely related to banking.

Investment funds (including investment companies) hold a substantial percentage of Belgian listed shares. Apart from Belgian and Luxembourg funds, foreign, especially US and UK institutional investors are more and more active on the Belgian markets. None has however crossed the 5% threshold, imposing disclosure. In a few listed companies, investment funds have been reported among the significant shareholders holding between 2 and 5%. With respect to Belgian and Luxembourg investment funds as well one should mention that these often are managed by companies that are closely related to Belgian banks, which are most of the time part of the group headed by the holding companies. It is unclear whether and to what extent in a critical case - e.g. a take-over - this feature might influence the portfolio manager's leeway whether or not to take account of its group 's interests

The public sector does not play any significant role as holder of shares in stock exchange listed companies. There are a few exceptions of companies[39]

37 Especially Belgolaise and Crédit Général, subsidiaries of General Bank and Kredietbank.

38 See the 100% stake of Royale Belge in Bank Ippa.

39 Barco, an electronics company; Cockerill, the steel producer.

restructured with the assistance of a public sector holding company and grown into a successful business.

Individuals as investors play a certain role, which is largely tributary to the presence of the larger shareholders, represented by the holding companies. Their role has decreased especially as more investors would indirectly access the markets through investment companies. There is a certain tax bias in favour of indirect investment.

The legislator has paid considerable attention to the reinforcement of the position of the individual investor. In 1989 he imposed a mandatory take-over bid upon transfer of control in a listed company, provided the transfer price exceeds the market price: the rule has been declared to be a rule of public order, and yields an individual right of action to each disappointed investor against the transferee who refused to bid for the remaining shares[40]. In 1991, the law extended the individual right of shareholders to whether sue the directors in liability, or sue in annulment of certain decision of the general meeting[41]. More recently, shareholders who own 30% of the shares in unlisted companies have the right to oblige the other shareholders to surrender their shares if they prove "serious motives" for expelling the latter[42]. On the other hand, 95% shareholders will have the right to compulsory acquire the shares of the remaining 5%, by freezing them out after payment of an indemnification established under the court's supervision[43].

3. *The Role of the Holding Companies*

In order to analyse the role of the holding companies in the Belgian economic system, and in the absence of comprehensive empirical research[44], one should first refer to their public declarations and annual reports. These reports give a limited, but authoritative insight into their beliefs and their actual functioning. Moreover one should warn against overly general statements as each of these holding companies has its own structure, its own objectives and business policy, depending on its historical background, its relationship to its controlling shareholder and its function in the larger group of which it forms part.

---

40 This is the Wagon Lits decision: Cass., 10 May 1994, Rechtskundig Weekblad, 1994-95, 431; Revue de droit commercial belge 1995, 15, note FR. GLANSDORFF, aff'ing Brussels, 6 August 1992, R.P.S., 1992, 248.

41 Art. 66 bis and art. 190 bis, Companies Act, modified in 1991 and 1995.

42 Art. 190 ter and quater, Companies Act, as modified by Act of 13 April 1995.

43 Art. 190 quinquies, Companies Act, as modified by Act of 13 April 1995.

44 L. RENNEBOOG, Ownership, managerial control and the governance of poorly performing companies listed on the London and Brussels Stock Exchanges, L.S.E., Ph. Diss., 1996.

There have been a fairly important number of limited analyses made especially by the holding companies themselves. Recently the debate about the role of the holding company has been activated under the influence of the actual discussion about the forms and techniques for reinforcing corporate governance in Belgian companies[45]. The debate about the often considerable difference between their asset value and their stock exchange price - see hereafter the discussion about this discount[46] - has been active for several decades.

Holding companies Belgian style have often been compared whether to the conglomerates of the 1960-1970s, or more recently to diversified closed ended investment companies. Both points of reference could usefully be invoked as guidelines for determining the function and position of the Belgian holding company.

A few striking elements can be inferred from the annual reports.

In terms of staff, holding companies are fairly small businesses. The number of their employees, although highly qualified, is limited and in several cases could be called embryonic. This characteristic may be attributed in part to their reliance on service contracts from other group entities, but also flows the limited nature of their function.

The following table gives some indication as to the number of employees as reported by the major Belgian holding companies[47]. Apart from Société Générale, engaged in a major turnaround after the Suez take-over, the other holding companies employ only a limited number of staff. This is motivated by the specific nature of the function, monitoring the investee without duplicating its management. A tendency to reduce or stabilise the number of their employees is visible.

---

45 See e.g. P. SCOHIER, Propos sur la guidance d'entreprise, Conférence, 26 January 1995, Société royale d'économie politique; among the older writings, one should mention: F. NEDEE, Holdings vandaag en morgen, Bank Fin. (1979) 549; C. LEMPEREUR, Holdings et sociétés à portefeuille: Le cadre réglementaire, Reflets et perspectives (1981) 213; E. NOLS, Importance et dynamisme des holdings, ib. 227; A.-M. KUMPS, Evolution et rôle économique des holdings, ib. 241; L. CUYVERS and W. MEEUSEN, The structure of personal influence of the Belgian holding companies, A quantative analysis, European Economic Review (1976) 51; A. VINCENT and E. LENTZEN, Les sociétés à portefeuille: rôle et moyens d'action, Courrier hebdomadaire du CRISP, Brussels, 17 October 1982, 2; A. VINCENT and E. LENTZEN, Groupes d'entreprises publics et privés, CRISP (1989) 46 p.; A. VINCENT, Le Pouvoir Economique dans la Belgique Fédérale, CRISP (1996) 288 p.

46 For further discussion of this topic, see R. KRAAKMAN, Taking discounts seriously: the implications of "discounted" share prices as an acquisition motive, 88 Colum. L.R., (1988) 891; B. DE LONG and A. SCHLEIFER, Closed-end fund discounts, 18, J. Portfolio Management, (1988) 46; also SEC Staff Report, Protection of Investors: a Half-Century of Investment Company Regulation, 29 May 1992, 432 et seq.

47 No data have been reported by Gevaert, NPM and Mecaniver.

Table 6: Staff and personnel of holding companies

	1991	1992	1993	1994	1995
Ackermans en van Haaren					
total		15	16	16	17
officers		5	5	5	5
Almanij					
total	3	3	4	3	3
officers	2	2	2	1	1
Berginvest					
total		0	0	0	0
officers		0	0	0	0
Brederode[48]					
total		4	4	2	2
officers		2	2	0	0
Cobepa					
total	12	12	11	13	14
officers	5	5	5	3	3
Definance					
total		3	3	3	2
officers		1	1	1	1
Electrafina					
total	13	12	9	9	9
officers	4	1	1	1	2
Electrorail					
total		2	1	1	
officers		0	0	0	
Fimeuse					
total		0	0	0	0
officers		0	0	0	0
Finoutremer					
total	6	6	5	5	4
officers	1	1	1	1	1
Floridienne					
total		11	11	10	0
officers		4	4	4	0
Groupe Bruxelles Lambert					
total	29	27	24	19	17
officers	12	11	7	5	5

48 Different figures for 1993 were reported in 1994.

Immobel					
total			36	28	28
officers			5	4	4
Powerfin					
total	x	x	x	0	0
officers	x	x	x	0	0
Sidro					
total		4	4	4	3
officers		1	1	1	1
Societe generale de belgique					
total	116	98	91	95	96
officers	41	31	29	31	31
Sofina					
total		34	36	35	33
officers		8	11	8	8

Most holding companies also seem to trade quite actively on the financial markets. This activity includes trading relating to the shares of companies in which they hold controlling blocks. Trading may be inspired whether by certain considerations of price stabilisation, or even by the simple motivation to realise a short term profit. Several holding companies have launched share repurchase programmes, in order to reduce the discount between their net asset value and their stock exchange price.

One should point here to the delicate issue of insider relating trading. Trading in the issuer's own shares, or in shares of investee companies would be considered as insider trading if the holding company has knowledge of specific information that is likely to influence the price formation. As major shareholders, often more or less actively monitoring the investee company, the holding companies will be considered as being in possession of price sensitive information during a greater part of the year.

Belgium has implemented the EEC directive on insider transactions. However the Belgian law of December 4, 1990 contains a significant and controversial exemption for trading by the parent holding company in the shares of companies in which the parent has invested. According to article 181 of the law "Is not considered inside information, the information in the possession of holding (or portfolio-) companies as a consequence of the role they perform in the management of the companies in which they hold a significant stake, provided this exemption only relates to information that should not be publicly disclosed according to the applicable legal and regulatory prescriptions which deal with the obligations flowing from listing of securities on a stock exchange"[49]. This exemption is ambiguous as it limits insider trading to the use of information other than the information which must be publicly disclosed. According to a decree of 1991, listed companies are obliged to disclose forthwith "all facts or decisions which, if disclosed, are liable to sensibly influence the price of their shares"[50]. Information not relating to specific facts or decisions, but flowing from the better overall knowledge of the situation of the company and its business may therefore lawfully be used by the holding company for trading in securities of the investee company. The question has often been raised whether this exemption was necessary, and if it is, whether it is compatible with the European directive.

Trading in shares by holding companies is documented only as far as their major transactions is concerned. Trading reports point to significant transactions relating to group companies, whether on the markets[51], or more frequently directly between major shareholders. The Société Générale group e.g. has engaged in a long term slimming down programme, leading to substantial disposals of subgroups. (C.B.R. Cementbedrijven, Compagnie Maritime Belge, Compagnie Royale Asturienne des Mines). At the same time, it reduced its holding in Union Minière, and in Recticel, while increasing its stake in the General Bank and in Accor, the French hotel group. Other groups regularly report similar large transactions.

A third significant feature is the existence of an often considerable price difference or "discount" between the net asset value of the holding company's portfolio and its market valuation. This discount has been well documented for a certain number of holding companies for which it amounted between 10% and 25%. Companies that experience higher discounts, some exceeding even 40%, do not disclose comparable figures. In any case, the calculation of the net asset value presents considerable difficulties, as both listed and unlisted shares are included. Criteria for the valuation of the unlisted shares are not always disclosed[52], and the approaches obviously are quite diverse[53]. Therefore the

---

49 Translation E. WYMEERSCH, The latter part of the sentence refers to the RD of 18 September 1990, detailing the disclosure obligations, especially the "ad hoc disclosures" which listed companies should meet. The question remains that not all information that should be disclosed under the "ad hoc" rules may be immaterial from the angle of the insider prohibition. The Commission of the EU has not taken steps against Belgium for defective implementation of the directive.

50 Art. 4, § 1, 1°, RD of 18 September 1990. See also Schedule C(5)(a) of the Directive 72/279/EEC of 5 March 1979.

51 Often transactions have been reported to have been executed on the London market. Seaq's share in Belgian shares is reported decreasing.

52 Cobepa gives a more detailed overview of its valuation criteria, Annual report (1995) 45.

53 The designation used by the holding companies differs considerably from "patrimonial value", to "intrinsic value" or "revalued own funds", and other similar expressions, the content of which is not defined. For the purpose of the

following figures should be analysed with caution, companies being inclined to undervalue their portfolio in order to reduce the gap with the stock exchange price. Moreover, in order to combat a discount which is regarded as excessive, some companies have started programmes to repurchase their own shares. Especially Cobepa and its subsidiary Ibel and more recently Compagnie Nationale de Portefeuille CNP-NPM Nationale Portefeuillemaatschappij are implementing widely announced repurchase programmes. These programmes further limit the comparability of the figures. Some holding companies have even implicitly indicated that their published valuation may not express the full discount[54].

Theoretically at least, if the holding companies' portfolios were mainly composed of listed shares, the percentage of the discount should remain more or less stable through the different stages of the market evolution: the holding company's value would follow the same trend as the value of the underlying assets. However, as the leading Belgian stock market index is based for at least 83% on holding companies shares[55], this criterion could not be used as a valid measure of the relative performance of the holding companies. At least one holding company has called attention to the cyclical nature of the discount: the discount increases in bear markets, which seems illogical as it allows investors to acquire at attractive conditions shares that would be worth much more than appears from the market price[56].

The following table gives an overview of discounts, based on a calculation of "net asset value", as published by the issuer itself.

Table 7: Discount-Decote

cnp/npm	**1991**	**1992**	**1993**	**1994**	**1995**
net asset value[57]	2188	1991	2589	2362	2393
market price	1975	1785	2120	2005	1900
difference	213	206	469	357	493
% of n.a.v.	9,73	10,35	18,12	15,11	20,60

present analysis, NAV has been used as the common denominator. A more detailed description of its calculation base was mentioned in CNP-NPM's 1991 annual report; shares of unlisted companies are valued at acquisition price, and for the significant blocks, according to the equity method (p. 16). Listed shares are valued at market.

54 CNP-NPM, upon launching its share repurchase programme recently declared that its discount amounted to about 40%, while according to the previously published figures it amounted to somewhere between 10% and 20%. See FD, "NPM koopt eigen aandelen om disagio te bestrijden", FET, 13 June 1996.

55 BFC Definition, 81% from 20 September 1996 on. See FD, "Analisten verwelkomen aanpassing Bel 20-index", FET, 20 April 1996.

56 See CNP-NPM, 1991, Annual report, p. 14.

57 Estimated share value.

Cobepa	**1991**	**1992**	**1993**	**1994**	**1995**
net asset value[58]	1164	1267	1461	1353	1423
market price	975	874	1154	1038	1110
difference	189	393	307	315	313
% of n.a.v.	16,24	31,02	21,01	23,28	22,00

Definance	**1991**	**1992**	**1993**	**1994**	**1995**
net asset value[59]	1650	1750	1820	1331	1300
market price	1278	1151	1496	998	810
difference	372	599	324	333	490
% of n.a.v.	22,55	34,23	17,80	25,02	37,69

Electrafina	**1991**	**1992**	**1993**	**1994**	**1995**
net asset value[60]	3566	2945	4094	3698	3845
market price	2630	2150	3250	2860	3060
difference	936	795	844	838	785
% of n.a.v.	26,25	26,99	20,62	22,66	20,42

Finoutremer	**1990-91**	**1992**	**1993**	**1994**	**1995**
net asset value[61]	3582	3602	4252	4193	5000*
market price					3540
difference					1460
reported discount %	39	44	30	30	29,20
*: pprox.					

G.B.L.	**1991**	**1992**	**1993**	**1994**	**1995**
net asset value[62]	3807	3585	5121	4705	4959
market price	3290	2780	4015	3770	4000
difference	517	805	1106	935	959
% of n.a.v.	13,58	22,45	21,60	19,87	19,34

Gevaert	**1991**	**1992**	**1993**	**1994**	**1995**
net asset value[63]	1431	1441	1858	2010	2245
market price	1067	1075	1500	1480	1850
difference	364	366	358	530	395
% of n.a.v.	25,44	25,40	19,27	26,37	17,59

58 Patrimonial share value.
59 Intrinsic value.
60 Estimated share value.
61 Liquidation share value.
62 Estimated share value.
63 Estimated share value.

Ibel	**1991**	**1992**	**1993**	**1994**	**1995**
net asset value[64]	3706	3570	4348	4778	5383
market price	2680	2390	3005	2730	3375
difference	1026	1180	1343	2048	2008
% of n.a.v.	27,68	33,05	30,89	42,86	37,30

Immobel	**1991**	**1992**	**1993**	**1994**	**1995**
net asset value[65]	3890	3747	3688	3203	2745
market price	3000	2600	3510	2800	2285
difference	890	1147	178	403	460
% of n.a.v.	22,88	30,61	4,83	12,58	16,76

Royal Belge	**1991**	**1992**	**1993**	**1994**	**1995**
net asset value[66]	4424	4804	6499	4917	6690
market price	3770	4135	5880	4870	5880
difference	654	669	619	47	810
% of n.a.v.	14,78	13,93	9,52	0,96	12,11

Societé générale de belgique	**1991**	**1992**	**1993**	**1994**	**1995**
net asset value[67]	2286	2288	2950	2740	2968
market price	1673	1727	2400	2160	2460
difference	613	561	550	580	508
% of n.a.v.	26,82	24,52	18,64	21,17	17,12

Holding companies exercise a variety of functions. These functions are reported on by several holding companies, although the smaller ones do not explicitly comment on the philosophy of their activity. Some are clearly more active than others.

Holding companies firstly act as professional investors holding non diversified portfolios.

As owners of large blocks of shares, they aim at exercising control or at influencing the investee companies' conduct. Motivated by profit maximisation, this attitude leads to a long term growth strategy and development of the investee's business, rather than to a short term dividend distribution policy. However, as the holding company has to serve a dividend to its own public investors, it cannot make abstraction of all investee's dividend policy. Often,

64 Patrimonial share value.
65 Intrinsic value.
66 Revalued own property.
67 Estimated share value.

the investee also is a listed company, and therefore bound to make regular distributions to its public shareholders. As a consequence the controlling holding company will follow an intermediate course, standing for a mix of long term growth and a reasonable dividend pay out.

In order to stabilise its income flow, several holding companies report about their efforts to earn additional income from other activities, mainly from short term trading on the financial markets, including in the shares of the investee companies or from rendering additional services to their investee companies, especially financial or fiscal engineering, for which separate fees are charged. As a consequence, some holding companies compared themselves to the English merchant banks

Some of these holding companies expressly underline their function as stable shareholders: it is not their intention to sell the shares on the market even if a interesting opportunity presents itself. Often, the volume of the portfolios would prevent any block sale of the shares, except to other investors with a comparable long term interest. This function of stable shareholder also is very welcomed by the management of the investee companies, which feels protected against the ebb and flow of the markets.

During the last decade most holding companies have slimmed down, reducing their portfolio to those assets that correspond to a sufficiently coherent investment strategy. Some have focused on their core business, as defined by the holding company's management. Others limit their sphere of business to a specific industry sector, such as financial services, pursuing an additional return from their presence in several subsectors in the same industry line. Others have kept a relatively diversified portfolio, more clearly geared to their approach as a service business. Finally in some cases, the holding company's activity comes quite close to that as an closed ended investment company.

Although each of the holding companies has its own characteristics, some of the above mentioned strategies can be documented by the following examples.

The Société Générale de Belgique has been the subject of substantial changes after its take-over by French Compagnie de Suez in 1988. It slimmed down its portfolio from a wide variety of business sectors to about seven areas: mining, chemicals, engineering and public utilities, banking and insurance, electric appliances. Other sectors have been disposed of or are announced to be: this applies to its interest in shipping, in cement and building materials and in steel. The volume of shares held is reduced up to the minimum majority level required for maintaining majority e.g. in Union Minière or Recticel, thereby underlining its will to maximise its control position with minimal ownership. In the banking and insurance field, it reinforced its - minority -share investment.

The Almanij Group is a financial services group with major interest in Kredietbank Belgium (38,57%) and in Kredietbank Luxembourg (39,12%). In addition it has substantial interest in a series of financial services companies, ranging from insurance, savings banks, leasing to asset management and investment banking.

The Cobepa group, a 66,92% subsidiary of French Paribas, has substantial interests in a wide variety of fields, including several subholdings. None of ultimate investees represent more than 10% of the overall portfolio value of Cobepa. This company also publishes "relative asset values" in the ultimate investee companies, called "transitive values", especially illustrating the sources of the group's income from and the distribution of its assets in the different investee companies. This issuer also describes part of its economic function in terms of "merchant banking", a function other companies expressly consider to be outside the scope of their action field.

Most holding companies serve as investors, more than as entrepreneurs in the sense that they do not frequently act as the starting point for new industry developments. Few of the companies in which they invest have been founded by today's holding companies, but rather were the fruit of entrepreneurial efforts to which the holding company has contributed, at a certain stage of the investee's development, by offering finance and expertise[68]. In that sense, the activity of the holding company has been compared to that of "investment" or "merchant" banks. But here again a wide variety of individual situations exist.

One of the major holding companies sees its function as organiser or supporter of the turnaround of firms that had lagged behind in market developments. The holding has developed substantial expertise and know-how in slimming down its investees, in refocusing their activity on their core business, selling off the peripheral activities and re-engineering the existing processes and activities. The holding company would normally acquire an initial small stake, which it will hold for the turnaround period, and consider to resell it to other partners, at a surplus value more rarely to the markets, after the turnaround has been realised.

Holding companies repeatedly act as major providers of capital to finance the expansion of their existing investee companies. These investments are funded whether by the holding companies public share issues, by re-employing the proceeds of previous disposals of investments, by dividend reinvestments, and finally by credit. Taking into account the infrequent share issues by non-holding companies as compared to public share issues by holding companies, one can infer that investee companies have been financed more readily by their holding companies than directly by the securities markets.

---

68 This feature is also based on the objective to invest only in firms that have sufficiently matured and have reached the level of a stable dividend flow, out of which the holding company can also service its own profit distribution.

In that sense the financing role has largely been internalised within the groups, thereby insuring the financing needs of the subsidiaries, and avoiding dilution of control.

Traditionally, there are relatively few public shares issues by stock exchange listed companies on the Belgian securities market. In order to provide funds to their controlled subsidiaries, the holding companies do regularly tap the public securities market. Apart from the investment companies, most private sector flotations of securities have been by banks or by listed industrial or commercial companies. The following table gives a overview of financing by public securities issues, specifying which part has been taken up by the financial holding companies, and which part of market securities financing is directly flowing to productive commercial or industrial companies, whether the latter are dominated by a holding company or not. The table illustrates the overwhelming financing function of the holding company, and the infrequency of direct market access by industrial or commercial firms[69]. Unfortunately, there are no tables available about the overall financing flows funding firms belonging to the group.

Table 8: Public Securities Issues (in mln. BEF)

		1990	1991	1992	1993	1994	1995*
A. Public share issues by domestic companies in Belgium							
Total		23406	21476	9890	21468	36538	7974
of which:	- holding companies		8418	6423	16461	26917	7960
	- holding comp.: % of total share issues		39,20	64,94	76,68	73,67	99,82
B. Public bond issues by domestic companies in Belgium							
Total		2988	12674	17812	11333	26811	1785
of which:	- holding companies		6867	2554	2603	5362	1567
	- holding comp.: % of total emission		54,18	14,34	22,97	20,00	87,79

* half year

These figures do not shed light on the sometimes considerable investments made by these holding companies, whether in existing subsidiaries, or by acquiring new stakes. Some of these companies publish detailed tables of changes in the financial position or "Tableaux de financement".

69 These figures do not include the "certificates of deposit", issued by commercial firms mostly to institutional investors. These certificates are not traded on the public markets.

Often, holding companies provide capital to the subsidiary by subscribing to additional shares, or providing long term loans. Unless relating to new firms, the acquisition of existing stakes from other shareholders has of course not the same character. These transactions have been financed most of the time it seems by reinvesting the proceeds from the realisation of existing holdings, by lending in the international markets, or by re deployment of retained earnings. Although public securities issues by the holding company would play a considerable role, it seems less significant than redeployment of existing group funds.

It is striking that several of these holding companies have invested relatively large sums in the acquisition of shares in more or less unrelated firms, shares that often represent very small percentages of the investee's company capital. These share investments are described as mainly serving as the basis for the provision of services and for the creation of a networking system. This networking function may also explain the frequency whether of cross shareholdings, and the formal exchange of shares with other business partners. No concept comparable to the Keiretsu has however emerged[70].

In deciding to make these sometimes - at least moneywise - large investment that would not yield influence on management, the investee's dividend policy would be given greater consideration. Also these small percentages in unrelated fields may serve the overall strategic interests of the majority shareholder. This explains the presence of some Belgian groups among the "actionnaires stables" of the privatised French former public sector companies (e.g. a 0,5% to 1% share in French Elf Aquitaine, a 2,7% in Bayer). In these cases the role of the holding company would come closer to that of an investment fund, except that holding of the shares might also aim at strategic considerations.

Until recently cross shareholdings constituted a essential part of the Belgian company structure and was inspired by a wide variety of motives among which of autocontrol, good neighbourhood, and networking played an important role. Starting with the 1991 amendments to the Companies Acts, cross holdings, whether between parent and subsidiary companies, or between unrelated firms were curtailed to a 10% level. The 1995 amendments further restricted the use of cross holdings, whether by assimilating parent and direct subsidiary cross holdings to repurchases of own shares or by suspending voting rights attached

70 A different impression was created by the notification of a 47 parties notifying each less than 2% of the shares of Almany. This could be situated within this companies policy of Belgian "anchorage". CNP-NPM also indicated the significance of networking "adhérences capitalistiques permettant de développer des relations réciproques porteuses d'avenir et d'investissements rentables" (1991 annual report, p. 15). A similar picture appears from the overview of small holdings in French formerly state owned enterprises, see FET, 7 June 1994.

to all cross holdings[71]. At present, a subsidiary cannot hold shares of its - direct or indirect - parent exceeding 10% of the parent's shares, and voting rights will be suspended. Cross holding between independent companies - i.e. between which no control relationships exists - is equally limited to 10% but voting rights will only be suspended for shares exceeding the 10% threshold[72].

Striking are the grandfathering clauses that have been maintained in order to facilitate cross holdings to be continued or reduced over time. These clauses especially address stock exchange listed companies[73].

As influential shareholders, holding companies would normally play an active role in the orientation of the business policy to be developed by the investee company, supervising its management and driving for long term profit maximisation. Here lies the basis for one of the most interesting aspects of their action. Holding Companies Act - or may act - as monitors of corporate conduct in a sense which is comparable to the stronger forms of monitoring exercised by large US investors, but going beyond the interventions that traditional institutional investors seem to have developed. Both in the UK and more strongly in the US, institutional investors are reported to actively oversight the companies in which they have invested to secure profit maximisation and guarantee maximum - often long term - returns to the beneficiaries of their investment activity. In the Anglo-Saxon economies, this type of monitoring has been welcomed to avoid that managers would not sufficiently respond to the shareholder's needs, engage in empire building, or otherwise their inaction to result in a weakening of the enterprise structure. Some of these interventions have been documented and proved very successful: the turnaround of General Motors, under the influence of investors as Warren Buffet often is cited as an example of this more activist stand taken by the large or institutional investors in general and the development of this new type of investor in particular. Also this type of monitoring serves as an alternative for the so-called Wall Street Rule, institutional investors not being able anymore to dispose of their shares in the markets due to the build-up of considerable blocks of shares. Some of the Belgian holding companies have also been exposed to the activist stand of US institutional investors, which were represented - and sometimes welcomed - at their general meetings.

Do the Belgian holding companies exercise this monitoring function which, as stable shareholders, could lie at the heart of their activities and economic function?

---

71 At least until the 1995 amendements of the Companies Act became effective. These amendments lead to a suspension of voting rights.

72 At the moment of writing, all voting rights are suspended, even relating to less than 10% stakes. This rule is planned to be changed, and only voting rights relating shares exceeding the 10% threshold will be suspended.

73 See art. 219, as modified by Act of 13 April 1995.

The monitoring function as exercised by the holding companies can be further documented by relying on their public statement, especially the description of their mission.

There is evidence that Belgian holding companies engage in monitoring activities, although the latter may considerably vary from case to case. These differences are due to the specific situation in which the group has found itself, e.g. in the case of the Société Générale where, even before the take-over by Suez, a major turnaround was considered necessary, slimming down the widely diversified conglomerate to a limited number of core businesses. During that process the company saw its function:

> as that of "continuous monitoring of the management of each of the subsidiaries, in order to be able to take account of all changing circumstances. Medium term strategy is fixed in concertation with the subsidiaries, while financial support, both in terms of means and of management, is actively put to work[74].

Other groups, more specifically Cobepa conceives its role as that of a "services business", acting as a "professional shareholder" and as a "merchant bank". In the first capacity, it will offer its investee support in order to increase growth, and create added value for the shareholders of the investee. Active and professional monitoring are the instruments to create added value in a long term perspective[75]. As a merchant bank Cobepa offers its services to its investees and third firms, earning fees from financial and service transactions.

It described its role as a "responsible" shareholder" or "active investor "and that of its subholdings as follows:

> serving the purpose, not only of providing the necessary capital, but also giving management financial and technical assistance, supporting the investee's strategic decisions, and striving at a lasting structure supporting the investee's autonomy by putting into place efficient, stimulating management procedures and systems[76].

Investments and disinvestments are regularly undertaken. Also intense monitoring and following-up on investments, especially of those that are confronted with strategic choices, refocusing of their activities or restructuration.

---

74 Société Générale de Belgique, Address to shareholders, Annual Report 1991, p. 5, and Annual report 1995, p. 8, stressing the function as reliable shareholder, with ample financial means. See also Interview with P. LIOTIER, Patron de Holding, c'est un métier ça?, in *Eco-Soir*, 5 April 1996, further detailing the monitoring function v.à.v. investee companies.

75 See P. SCOHIER, annual meeting 26 April 1996. In the annual report for 1995, this is further described as "investments and disinvestements in order to achieve the necessary rejuvenation of the portfolio, and also intense follow-up of a number of investees, especially those that are confronted with strategic choices, or that are bound to refocus their activities or rationalise their business.

76 Cobepa Annual Report 1991.

CNP-NPM[77] described its objective "as the increase, in a long term perspective, of surplus value of its assets, and therefore of its shares". Shareholders should take into account this long term perspective, measuring achievements by the evolution of the estimated value of the shares and of the dividend.

In further enumerated the five fundamental functions exercised by a holding company of the Belgian type as a professional shareholder:

- to decide on strategic choices, including risk management and management of expected profitability;
- to approve investments or disinvestments;
- to provide long term resources, their amounts and types, and determination of dividend policies;
- to select and motivate the top management;
- to develop contacts between group firms, to their mutual benefit.

Intervention in crisis situations also form part of their mission.

A different type of monitoring can be attributed to the group direction that sees its function as including that of an umpire between the conflicting interests between the different investee companies that are engaged in competing activities within the same market segment.

In other cases, monitoring would be less fargoing, the holding company mainly serving as an instrument for long term investment, following up the situation from an essentially financial point of view. Here one finds holding companies with widely diversified minority, or even smaller holdings in stock exchange listed firms (e.g. Electrafina). These holdings often serve as support for wider control strategies, developed by other holdings.

Sometimes the possibility of creating synergy between the different investee companies is considered a considerable advantage for acquiring or disposing of block of portfolio shares. This objective may explain the relatively frequent regroupings of activities or restructuring of business segments within groups or among them. The shares of these holdings reflect a greater discount than those of the actively monitoring ones.

Basically, the long term investment function of the holding company would not be fundamentally different from that of a closed end investment company: it would also hold securities with a view of their resale at a profit once their value has plainly matured, possibly under some monitoring influence by the holding company.

Said trading activity rarely takes place on the securities markets, even if ultimately listed securities are involved, but is effectuated by transferring the shares in intermediate holding companies. This feature explains the prevalence

---

77 CNP-SNP, Annual report 1994, 3.

of transactions in blocks of shares in the Belgian - and French as well - industrial structure. Often these blocks represent - full or partial - control. The Belgian holding company's control is to be analysed in conjunction with shares owned by other - holding or other - companies belonging to the same group. This feature explain the complex nature of the company structure in Belgium.

Corporate governance issues are recently receiving more attention in the action and public statements of the Belgian holding companies.

Cobepa extensively developed its function as a professionals shareholder in a "corporate governance" perspective. Maximising shareholder value and respecting minority shareholders prerogatives are considered essential objectives. Instruments for more efficient governance include the appointment of independent directors, a charter provision imposing pre-emptive rights in case of new share issues, along with ample disclosure.

One of the other prominent holding companies referred to governance issues to change its policy of free of charge central administration and support for subsidiary or affiliated firms. Henceforth, services will be provided against a fee based on a "correct valuation" of the services rendered[78]. Greater awareness of governance issues lies at the basis of the increased separation of the functions of chairman of the board and CEO, still not the prevailing pattern in Belgian listed company[79].

In the Belgian approach, monitoring instruments would mainly consist of the - not necessarily majority - representation of the parent shareholder on the board of the investee company. According to Belgian law, board members can be revoked by the general meeting without notice nor indemnification: this rule has been declared a principle of "economic public order"[80]. As a consequence, subsidiary directors rarely resist policy decisions supported by the group management. It is not usual for most parent companies to give formal instructions: Belgian law refuses to recognise a parent's legally enforceable right to give instructions[81]. In practice, these instructions flow from the common determination of policy lines and collective decision making.

In most cases, at least one of the directors of the parent is also a member of the board of the subsidiary, enabling him to directly influence decisions in accordance with the group interest. In more tightly controlled subsidiaries the parent would also approve and follow up on the budgets established by the subsidiary. Major decisions, especially changes of the company charter,

---

78 See CNP-NPM, Annual Report 1995, 9.

79 See for statistical data E. WYMEERSCH, European Financial Services Law (1996) 130-141.

80 Cass., 22 January 1981, R.P.S. (1981) no. 6165, 285. As a consequence, contracts may not set aside the rule, nor offer techniques for evasion.

81 See E. WYMEERSCH, The Groups of Companies in Belgian Law, in: Groups of Companies in the EEC (1993) no. 57, 42.

reorganisations, major investments or disinvestments would as a rule be submitted to the parent company. Decisions about investment projects usually are subject to the group management deciding on the allocations between the different business segments and on financing out of available group funds. In some groups, the holding company also serves as the basis for group cash management. The Belgian tax law has however incited international groups to domicile this function in specialised entities, called "co-ordination centres" that benefit from a very favourable tax status. The entities would normally be subject to the direct supervision of group management. The relatively important differences in staff employed could serve as a criterion for the involvement of the holding company (see supra table no. 6).

With respect to day-to-day running, the parent's role would seem to be relatively limited. The parent's agreement has to be obtained for major investment projects, and for decisions relating to the shareholding structure. Decisions with respect to the latter will normally be initiated by the parent.

Directors are supposed to take account only of the interests of the company on the board of which they serve. The legal system and the traditional legal opinion would seem to bend in favour of parents not intervening too heavily in the functioning of the subsidiary. From the legal point of view this creates tension, as directors, being the representatives of the investee company, should act in the latter company's interest, while in practice directors normally adhere to the policies developed by the group management. Belgian judiciary and administrative practice - especially of the BFC - have developed a more refined reasoning for dealing with the parent-subsidiary relationship, and the possible oppression that may result. This doctrine is fundamentally not very different from the "Rozenblum"-doctrine which French Supreme Court has developed[82].

The Belgian law on groups of companies recognises the existence of the parent company's interest: the board of directors of a subsidiary may strike a reasonable balance between the subsidiary's interest and the parent company's interest. Their the decision will withstand judicial scrutiny, if in the longer term, it is in the overall interest of the subsidiary to take account of the proper interests of the parent company, especially if the subsidiary directors are entitled to expect a just and equitable return that is likely to offset the charges imposed to the subsidiary. But if the balance of pros and cons would be grossly detrimental to the subsidiary, or if no just return could reasonably be expected from the parent company, the decision will be set aside, mostly on the basis of "abus de majorité", referring to the basic rule that the company should be run

82 See about the Rozenblum decision, Cass. crim. fr., 4 February 1985, Jurisclasseur (1986), éd. G, II, 20585, nt. W. JEANDIDIER; Dalloz (1985) 478, note OHL; Rev. Sociétés (1985) 648, note B. BOULOC.

in the interest of all shareholders[83]. This criterion would be considered applicable to decisions of the board of directors and of the general meeting of shareholders as well.

The former rule would therefore allow subsidiary directors to follow the parent company's instructions, at least in the normal course of business. Caution is required as the parent company could not offer any return, e.g. if it is likely to become insolvent, or if the imbalance in the trade is so great that even on the very long term, no equivalent return is to be expected. As several of the investee companies are stock exchange listed, the extent to which the interest of this subsidiary could be ignored or jeopardised, will also be influenced by the reaction of the markets and by the protective action of the supervisory authorities, in this case the Banking and Finance Commission. In an increasing number of cases, the judiciary has been called upon to investigate, both from the angle of criminal law and of investor protection, decisions or behaviour that was considered detrimental to the subsidiary. There undoubtedly is a greater awareness of the responsibilities of the parent company dealing with listed subsidiaries.

In the past, shareholders with minority positions do not always have been able to fully impose their views, the company's directors considering that the company should be run "in the company's interest". Here one touches upon one of the most delicate issues in the group context, i.e. this question of conflicts of interest between the parent and its subsidiary.

It is unclear to what extent the monitoring function of the Belgian holding companies could be considered significant or intensive. The absence of a considerable monitoring infrastructure and the wide interconnection of business relationships has certainly prevented in some instances unsatisfactory situations to continue over time. Apart from rare open fights between shareholders, cases have been reported in which a company has been paralysed for many years due to the unwillingness of the shareholder to actively intervene and settle their disputes. On the other hand, there have been several cases in which ineffective managers were removed, probably at the instigation of the controlling shareholders. This traditional rule of thumb for measuring effectiveness of monitoring would point towards more aggressive monitoring at least these last years. Data are lacking to measure this phenomenon with greater precision[84].

The conclusion of this partial analysis could be double: whether active monitoring takes place may be controversial, and very much depending on the

---

83 See for further details E. WYMEERSCH, The Groups of Companies in Belgian law, in: Groups of companies in the EEC (1993) no. 99, 70.

84 See however for further details and data, L. RENNEBOOG, Ownership, managerial control and the governance of poorly performing companies listed on the London and Brussels Stock Exchanges, L.S.E., Ph. Diss., 1996.

individual case. Whether stronger monitoring by shareholders might be necessary on the other hand certainly is to be affirmed. Monitoring the investee companies might be one of the most useful functions holding companies can exercise.

The financial markets and the public opinion in general have been rather distrustful of the function of the Belgian holding companies which have been considered as wielding large economic power and not always sufficiently taking account of the interest of the investors, or of the local economy. In the 1970 there existed a lively debate about whether these holding companies exercised their economic power in the general interested, especially whether they invested sufficiently in Belgium or preferred to invest abroad, or even convert their industrial investments in mere trading assets. The success of more market oriented doctrines and the further internationalisation of the economies in the 1980 and 1990's have stopped the latter line of thinking.

The public perception of the holding companies can in part be explained by the negative valuation of the holding company shares v.à.v. the value of their underlying assets. This is the so-called "discount" problem that has received wide attention in Belgium (see supra table 7). There has been considerable debate about the explanation of the discount of the value of their shares, some even underlining that the positive value of their intervention, in fact that their monitoring function should result in a valuation above market, the free shareholders free riding on their monitoring efforts by the other shareholders. Investors perception of the value of this monitoring effort is probably offset by the feeling of powerlessness major transactions taking place without consultation of investors, or being entered into in the interest of other, upstream entities in which they hold no interest.

The functioning of this multi-layer holding company structure raises the question of the overall charge imposed on the income flow between the ultimate investee and the ultimate investor. Comparing investments directly in the ultimate investee or indirectly through a holding company, the difference stands for the dilution in terms of asset value, or of income flows. could be measured. The differences in terms of income flows are easily measurable. The yardstick is somewhat imprecise, as holding companies also hold bonds, deposits and other trading securities. However, the comparison gives an indication about the overall loss of income as a consequence of the interposition of holding structures.

From the annual reports of the holding companies, the financial income flows between the original dividend distributed by the ultimate investee, and the dividend distributed to the ultimate investor at the other end of the investment chain, have been collected. Income received includes both interest income from loans paid out by the investee, and dividends paid to the holding company, excluding extraordinary income, most of the time flowing from the realisation of previously built up stakes. It appears that on average 72% of the portfolio income is distributed to the shareholders, varying largely from case to case but also over time. The smaller companies would probably show less largesse. Some holding companies also distribute more than income received: the difference may be explained, whether from undistributed income from previous years or from realised surplus (extraordinary income). Extraordinary income is sometimes distributed to shareholders, although most holding companies would prefer to reinvest in other ventures. The claim that some of this income also is derived from the holding company's own trading activity cannot be substantiated from the published figures, but does not seem likely as the phenomenon is not recurrent.

Table 9: Pay-out ratios

						Average
Ackermans en Van Haaren						
portfolio		1992	1993	1994	1995	
dividends + interest		517353	212538	490445	503513	
paid to shareholders		215639	223730	244442	262500	
ratio		41,68	105,27	49,84	52,13	62,23
Almanij						
portfolio	1990/91	1991/92	1992/93 18 months	1994	1995	
dividends + interest	1945178	2271039	3360894	2749133	2936182	
paid to shareholders	1221494	1377462	2236179	1674988	1922861	
ratio	62,80	60,65	66,54	60,93	65,49	63,28
Belcofi						
portfolio		1992	1993	1994	1995	
dividends + interest		293459	359568	386170	220091	
paid to shareholders		146160	157479	167321	194880	
ratio		49,81	43,80	43,33	88,55	56,37
Brederode						
portfolio		1992	1993	1994	1995	
dividends + interest		315065	372016	475632	468477	
paid to shareholders		212176	232001	290335	317687	
ratio		67,34	62,36	61,04	67,81	64,64

CNP/NMP

portfolio	1991	1992	1993	1994	1995	
dividends + interest	2053417	2052358	2415166	2711783	3194392	
paid to shareholders	2079710	2079710	2123958	2485825	2552188	
ratio	101,28	101,33	87,94	91,67	79,90	92,42
discount %	9,73	10,35	18,12	15,11	20,60	14,78

Cobepa

portfolio	1991	1992	1993	1994	1995	
dividends + interest	3177274	3374134	2895733	2806351	2611442	
paid to shareholders	1856537	1902080	1928808	2277417	2430510	
ratio	58,43	56,37	66,61	81,15	93,07	71,13
discount %	16,24	31,02	21,01	23,28	22,00	22,71

Elektrafina

portfolio		1992	1993	1994	1995	
dividends + interest		4944439	3655066	3159836	4257437	
paid to shareholders		3306727	3389666	3865441	4171065	
ratio		66,88	92,74	122,33	97,97	94,98
discount %		26,99	20,62	22,66	20,42	22,67

Fimeuse

portfolio		1992	1993	1994	1995	
dividends + interest		30407	58553	58517	60591	
paid to shareholders		34248	34209	34209	0	
ratio		112,63	58,42	58,46	0,00	57,38

Finoutremer

portfolio	1991	1992	1993	1994	1995	
dividends + interest	273760	227337	290650	285721	307788	
paid to shareholders	197448	215963	241040	249648	246209	
ratio	72,12	95,00	82,93	87,37	79,99	83,48
discount %	39,00	44,00	30,00	30,00	29,20	34,44

Floridienne

portfolio		1992	1993	1994	1995	
dividends + interest		78448	68562	28266	69621	
paid to shareholders		0	0	0	21957	
ratio		0,00	0,00	0,00	31,54	7,88

GBL

portfolio	1991	1992	1993	1994	1995	
dividends + interest	3939907	5691771	4055108	5691771	5433932	
paid to shareholders	4355332	4476773	4462762	4590930	4591981	
ratio	110,54	78,65	110,05	80,66	84,51	92,88
discount %	13,58	22,45	21,60	19,87	19,34	19,37

Gevaert

portfolio	1992	1993	1994	1995	
dividends + interest	2240020	1993844	2160403	2175385	
paid to shareholders	1374912	2187360	1562400	1718640	
ratio	61,38	109,71	72,32	79,00	80,60
discount %	25,40	19,27	26,37	17,59	22,16

Imp. Invest

portfolio	1992/93	1993/94	1994/95	
dividends + interest	94303	134058	157897	
paid to shareholders	70561	76313	80632	
ratio	74,82	56,93	51,07	60,94

Mecaniver

portfolio	1991	1992	1993	1994	
dividends + interest	496858	401622	614167	534688	
paid to shareholders	410457	452918	464630	476554	
ratio	82,61	112,77	75,65	89,13	90,04

Powerfin

portfolio	1991	1992	1993	1994	1995	
dividends + interest	9840433	5566938	5865639	6543320	7205932	
paid to shareholders	5720610	3195872	3357279	3518654	3675171	
ratio	58,13	57,41	57,24	53,77	51,00	55,51

Sidro

portfolio	1992	1993	1994	1995	
dividends + interest	213005	121584	175641	173260	
paid to shareholders	153920	155475	155475	153920	
ratio	72,26	127,87	88,52	88,84	94,37

Societé générale de belgique

portfolio	1991	1992	1993	1994	1995	
dividends + interest	8804861	7522856	8753923	6494891	7085259	
paid to shareholders	5583512	6803449	7097673	8082277	8189724	
ratio	63,41	90,44	81,08	124,44	115,59	94,99
discount %	26,82	24,52	18,64	21,17	17,12	21,65

Sofina

portfolio	1992	1993	1994	1995	
dividends + interest	1460659	1211727	1190932	1140882	
paid to shareholders	1042402	1087195	1257513	1296646	
ratio	71,37	89,72	105,59	113,65	95,08

From these figures there would appear as loss of income of more than 1/4 of the original current income earned. Taking into account the time factor - it takes at least one additional year for dividends distributed by investee to transit through the holding company - one will understand that investors charge a discount for this type of indirect investment.

Arguments are often made in support of the holding companies' function. The claim is often made that holding companies offer a better protection against the unfavourable market development of individual shares: the argument comes down to risk diversification[85]. There is no evidence that individual investors are better or worse stock pickers than holding companies, especially as the latter may follow their "strategic interests" that would influence their investment decisions, but which are not necessarily to the benefit of the investors in that particular company. Also the idea that holding companies offer the advantage of long term strategies, may be valuable in macro-economic terms, but does not help today's investors and their strive for wealth maximisation.

Several of the disadvantages of the holding companies are multiplied as a consequence of the existence of multi-layer holding structures: if income flows have to be submitted to repeated charges and delays caused by the interposition of several holdings, the negative factor will multiplied.

The functioning of holding companies necessarily implies a number of charges. The overall charge of the management function - i.a. directors and employee remuneration - has already been mentioned, and although relatively limited in comparison to the income flows, is not negligible. Structural factors, such as the legal and tax charges resulting from the functioning of separate legal entities, can be identified. In the Belgian case, the tax burden is relatively

85 See CNP-NPM, Annual Report 1991, 15. Due to the high concentration of holdings in investee companies investors obviously prefer to diversify by acquiring investment funds shares.

minor, as the tax code largely - in fact up to 95% - exempts dividends from share investments from company taxation. Holding company income taxes therefore are if not negligible, not very material. An attempt to quantify some of these charges was made supra table 5.

As the multi-layered functioning of these holding companies constitute an undeniable burden on the dividend flows, several have attempted to supplement their income by generating independent business, such as investment advice, financial and fiscal engineering, trading in portfolio securities, etc. The aim of this activity has been stated as not to burden the holding function with charges that are merely related to the existence of these intermediate structures. Cobepa e.g. has strived very hard in pursuing this goal and may have succeeded in its attempt, its discount being comparatively small, while its distribution policy was moderately liberal. However, another factor may help explain the lower discount: Cobepa has a share repurchase programme running that certainly has sustained the market price of its shares.

Other factors are almost impossible to substantiate. The fact that control is maintained at the holding company level, and that if control changes, the premium does not go to the ultimate investors, but is systematically reinvested, is an element that drives valuation of the holdings company's shares and of the underlying shares apart. As the holding company itself is in fact not exposed to a take-over threat, its shares will not express any premium, while such premium attaches to most of their portfolio shares. Therefore the rule mandating a take-over bid is applicable only if control is transferred at a price above market price. It should be mentioned that Belgium has introduced, already in the 1960's a mandatory bid rule, now legally enforceable since the 1989 legislation: the rule was originally aimed at avoiding holding companies taking advantage of their power to negotiate at substantial premiums on trading their controlling blocks of shares, without sharing any of this premium with their fellow investors. Since the 1989 change of the law, the investors have a legally enforceable right to be bought out at the same price as obtained by the selling controlling shareholder[86]. The rule does not apply to unlisted companies, or companies the shares of which have not been issued to the public[87].

In the more popular press the issue of conflicts of interests also is often referred to: holding companies often run their investments in their own interests, not in that of the investee and of its investors. Cases have been cited in which the subsidiary has been obliged to acquire assets of the parent in order to replenish the parent's cash reserves or where share transactions between

86 See Cass., 10 March 1994, Rechtskundig Weekblad (1994-95) 431; Revue de droit commercial belge 1994, 12, note FR. GLANSDORFF (Wagon Lits Case).

87 See for the precise definition, art. 1, RD of 8 November 1989.

group entities merely served to realize a surplus on the value of the shares which had not appeared before in the non-consolidated accounts. These cases constitute specific examples of conflicts of interest between the parent company and its subsidiary, itself often a listed company.

The 1995 amendments of the Belgian law have introduced specific procedures submitting this type of transaction to the appreciation of independent directors, acting on the report of an independent expert[88]. The rule applies only to transactions between Belgian stock exchange listed companies and their important shareholder - defined as a shareholder with a controlling or with a significant influence - whether these are holding companies, or other entities. It calls for the transaction to be submitted, before decision by the board, to a committee of three directors, that are independent "vis-à-vis the transaction or decision". These are not independent directors in the Anglo-Saxon sense[89], as their independence is limited to the single deal involved. This committee will be assisted by a expert which has to be equally independent "vis-à-vis the transaction or decision". This committee will report on the conditions of the transaction, whether it is in the interest of the company and all its shareholder, and does not confer, directly or indirectly, any undue advantage to one of the shareholders. The conclusion of the report is included in the annual report and is disclosed to the public. In case of non-compliance, the directors might be liable, and the transaction can be voided.

On the basis of these independent opinions, boards will not lightly engage their reputation, and possibly their liability as well, by agreeing to transactions that could be criticised as constituting a transfer of financial substance to the parent company.

At least one company has already published a report called for by the said company law provision, although the latter has entered into force only on the 1st of July 1996[90].

Conclusion

The issue whether this interposition of holding companies of the Belgian type results in added value, or rather would constitute a limitation on investors' wealth maximisation, especially as imposing a burden on dividend flows, remains a fascinating question. Any answer to this question would constitute a

---

88 See FR. VINCKE, Een eerste poging om "corporate governance" toe te passen op Belgische vennootschappen, T.R.V. (1995) 41.

89 Due to the presence in most companies of dominant shareholders one can question the possibility to appoint really independent directors.

90 Art. 60 bis, Companies Act; for an extensive analysis see E. WYMEERSCH, Het belangenconflict in de vennootschappen (1996).

value judgement for which at present there is not sufficient evidence. The purpose of the present paper has mainly been to sketch some perspectives that could offer a valid alternative to the sometimes raised question whether there is a future for financial holding companies. The answer is that the future will depend on the functions assumed and to the added value achieved. Effective monitoring of the investee companies could certainly contribute to support this double objective.

Appendix: Principal Shareholders of Listed Companies (1/7/1996)

1. Full majority control

Listed Company	Principal shareholder	% of direct and indirect ownership	declaration date
Afrifina	Brederode	71,35	21-12-95
Agricom	Finoutremer	94,96	14-4-95
Ans et Rocour	Dorchester	85,52	12-2-96
Asturienne	Foncière du Chateau d'Eau de Paris	56,61	31-12-95
Aurex	Hoste	71,73	27-12-95
Axa belgium	Finaxa/Axa S.A. (France)	91,07	30-4-96
Behermann	Behermann O.B.A.	65,1	9-10-95
Belcofi	Ackermans	55,1	31-12-95
Belectric	Lonrho	77,9	30-4-96
Belg. Beton	CMS and concert parties	50,29	31-12-95
	Trustmetal	20,55	31-12-95
Belgo-Katanga	Auximines/La Lieve	61,64	20-5-96
Belgolaise	Gen. Bank	55,24	31-12-95
Bemat	Moury family	58,52	31-12-94
Berginvest	Concert parties	72,2	18-1-96
Bernheim-Comofi	Concert parties	77,36	31-12-95
Bois Sauvage	Surongo c.s.	62,02	20-5-96
Brederode	Auxiliaire	59,41	31-12-95
Campine	Hempel/Erze	59,44	31-12-95
Chanic	Finoutremer	55,94	31-12-94
City Hotels	Europ Invest	50,1	8-3-95
CMB	Almabo/Naviga	50,07	22-4-96
Cobepa	Paribas	66,92	31-12-95
Cockerill Sambre	SWSID	78,77	31-12-95
Colruyt	Colruyt Family	63,66	31-3-95
Corona-Lotus	Bisinvest + physical persons	70	30-4-96
Credicom	Vaturi	86,16	30-1-96
Crédit général	Kredietbank	63,93	7-12-95
	in concert with Kredietbank	37,58	
Creyf's Interim	Ciparco/Sticht. Martine	51,51	12-7-95
D'Ieteren	Concert parties	57,43	31-12-95
Distrigaz	Tractebel	57,53	20-6-96
Egecim	Finoutremer	50,87	31-12-94
Electrafina	GBL/Royale Belge	56,29	28-6-96
	Compagnie des Eaux	23,96	30-4-96

Engrais Rosier	Elf Acquitane	56,86	30-4-96
Fabr Fer Charleroi	Concert parties	50,57	30-6-94
Fimeuse	Tractebel	91,99	22-5-96
Finoutremer	Société Générale	55,16	31-12-95
Her-Fic	Armurerie Liégoise	79,96	31-12-93
Franki	Frankipar/Van Roey	60,48	31-12-95
Ford motor	Ford Motor Cy	84	30-4-96
Generale Mij	Suez	62,47	31-12-95
Gevaert	Cobepa	35,38	31-12-95
	concert parties	60,75	
Glaverbel	Asahi Glass	67,25	30-4-96
Gouffre	Surongo	50,42	30-4-96
Henex	Boël	54,52	30-4-96
Herseautoise	Coorevits	82,33	31-12-94
HSPL	Hilos	53,13	15-9-95
Ibel	Cobepa	77,2	30-4-96
Immobel	Concert parties	61,01	31-12-95
Imperial Invest	Concert parties	50,58	2-3-96
La Lieve	Auximines	90,8	28-6-96
Lonrho Belg.	Lonrho Plc.	82,48	30-4-96
Mecaniver	Danone (ex BSN)	88,99	12-6-96
Mercantile Beliard	Gimvindus	99,76	30-4-96
Monceau Zolder	Brederode	82,56	31-12-95
Mosane	Cobepa	76,34	28-12-95
Musson et Halanzy	LB Holding	69,79	27-6-96
BNB/NBB	Belgium	50	31-12-95
Nord Sumatra	Socfin/Socfinasia/Socfinal	50,2	30-4-96
CNP/NPM	Concert parties	55,8	31-12-95
Obourg Fin	Fam. Janssen/Tubize Fin.	71,98	29-11-95
PCB	Brugefi/OCP participations	86,83	30-4-96
Picanol	Steverlynck	57,91	30-4-96
Powerfin	Tractebel	59,96	31-12-95
Profrigo	Kredietbank	94,98	30-4-96
Prominter	De Eik	66,67	30-4-96
Quick	GIB	57,44	31-12-95
Recticel	Société Générale	69,98	31-12-95
Roton	Rota Finance	80,35	30-4-96
Royale belge	Concert parties	69,28	31-12-95
Sabca	Dassault	52,96	30-4-96
	Fokker	42,8	
Sabech	Mofima	96,58	30-4-96
Sait Radio	Cobepa	64,34	31-12-95

Sapec	Financiere Frederic Jacobs	54,23	30-4-96
SCF	Gedimo	78	31-12-95
Sidro	Sofina	70,06	30-4-96
Socobom	Deferm	71,1	30-4-96
Sogefor	Finoutremer	53,39	30-4-96
Spector	Fotoinvest	56,99	31-12-95
Sun International	Van Moerkerke	54,79	31-12-95
Surongo	Paquot	63,44	31-12-95
Ter Beke	Coopman	54,2	30-4-96
Koramic (ex-Terca)	Stichting Adm. kantoor Terca:	80,94	23-5-96
Texaf	Cobepa	82,1	5-4-96
Trustmetal	Tytgadt	55,89	19-12-95
Tubize Fin	Fam. Janssen	67,87	29-11-95
UCO	Cobepa	57,72	6-5-96
Union Minière	Société Generale	50,19	31-12-95
Verelst	Mr. D. Mackarness/LVH	94,88	30-4-96
Walibi	Concert Parties	53,76	23-4-96
Werister	Soter c.s.	51,92	31-12-94
	90 companies	**65,69%**	

2. Between 50% and 45%

Bekaert	Concert parties	47,65	31-12-95
CBR	Heidelberger Zement	48,89	31-12-95
Charleroi	Boël and partners	45,53	30-4-96
GBL	Pargesa Holding	48,8	31-12-95
	UAP/Royale Belge	15,89	
Spadel	Dubois	49	30-4-96
	Brewfin	34,83	
Wittock	Gevalmo	48,57	31-12-95
	6 companies	**4,38%**	

3. Between 45% and 40%

Agridec	Etoile	40,65	30-4-96
CFE	Lyon Dumez	43	31-12-95
Clabecq	Société Wallone Pour la Sidérurgie	40,45	17-6-96
Electrabel	Tractebel	44,73	31-12-95
Definance	Defi	40,17	31-12-95
Co.Bra.Ha	Interbrew	35,28	31-12-95
	Finabra/Gefi	44,93	

Moustier	Boël	43,64	30-4-96
Petrofina	Concert parties	43,1	12-1-96
Socfin	Cie des Glenans	44,43	31-12-95
	Geselfina	24,99	
Sofina	Solvay en co	40,99	31-12-95
Telinfo	Sidmar/Gimvindus	44,82	31-12-95
Tessenderlo	EMC Belgium	40,61	30-5-96
Tractebel	Société Générale	40,45	31-12-95
	G.B.L.	24,5	
	13 companies	**9,49%**	

4. Between 40% and 30%

Almanij	Concert parties	38,30	31-12-95
	ex concert agreement	53,40	
Barco	GIMV	39,11	31-12-95
BBL	Joint control	37,19	19-1-96
	Winterthur included	45,42	15-5-96
BBL	ING	20,06	28-9-95
Befimmo	Bernheim Comofi	33,61	30-4-96
BMT	Seynaeve	38,21	31-12-95
Cimescaut	CBR	33,52	30-4-96
	NIFRAC Finance	20,33	
Fortis AG	Concert parties	35,2	16-2-96
Kredietbank	Almanij	36,23	31-12-95
PEK	Vanhool	39,49	
Sococlabecq	Dessy	31,75	31-12-95
	Fibepa	29,19	
UCB	Obourg Financiere	36,99	18-1-96
Uniwear	Connie	39,84	31-12-95
	12 companies	**8,76%**	

5. Less than 30%

Ackermans	Belfima	28,31	31-12-95
Anderlues	Wittmer	19,48	30-4-96
	Ch. Ducarme ets	17,05	
Auximines	Holdicam	13,65	30-4-96
Catala	Concert parties	26,01	30-4-96
Cofinimmo	Assubel/De Schelde/AGF	8,54	29-3-96
	Rodamco	9,93	
	P&V verzekeringen	5,91	

	Degroof	5,07	
De Ceuninck	Plastec Int.	25,61	31-12-95
	Royale Belge	14,99	
Delhaize	No Shareholder over 5%		31-12-95
Electrorail	Kamobel	20,89	31-12-94
Floridienne	Cobepa	28,1	31-12-95
General Bank	Société Générale	28,23	31-12-95
GIB Group	Cobepa	14,82	31-12-95
Sipef	Bracht	10,87	30-4-96
	De Vaderlandsche	5,03	30-4-96
	Darier Hentsch	5,22	18-8-95
Solvac	No shareholder over 5%	3	0-4-96
Solvay	Solvac	26	30-4-96
	Physical persons	29	
Usines Porph	Porphyroc	20,08	30-4-96
Willem-Sophia	Partindus	21,25	30-4-96
	16 companies	**11,68%**	

The Corporate Governance Debate in Belgium[1]

François Vincke

Contents

I. Introduction

Writing about the corporate governance debate in Belgium presents an exciting but also a risky challenge. Many reasons induce me to be modest in my approach and prudent in my evaluations. Indeed, when studying the rich literature on governance from the United States, I am impressed - not to say depressed - by the large numbers of books and articles written on the subject. In addition, a few major economic indicators will bring me back to a natural humility: Belgian market capitalization is small, the market is relatively illiquid and it can hardly be said that our country is in the front line of change.

---

1 Article written with the help of C. JOHNSON, member of the Fina Legal Team in Brussels and member of the Californian Bar (J.D., University of California, Berkeley; A.B., Princeton University).

But turning a disadvantage into an opportunity is one of the lessons of modern management. Admittedly, our country is a relative latecomer to this debate, but this is no reason to be only passive followers or lazy onlookers.

Belgium, with its cultural tradition, has naturally shied away from fundamental debates about the structure of its capital markets and the division of power in its corporations. Boardroom activity is not the obvious subject of academic work or intellectual scrutiny but, on the positive side, I can point to some major changes in corporate law.

II. Recent developments in corporation law

Taking the risk of being too schematic, one could say that our corporations law has experienced two main periods of sweeping changes in its history.

The first one occurred in the thirties with a series of legislative measures which separated banks and holding companies, instituted the Banking Commission and reorganized the stock exchange.[2] While all companies stayed with the single-tier structure, banks adopted the two-tier structure. The stock exchange imposed the one-share one-vote rule and share issues were organized under the control of the newly created Banking Commission.

The attempted take-over in 1988 of the Société Générale de Belgique, the famous holding company which played a historic role in so many industrial and financial ventures of the Kingdom[3], and ensuing events, introduced a second era of change and reform. After an initial reaction of fear which led to the so-called "ancrage/verankering" debate, the Parliament would visit[4] and revisit[5] the law on corporations, make transparency declarations compulsory, lay down a number of specific rules on take-overs[6] and, more recently, reorganize the stock exchange[7]. A number of court decisions would during the same period of time revolutionize the small world of listed companies.

When the Cadbury report[8] was produced, it found in Belgium both interested readers who were seduced by the idea of self-regulation and Belgian financiers who were concerned to maintain the attractiveness of their market for international investors. Because Belgium is a small country with a major proportion of its economy dependent on international trade, supranational

---

2 Royal Decree n° 2 of 22 August 1934.
3 See, for a historical description, E. WYMEERSCH in: Institutional Investors and Corporate Governance (1993) 347 and notes.
4 Law of 18 July 1991.
5 Law of 13 April 1995.
6 Law on Transparency and Takeover Bids of 2 March 1989.
7 Law of 6 April 1995.
8 Report of the Committee on the Financial Aspects of Corporate Governance and the Code of Best Practice, 1 December 1992 (Cadbury Report).

integration in the European Union and international cooperation at large are a matter of survival. The evolution of Belgian listed companies can therefore not be seen outside the international context.

III. The Belgian equity market - some statistics

The Belgian market is small, having only 0.58 percent of total world stock market capitalization. As appears from table 1, the Belgian Stock Exchange ranks 23rd in the world.

Table 1

Stock exchange	Rank	Market capitalization in million of US$	% of World Stock Market Capitalization
NYSE	1	4,147,936	28.48
Tokyo	2	3,592,193	25.54
London	3	1,158,016	7.95
NASDAQ	4	793,668	5.45
Frankfurt	5	499,278	3.43
Paris	6	452,049	3.10
...	...		
Taiwan	10	247,325	1.7
...	...		
Mexico	20	130,248	0.89
...	...		
Brussels	23	84,421	0.,58

Source: FIBV/Brussels Stock Exchange.

About 155 companies were quoted on the Belgian Stock Exchange at the end of 1994. Table 2 allows to compare such position with some leading financial markets.

Table 2

Country	Listed domestic companies
Germany	664
France	726
Netherlands	239
United Kingdom	1,927
European Union (12)	4,871
Japan	1,667
NYSE	1,788
NASDAQ	4,310

Source: FIBV, CEPS.

The number of corporations listed on the Brussels Stock Exchange has been decreasing in the last decades. Table 3 shows this evolution in the period spanning the years 1973 to 1994.

Table 3

Year	Number of listed companies
1994	155
1993	159
1990	182
1980	225
1973	328

Source: Brussels Stock Exchange (Société de la Bourse de Valeurs Mobilières de Bruxelles, annual report, 1994).

New listings on the Stock Exchange are fairly rare in recent years[9]. Table 4 shows the most recent listed companies, the year of their floatation and their area of activity.

9 For an original view on the reasons for the scarcity of new stock exchange listings, see E. DE KEULENEER, Levert een beursnotering in België voldoende voordelen op?, Bank- en Financiewezen (1994) 534. See also L. WAUCQUEZ, Etude de la faisabilité d'une introduction en bourse, Ecole de Commerce Solvay (1994-1995).

Table 4

Company	Year	Activity
Cofinimmo	94	Real estate
Spector Photo Group	94	Photo
Terca	94	Building materials
Quick	93	Fast food
Imperial Invest	93	Holding
City Hotels	91	Real estate
AG 1993	91	Insurance
Desimpel	90	Building materials
Creyf's Interim	90	Interim

Source: Générale de Banque - Corporate Investment Banking/Annual report Brussels Stock Exchange.

Belgian Stock Exchange capitalization compared to Gross Domestic Product is at 38.6%,[10/11] below the average of the European Union of Twelve, which stands at 44.3%. Table 5 shows the Belgian Stock Exchange capitalization as a percentage of GDP in European and international contexts.

Table 5

Country	% of GDP
Belgium	38.6
Germany	25.1
France	37.9
Netherlands	61.5
United Kingdom	132.4
European Union (12)	44.3
Japan	73.8
NYSE	70.3
NASDAQ	13.2

Source: FIBV, CEPS.

The size of Belgian listed companies is relatively small. Only 4 companies are in the FORTUNE 500 classification of 7 August 1995, which is based on sales. Table 6 lists these 4 companies.

10 *CEPS*, Corporate Governance in Europe, Working Party Report n° 12 (June 1995), p. 7.

11 The annual report of the Brussels Stock Exchange mentions for 1994 a percentage of 34.96 (p. 71).

Table 6

Company	Rank (1994)	Revenue $ millions (1994)	Profits $ millions
Delhaize	312	11,564.7	120.2
Petrofina	318	11,399.1	324.9
Tractebel	428	9,131.3	320.7
Generale Bank	465	8,426.8	378.4

Source: Fortune, 7 August, 1995

Total volume of transactions on the Brussels Stock Exchange in 1994 appears in Table 7 and puts Brussels in 15th position.

Table 7

Stock Exchange	Volume in billion US$	Rank
New York	4.908,5	1
Tokyo	3.257,6	2
London	2.072,7	3
Frankfurt	1.301,9	4
Zürich	501,1	5
Paris	420,5	6
Milan	234,4	7
Australia	200,8	8
Amsterdam	179,3	9
Stockholm	177,4	10
Singapore	169,4	11
Madrid	111,1	12
Copenhagen	57,3	13
Oslo	36,8	14
Brussels	34,8	15
Helsinki	29,1	16
Vienna	17,8	17
Athens	10,5	18

Source: The Amsterdam Stock Exchange in 1994 (annual report).

Institutional investors account in Belgium for around 22 percent of total shareholdings.[12] This figure seems rather low, especially when compared to the United States, where institutionals have seen their participation rise constantly.

12 WYMEERSCH (supra note 3) 351.

In 1950 they held 8 %, by 1980 they stood at 33 percent and in 1990 they owned 45 percent of all outstanding equities.[13] One must be careful, though, in such comparisons, because there seem to be vast differences in what is encompassed by the different definitions of "institutional investor". Table 8 shows the large differences which may exist in institutional shareholdings between some major industrialized countries.

Table 8

Country	Year	%
Germany	90	22
France	92	23
United Kingdom	93	59
Japan	92	48

Source: CEPS, Lightfoot, see note 12.

Shareholding in major Belgian corporations is not broadly dispersed[14]. In order to evaluate the share dispersion rate in the Belgian stock market, I have researched, based on the legally compulsory transparency declarations, as they appear in the 1994 reports, of the Bel-20 corporations, the holdings of their 5 largest shareholders. Table 9 shows the Bel-20 companies and their 5 largest individual shareholders.

Table 9

Bekaert		Generale Bank		Electrabel		C.B.R.		Solvay	
Foundation Bekaert	21.4	Gén Belgique	27.31	Gén. Belgique	28.35	Heidelberger	48.89	Solvac	25.01
Family	12,64		3	Tractebel	16.25				
Davbury Ltd	6.01			Fortis	2.29				
Tirhold Inc.	4.88			Cofidel	1.08				
Int. Ind. Invest	1.92								
Total	46.85		30.31		47.97		48.89		25.00

13 R.W. LIGHTFOOT, Note on Corporate Governance Systems: the United States, Japan and Germany, prepared as the basis for class discussion at Harvard Business School (1991).

14 On the effects of liquidity of stock markets on the managers-shareholders relationship, see the critical views of A. BHIDE, Deficient Governance, Harvard Business Review (November-December 1994) 129-139.

Delhaize*Fortis		G.I.B.		UCB		Royale Belge			
(Family)	(35)	Gén. Belgique	19.22	Cobepa	15	Financ. d'Obourg	28.4	R. Vendôme	52.4
		Asphales	9.73	Vaxelaire	6.4	Bq. du Luxem-bourg	4.88	UAP	9,5
		Asahi	7.09			Financ. Drogenbos	3.56	Sofina	4.4
		Anhyp	6.70					C.N.P.	3.1
		Selstra	1.38						
Total	(35)		44.12		21.4		36.84		69.4

* No transparency declaration was required for Delhaize as no individual shareholder held more than 5%. The media mention however that family participation reaches 35%.

Tractebel		Petrofina		BBL		Gén. Belgique		GBL	
Gén. Belgique	40.59	GBL	29.84	GBL	12.44	Suez	61.53	Pargesa	47.4
GBL	24.59	Gén. Belgique	10.32	Royale Belge	12.36	Fortis	14.60	UAP	10,2
Fortis	2.29	Elf	2.26	ING	12.06			Royale Belge	5.0
Sofina	0.03	Sofina	1.20	Créd. Comm.	10.76				
		Fortis	0.36	Winterthur	8.30				
Total	66.39		43.98		55.92		76.13		62.6

Colruyt		KB		UM		CMB		Cockerill	
H.I.M.	17.4	Almanij Group	40	Gén. Belgique	50.19	Almabo Group	52.25	S. Wallone	79.79
D.I.M.	13.8					Naviga	1.16		
Family	7.1					Belgamar	0.26		
Staff	5.5					Boreas	0.14		
Sofina	5.2					Boreas Leven	0.05		
Total	48.0		40		50.19		53.86		79.79

Overall, the average holding of the five largest shareholders in the Bel-20 corporations is 49.23%.

IV. A first reaction

In such a restricted financial market, the governance debate could have been regarded with mixed feelings. Was it just a new trend in those fashionable

American management theories? Was it a kind of company law for non-lawyers? Was it a hidden and mysterious tool for corporate revolution?

After a moment of hesitation, the Cadbury report forced some prudent respect. It was practical in some respects and it laid down some fundamental principles such as the accountability of boards of directors to their shareholders' interests.[15] At the same time, as indicated above, the Belgian legislator was at work reformulating some elements of corporations law, and the parliamentary reports leading to the 1995 law already bear the imprint of the governance debate.[16]

Even more recently, the first publications have appeared and lectures have been given,[17] and articles in the press have revealed a rising interest in the matter.[18]

This new awareness should not surprise us: all corporations have to compete in difficult financial markets for the lowest-cost financing. Rating agencies, professional financial analysts, financial reporters, and, most importantly, institutional investors will coldly analyze each company's behavior, not only as regards governance,[19] but also as regards financial information or reporting and

---

15 Cadbury Report, p. 16, n° 3.4.

16 Documents Parlementaires, Sénat, 1 086-2, pp. 112, 118 and 152.

17 Apart from the works of Professor E. WYMEERSCH, see the lecture given by P. SCOHIER, Propos sur la guidance d'entreprise, Société royale d'économie politique de Belgique, and my own participation in a corporate law seminar at the Katholieke Universiteit Leuven, organized by Professor K. GEENS. Een eerste poging om 'corporate governance' toe te passen op Belgische vennootschappen, Tijdschrift voor Rechtspersoon en vennootschap (February 1995) 41.

18 See "Le Corporate Governance, on ne parle plus que de ça!" Le Soir, 28 October 1994; "'Corporate Governance' et droit français: convergence ou opposition?", Les Echos, 17 January 1995; "Scohier: Retour a la separation des pouvoirs dans l'entreprise?", L'Echo, 2 February 1995; "Des conseils d'administration plus British en Europe?", L'Echo, 25-27 February 1995; "Jean Peyrelevade pleit voor Angelsaksisch model van 'corporate governance'", Financieel Economische Tijd, 22 March 1995; "Suez sans stratégie? Worms contre-attaque", L'Echo, 13 April 1995; "S.G.B.: premiers pas vers le 'corporate governance'", L'Echo, 18 May 1995; "Elf à l'avance du Corporate Governance", L'Echo, 23 July 1995.

19 CalPERS (Californian Public Employees' Retirement System), a very large US institutional investor, in May 1994 sent a letter to the CEOs of the 200 largest companies in its portfolio asking them how they measured up against the General Motors guidelines on boardroom practices. (For the General Motors "Board Guidelines on Significant Corporate Governance Issues", see Corporate Governance, An International Review, Basil Blackwell, Volume 3, Number 1, January 1995). CalPERS graded the companies on their answers and used them in its decisions for proxy voting. (Business Week, 17 October 1994, pp. 70-72). In June 1995 CalPERS announced that it would launch a campaign in the UK, Germany or Japan by holding discussions with companies in which it owns equity and which are performing poorly (Financial Times, "US shareholder activity to launch campaign abroad", 8 June 1995).

accounting practices. These two latter subjects, which we will not discuss here, will inevitably be part of a global assessment of a corporation's performance.

V. Board practices

The centerpiece of the governance debate will undoubtedly be, in Belgium as elsewhere, the Board of Directors. What are its duties, how will its members be chosen, what degree of autonomy will it have, how will it organize its procedures? In this discussion there will be both issues of principle and practical matters of organization.

1. Main duties

The law entrusts directors with the "administration" or "management" of the corporation.[20] This wording, as it is still used in the Belgian corporations law, should probably be considered to be antiquated. Nobody seriously believes that a board that meets perhaps 6 to 12 times a year for 2 to 4 hours at a time can act as the management of a corporation.[21] On the contrary, they will, with notable exceptions such as in times of crisis, broadly oversee the conduct of the corporation's business. In so doing, the directors will avoid over-involvement, leaving to the CEO, the other executives and the staff full responsibility for implementing corporate policies. The Viénot report[22] represents a useful effort in trying to define more precisely the tasks entrusted to the board of directors and namely: (1) definition of the strategy of the enterprise; (2) designation of the company executives entrusted with the management ("mandataires sociaux") within the framework of this strategy; (3) control of this management and (4) control of the quality of the information given to the shareholders as well as to the markets in the annual report and at the time of important transactions.

---

20 Law on Corporations, article 53.

21 See also A. TUNC, Le gouvernement des sociétés anonymes, le mouvement de réforme aux Etats-Unis et au Royaume-Uni, Revue internationale de droit comparé (1994) 60.

22 Association Française des Entreprises Privées and Conseil National du Patronat Français, "Le Conseil d'Administration des Sociétés cotées" (July 1995) 6 and 913 (Viénot Report).

2. *"Intérêt social"*

The directors have a mandate which is revocable at any time ("ad nutum")[23] Their responsibility, as holders of this mandate, is to carry it out and to be answerable for any mistakes they have made during their management.[24]

They must act in the interest of the corporation ("intérêt social")[25] Conformity with the interest of the company is the touchstone for determining the propriety of corporate decisions. If they disregard this interest, they may be set aside, at least within the internal framework of the company, and the directors will be liable for them.[26] This concept, which is often referred to in legal texts[27] and in legal doctrine, is almost unanimously recognized as vague. Certain authors consider that the interest of the corporation is identical to the interest of the shareholders; others broaden the notion to also encompass the customers, the suppliers, the managers, the work force and even the region and the country (the so called "stakeholders").

Professor van Gerven has noted that, under the influence of American opinion on the primary role of the shareholders, and also as a result of the neo-liberal economic philosophy of the last decade, the interests of actors other than the shareholders are considered more often to be of lesser importance.[28]

Professor Heenen criticizes too broad definitions of the interest of the corporation, alleging that, if they are too encompassing, they become useless. How can the interest of the corporation also comprise the interests of the suppliers, the customers, the banker and the staff, as those interests are often divergent? Professor Heenen proposes an original definition: for him the interest of the corporation is identical to the interest of any person, physical or corporate, who exercises an economical activity, and that is to improve the position of its products and services in the market[29].

Professor Nelissen Grade, after having reviewed the most recent evolution of doctrine in Belgium and the Netherlands, concludes that the interest of the

---

23 Law on Corporations, article 55, para. 3, This principle was reaffirmed in rather strong terms by the Supreme Court ("Cour de Cassation") in its judgment of 13 April 1989, see Journal des Tribunaux (1990) with a note by D. MICHIELS, 751-758. The Court declared "ad nutum" revocability by the shareholders in general meeting a rule of public policy.

24 Law on Corporations, article 62, para. 1.

25 On the concept of "interest of the corporation", See Professor X. DIEUX'S opinion in Documents parlementaires, Sénat, 1086-2 (1993-1994), p. 145.

26 J. HEENEN, L'intérêt social, Liber Amicorum Paul De Vroede (1994) 891.

27 The interest of the corporation is used as a reference in the following articles of the Law on Corporations: art. 29bis, art. 29quater, art. 34 §2, art. 34bis § 3, art. 41 §2, art. 60bis, art. 65, art. 67, art. 74ter and art. 191.

28 W. VAN GERVEN "De overneming van vennootschappen naar Belgisch recht. De rol van de Bankcommissie", Van vennootschappelijk belang. Opstellen aangeboden aan Professor J.M.M. MAEYER (1988) 47-48.

29 J. HEENEN (supra note 26) 894.

corporation implies its existence, its continuity, its development, its capability to produce profits, all in the interest of the totality of its present and future shareholders.[30]

So in Belgium too we are confronted with the "shareholders v. stakeholders" debate,[31] but there is no serious doubt in my mind that in the short and the long term, the direct and indirect interests of the shareholders taken as a whole are, and will even more in the future be, the leading concern of every Board of Directors. I would, however, plead for a thorough professional debate on this subject in order to reach a clear definition of such an important concept. I think one will accept from me, as a practitioner of corporate law, that it is hard to have to answer directors' questions about the interest of the company with - "it's a vague concept"...

3. *How are directors chosen?*

I do not want to speak yet about the independent or non-executive director; I only want to address briefly the matter of election v. cooptation. Law[32] and doctrine[33] are quite adamant on the subject: directors are to be elected by the general shareholders meeting; only if a place becomes vacant will the remaining directors proceed with a temporary replacement. In reality, however, cooptation takes place in the absence of a vacancy or when there is no urgent need for an immediate replacement. By coopting someone to the board as an additional member or as the replacement for a deceased or resigning director, when there is no urgent need to do so, the directors narrow the power of the general meeting of shareholders. This practice should not be encouraged.

4. *How many directors?*

A number of American authors are quite explicit on this subject. Charles Waldo provides statistics showing that the total number of members on the average

30 J.M. NELISSEN GRADE, note "De la validité et de l'exécution de la convention de vote dans les sociétés commerciales" under the judgment of 13 April 1989, Revue critique de jurisprudence belge (1991) 234.

31 See W.G. BOWEN, Inside the Boardroom: Governance by Directors and Trustees (1994) 9. See also J.W. LORSCH with E. MACIVER, Pawns or Potentates: the Reality of America's Corporate Boards, Harvard Business School Press (1989) 37-54. (LORSCH distinguishes between the "traditionalists" who believe directors are accountable to shareholders alone, the "rationalizers" who hold the view that what is good for the shareholder will be good for other constituencies and the "broad constructionists" who consider that directors' responsibilities encompass more than shareholders).

32 Law on Corporations, article 55, para. 2.

33 RESTEAU, Traité des Sociétés Anonymes, Volume II, 87-88.

board has remained remarkably constant from 1966 to 1982.[34] Martin Lipton and Jay Lorsch recommend that a board should have no more than 10 directors (with 2 independent directors for each director from management).[35] William Bowen refers to the Korn/Ferry Board of Directors Study for 1992 to show that American boards have on average shrunk from 14 members in 1987 to 12 in 1991,[36] while he proposes as his first "presumptive norm" that the "size of for-profit boards should normally fall within a range of say 10 to 15 members ...".[37] This he justifies by reminding us that there is general agreement that a board's capacity to perform its functions is critically dependent on its size. He warns that achieving a genuinely interactive mode of discussion for decisionmaking will be harder when a board becomes too large, but he also stresses that a board with fewer than 10 or 12 members runs the risk of being insufficiently diverse. At present the average number of directors, in the United States stands at 12 and that figure is stable since 1990.[38/39]

The Canadian answer to this question is somewhat more involved.[40] The Toronto Stock Exchange Committee on Corporate Governance in Canada puts forward as a guideline that "Every board of directors should examine its size and, with a view to determining the impact of the number upon effectiveness, undertake where appropriate, a program to reduce the number of directors to a number which facilitates more effective decisionmaking." The Committee was in fact split between a majority which believed that when the number of directors increases beyond a particular threshold (approximately 20), the effectiveness of the board decreases and a minority which thought that in large boards there could be diversity of views and experiences as well as an opportunity for broad geographic representation.

Belgian boards are larger than their American counterparts. While the solution of Lipton and Lorsch is probably too radical and does not take into account the vast differences one finds in the corporate world, I nevertheless believe that the Belgian corporate community should study the matter further.

---

34 C.N. WALDO, Boards of Directors, their changing roles, structure and information needs (1985) 45-47.

35 M. LIPTON and J. LORSCH, Boards with Backbone, Financial Times, 25 November 1992 and "A Modest Proposal for Improved Corporate Governance", The Business Lawyer (November 1992) 67.

36 BOWEN (supra note 31) 43.

37 Ibid.

38 See further Table 14 and footnote 63 for the 1994/95 situation.

39 The SpencerStuart Board Index (SSBI) 1994 Proxy Report records an average size of boards of 100 multi-billion USD corporations of 13. Five years ago, that average was 14 and ten years ago 15. It is anticipated that further reductions over the next three to four year will bring the average down to 12.

40 Report of the Toronto Stock Exchange Committee on Corporate Governance in Canada, "Where were the Directors?: guidelines for improved corporate governance in Canada" (December 1994).

Table 10 shows the number of directors of the Bel-20 companies, based on their 1994 annual reports.

Table 10

Company	Number of Directors
BBL	29
Bekaert	12
C.B.R.	10
CMB	17
Cockerill	12
Colruyt	12
Delhaize	11
Electrabel	27
Fortis	12
GBL	20
Générale de Banque	26
Générale de Belgique	21
GIB	16
Kredietbank	17
Petrofina	20
Royale Belge	20
Solvay	15
Tractebel	24
UCB	10
Union Minière	19

5. *Can a corporation be a director?*

In Belgium there are some cases where a corporation is designated as a member of the board of directors of another corporation. The corporation, so elected or designated, then designates a physical person to represent it on the board. The law is silent on this subject and the commentaries are unenthusiastic.

I realize that such a structure, which is quite imaginative, will fit certain specific purposes in special circumstances, but at the same time I can see that personal accountability and interactive board participation will not be enhanced by such a practice. I doubt that it should be encouraged.

6. *Should board meetings bring the directors together physically?*

To many, this question will appear as either a provocative or a rhetorical question. In our country, paper board meetings have almost become a reality even for listed companies. Indeed, a number of company lawyer colleagues with good intentions endorsed a proposition to our Parliament for a law which would have allowed boards to make decisions on the basis of unanimous written consent. A certain number of other actors, insisting that public companies should be managed by an active and responsible board of directors,[41] warned against such a practice, which would weaken the board's function as a deliberating body. The Parliament amended the proposition and restricted the possibility of paper board meetings to exceptional circumstances, justified by urgency and the "interest of the corporation".

At a seminar in Liège, I referred to corporate governance and more specifically to the Cadbury report in stressing that the board of directors, as the central organ of the corporation, should be in a position to be truly pro-active[42]. Real deliberation on the agenda items of a board meeting will normally require that the board members come together physically.

7. *Can a CEO also be Chairman of the Board?*

This question has been heavily debated in governance circles and a fair amount of literature has been produced on the issue. Interestingly enough, the answer is not unequivocal and it shows that corporate governance is, fortunately, not a religion: there is no single, universal answer to the question.

In the United States, even if arguments to split the two functions have been very strong,[43] boardroom reality shows that the CEO is also the chairman in more than 80 % of US public companies.[44] Recent publications also reveal that governance scholars are reconciled with the Chairman-CEO practice.[45]

The argument for a split between the functions has at times been very heated. Bowen quotes one author who writes: "One-man rule is a bad idea. A single CEO-Chairman can do great damage before being reined in - often when

---

41 Parliamentary reports for the law of 13 April 1995, Sénat, Session 1994-1995, 1086-2, 176-177.

42 Seminar of the Commission Droit et Vie des Affaires of January 1994, published in: Revue Pratique des Sociétés, n° special, "Le projet de loi modifiant les lois coordonnées sur les sociétés commerciales. Quels changements dans la vie des entreprises?", pp. 151-153.

43 LORSCH with MACIVER (supra note 31) 184-187. Notes at the bottom of p. 185 give references to previous literature favorable to the "separate chairman" solution.

44 J.W. LORSCH, Empowering the Board, Harvard Business Review, January-February 1995, p. 107.

45 LIPTON and LORSCH, A Modest Proposal (supra note 35) 70.

it is too late..."[46] Bowen also cites a writer who declares that "All [his] experience and study has convinced [him] that the

Chairman of the board should not be the CEO - not in an American public corporation ...". This author further states that "a chairman/CEO wears two hats at the same time and you just can't do that and look good in both roles". He then goes on to describe these two roles and concludes: "When one does all that and in addition usually picks his/her fellow board members, you have in my opinion a dictatorship".[47]

Lorsch and MacIver were more nuanced but nevertheless pretty firm in expressing their view. They stated that one major need is to diminish the CEO's power as leader of the board. To do this they suggested that, by law and by custom, the position of chairman and CEO be separated. Having a separate chairman would help directors prevent crisis, it would give them a strong voice in setting the agenda, in conducting meetings, and in selecting directors. The chairman could also use control of the meeting process to encourage more open discussion. Finally this reform would reinforce the board's right and obligation to govern.[48]

As the debate continued, only a minority of American corporations[49] opted for a separate chairman system and some that did, like American Express and Westinghouse, afterwards recombined the two positions. Facing very strong opposition, even Lipton and Lorsch, the two strong proponents of separation, backed down from the idea of a separate chairmanship,[50] and now favor instead the principle that there should be, next to the Chairman-CEO, a lead director.

Bowen partly follows this route[51] when he proposes as his presumptive norm number 11 that "the board should have either a non-executive chairman or an alternative structure (such as a strong committee on the board led by an outside director) that will allow the board to discharge its obligations without usurping managerial functions". I will come back later to the idea of a committee on the board when we review the committee structure. In Bowen's view the lead director would register concerns and check impressions, especially when an organization seems to be in trouble or to be missing opportunities. He would therefore function on standby and serve as an insurance policy on which the board hopes not to collect. But Bowen hastens to add that the lead director should not be competing with the CEO for authority.

---

46 BOWEN (supra note 31) 83 (quoting John Whitehead).
47 Ibid, pp. 83-84 (quoting Kenneth Dayton).
48 LORSCH with MACIVER (supra note 31) 184-185.
49 The SpencerStuart Board Index (SSBI) 1994 Proxy Report records that currently 10 of the 100 SSBI boards have done the separation of the offices of chairman and CFO. At 7 of these boards, the chairman is the previous CFO who has retained the chairmanship role and title to assure continuity.
50 LIPTON and LORSCH, A Modest Proposal (supra note 35).
51 BOWEN (supra note 31) 81 and 89-93.

The English position and experience on this issue is quite different. In that country the practice of having a chairman separate from the CEO is engrained in the system.[52] The Cadbury report simply states that "given the importance and particular nature of the chairman's role, it should be separate from that of the chief executive. If these two roles are combined in one person, it represents a considerable concentration of power.[53]

As a consequence, the Cadbury Committee recommends that "there should be a clearly accepted division of responsibilities at the head of a company, which will ensure a balance of power and authority, such that no one individual has unfettered powers of decision". Nevertheless, the Committee does not go so far as imposing such a division of powers and states that "where the chairman is also the chief executive, it is essential that there should be a strong and independent element on the board."[54]

In the period 1993/1994[55] and within the sample analyzed by the Cadbury Committee, compliance on the Chairman/CEO recommendation was as follows:

Table 11

Companies; market capitalization down to	separate (%)	combined with independent element of non-executive directors	combined without independent element of non-executive directors
GBP 1.4 bio	82	15	3
400 mio	83	15	2
120 mio	82	11	7
45 mio	73	17	10
25 mio	81	13	6
10 mio	74	15	11
1 mio	72	5	23

The Canadian solution is also quite balanced. The Toronto Stock Exchange Committee puts forward the view that "the board should be able to function independently from management".[56] The Committee suggests that the simplest means for implementing this guideline is for the board to appoint a strong non-executive chair of the board whose principal responsibility is managing the board of directors. The Committee expresses a preference for this solution but

52 Cadbury Report, 20-22; Code of Best Practice, p. 6, no 12; see also LORSCH with MACIVER (supra note 31) 185.
53 Ibid.
54 Ibid.
55 Report of the Committee on the Financial Aspects of Corporate Governance, Compliance with the Code of Best Practice, 24 May 1995, pp. 11 and 16.
56 Toronto Stock Exchange Committee Report, p. 41.

recognizes that there are other means to achieve it, as for instance a committee on the board or a lead director.

What is the present situation in Belgium?

I made a quick check of the situation prevailing in the BEL-20 companies. The conclusion is that the vast majority of these companies have a separate chairman and CEO. In a small minority of cases, it may be that the chairman also has an executive position distinct from that of the CEO. I gather that the chairman/CEO split generally functions to the satisfaction of both and that while the chairman oversees and directs the board's processes, the CEO has sufficient room for effectively managing the company. In addition, the perception of the outside world is positive: the CEO is considered to be the person really in command of the workings of the enterprise, while the chairman is seen as the organizer, animator and leader of the supreme body of the corporation, that is the board .

In such a context, a lead director or a "committee on the board" appears unnecessary, not only because in the studies I have just mentioned, they are put forward as second best solutions, but also because a third power - in addition to the chairman and the CEO - would most probably confuse the situation or blur the perception of the power structure. Indeed, we should never forget that effective governance requires not only adequate checks and balances but also a clear and unequivocal division of work between a small number of actors.

8. *Executives v. non-executives*

The relationship between executive directors and non-executive directors is at the very heart of the corporate governance debate. Their relative numbers and their relations will be determining factors for the empowerment of a board, and empowerment means that outside directors have the capability and independence to monitor the performance of top management and of the company, to influence management to change the strategic direction of the company if its performance does not meet the board's expectations; and in the most extreme cases, to change corporate leadership.[57]

a) The American Bar Association states that boards should be structured in a way to encourage their role as an independent and informed monitor of the conduct of the corporation's affairs and the performance of its management.[58] To function effectively, the board must exercise independent judgment. To reach that goal, the ABA puts forward that at least a majority of members of

57 LORSCH, Empowering the Board (supra note 44) 107.
58 American Bar Association, Section of Business Law, Corporate Director's Guidebook (2d ed., 1994) 17-18.

the boards of publicly held corporations should be independent of management. They go further and define as independent, the non-management director free of any material business or professional relationship with the corporation or its management.[59] The ABA definition is, however, silent on the matter of shareholding by directors or their environment.

b) The American Law Institute (ALI) in its recommendations on corporate practice follows the same trend but makes some exceptions for companies with a specific shareholding structure.[60]

The ALI recommends that the board of every large publicly held corporation (2000 shareholders or more and USD 100 million or more in total assets) should have a majority of directors who are free of any significant relationship with the corporation's executives, unless a majority of the corporation's voting securities are owned by a single person, a family group or a control group. And all publicly held corporations should have at least three directors who are free from such a relationship.

c) The citations above are only recommendations, but in the United States there are also stock exchange requirements. The New York Stock Exchange requires that listed companies have a minimum of two directors independent of management, as does NASDAQ. The American Stock Exchange recommends a minimum of two independent directors.

d) The guideline offered by the Toronto Stock Exchange Committee[61] is that every board should have a majority of individuals who qualify as unrelated. The definition of an "unrelated" individual is quite close to the ABA definition of "independent", but the Canadians are explicit on the issue of shareholding by directors. In its Draft Report, the Toronto Committee had been of the opinion that a shareholder who is in a position to control or influence the control of the company should be treated as a related director. In the final analysis, it changed its position and now considers that a significant shareholder or a director who has a relationship with a significant shareholder should not be considered a related shareholder. The Committee points to a number of considerations which

59 See also Ph. DEVESA, Les Administrateurs indépendants, Revue de Droit des Affaires Internationales (1994) 543-566.

60 The American Law Institute, Principles of Corporate Governance: Analysis and Recommendations, as adopted and promulgated by the ALI in Washington, D.C., 13 May 1992. Volume 1, § 3 A.0.1 (p. 110). These Principles took some 14 years to be finally adopted. They have been and still are heavily debated. Some comments are enthusiastic, as for instance: J.T. SUBRAK, This baby was worth the wait, Business Law Today, September-October 1994, pp. 58-61. See also Professor A. TUNC (supra note 21).

61 Toronto Stock Exchange Committee Report, 24.

lead to the conclusion that a significant shareholder or its representative should not be excluded from the ranks of unrelated directors. One of these considerations is that investors who acquire shares in corporations with a significant shareholder are generally aware of the shareholding, and rely in many cases on the significant shareholder to exercise control and implement his or her strategy for the corporation. It is also argued that treating a significant shareholder as a related director "would compromise the ability of the significant shareholder to exercise control".[62] So during its examination, the Toronto Committee made an impressive u-turn and recognized the significant shareholder's role in the composition of a board. The Committee adds, however, that the board of a corporation which has a significant shareholder should include a number of directors who have no relationship either to the management or to the significant shareholder, so as to reflect the investment in the corporation of the other shareholders.

e) The Cadbury Report recommends a minimum of three non-executive directors on all boards, two of those three being independent. Independence, in the British Committee's understanding, means being independent of management and free from any business or other relationship which could materially interfere with the exercise of independent judgment.[63]

The Cadbury Committee has found that a very large proportion of the English listed companies is complying with such recommendation, as appears in Table 12.[64]:

Table 12

companies; market capitalization down to	3 or more non-executive directors (%)	2 non-executive directors (%)	1 non-executive director (%)	nonon-executive director (%)
GBP 1,4 bio	97	2	1	0
400 mio	91	7	1	1
120 mio	84	11	4	1
45 mio	74	22	4	0
25 mio	71	19	6	4
10 mio	54	31	15	0
1 mio	39	33	25	3

62 Ibid., 25.
63 Cadbury Report, no. 4.11 and 4.12 (p. 22).
64 Cadbury Committee, Compliance with the Code of Best Practice, 24 May 1995, 11, 12 and 29.

Are non-executive directors also independent? The following figures show that the larger the company, the higher the percentage of compliance with the requirement that a majority of non-executive directors also be independent.[65]

Table 13

companies; market capitalization down to	% with all or majority of non-executive independents
GBP 1,4 bio	92
400 mio	86
120 mio	80
45 mio	82
25 mio	75
10 mio	72
1 mio	58

f) The Listing Rules of the London Stock Exchange (the Yellow Book) provide (Chapter 3, paragraph 3.13) that "[an] applicant [to the London Stock Exchange] must (also) demonstrate that the composition of its board is such that all significant decisions are taken by directors of whom the majority are independent of any controlling shareholder". A controlling shareholder is "any person who is entitled to exercise, or to control the exercise of 30 % or more of the rights to vote at general meetings (...) or able to control the appointment of directors who are able to exercise a majority of votes at board meetings (...) (Chapter 3, paragraph 3.12).[66]

g) The Viénot Committee[67] stresses first that the presence of independent directors in French boards is less of an issue than in other countries. French corporations law already caps the number of directors having an employment contract with the company at one third of the total.[68] While the committee recommends the presence of at least two independent directors in each listed company, it reaffirms the need for the board to act collegially and the requirement for each director to represent all the shareholders. The French committee views independence as the absence of ties to the management of the

65 Ibid.

66 See also "A Practitioner's Guide to the Stock Exchange Yellow Book", overview by N. ATKINSON, (1994) 58.

67 See note 22.

68 See also on that topic A. COURET, Le gouvernement d'entreprise, la corporate governance, Recueil Dalloz Sirey (1995) 164.

company or of the group, and also to any important shareholders of the company or of a company of the group.[69]

h) The King Report on Corporate Governance[70] by the Institute of Directors in Southern Africa states that a board needs to be balanced with at least an equal number of executive and non-executive directors. The chair should be independent and non-executive. When this is not the case, there should be at least two non-executive directors who would carry significant weight in the board's deliberations and resolutions.

From this overview, we can already conclude that it is generally accepted that a publicly held corporation should have a board component which is not tied to management so that the oversight function can be performed in an objective manner. This element of objectivity will give additional credibility to the oversight performed. The size of that component in relation to the total number of members of the board is a matter of evaluation and circumstances. There is general acceptance that "independent directors" should have no ties to management, while the relationship to shareholding is debated.

What is the current state of affairs in the United States? The Korn/Ferry Board of Directors study for 1995 mentions an average number of three insiders for nine outsiders.[71]

Table 14

Type and Size of Company	Average Number Inside Directors	Average Number Outside Directors	Average Number
Industrials			
$ 600 million - $ 999 million	3	7	10
$ 1 billion - $ 2.999 billion	3	8	11
$ 3 billion - $ 4.999 billion	2	9	11
$ 5 billion and over	3	10	13
Banks	3	14	17
Other financial institutions	3	9	12
Insurance companies	3	10	13
Retailers	3	8	11
Service companies	3	8	11
Average	3	9	12

Source: Korn/Ferry International 22nd Annual Board of Directors Study.

69 French doctrine has shown interest for corporate governance at an early stage, see for instance A. TUNC, Supprimer ou renforcer le conseil d'administration des sociétés anonymes?, Revue de Droit des Affaires Internationales (1991) 669-687.

70 The King Report on Corporate Governance, Institute of Directors in Southern Africa, 29 November 1994, see in particular p. 6.

71 Korn/Ferry International, 22nd Annual Board of Directors Study (1995) 10 (The Korn/Ferry study is based on the analysis of Fortune industrial and service corporations.

The Spencer Stuart Board Index (SSBI) 1994 records a ratio of 1 insider to 4 outsiders at half of the SBBI boards. At a third of the same boards, the ratio is 1 or more to 5.[72]

i) The Conference Board Europe[73] stresses that outsiders in the United States are the majority on 94 percent of the boards of manufacturing companies and financial firms and on 93 percent of non-financial service company boards.

The situation in Belgium is much more difficult to evaluate. As far as I know, there are no reliable figures available. When one tries to appraise pragmatically the situation, without scientifically established data, the presence of outside directors, which was up to now fairly modest, has risen in recent years,[74] probably also under the influence of Anglo-Saxon corporate governance ideas. A fair number of the BEL-20 companies can be said to have outside directors[75]. Later on, when I will touch upon the new conflict of interest rules in Belgium, I will revert to the issue of the presence of independent directors on Belgian boards.

9. *Committees*

One of the main tenets of corporate governance thinking is that, in order to further an in-depth analysis of some of the fundamental issues which must come before the board, the directors should be in a position to gather in small committees having very few executive directors or none at all. Governance textbooks, reports and other analyses seem to be unanimous on this score.[76]

---

72 SpencerStuart Board Index 1994, 3.

73 The Conference Board Europe, Corporate Boards and Corporate Governance (1993) 6.

74 Contra: E. WYMEERSCH writes that "As a rule there are no outside directors ... [in Belgian boards]" in his contribution "Elements of comparative corporate governance in Western Europe" in: M. ISAKSSON and R. SKOG (eds.), Aspects of Corporate Governance, (December 1993), p. 113.

75 See article with Mr J. HUYGHEBAERT, Chairman of Almanij, in which he declares that his company has always had independent directors, La Libre Belgique, 8 June 1995.

76 American Law Institute (supra note 60) Volume 1, § 3 A.02 and § 3 A.03 (Audit Committee), § 3 A.04 (Nominating Committee), § 3 A.05 (Compensation Committee). Corporate Director's Guidebook, Audit Committee p. 27; Compensation Committee p. 33; Nominating Committee p. 38. LORSCH with MACIVER (supra note 31) 179 in the conclusions, 58-60, 82-83 and 87. BOWEN (supra note 31) 96-100. Toronto Stock Exchange Committee Report, general, p. 42; audit committee, p. 43; executive committee, p. 43; nominating committee, p. 28; governance committee, p. 39. Cadbury Report, general, p. 25; nomination committees, p. 27; audit committees, p. 27-30, and Code of Best Practice, no. 4.3. R.T. LANG and S.G. SMUL, Caution: Monitors on board. It's time to cast outside directors in a new role, Business Law Today (Jan./Feb. 1994).

Actually, the existence of certain committees is commanded not by self-regulation but by stock exchange requirements or SEC regulations. Already in 1939 the New York Stock Exchange recommended the creation of an audit committee. For some time, the New York Stock Exchange, the American Stock Exchange and Nasdaq have required the establishment and maintenance of an audit committee by all listed companies.

Many other committees have appeared: the nomination committee, the compensation or benefits committee, the executive committee, and also the governance committee or the committee on the board, the strategic planning committee, as well as ad hoc committees.

The audit committee, according to the American Law Institute, should implement and support the oversight function of the board by reviewing on a periodic basis the corporation's processes for producing financial data, its internal controls, and the independence of the corporation's external auditor. As the stock exchanges require all listed companies to have an audit committee, it is not surprising that all corporations reviewed by Korn/Ferry indeed have one.[77]

Table 15

Committee	% of reviewed US companies
Audit	100
Compensation	99
Nominating	71
Executive	67
Stock options	61
Finance	34
Board organization	28
Succession planning	28
Investment	20
Corporate responsibility	19

Source: Korn/Ferry International 22nd annual board of directors study.

According to the Cadbury Report, around two-thirds of the top 250 UK listed companies had an audit committee in place.[78]

The nomination or nominating committee should, according to the ALI, recommend to the board candidates for directorships and directors to fill the seats on board committees. In 1993 60 percent of the US companies reviewed

77 Korn/Ferry (supra note 71) 13.
78 Cadbury Report, p. 27, no. 4.33.

had such a committee; in 1994 that number had risen to 67 percent, and in 1995 it stood at 71 per cent.

The Cadbury Committee found a dramatic increase of nomination committees in the companies it reviewed[79]: Table 16 compares for the periods 1991/1992 and 1993/1994 the percentages of companies with such a committee in the United Kingdom.

Table 16

companies; market capitalization down to	% of viewed UK companies	
	1991/1992	1993/1994
1.4 bio GBP	9	69
400 mio	7	60
120 mio	1	36
45 mio	0	27
25 mio	0	23
10 mio	0	26
1 mio	0	9

The compensation or benefits committee should, according to the ALI, review and recommend to the board or set the annual salary, bonus, stock options and other benefits of the senior executives, review new executive compensation programs and also take steps to modify compensation programs that are not reasonably related to executive performance. The SEC has prescribed how compensation committees should report top management's pay to shareholders. In 99 percent of US companies there is a compensation committee.[80]

The UK figures came close to the US figures in the most recent years, specially in larger companies. Table 17 shows the significant increase in the percentage of companies having what the Cadbury Committee calls a Remuneration Committee[81]:

79 Cadbury Committee (supra note 64) 16 and 30.
80 Korn/Ferry (supra note 71) 13.
81 Cadbury Committee (supra note 64) 20 and 30.

Table 17

companies; market capitalization down to	% of viewed UK companies	
	1991/1992	1993/1994
1.4 bio GBP	71	98
400 mio	53	97
120 mio	26	86
45 mio	11	88
25 mio	7	79
10 mio	11	67
1 mio	5	56

The executive committee is called upon to act between full board meetings and receives powers to do so. Their number is decreasing in the US, where 78 percent of the companies under review had such a committee in 1992 and 75 percent in 1993. In 1994 that figure has fallen back to 67 percent[82] The Toronto Committee notes that "boards of directors have become much less reliant upon executive committees".[83]

The committee on the board, as proposed by Bowen[84], would exercise primary responsibility for the effective functioning of the board, its membership, its structure and work habits. Such a committee would be established in corporations where the functions of chairman and CEO are exercised by a single person.

It is unanimously prescribed that the various committees described above be composed in a large proportion of non-executive or outside directors. In such a way, it is hoped that when exercising their oversight function, the directors will be in a position to make independent judgments on the important matters which they review.

10. Advisory v. decision-making functions of committees

While the creation of committees appears to be largely endorsed by the literature, some important nuances must nevertheless be noted. Lorsch and Maclver have stated that "committee reports to the board are almost a formality, and little time is devoted to them, suggesting that directors do trust their colleagues to have considered properly the issue in question".[85] Such an

82 Korn/Ferry (supra note 71) 13.
83 Toronto Stock Exchange Committee Report, p. 43.
84 BOWEN (supra note 31) 93-96.
85 LORSCH with MACIVER (supra note 31) 62.

attitude is probably warranted by the principle expressed by the ALI that a director in good faith may rely on the decisions, judgments, and performance of a duly authorized committee of the board upon which the director does not serve.[86]

Bowen, on the other hand, puts forward as one of his presumptive norms that "committees should not make major policy decisions for the board as a whole" and he further suggests that all members of the board should be kept fully informed of the activities of the committees and included in policy discussions.[87]

Concerning executive committees, the Toronto Stock Exchange Committee notes that the historical model of the executive committee comprised of the real decision-makers within the board has virtually disappeared. It even considers that executive committees tend to create two classes of directors, those on the inside and those on the outside, with the result that those directors on the outside may lose interest and feel little sense of accountability for corporate decisions.[88]

The Viénot report declares itself very favorable to the creation of committees, but stresses that such creation may not seize power from the board, which is the sole legal body which may take decisions and that committees may not lead to a dismembering of the college of the board, which is and has to remain collectively liable for fulfilling its tasks.[89]

In Belgium the committee structure is not unknown, but has certainly not experienced the same expansion as in a number of countries which we have discussed.[90]

I read that committees are meant to enable directors to cope with two of the most important problems they face, which are the limited time available and the complexity of the information they must deal with.[91]

The time-saving argument surprises me, as directors are required to attend regular board meetings and will have to devote additional time to committee work. The argument of being better able to cope with complexity is only valid if the report produced by a committee succeeds in simplifying for the whole board what was originally a complex matter.

---

86 ALI (supra note 60) part IV, § 4.03.
87 BOWEN (supra note 31) 96-97.
88 Toronto Stock Exchange Committee Report, p. 43.
89 Viénot report, p. 20.
90 As a result of superficial research, I can find following committees in Belgium: Audit Committees: Société Générale de Belgique, Générale de Banque, Fortis AG, GIB Group, Kredietbank; consultative shareholders committee: Société Générale de Belgique; compensation committee: GIB Group.
91 LORSCH with MACIVER (supra note 31) 59.

I agree with Lorsch that corporate governance is all about empowering the board.[92] The question I am now confronted with is this: will directors be more empowered if they approach complex issues, like auditing and compensation, in small committees rather than in a unified board? Will being assembled in a number of committees, which usually meet just before the full board, create a feeling of cooperation, consensus and collegiality?[93]

Committees are meant to be small. On average in the US they range from 4 to 5 members.[94] Necessarily, the diversity of backgrounds, perspectives and experiences will be less broad in a small committee than in a full board.

11. Conflicts of interest

As I indicated earlier, the Belgian Parliament recently modified a number of aspects of the law on corporations and one of the most hotly debated subjects was conflicts of interest. The relevant article of the law had already been amended once in 1991 and was reworked and completed with a new rule on intra-group transactions in 1995.[95]

With the latter amendment, a new procedure applies to all listed Belgian companies. Each time a decision falling within the competence of the board may produce an economic advantage for a shareholder having a decisive or significant influence on the designation of the directors, the board will have to designate three directors chosen for their independence on the matter in question. These three directors will, with an expert, who shall likewise be independent, draw up a report describing and evaluating the financial consequences for the company of the proposed transaction. The report must

92 LORSCH, Empowering the Board (supra note 44) 107.

93 See for a nuanced view on committees, the opinion of Jacques THIERRY (at that time Chairman of the boards of BBL and Interbrew) in: Le Soir-Eco-Soir of 19 March 1993, p. 2.

94 Korn/Ferry (supra note 71) 14.

95 See E. WYMEERSCH, L'article 60 et le droit belge des groupes de sociétés, Mélanges Heenen (1994) 633-655 (article published just before the adoption of the newest version of the conflict of interest rule); X. DIEUX, Les nouveaux articles 60 et 60bis des lois coordonnées sur les sociétés commerciales: un faux pas en avant, un vrai en arrière, in: La nouvelle réforme du droit des sociétés, Seminar Vanham & Vanham of 17 May 1995. G. KEUTGEN, Conflits internes d'intérêts: articles 60 et 60bis, in: Réforme du Droit des Sociétés, Seminar "L'Echo" of 30 May 1995. J.-L. DUPLAT, Conclusions: du droit des sociétés au droit financier", Seminar "L'Echo" of 30 May 1995, 17-19. M.P. LEMAITRE, La réforme du droit des sociétés: l'article 60 et la procession d'Echternach, DAOR, 16 June 1995. H. LAGA, Belangenconflicten, aantal bestuurders, schriftelijke besluitvorming in de N.V. in de Wetten van 7 en 13 April 1995, Jan Ronse Instituut (1995). C. DARVILLE and G. KEUTGEN, La nouvelle réglementation des conflits internes d'intérêts, Cahier du juriste, ABJE (1995) 59-69.

establish that the proposal is in the interest of the corporation and of the shareholders in general, as well as the absence of any advantage which would be a privileged remuneration directly or indirectly benefiting a shareholder. Once the report has been presented to the full board, the latter may deliberate and vote on it. In enacting this provision, the Parliament made significant innovations. Indeed, the concept of "independent director" or at least of "the director independent towards the transaction at stake" is new. Also new is the notion of "shareholder having a decisive or significant influence on the designation of the directors". In introducing such new concepts, the Parliament referred a number of times to corporate governance and related concepts.[96] Chairman of the Banking and Finance Commission, Jean-Louis Duplat, wonders if this reference is appropriate, as corporate governance rules or norms are generally based on voluntary compliance rather than on statutory rules. This is basically true, but one will remember that the creation of an audit committee in the United States is a matter not of voluntary compliance but of stock exchange requirements. Likewise, the Cadbury report is based on typically British self-regulation, but as announced in the report,[97] the London Stock Exchange requires listed companies registered in the United Kingdom (with the exception of listed overseas companies) to state whether they comply with the Code and to give reasons for any areas of non-compliance.[98] This is not a legal requirement but it is very close to being one. Compliance with the Code is addressed by the Cadbury Committee in a report of 24 May 1995.[99] Chairman Duplat also stresses that Belgian independent directors are not the counterparts of Anglo-Saxon non-executive directors. I concur with him. The non-executive or outside director definition, as we saw above, is often used in determining which board members will serve on a given committee.[100] Basically, a non-executive director is not a member of management and has no ties with it. In contrast, the Belgian independent director is closer to the American disinterested director. The American statutes and courts have imposed, among the fiduciary duties of directors, the duty of loyalty. This duty requires directors to exercise their powers in the interests of the corporation and not in their own interest or in the interest of another person or organization. When

96 Documents parlementaires, Sénat, 1086-2, 112, 118 and 152.
97 Cadbury Report, 11.
98 Listing Rules of the London Stock Exchange (The Yellow Book), paras. 12.43a) and 17. 12.
99 Report of the Committee on the Financial Aspects of Corporate Governance, Compliance with the Code of Best Practice, 24 May, 1995.
100 Toronto Stock Exchange Report, 26.

such an interest is present, the interested director should seek approval by disinterested directors of the relevant transaction.[101]

It is also interesting to compare the new Belgian conflict of interest rule to the provision laid down in Chapter 3, paragraph 3.13 of the Yellow Book of the London Stock Exchange. Such rule provides for applicants that "where potential conflicts exist between the interests of the applicant and those of a controlling shareholder, the applicant must demonstrate that arrangements are in place to avoid detriment to the general body of shareholders of the applicant". All three learned authors who have commented on the new provision, Chairman Duplat,[102] Professor Dieux[103] and Professor Keutgen[104] have regretted that the Belgian legislator has not opted in his most recent reform for a two-tier board system. The two-tier system distinguishes clearly between oversight and management, but it doesn't offer as such any solution in cases of conflict of interest in intra-group transactions. Moreover, I am not sure that the two-tier system promotes the necessary interactive dialogue between the managers responsible for knowing and carrying on the business and the overseers responsible for advising and monitoring them.

VI. Corporate Governance - Practical and Conceptual

The last topic we have discussed shows us that corporate governance deals with basically two types of subjects. The first is more visible or tangible: the composition of the board, the separation of the functions of chairman and CEO, the number of directors, the committees. These subjects are relatively easy to apprehend. They also may serve to convey a message to investors - that a company wants to adapt its structures to their perceived needs. But these visible elements are only the top of the iceberg: they are extensions of fundamental concepts which require much more study to be understood and fully appraised. And here I am referring to the duty of loyalty which I have briefly mentioned, but also the duty of care and the business judgment rule. When we in Europe pay attention only to the first elements, not concerning ourselves with the second ones, we do as someone who would go to Mass without having learned the creed.

---

101 Corporate Director's Guidebook, 12. See also L.D. SOLOMON, D.E. SCHWARTZ and J.D. BAUMAN, Corporations, Law and Policy, Materials and Problems (2d ed.) 683 et seq.

102 DUPLAT (supra note 95) 19.

103 DIEUX (supra note 95) 21.

104 G. KEUTGEN, in Revue pratique des sociétés, numéro special consacré au colloque de Liège du 20 septembre 1994, 161-166.

VII. Beyond Corporate Governance

Corporate governance mainly aims at monitoring management while carefully avoiding that directors would cross the line and involve themselves in management.[105] John Pound proposes in an article of March 1995 a new approach.[106] He distinguishes a new model of governance, which is no longer based on the "managed corporation" but on the "governed corporation". In the managed corporation, the focus is on power, on the checks and balances between board and management. In the governed corporation, there would be a reconnection between shareholders and board. Pound reviews a number of corporate failures and concludes that what matters is not the monitoring of managers but the improvement of decisionmaking. Three critical constituencies should be involved in setting corporate policies and decisionmaking: managers, directors and shareholders. He makes a comprehensive proposal to make the board more effective and to bring about a better contact between the company and its shareholders.

Shareholders in general and institutional investors in particular are on the move, but we should bear in mind the real proportions of such movement. When asked if they had been formally contacted by institutional investors about criticism relating to corporate governance in 1993, 81.5 percent of the US companies answered no. If the answer was yes, the next question was "has such approach had an impact?" and 41.5 % answered no.[107]

Between the directors, the shareholders and the managers a dialogue has been initiated. In Belgium, as I said in my introduction, we are only beginning this dialogue, but maybe we will have something like beginners' luck.

---

105 LORSCH, Empowering the Board (supra note 44) 114.

106 J. POUND, The Promise of the Governed Corporation, Harvard Business Review (March-April 1995) 89-98.

107 Korn/Ferry, 21st Annual Board of Directors Study (1994) 21.

A Note on the Typology of Financial Systems

Erik Berglöf

Contents

I. Introduction

Until recently corporate finance and corporate governance were two separate literatures in two different academic disciplines. Corporate finance concerned financial economists, whereas corporate governance was a preoccupation of legal scholars. The literature on corporate finance dealt primarily with the choice between debt and equity, or the irrelevance of this choice. Over the last decade these two bodies of work have engaged in a fruitful interchange. Today it is hard to discuss corporate finance without considering corporate governance implications, and to analyse corporate governance as isolated from how the corporation is financed. In particular, corporate governance is important for understanding differences in corporate finance across countries.

Much of the public and academic debate has taken a narrow view of corporate governance. Reflecting an Anglo-American bias, the focus has been on the role of equityholders. However, the recent corporate finance literature has broadened and deepened our understanding of the relationship between the firm and its investors, but also for the larger context in which this relationship is embedded - the financial system. For legitimate reasons economists have been reluctant to address such complex notions as financial systems. But the new finance literature offers concepts, and even formal models, which allow us to think more systematically about such clusters of institutional arrangements and compare their economic properties. Together with similar developments in other fields of economics, this literature has contributed to a research program called *comparative institutional analysis*.[1]

---

1 M. AOKI, Towards a Comparative Institutional Analysis: Motivations and some Tentative General Insights, mimeo, Stanford University (1995); TH. BAUMS,

Prior to the revolution of modern finance triggered by the publication of Modigliani's and Miller's seminal article in 1958 there was a considerable institutional literature emphasizing the differences across financial systems (with Alexander Gerschenkron as its most prominent representative). The contributors to this literature also claimed that these differences had important implications for how the systems functioned, and ultimately for economic growth.[2] While the institutional tradition survived in economic history, it had little impact on the mainstream of corporate finance. It was not until the 1980s that financial economists came to be interested in international variations in financing patterns. Since then a number of attempts have been made to examine more closely the intuition of the institutionalists, using a more solid theoretical base and more advanced empirical methods.

While recognizing the limitations of such crude classifications the institutionalists distinguished between two types of financial systems - one Anglo-American and one Continental European (sometimes including Japan). Some authors would divide the latter category in two or more subcategories, typically distinguishing between the German and the French models. The institutionalists focussed on differences in the relative importance of banks and markets. More recently, similar attempts have been made at classifying systems along similar dimensions. Among the typologies used are *bank-oriented* vs. *market-oriented* financial systems,[3] *market-based* vs. *credit-based* systems[4], *debt-based* vs. *equity-based* systems, *intermediated* vs. *securities-based* systems, *market-based* vs. *universal banking* systems[5] and *insider* vs. *outsider* systems[6].

The purpose of this note is to briefly discuss the strengths and weaknesses of these typologies and suggest an alternative classification scheme. Ultimately, the objective is to identify the critical dimensions along which to compare financial systems and suggest some operational measures for establishing differences and studying the properties of various systems. In evaluating a particular typology we focus on two criteria: first, a typology should be based on a microeconomic analysis of the features distinguishing systems; and second, it should be consistent with empirical evidence. We will start by confronting existing

Corporate Governance in Germany - System and Recent Developments, in: ISAKSSON and SKOG (eds.), Aspects of Corporate Governance (1994); E. WYMEERSCH, Elements of Comparative Corporate Governance in Western Europe, in: ISAKSSON and SKOG.

2 See, for example, A. GERSCHENKRON, Economic Backwardness in Historical Perspective, Harvard University Press (1962).

3 T. RYBCZINSKI, Industrial Finance Systems in Europe, United States and Japan, Journal of Economic Behavior and Organizations, vol. 5 (1985).

4 J. ZYSMAN, Governments, Markets and Growth, Cornell University (1983).

5 O. YOSHA and Y. YAFEH, Anatomy of Financial Market Reform: An Industrial Organization Perspective, mimeo, Hebrew University (1996).

6 J. FRANKS and C. MAYER, The Ownership and Control of German Corporations, mimeo, London Business School (1994).

typologies with the limited quantitative data available regarding differences across financial systems.

II. International Variations in Financing Patterns

In studying differences in corporate finance patterns across countries essentially two types of data have been used: aggregated national accounts or surveys of enterprises (published yearly in OECD Financial Statistics). Goldsmith[7] (1969 and 1985) makes use of information from national accounts to examine differences in stocks of financial assets, and the ratio of financial to real assets, across industrialized and developing countries. Mayer,[8] and later Corbett and Jenkinson,[9] draw on flows-of-funds, rather than stock, data since the former data is less susceptible to differences in accounting standards and other valuation problems. More precisely, they focus on the net contribution of different sources of funds to financing the capital stock in place at a particular point-in-time (by using net figures certain double counting can be avoided).

Figure 1: Net Sources of Industrial Finance

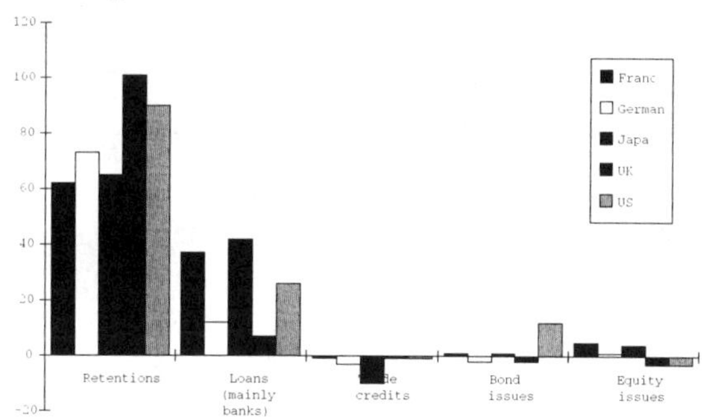

* The net contribution of a particular source of funds to the capital stock in place in 1985; weighted by level of investment each year.
Source: C. Mayer, "New Issues in Corporate Finance, inaugural lecture given at the City University Business School (1987).

7 R. GOLDSMITH, Financial Structure and Development, Yale University Press (1969); R. GOLDSMITH, National Balance Sheets for 20 Countries, Yale University Press (1985).

8 C. MAYER, New Issues in Corporate Finance, inaugural lecture at the City University Business School (1987); C. MAYER, Financial Systems, Corporate Finance, and Economic Development, in: G. HUBBARD (ed.), Asymmetric Information, Corporate Finance, and Investment, National Bureau of Economic Research, Chicago University Press (1990) 307-332.

9 J. CORBETT and T. JENKINSON, The Financing of Industry, 1970-89: An International Comparison, Working Paper 948, Centre for Economic Policy Research, London (1994).

While much of the early discussion of the findings in these studies focussed on the differences across countries, the systems appear have to many features in common.[10] In particular, Mayer finds that retentions is by far the most important source of finance, and debt the most important external source, during the period he studies (see Figure 1). External equity capital raised through new issues seems to play a limited role in financing investment according to these studies. Using more recent data and a slightly more refined methodology, Corbett and Jenkinson make similar observations but emphasize the peculiarity of Japanese industry as relying more heavily on external finance (see Table 1).[11]

Table 1: Net Financing In Five OECD Countries

(Period I: 1980-84; Period II: 1985-1989; in the case of Sweden, 1981-1985 and 1986-1990, respectively)

	United States		Japan		Germany		UK		Sweden	
	I	II	I	II	I	II	I	II	I	II
Internal funds	89.6	103.7	74.6	70.7	79.8	89.1	115.4	81.0	110.4	142.0
Bank	12.9	15.0	31.7	23.1	11.1	9.3	12.4	29.9	9.8	66.0
Bonds	10.9	24.8	0.6	8.6	-2.1	0.4	2.0	8.8	-3.0	-38.2
Shares	-4.8	-29.6	3.6	4.4	-0.5	2.4	-7.6	-20.6	-10.9	-51.9
Trade credits	-1.7	-4.7	-8.4	-5.7	-2.8	-1.8	-3.1	-0.6	-4.6	-0.1
Others	-0.6	1.8	-2.1	-1.1	4.7	-7.9	-12.2	-0.8	-0.8	-6.3
Transfers within corporations	..	..	..	..	9.7	8.4	1.6	0.4	-0.9	-11.4
Statistical adjustment	-6.3	-11.0	..	..	..	..	-8.4	-1.8	..	..
Total	100	100	100	100	100	100	100	100	100	100

Source: Corbett and Jenkinson (*supra* note 9); and Berglöf and Sjogren (*supra* note 11) (for Sweden).

10 Analyses of historical data suggests that there may have been significant differences in the degree of intermediation, and the relative importance of banks in external financing, in the early post-war period (for an analysis of Japanese data, see AOKI et al. (supra note 1).

11 It is worth noting in Table 1 that Sweden, traditionally viewed as a bank-oriented financial system, resembles United Kingdom in the early part of the 1980s in terms of the relative importance of different sources of funds. However, in the latter half of the decade becomes an outlier with very high liquidity in the corporate sector and a rapid expansion of bank lending, leading up to the banking crisis in the early 1990s (E. BERGLÖF and H. SJÖGREN, "Combining Arm's-Length and Control-Oriented Finance - Main Bank Relationships in Sweden," mimeo, Université Libre de Bruxelles (1996).

The quality of the aggregate data is poor, and the types of questions that can be addressed using the data are limited. To allow a discussion of more precise and interesting theoretical issues,[12] Rajan and Zingales (1996) draw on a new data base with balance sheet information for large firms in the G-7 countries. While there are some questions as to the comparability of the samples for the different countries, Rajan and Zingales also emphasize the similarities rather than the differences. In particular, after controlling for firm characteristics they find no evidence that debt finance would be systematically more important in some countries than in others, at least not along the distinctions made in the institutional literature.

How then can this evidence of important similarities between financial systems be reconciled with the observations of the institutionalists? For example, if bank finance is approximately as important in the Anglo-American financial systems as in those on the European continent, how could the institutionalists have been so struck by the differences in the role of banks in corporate finance? Or if the share of markets in the provision of funds is so small, why would so many observers have focussed on them as the feature distinguishing financial systems?

We suggest here that there are indeed important differences in the roles of banks and markets. These differences concern not the sources of finance, but the conditions under which finance is provided or, more precisely, the corporate governance arrangements. They are not captured by the aggregate financial statistics or the analysis of balance sheets of individual firms. It is not until we examine the concentration of ownership and the identity of controlling investors that some of the differences among financial systems become apparent. Unfortunately, there are no systematic international studies of ownership patterns, and the most reliable information for individual countries is rather dated. Table 2 summarizes a number of studies of ownership concentration in different countries. The differences in underlying samples and methodology rule out direct comparisons, but the table is suggestive. Levels of ownership concentration are clearly much higher in Germany and France than in United Kingdom and United States. Ownership in Sweden also stands out as highly concentrated.

12 R. RAJAN and L. ZINGALES, What Do We Know About Capital Structure? Some Evidence from International Data, Journal of Finance, XX (1996).

Table 2: Concentration of Ownership

<table>
<tr><th></th><th>(1)</th><th>(2)</th><th>(3)</th><th>(4)</th><th>(5)</th><th>(6)</th><th>(7)</th><th>(8)</th></tr>
<tr><th>Largest owner's share</th><th>France (1982)</th><th>Germany (1985)</th><th>Italy (1993)</th><th>Spain (1990)</th><th>Sweden (1987)</th><th>UK (1990)</th><th>Japan (1983)</th><th>US (1981)</th></tr>
<tr><td>> 50</td><td>55</td><td>66</td><td>89</td><td>49</td><td>42</td><td>5</td><td>5</td><td>9</td></tr>
<tr><td>30-50</td><td rowspan="6">42</td><td rowspan="4">23</td><td rowspan="3">9</td><td rowspan="6">49</td><td>31</td><td rowspan="3">29</td><td rowspan="6">70</td><td rowspan="4">29</td></tr>
<tr><td>25-30</td><td rowspan="2">12</td></tr>
<tr><td>20-25</td></tr>
<tr><td>15-20</td><td rowspan="4">2</td><td rowspan="2">11</td><td rowspan="2">27</td></tr>
<tr><td>10-15</td><td rowspan="3">12</td><td>10</td></tr>
<tr><td>5-10</td><td rowspan="2">4</td><td>30</td><td>29</td></tr>
<tr><td>< 5</td><td>2</td><td>2</td><td>9</td><td>25</td><td>23</td></tr>
</table>

The institutionalists also point out the importance of international variations in the identity of controlling owners. The systematic evidence is here even more scarce. Table 3 shows data for three countries. In the 1980s family control was still important in Germany and France Institutions - either other corporations or banks, directly or through their various instruments - were important controlling owners in all the three countries. The identity of controlling owners is closely connected to the different orientation of institutional ownership. Institutional ownership has increased in most industrialized countries - perhaps it is the most remarkable transformation of capitalism over the last twenty years. But the types of institutions, and their role in the economy, are quite different. In the Anglo-American systems, mutual funds, pension funds and insurance companies have become the most important owners. On the European continent, industrial corporations, banks and sometimes insurance companies have increased at the expense of individual investors. The orientation of these institutions as owners differs substantially from that of their counterparts in United States and United Kingdom; they are much more likely to exercise control over investment decisions.

Table 3: The identity of Controlling Owners (%)

	France[a] 1982	Germany[b] 1980	Sweden[c] 1985
Individuals	42,3	34.5	36.0
Non-financial enterprises		17.3	25.0
Investmentcompanies			26.0
Banks		12.2	
Insurance companies		2.5	6.0
Government	18.0	14.2	
Foreign owners	39.6	17.3	
Others		2.0	7.0
Total	100.0	100.0	100.0

a. Data refer to 249 firms with a majority shareholder (out of 500 largest firms).
b. Majority shareholder in listed firms.
c. Largest shareholder in 107 largest privately-owned firms.

Source: Berglöf (1988).

III. Competing Typologies

This brief examination of the stylized facts thus lends some support to to the distinction made by the institutionalists and others between Anglo-American systems and Continental European systems, not in terms of the relative importance of different sources of finance but in corporate governance patterns. The stylized facts also allow us to evaluate the typologies used by previous authors to capture these differences between systems.

The perhaps most frequently used distinction in the literature on comparative finance is that between market-oriented and bank-oriented, or bank-based and market-based, financial systems (often attributed to Rybczinski[13]). This typology is misleading, if referring to the relative importance of banks and markets as sources of funds for corporations; bank finance was the most important external source of finance in all the countries studied, and markets did not play a prominent role in this respect anywhere. The term bank-oriented, or bank-based, places too much emphasis on the role of banks without distinguishing between different forms of bank finance and bank involvement in corporate governance. The bank-oriented category would exclude Germany if defined based on the relative importance of banks in the provision of corporate finance,[14] and Italy if the term referred to the role of banks in the ownership

13 RYBCZINSKI (supra note 3).
14 C. MAYER and I. ALEXANDER, Banks and Securities Markets: Corporate Finance in Germany and the U.K., Journal of Japanese and International Economies (1991);

and control of corporations.[15] Yet, the institutionalists would tell us that these systems have important traits in common.

Another typology suggested by Zysman[16] is "credit-based" vs. "market-based" financial systems. He places Germany in the former category, and United States and United Kingdom in the latter. (He refers to the French system as one where prices are set administratively, rather than by private actors in markets, thus emphasizing the role of the state.) Zysman's terminology suggests that firms in credit-based financial systems are more dependent on debt, and this is not supported by the data. In any case, "credit" and "market" are two different dimensions: credit could be both market-based and provided by intermediaries. Corporate bonds have, at least until recently, only played an important role in US firms, but not in UK firms. In a more generous interpretation, it is in monitoring - or corporate governance - that the "credit-based" features of the Continental European systems stand out. Large creditors, in particular banks with large holdings of both debt (and often equity), yield considerable influence over strategic decisions - a feature largely absent in the Anglo-American systems.

A common distinction, too widely used even to be given a specific reference, in the literature is that between "intermediated" and "securities-based" systems. This terminology is also misleading. The data show no significant difference in the share of intermediated finance - most funds are internally generated and intermediated finance dominates among external sources in all countries. The differences between Anglo-American and Continental European systems regard the type of intermediation provided, in particular the extent to which institutions monitor the use of funds. The distinction between "market" and "intermediated" financial systems could make more sense if understood as referring to the exercise of control. In the Anglo-Saxon systems the market for corporate control is often believed to play an important role in monitoring, whereas this function is performed by large controlling investors in the Continental European systems; the exercise of control is an important form of intermediation. However, there is also a considerable trade in controlling shares in the latter countries, even though these transfers typically take place outside the official exchange. Furthermore, the distinction "market-intermediated" is not adequate since monitoring can also be performed directly by individual investors and families - an important feature of corporate governance in many countries on the European continent.

J. EDWARDS and K. FISCHER, Banks, Finance and Investment in Germany, Cambridge University Press (1994).

15 F. BARCA, On Corporate Governance in Italy: Issues, Facts and Agenda, paper presented at OECD Conference "The Influence of Corporate Governance and Financing Structures on Economic Performance" (1995).

16 ZYSMAN (supra note 4).

In an interesting and insightful discussion of the transformation of the Israeli financial system Yafeh and Yosha[17] distinguish between systems based on market finance and those with universal banking. While this typology captures some of the differences in the nature of bank activities in the two types of systems, whether or not a particular system have universal banking is not the generic feature. First of all, the term "universal" is vague; the degree of universality differs substantially across countries with such banking regulation. Second, in principle United Kingdom has universal banking, whereas United States does not, and many systems classified as belonging to the Continental European category do not have universal banking, at least not in the legal sense (e.g., Italy, Sweden and Japan).

The typology that comes closest to capturing the corporate governance features distinguishing Anglo-American and Continental European systems is the distinction between "insider" and "outsider" systems.[18] However, these terms could also be misleading. "Insider control" is commonly used to denote a situation with strong control by management - a characteristic more closely associated with arm's-length systems than control-oriented systems. Who is an "insider" and who is an "outsider" are also matters of definition, or legal interpretation. For example, in the US legal tradition an insider is someone who exerts control over investment decisions; the notion of "outsider control" then becomes somewhat confusing. Finally, and more importantly, Franks and Mayer terminology does not, at least not explicitly, have a base in microeconomic analysis in the sense of a formal analytical model explaining corporate finance arrangements using first principles. In the following, we will suggest a conceptual framework with foundations in a reasonably well-established theoretical literature.

IV. Arm's-Length vs. Control-Oriented Finance

The conceptual framework we propose here, and more thoroughly developed elsewhere,[19] builds on the recent literature on financial contracting and corporate governance. The implicit claim of this literature is that *debt-equity* or *direct-intermediated* finance are not the only, and perhaps not even the most important, distinctions in corporate finance; a crucial feature distinguishing financing arrangements is how they attempt to mitigate the basic agency

17 YOSHA and YAFEH (supra note 5).

18 FRANKS and MAYER (supra note 6).

19 E. BERGLÖF, "Corporate Governance, Financial Systems and the Transition to Capitalism - Towards a Conceptual Framework, in: J. ROEMER (ed.), Property Rights, Incentives and Welfare, MacMillan Press (1997; forthcoming).

problem of capitalism, i.e., the credibility problem facing entrepreneurs or firms as they seek to convince outside investors to contribute funds.

There are two generic solutions to this problem. Under *arm's-length finance* investors maintain a distance to the firm, at least not as long as payment obligations are met. Intervention in management typically is engineered by a third party, via the market for corporate control or through a court in the case of bankruptcy. Under this form of finance the firm can commit to behave efficiently and repay investors by contracting on individual well-specified, and verifiable, assets or cash flows.[20] The other generic form of corporate finance - *control-oriented finance* - allows investors to intervene in investment decisions.[21] This is done, for example, through a control block of equity or a position as exclusive or dominant creditor.

The choice of typology is admittedly somewhat arbitrary. Holmström[22] and Holmström and Tirole[23] use interchangeably the terms "intermediated" and "informed" for what is here called control-oriented finance, and "uninformed" for arm's-length finance. None of these terms are ideal. Monitoring is just one form of financial intermediation. The dichotomy "uninformed-informed" highlights on the information available to investors whereas the crucial distinction is whether or not investors influence investment decisions. Furthermore, "uninformed" misleadingly suggests that assessing collateral and cash flows requires no information. Whereas the amount of information generated under the two forms of finance may differ, it is the differences in informational requirements that separates the two: arm's-length finance requires that information be verifiable by courts, whereas under control-oriented finance only monitoring investors need to be informed. The term "control-oriented" also may suggest that there is no exercise of control under arm's-length finance.

---

20 O. HART and J. MOORE, A Theory of Debt Based on the Inalienability of Human Capital, Quarterly Journal of Economics 109 (1994) 841-79; P. BOLTON and D. SCHARFSTEIN, A Theory of Secured Debt: Constracting with Multiple Investors, mimeo, Université de Bruxelles (1993); E. BERGLÖF and E.-L. VON THADDEN, Short-Term vs. Long-Term Interests: Capital Structures with Multiple Investors, Quarterly Journal of Economics, CIX, (1994) 1055-1084.

21 S. GROSSMAN and O. HART, The Costs and Benefits of Ownership: A Theory of Vertical and Lateral Integration, Journal of Political Economy 94 (1986) 691-719; P. AGHION and P. BOLTON, An 'Incomplete Contract' Approach to Bankruptcy and the Financial Structure of the Firm, Review of Economic Studies, 59 (1992) 473-494; M. DEWATRIPONT and J. TIROLE, A Theory of Debt and Equity - Diversity of Securities and Management-Shareholder Congruence, Quarterly Journal of Economics, CIX (1994) 309-40.

22 B. HOLMSTRÖM, Financing Investment in Eastern Europe: A Theorectical Perspective, mimeo, Yale School of Organization and Management (1993).

23 B. HOLMSTRÖM and J. TIROLE, Financial Intermediation and the Real Sector, mimeo, Centre for Economic Policy Research (1993).

This is, of course, not true, but investor intervention is limited during the contracting period, and typically relies on third-party mechanisms.

The emphasis on the "arm's-length"-"control-oriented" dimension does not imply that the traditional distinction debt-equity is unimportant. The choice between debt and equity finance, and between debt contracts with different priority and underlying collateral, will play an important role in determining the outcome if the firm cannot, or does not want, to meet its payment obligations. The form of finance also influences the nature of influence and the incentives of investors in such renegotiations; shareholders are likely to be soft whereas creditors are more inclined to be hard.[24] A firm may also choose to issue short-term and long-term claims to different investors, and provide them with different collateral, so as to improve its ex ante commitment ability.[25] In a control-oriented arrangement the choice between debt and equity also influences when investors can intervene. A control-oriented creditor is often limited to intervening in situations where the firm has liquidity problems, whereas shareholders can intervene in all states, or at least in non-default states.

The distinction between direct, or market, finance, and intermediated finance can also help us understand better the nature of corporate governance. Control can be exercised directly by an individual investor, but can also be viewed as a form of intermediation. An intermediary with liquid claims (e.g., short-term deposits and listed equity) on the liability side of her balance sheet collects information and exercised control over illiquid claims (e.g., debt and equity holdings in client firms) on her asset side; intermediation transforms illiquid claims into liquid ones. It is the combination of the information collected and the control rights exercised which allow such intermediation.

Figure 2 illustrates how the three distinctions in corporate finance - *debt* vs. *equity, direct* vs. *intermediated,* and *arm's-length* vs. *control-oriented finance* - can be reconciled, and used to classify specific financial instruments and arrangements (the italics in the figure indicates that the form of finance should find itself at the back of the box, i.e., it is intermediated). The figure suggests that the absolute and relative size of a holding of debt or equity in a particular firm play an important role in determining whether the financial relationship should be viewed as arm's-length or control-oriented. For example, bank debt can be both arm's-length and control-oriented. Most US banks refrain from large exposures in individual firms and maintain arm's-length relationship with their client firms. However, house banks in Germany and main banks in Japan can have large shares of in individual firms' debt, often combined with sizeable equityholdings. Evidence from Sweden suggests a strong correlation between the importance, and stability, of bank-firm relationships and the size of

---

24 DEWATRIPONT and TIROLE (supra note 21).

25 BERGLÖF and VON THADDEN (supra note 20).

equityholdings by banks and its related institutions (Berglof and Sjogren, 1996).

Figure 2: The Three Dimensions of Corporate Finance

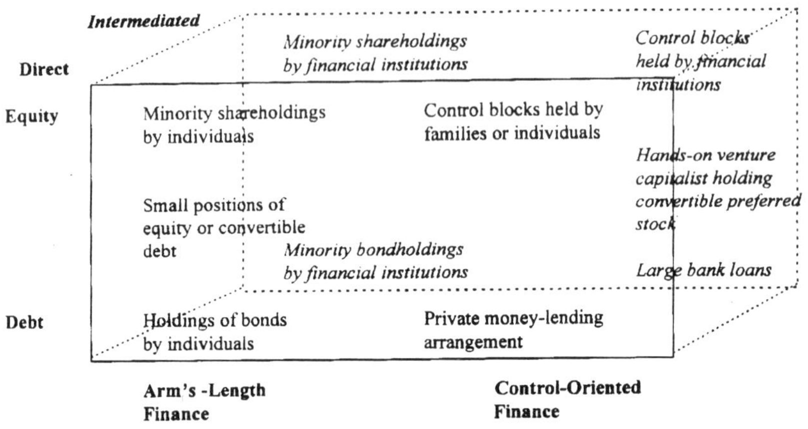

The figure can also be used to characterize such mixed forms of finance.Other examples include convertible preferred stock - the preeminent form of finance in venture capital finance - or mezzanine financing common in, for example, real estate development.

While the degree of separation of ownership and control may not be reflected in the role of external finance or in the relative importance of debt and equity finance, it should be visible in other aspects of capital structure, in particular in the degree of concentration. The prevalence of monitoring arrangements can also be inferred from the portfolios and orientation of individual investors. Under control-oriented finance investors' portfolios are likely to be concentrated , and investors control-oriented, whereas investors extending arm's-length finance should tend to focus on diversification. In addition, given the potential complementarity of debt and equity control we should expect such investors to hold both types of instruments. For example, Figure 2 allows us to make a distinction between the different forms of venture capital finance, in particular between "hands-on" venture capitalists focussing on a smaller number of firms and venture capitalist funds with highly diversified portfolios. Under hands-on venture capital arrangements finance is control-oriented with important investor representation on the board of directors and sometimes majority control.

Our main claim is that the relative importance of the two generic forms of finance - arm's-length and control-oriented finance - is the most important distinction between different governance arrangements, and financial systems. To emphasise the link between our analysis of financial systems and its microfoundations we use the terms *arm's-length* and *control-oriented financial systems* (Table 4). In other words, the crucial distinguishing feature between different capitalist financial systems is the extent to which investors get involved in investments decisions in individual firms, what we denote the degree of separation of ownership and control. The economies of United Kingdom and United States are characterized by considerable separation of ownership and control, whereas ownership and control still are closely associated in Japan and on the European continent. The differences in the degree of separation is reflected in a number of other aspects of the financial system, e.g., the liquidity of equity markets, the predominant conflicts in corporate finance, accounting practices, disclosure requirements, takeover regulation, and basic company law.[26]

Table 4: Financial systems and capital structure

	Type of financial system	
	Control-oriented	Arm's-length
Share of control-oriented finance	high	low
Liquidity of financial markets	low	high
Ownership of debt and equity	concentrated	dispersed
Investor orientation	control-oriented	portfolio-oriented
Dominant agency conflict	controlling vs. minority	management
Role of board of directors	limited	important
Market for corporate control	outside exchange	official exchange

The institutional differences outlined in Table 4 suggest important implications for how conflicts are resolved. Empirical research on firms in United States and Japan also show that the mechanisms for investor intervention differ substantially.[27] Despite these differences Kaplan[28] (1994) fails to distinguish the

26 See BERGLÖF (1996) (supra note 20).
27 S. GILSON, The Political Ecology of Takeovers: Thoughts on Harmonizing the European Corporate Governance Environment," 61 Fordham Law Review 161 (1992); S. GILSON, K. JOHN and J. LANG, Troubled Debt Restructurings: An Empirical Study of Privat Reorganization of Rims in Default, Journal of Financial Economics, vol. 27, (1990) 315-353; ASQUITH, GERTNER and SCHARFSTEIN, Anatomy of Financial Distress: An Examination of Junk Bond Issuers, Quarterly Journal of Economics 109 (1994) 625-58; S.N. KAPLAN and B.A. MINTON,

systems in terms of performance; managers are as likely, or unlikely, to be fired or penalized financially following poor performance.

V. Concluding Remarks

The clustering and apparent complementarity between different features of financial systems have important implications for public policy. Institutional reform is likely to be much more complicated than commonly believed and efforts to harmonize institutions across countries may be counterproductive. A particular institutional arrangement may function perfectly well in one environment but not in another.

The discussion also has implications for how we can learn more about these systems and their properties. In particular, it seems virtually impossible, at least given our present state of knowledge, to make statements about the effects of a particular institutional feature on economic performance. If features are closely related, breaking out one aspect is likely to be misleading. There is also an implicit suggestion in the perspective taken here that a particular organization adopts the governance arrangement most suitable to its needs. While there are reasons to doubt strong versions of this evolutionary view, it implies that there may important selection biases in comparisons of the economic properties of different institutional arrangements.

Outside Intervention in Japanese Companies: Its Determinants and Its Implications for Managers, Journal of Financial Economics, 36 (1993) 4.

28 S.N. KAPLAN, Top Executive Rewards and Firm Performance: A Comparison of Japan and the U.S., Journal of Political Economy, 102 (1994) 510-46.

Path Dependence, Political Options, and Governance Systems

*Mark J. Roe**

Contents

In this essay, I refine the evolutionary model from law and economics by modifying it to accommodate three related concepts, one from chaos theory, another of path dependence, and a final one from evolutionary theory itself. I then apply this model to national corporate governance systems.

The thesis here can be seen as a group of metaphors, beginning with a standard one from law and economics: Economic evolution selects out for extinction very inefficient results, and efficient results tend to survive. This metaphor, however, is by itself not rich enough to explain enough of what we see surviving, nor is it rich enough to explain fully how what survives survived. Within the looseness of acceptable efficiency[1], what survives depends not just on efficiency but on the initial, often accidental conditions (chaos theory), depends on the history of what problems had to be solved in the past - problems that may be irrelevant today (path dependence), and depends on evolutionary accidents - what might do best today could have been selected out for extinction in the past when a feature, which might survive if competing today, met its evolutionary demise. Although institutions cannot be *too*

---

* This paper draws on my Chaos and Evolution in Law and Economics, 109 Harv. L. Rev. 641 (1996).

1 It's the cost of change - informational, organizational, and political - when the value of change is uncertain, that yields the "give" at the joints.

inefficient if they have survived, evolution toward efficiency constrains but does not fully determine the institutions we observe.

I. The Evolutionary Paradigm

The evolutionary paradigm has a strong grip on American law and economics scholarship. What survives is presumptively efficient. If it were inefficient, the practice, the law, the custom would be challenged by its more efficient competitor. The success of the more efficient practice or law allows it to prosper, while its less efficient competitor withers and dies. Entrepreneurs without a clear understanding of what they are doing stumble on an efficient practice. They make money and their firms grow at the expense of firms that failed through bad luck or poor skill to adopt the efficient practice. States compete by producing efficient law. States that fail to provide efficient law get less of the regulated activity. Inefficient rules are challenged, because the challengers find it profitable to do so.[2]

Here I shall examine this paradigm of a Darwinian survival of the fittest in law and economics. While the evolution-to-efficiency paradigm explains much, but if we want a finer approximation to explain resultant reality, we must add two or three other paradigms.

The first comes from the science of chaos. Some phenomena are extremely sensitive to the initial position. Small changes in the original position make for very large changes in outcome.[3] Some American bankruptcy and corporate structures are better explicable with this paradigm in mind than a natural selection paradigm alone. Moreover, although the surviving practices *could* be perfectly efficient, if they became satisfactory they did so because they were subjected to *further* adaptations that decreased their costliness. Furthermore, the resulting structures, even if acceptable, may be imperfect when compared to what could have been had the original conditions differed.

The second paradigm comes from modern thought on evolution. The observed evolutionary outcome may well be the most efficient of the *available*

---

2 Several classics of natural selection in economic and organizational evolution are A. ALCHIAN, Uncertainty, Evolution and Economy Theory, 58 J. Pol. Econ. 211 (1950); A. ALCHIAN, Comment, 43 Am. Econ. Rev. 600 (1953); M. FRIEDMAN, Essays in Positive Economics 3 (1953); R.R. NELSON and S. WINTER, An Evolutionary Theory of Economic Change (1982); O. WILLIAMSON, The Economic Institutions of Capitalism (1985). For a few of the legal analyses of evolution, efficiency, and the common law, as well as citations to the literature, see E.D. ELLIOTT, The Evolutionary Tradition in Jurisprudence, 85 Colum. L. Rev. 38 (1985); R.A. POSNER, Economic Analysis of Law 493-98 (3d ed. 1986); G. PRIEST, The Common Law Process and the Selection of Efficient Rules, 6 J. Legal Stud. 51 (1977).

3 J. GLEICK, Chaos: Making a New Science 8 (1988).

competitors. But that does not mean that evolution is an onward and upward process. A competitor survived because it was best suited for yesterday's environment, an environment that was destructive of others with which the survivor had competed. But the destroyed group may be best suited for *today's* environment. Yet nothing in evolution assures that the destroyed group will reappear.[4] Evolutionary biologists use the metaphor of natural selection leading us to the top of this local hill. To achieve the next, much higher summit in the chain of hills, however, we would have to go *down* this hill, and then *up* the next one. But natural selection, by selecting only upward-bound characteristics, stymies us from going down the hill. We are stuck in a local equilibrium, yearning for the higher hill. Survival does not imply superiority to untried alternatives.

The third paradigm is path dependence. All three paradigms overlap, and it's with the last that I'll begin to detail this inquiry.

II. Path Dependence

Consider the most basic instance of path dependence. We are on a road and wonder why it winds and goes here instead of there, despite that a straight road would be a much easier drive. Today's road depends on what path was taken before. Decades ago, a fur trader cut a path through the woods, and the trader, bent on avoiding a wolves' den and other dangerous sites, took a winding indirect route. Were the fur trader a better hunter of wolves, the trader might have chosen a straighter path. Later travellers dragged wagons along the same winding path the trader chose, deepening the grooves and clearing away some trees on the winding path. Travellers continued to deepen and broaden the road even when the dangerous sites were gone. Industry came and located in the road's bends; housing developments went up that fit the road and industry. Local civic promoters widened the path and paved it into a road suitable for today's trucks.

It's time to resurface the road. Should today's authorities straighten it out at the same time? They see no reason to raze to the ground the factories and housing developments that arose on the path's bends and may not even bother to consider straightening it out. Today's road, dependent on the path taken by the trader decades ago, is not the one that the authorities would lay down if they were choosing their road today. But society, having invested in the path itself and in the resources alongside the path, is better off keeping the winding road on its current path than paying to build another. (Occasionally, the path

4 Recessive genes and sexual reproduction increase the chance that diverse life forms survive and could flourish later. Law's rough equivalent to a recessive/dominant genetic system is federal competition.

dependent road is so costly that a society rips it up and builds a new one. More about that below.[5]) If the road winds too much, new technologies will develop that allow the vehicles on the road to hug the road well without giving up too much speed. If the new technologies are too noisy, sound walls may go up along the road. Drivers may have to be better trained and controlled than if the road were a simple straight one. The result won't be ideal, but the transportation system will adapt.

III. Corporate Structures

Corporate law's academic work has analyzed the relationships among stockholders, senior managers, and board of directors of large public corporations. With American stock ownership scattered for large firms, managers are freer than they otherwise could have been to pursue their own agenda. The history of these relationships illustrates path dependence.

The U.S. developed corporate structures with strong managers and weak owners (instead of, say, strong owners and weaker managers) partly due to path dependence. The analogue to the fur trader could be to Andrew Jackson's destruction of the Second Bank of the United States in the 1830's, which (along with the rest of 19th century American financial politics) yielded weak financial institutions that today in the late 20th century would be out of place in the U.S., which is a nation of large businesses and could well absorb large-scale finance.

After the destruction in the 1830's of the Second Bank of the United States, which operated a nation-wide network of branches, the U.S. had neither a central bank to mold a truly national financial system nor a model for a national private banking system. In the one hundred and sixty years after it's destruction, no American bank has had similar national operations. America's many "national" banks have been national only in name; they could branch only locally, and only in the 1990's are they getting authority to operate interstate branches.[6]

These rules arose because the American public historically abhorred private concentrations of economic power, concentrations that more powerful financial institutions would create, concentrations that a more powerful central government would have made politically palatable, concentrations that if they were first arising today would probably be regulated, not destroyed.

---

5 See infra "Punctuated Equilibrium."

6 For details about American financial history, but without either the path dependent argument outline here or the evolution of corporate institutions outlined below, see M.J. ROE, Strong Managers, Weak Owners: The Political Roots of American Corporate Finance (1994).

Concentrations of private economic power are the wolves that the U.S. feared and built a winding road to avoid. Had the U.S. had a stronger central government back then - were the fur trader a better hunter of wolves - the U.S. might have tolerated but regulated the strong financial institutions.

As American large-scale industry arose at the end of the 19th century, it faced two financing problems that the absence of nation-wide financial institutions created: big industry needed to gather lots of capital nationally and certain types of organizational forms that worked well with strong financial institutions were unavailable. So the U.S. developed very good substitutes. The U.S. developed, for example, high quality securities markets, which allowed firms to raise capital in a national market to remedy the absence of a truly national financial institutions - a bank with a nation-wide network of branches.[7] The U.S. developed antitrust rules that promoted competition, an antidote to the corporate governance problems that are exacerbated when financial institutions are weak. (And the existence of a continental-sized economy allowed for enough competition that the corporate governance problems were not too costly.)

In time, the U.S. adopted new institutions, legal and economic, that are not as well-developed in other advanced nations. Corporate boards have well-defined legal duties that partly constrain managers, and an active bar pursues lawsuits, some of which are legitimate and functional. A professionalism motivates some managers. A constant goal of corporate law reformers has been to upgrade the board of directors, to make it a counterweight to managers. American firms have well-developed incentive compensation for managers and, increasingly, directors. Hostile takeovers developed in the 1980s to further constrain managers.

Whatever tasks strong financial institutions might have done, other institutions developed to do. Although in this take there is efficiency-driven evolution, to *explain* what institutions we have, we must resort to examining the original conditions. We did not have an economic battle in the U.S. between one form of corporate ownership and another (ownership through decentralized securities markets versus ownership through powerful financial institutions), with one winning and other losing. The U.S. barred the second type, allowed only the first type, and the consequential evolution was to make that which was available work satisfactorily.[8]

---

7 In many respects securities markets are superior to banks in financing industry; the point is that the American markets are even better than they would otherwise have been, or at least bigger, to substitute for the relative weakness of banks.

8 This obviously corresponds to current thinking about evolution in two senses: First, evolution is now often not thought of as a relentless drive toward efficiency, but a drive to survive a crisis and then to stay stable. E.g., S.J. GOULD, Is a New and General Theory of Evolution Emerging?, 6 Paleobiology 119 (1980). Second,

Below I develop this problem further with two ideas. First, I will ask, what happens when the American system walks out into a globalized economy where different corporate ownership systems prevail? Second, what inefficiencies might there be in the system that prevails, and would domestic competition have been enough to weed out those inefficiencies?

Let us first though develop a typology of the consequences of path dependence. Our subsequent investigation will be better if we have a typology of what path dependence could in theory do for our understanding of business and legal institutions.

IV. Three Analytic Uses

Path dependence could explain the forms we see. Multiple, equally efficient results might abound and path dependence - a nation's political and culture institutions, or chance events - could determine which among equally efficient end-results we have. Or path dependence could permit structures that were once satisfactory to become inefficient, but not be worth changing; the path-determined structures are regretted but persist. Or path dependence could lead to highly inefficient structures that society cannot get itself rid of. The first two types are common. There's less reason to believe the third is a serious problem (or better put: even if it's a serious problem, it's hard to identify and there's not much we can do about it).

1. Weak-form Path Dependence

Path dependence can explain the form of the institution that survives. The U.S. has strong managers and weak financiers, Germany and Japan have stronger financiers. The results are due to path dependence: Way back when, the U.S. was populist and comfortable with neither a strong central government nor strong private financial institutions; and way back when, the foreign countries were centralized and feudal, with the populace (to the extent they had a say) comfortable with powerful institutions. Building on that base, American business developed satisfactory substitutes for strong intermediaries - good securities markets for raising capital, independent boards for checking managers, hostile takeovers when things got far out of line; the foreign nations developed satisfactory substitutes for strong boards and good securities

---

many of biology's great "decisions" did not result from direct contests. Mammals did not beat the dinosaurs in a head-to-head struggle for survival; rather a climactic debacle, probably from the earth's collision with an asteroid, destroyed the dinosaurs. Mammals, which had been peripheral, filled the newly opened biological space.

markets, i.e., strong financial institutions that could act on managers directly and could provide financing directly without the intermediation of the securities markets.

For path dependence to be relevant in the first sense, neither institutional result needs to be better than the other; each can be good enough. Path dependence explains the resulting forms, but says nothing about relative efficiency. I call this "weak" form path dependence, because the original path does not have to be very strong for path dependence to explain how we got to where we are. "Weak" does not mean unimportant or trivial: Quite a few institutions cannot be well-explained by evolution to efficiency alone and are explicable only when we invoke path dependence. Several satisfactory formats were available, path dependence explains which one we got.

2. *Semi-strong Form Path Dependence*

Path dependence of the second type leads to inefficient paths. A decision is made to use this form, instead of that. The road goes in what eventually turns out to be an inefficient direction. Had we known then what we know now, we would not have made that investment. However, with capital stock already in place, it's not worth rebuilding our system. We regret the result, but will not pay up to change it. The QWERTY typewriter is claimed to be of this type, which I call "semi-strong" path dependence.[9]

In the abstract one can think of this model: Way back when, the cost of wiping out the wolves equalled the benefit from a straight path. Society could have gone either way, but the first trader through the woods was a bad hunter, so we got a winding road with wolves. Today, the cost of straightening the road out is quite high; we regret what we've done. It may, however, be inefficient to change, because today's saved transportation costs from a smooth and straight road are not as great as today's costs of straightening. This is semi-

---

9 The QWERTY keyboard forces our weaker fingers to type common letters, an advantage in the 19th century when keys jammed easily. Whether the QWERTY keyboard is really as inefficient as has been claimed, B. ARTHUR, Competing Technologies, Increasing Returns, and Lock-In by Historical Events, 99 Economic Journal 116-31 (1989); B. ARTHUR, Positive Feedbacks in the Economy, Scientific American, Feb. 1990, at 92-99; P.A. DAVID, Understanding the Economics of QWERTY: The Necessity of History, in: W.N. PARKER (ed.), Economic History and the Modern Economist 30-39, has been disputed. S.J. LIEBOWITZ and S. MARGOLIS, The Fable of the Keys, 33 J. Law and Econ. 1-26 (1990). One can think of semi-strong path dependence in terms of economic substitutes. A legal rule that bars oranges will have semi-strong consequences. It will explain why we drink grapefruit juice in the mornings and why my kids eat tangerines instead of oranges. For a few people, the switch to other citrus fruits will be a poor one and they will bear costs.

strong path dependence; we regret the result, but it's inefficient to do anything major about it now.

Does corporate history exemplify much semi-strong path dependence? In the U.S., firms developed with weak owners, and this may have had costs in three areas: agency costs, time horizon costs, and industrial organization costs. The first, agency costs, arises from the fact that managers and shareholders have different agendas; managers might not pursue shareholders' agenda wholeheartedly.[10] And corporate academic work in the U.S. has sought to minimize agency costs of managers who did not do their owners' bidding. One mechanism to reduce agency costs might have been tighter links between financiers and industrial managers.

The second, time horizon costs, arises from the possibility that distant shareholders excessively rely on short-term performance numbers. Although controversial and disputed, influential commentators have urged that the U.S. restructure its financial system to more closely parallel those of its competitors.[11] Financiers inside the boardroom might have avoided these possible costs.

The third, industrial organization costs, arises from the possibility that financial institutions can link together related firms, such as suppliers and customers, without forcing them into a bureaucratic vertical organization.[12] Strong financial intermediaries could have helped build these linkages which, at least in theory, could sometimes be more effective than pure vertical integration.

Foreign systems have had stronger financial intermediaries, and although they therefore might not have incurred these costs as severely, they would have faced other costs. The German and Japanese corporate system, for example, has usually been said to involve substantial bank ownership or voting of stock and greater bank presence in corporate policy making.[13] Although the foreign systems would then have not experienced the managerial agency costs, short horizons, and hybrid industrial organization links to the extent that American corporations faced, the foreign systems would have faced other costs, such as

---

10 Whether the shareholders' interest on average equals the social interest is worth debating, but here to make it simple I'm adopting without question the usual corporate perspective.

11 See, e.g., Capital Choices: Changing the Way America Invest in Industry (research report of The Council on Competitiveness, principal author: M.E. PORTER); M. PORTER, Capital Disadvantages: America's Failing Investment System, Harv. Bus. Rev., Sept.-Oct. 1992, at 43. But see sources cited infra note 24.

12 See R.J. GILSON and M.J. ROE, Understanding the Japanese Keiretsu: Overlaps Between Corporate Governance and Industrial Organization, 102 Yale L.J. 871 (1993).

13 To be sure, even this "fact" is now disputed, at least for Germany. See J. EDWARDS and K. FISCHER, Banks, Finance and Investment in Germany (1993).

financial institution agency costs, *over*-investment in long-term capital projects, and *too many* loose supplier-customer linkages that could have reduced, say, the incidence of entrepreneurial innovation.

The point here, if we have a semi-strong path, is that each path dependent ownership system has costs: a system bent on destroying financial power facilitates more managerial agency costs, may encourage industrial short-term investments, and discourages loose supplier-customer linkages. In each case, a bank-centered system encourages the contrary cost. It's not obvious which system's costs are greater. When the underlying economic imperatives are for, say, liquidating current capital and investing in new technologies, a securities-based system should do better; when the underlying imperatives are for, say, increased investment in known technologies, a bank-centered system would do better.

Yet it would be serendipitous that, if we could measure the net costs of each system, they would be perfectly equal over time, so that each is equally efficient. If we lack serendipity, we have semi-strong form path dependence. Each system depends on whether its political past had Andrew Jackson or the feudal manor; absent serendipity, one of these path dependent systems is more costly than an obvious and extant alternative.

Again, this does not mean that the less efficient system, even if one could identify which one is less efficient, should change: once a society has invested in its institutions there is plenty of reason for it not to change them radically, or at all; the costs of change might outweigh any advantages from change. Once the winding road is in place, authorities will not raze the factories and suburban housing developments in the bends of the winding road. We resurface, we do not revolutionize. Both systems may persist, and rationally persist. Yet both could have been path determined. And one of them, if we had all the information, is probably better than the other, unless we are the happy beneficiaries of serendipity.[14] (And each pure type may be less efficient than a hybrid that used both financing systems.)[15]

The next step, if we were not to attend to the last type of true path dependence, would be to think about what could happen when two different semi-strong path-determined systems emerge from their own histories to compete with one another. We'll think about this after we discuss strong path dependence.

---

14 Or, as I speculate below, a very finely-gauged evolution toward efficiency.

15 *Both governance* systems show semi-strong path dependence. My policy bet is that an economic system in which institutional-centered governance competed with managerial-centered governance would be better than one with either alone, because each governance system has special strengths and fits differing kinds of production better than the other does.

3. Strong-Form Path Dependence

There's another kind of inefficient path. We've done it, the road is built, and it *would* be worthwhile to transform the road in terms of present costs. That is, the cost of tearing down the buildings we'd have to condemn, added to the cost of a new road, is less than the value of the straight road. However, we cannot rebuild because of inefficiencies due to public choice or information problems.

The new road builders are uninfluential in the legislature; the incumbent groups - created because of the path taken - are influential and block change. Or, the information justifying the change, and what the change should be, is hard to assess, so the status quo persists.

This third form, which I'll call strong-form path dependence,[16] entails costs. We can reinterpret it as a variant of the second form: Public choice and information *are* real costs of action. If they block reconstruction, because the cost of overcoming the incumbents or the informational uncertainties, then we regret how the path turned out, but the current costs of change - costs that could be political and not just technical construction costs - are too high.[17]

"False" path dependence could be confused with these three "true" types. Today, we're upset that we have a winding path, because a straight road would be so much better. We regret that we didn't build the straight road way back when; and we feel trapped with the winding, inefficient road. We *think* we are the victims of path dependence, but we are mistaken, because this time we would have been *poorer* had we invested early on in the straight path. The cost of hunting down those wolves *was* higher than the value of having the straight road today.[18] Net of costs and benefits, we are *better* off having the winding road (and having avoided the heavy burden of wolf-hunting). The suspicion that *all* path dependent stories are of this type - and that none are of the other three "true" types - makes some wary of path dependence.[19] I call this type, where the costs right from the beginning and when added up *always* favored the path taken, "False Path Dependence," which should be distinguished from the Weak, Semi-Strong, and Strong varieties.

---

16 Capital markets typologies of efficiency use an analogous, weak, strong, semi-strong classification system. For capital markets, the weak form is the most justifiable, most likely to exist, and strong-form is the least likely to exist.

17 See D. NORTH, Institutions, Institutional Change and Economic Performance (1990) 94-95; B.W. ARTHUR, Self-Reinforcing Mechanisms in Economics, in: P.W. ANDERSON, K.J. ARROW and D. PINES (eds.), The Economy as an Evolving Complex System 10 (1988). Arthur discusses how adoption of technologies induces lock-in; North applies the concept to institutions. Note that these typologies can coexist with either Pareto or Kaldor-Hicks concepts of efficiency.

18 The hunting costs have to be adjusted for time, i.e., society gained by investing elsewhere the resources saved by not spending on wolf hunting.

19 And with information costs and public choice costs we *can make* all path dependent stories of this type.

V. An Application to Corporate Governance

I have described America's corporate governance as arising from politically-induced weak intermediaries, which led to strong managers, superb securities markets, and professionalized directors. Although perhaps sometimes seen as the only efficient path imaginable, the American results should be seen as adaptations to the American environment that disallowed strong financial intermediaries.

When international competition hit business consciousness in the 1980s, U.S. firms for the first time had to compete against firms with different ownership structures. Germany and Japan had stronger financial intermediaries that owned and controlled big blocks of stock in their largest industrial companies. The U.S. system was not the inevitable end of corporate evolution, but one of at least two possible results, each reasonably satisfactory.[20]

There were thus at least two models for corporate governance in economically advanced economies. While the American system invested authority disproportionately in the CEO (subject to check by occasional director activism and by takeovers), the German and Japanese structures were more bank-centered, with their CEO's lacking the central authority that the American CEO's had. American CEOs were confined by hostile takeovers; German and Japanese CEO's were confined, it was said, by their banks. Neither the American nor the foreign systems were perfect, each had lapses and limitations, but what is important is that both have been seen as different.

Could both be equally efficient?[21]

Or, to pose the question first in a way that is easier to answer, could either be highly inefficient?

The answer has to be no. Neither could be highly inefficient. One, the economies, which we have assumed to be advanced, could not have had a governance system that shackled their largest firms from operating satisfactorily. (If evolution had led to *highly* inefficient corporate governance, the economy of that nation would not have been advanced. To emerge as a

---

20 To be sure, serious academic research on how governance systems function was nearly non-existent in the 1980s and is spotty even today. Rather, the intellectual challenge came from the brute observation that with all those Japanese cars on American roads, Japanese car-makers - the biggest governed firms there as well as here - and their banks could not be so bad.

21 "Corporate governance devices that have survived in many firms for extended periods are particularly unlikely candidates for challenge as mistakes. We have emphasized that the durability of a practice both enables people to gauge its effects and allows competition among firms to weed out the practices that do not assist investors. There is no similar process of weeding out among academic ideas or regulations. Quite the contrary, mandatory terms prescribed by law halt the process of natural selection and evaluation." F.H. EASTERBROOK and D.R. FISCHEL, The Economic Structure of Corporate Law 31 (1991).

competitive player in the global economy, corporate governance had to have been satisfactory. Path dependence may have led this or that nation down a highly inefficient path, but that nation would not have emerged as a global competitor.[22])

Two, global product competition should reduce or eliminate the most inefficient features of a governance system. Firms that have weak governance systems would, in the long-run, decline.

Three, cheap telecommunications and frequent international corporate governance conferences mean there are few secrets left. Nations and businesses can consciously copy one another's better features, can understand that domestic varieties previously thought to be impossible survive abroad, and can find ways to fix their systems' worst features.[23]

Global competition challenged national corporate governance systems in two dimensions, one intellectual and one real. In the intellectual dimension, efficiency explanations for the *forms* of American ownership and corporate power had to seem weaker. Other systems were possible and not grossly inferior. The possibility that the American path to the corporate present was heavily influence by American politics seemed plausible when other systems worked differently.

Yet for each system to survive, it could not be grossly inefficient. At a minimum, it's inefficiencies had to be counterbalanced by efficiencies elsewhere in the system. True, it is possible that inefficient institutions could become embedded in a society, and that society's economy might not prosper. But with the European, American and Japanese economies roughly equally successful, each national corporate governance system could not have been grossly debilitating.

For example, consider the most basic of corporate governance issues: firing the CEO. Steven Kaplan has found that CEO's leave their jobs in all three nations at roughly the same rate after a precipitous decline in stock price or

---

22 True, a global player may have a high standard of living *and* a defective corporate governance system, *if* its wealth comes from an advantage outside. its corporate system. Saudi Arabia, for example, has a high standard of living based on resource exploitation, and still probably has a defective corporate governance system. The same argument shouldn't apply to Europe, Japan and the U.S., since all three compete mainly by making and selling modern manufactured goods and services. When Europe and Japan lagged the U.S. economically, it was plausible to believe that their corporate governance systems were highly defective; now that they compete roughly equally in arenas where governance is relevant, their governance systems cannot be highly deficient. Defects must be small, and it's unclear which governance system has more defects.

23 Human consciousness makes metaphoric comparisons with natural selection inapt, or at least only partial: natural selection operates without the subject's consciousness of the selection process. See infra "Punctuated Equilibrium."

profits.[24] This data suggests rough equivalence in basic governance tasks, although more confirming studies are needed and there are unanswered questions.[25]

How would one fit rough equivalence in basic tasks into the path dependent paradigm? In stark form, I believe that although America started with comparatively weak financial intermediaries, it eventually developed comparatively strong boards. And while Germany and Japan started with relatively strong intermediaries they developed comparatively weak boards.

The American case can be well-documented. For decades a key task of corporate reform has been to upgrade our boards of directors, to professionalize them, to make them (and senior managers) own stock or receive other incentive compensation, to make directors independent of managers, to set up monitoring committees of outsiders.[26] True, directors have often been tools of the CEO, and for years the independence of directors was a formality: they depended on the CEO for information and they were loyal to the CEO, who had hired them. They were well-qualified people who could give good advice. Yet, it may have made a difference by the late 1980's that good, formally independent people were in place, because, if the anecdotes are right, the directors started then to become more active. They do not take the CEO's word for granted, and sometimes they actually fire the CEO. Although one can criticize many boards for waiting too long, for not checking sooner, and so on, the anecdotal facts are that boards acting up in ways that they didn't only ten years ago.

And the formal structures are changing as well. Independent committees - an artefact once perhaps of extensive derivative litigation - are taking over substantive business decisions. Independent directors are getting their own legal counsel. The notion of separating the CEO's position from chairman of the board or installing a "lead" independent director has become popular to discuss and occasionally to implement.

---

24 S.N. KAPLAN and B.A. MINTON, Appointments of Outsiders to Japanese Boards: Its Determinants and Implications for Managers, 36 Journal of Financial Economics 225 (1994); S.N. KAPLAN, Top Executives, Turnover and Firm Performance in Germany, 10 Journal of Law, Economics, and Organization 142 (1994). Ronald Gilson has used Kaplan's (and Kaplan's co-author's) data to make the textual point orally.

25 Do the CEO's leave at equal rates after modest firm declines? Is one system better at *avoiding* the decline, or in dampening its severity, allowing CEO's to survive because the declines are not as frequent or severe? And is it the *governance system.* that induces them to leave, or do they leave because they disdain the pain of failure? Is one system better than the other at picking a replacement for the fallen CEO?

26 E.g., American Law Institute, Principles of Corporate Governance: Analysis and Recommendations (1994); Smith v. Van Gorkom, 488 A.2d 858 (Del. 1985) (directors liable for failure to scrutinize merger offer favored by company CEO)

The bottom line is that the American structure was in place to upgrade the board and, while critics could point out gross deficiencies that remain, the board seems to have been upgraded. Moreover, managers are confined by other economic institutions. They must compete in product and capital markets; they are socialized to do their jobs properly. They face lawsuits for some derelictions. In the 1980s, and somewhat still today, they faced hostile takeovers.

The point here is that when one technique of control - say, financial institution monitoring - is absent, one would predict that other control techniques would strengthen if and when weak corporate governance is seen by the corporate players to be important. In the U.S. it was first takeovers in the 1980s and activist boards in the 1990s.

Or, if other institutions of control are strong - say, product market competition in the U.S. - the incentives to develop strong financial institution monitoring become weak. The history of American ancillary institutions - strong competitive markets, weak institutional monitoring - is consistent.

The German and Japanese facts exhibit a similar but converse history vis-à-vis the board. That is, with financial institutional influence relatively greater, boards there became relatively even weaker than the old U.S. boards and certainly weaker than the current U.S. boards. The Japanese board is made up of insiders, with outsiders entering during crisis. The Japanese president's council (in which the presidents of affiliated companies meet informally once a month) has pale, board-like functions. But the council is big, and due to its size and to the time constraints on the presidents, it cannot operate as a perfect substitute for a good board of directors meeting once a month to discuss *one* company. It is, at most, a "soft" board.

German supervisory boards do not meet as often as American boards do and their meetings are often merely formal.[27] Codetermination - employees have half the board seats in large German firms - may weaken the board as a supervisory mechanism, because managers and bankers may prefer not to make the supervisory board strong, which would give employees more authority than a managerial-banker alliance would want. Thus, although the direct financial presence in the supervisory board is stronger than that found in the large American firm, the board is less powerful than the American board.

So, to overly abstract the situation we are describing, America developed weak intermediaries but eventually compensated with strong boards; Germany and Japan developed strong intermediaries but have not yet developed strong boards. The net governance results: Each performs about as well (or as badly) as the other. From the smattering of evidence now available, each fires senior managers at about the same rate after gross failure.

---

27 See EDWARDS and FISCHER, supra note 13.

This does not mean that national business institutions converged to have the same institutions. Rather, each system solved basic problems by modifying their its own path dependent institutions, the U.S. with weak intermediaries, the foreign systems with strong intermediaries. If they had failed miserably, their nations would not have become global economic players. The solutions are not usually beautiful and often are imperfect. Biological evolution is similarly imperfect, based on pre-existing structures that adapt to survive, not to be perfect.

Thus two competing forces interact here. Path dependence helped to create the institutions; adaptations reduced their *functional* failures. The forms may look different, but the very basic functions must be satisfactorily resolved. To make another biological analogy, whales, which are mammals, and fish, which are not, have very different "institutional" features. Yet both learned how to swim.

So does it matter?

Yes. In three ways. First, we sometimes want to *understand* why we have the institutions we have and efficiency alone cannot explain them all. Second, satisfactory resolution does not mean optimal resolution. Some systems would do better by having more techniques available. Third, sometimes the underlying production technologies change so radically that a path dependent institution is maladapted but cannot adapt. It must die.

When the systems emerge to compete, what happens? German and Japanese firms developed with weak boards and strong intermediaries; the U.S. developed the converse institutions. Each was sufficiently satisfactory to allow the three nations to become global competitors by the 1980s. Would competition lead competitors to adopt *both* constraints on managers? I see evidence that this is happening. In the U.S., institutional intermediaries are strengthening. True, they don't hold big blocks of stock in the biggest companies (as is true abroad). True, they generally don't sit in the boardrooms of the biggest firms (as is true abroad). But in recent years institutions have been pressing the boards of poorly performing companies to act up, and they've been pressing the boards of all companies to strengthen their own boards. The U.S. system is adopting some of the foreign techniques of financial institutional strength (not too many and not too strongly, to be sure) but mediated through America's path dependent strength, i.e., a system with the potential to develop a good board.[28]

---

28 Although American financiers began in the last decade to experiment with new relationships, the evidence of functionality is slight. One study, commissioned by a public pension fund, found large gains from activism. Wilshire Associates Inc. Long-Term Rewards From Corporate Governance (Jan. 5, 1994) (unpublished study of stock price changes of companies targeted by CalPERS for corporate

Although I know of no confirming Japanese anecdotes yet, the predictions for Germany fit an adaptive model. That is, as German firms face competition and experience failure, they should seek to strengthen their weak governance link, the boardroom. And in the past year or two, there's been increased attention to the potential for the supervisory board, with the board meeting in many firms moving from being merely formal to something closer to being a real monitoring board.[29]

These two moves - stronger influence of American intermediaries and a strengthening of the German supervisory board - are what competition should produce. Each firm and each nation wants to adopt *all* the best features. And competition induces them to, either consciously or because (in the long run) only the strongest survive.

Why, one might ask, didn't *domestic* competition induce American firms to adopt alternative governance mechanisms? Why didn't some American firms develop strong intermediaries with boardroom presence? After all, competition was domestic before it was global, and one must explain why domestic competition didn't produce the full range of corporate governance options. Was there something preventing change?

One explanation is imagination, which we never have enough of. We often lack the imagination to try non-existent alternatives if the current system works more or less ok. This is not, net, a bad result: If we were always experimenting with basic institutions - most of which work satisfactorily and many of which work ideally - progress would slow.

This roadblock to change could be thought of as an information cost, and we Americans might have been especially susceptible to it for business institutions, because we tended to think of our governance system as optimal.[30] Only when

---

governance activism). Two recent academic studies found, however, that firms targeted for institutional activism have only low or no stock price gains afterward. S. WAHAL, Pension Fund Activism and Firm Performance (University of North Carolina Working Paper) (March 1995); S. GILLAN and L. STARKS, Relationship Investing and Shareholder Activism By Institutional Investors: The Wealth Effects of Corporate Governance Related Proposals (University of Texas at Austin Working Paper) (1994).

29 Comments of E.-M. LIPP, Senior General Manager, Corporate and International Division, Dresdner Bank, at OECD conference on The Influence of Corporate Governance and Financing Structures on Economic Performance, February 24, 1995. After several spectacular failures by the banks to monitor well, political proposals arose to limit the number of supervisory boards on which a single person can serve, a limit that would make it harder for a director to be spread too thinly. J. TEMPLEMAN, Suddenly Germans Love to Hate Their Banks, Bus. Wk., Feb. 20, 1995, at 56; Central Europe's Model Bank, The Economist, Aug. 27, 1994 (discussing German banks' Metallgesellschaft and Schneider real estate debacles).

30 EASTERBROOK and FISCHEL, supra note 21.

faced in the 1980's with alternative and roughly equally successful European and Japanese systems did we realize that our system was not unique in its success.[31] This aspect is, I believe, potentially quite important for understanding legal and institutional evolution: if the climate of opinion about a system does not admit the possibility of radical alternatives, evolution and change might not emerge.[32]

Another explanation is that corporate governance is not *the* key indicator of national economic success or even an individual firm's economic success. So firms adapted elsewhere. Internal competition among middle managers may have yielded whatever superior governance at the top might have yielded. Similarly, a competitive product market in the U.S. yielded good economic performance, on top of which even better corporate governance might have done little for the national economy. Governance just wasn't important enough.[33]

Another explanation is organizational costs. American politics barred some corporate forms, and no single firm could alone change these rules. When American firms' principal competitors were other American firms, all were playing by the same organizational rules. Law did not allow for some types of gross innovation even if a firm and its financiers wanted to use the alternative.

And keep in mind that the American system did adapt, it just didn't adopt *every* control mechanism imaginable: For example, the hostile takeover and charged-up boards could be seen as America's lowest cost innovations to cure severe governance failures.[34]

VI. Punctuated Equilibrium

What if for most of the time legal institutions did not evolve in any important way? Things stayed the same, minor changes occurred below the surface of the big structures.

Moreover, imagine that when there are significant changes they are linked as part of a general upheaval.

---

31 Porter's prescription, see supra note 11, which grew out of a government-industry research project, and the business-finance Compact for Corporate Governance (Harvard Business Review) were both explicitly influenced by perceptions of German and Japanese corporate governance.

32 Cf. C. BECKER, The Heavenly City of the Eighteenth-Century Philosophers (1932).

33 And, relatively speaking, may still not be.

34 In a related paper, Chaos and Evolution in Law and Economics, I develop a similar path dependent adaptation of an American bankruptcy legal and financial mechanism, that involving out of court work-outs of failed bond issues.

In recent evolutionary theory, biological evolution is not seen as proceeding incrementally. Genotypes congeal rapidly and then are stable until a crisis afflicts the species, which dies quickly or adapts quickly. After the crisis is resolved by adaptation or extinction, there is little incremental change. There's genetic drift and minor random change, but most of the time there's neither creativity nor adaptation.[35] What does this tell us, metaphorically, about legal change?

Institutions and rules would be comparatively rigid until a shock hits the system: an economic depression or political crisis for us, an asteroid smashing into the earth for the biologists. What survives is what is best adapted to persist during the crisis; once the survivors survive the crisis and the maladapted become extinct, nothing much important happens until the next crisis. The survivors are filled with efficiencies and inefficiencies; all that evolutionary theory would tell us is that, net, the species was good enough to survive, but any one of its features may be maladapted.

We can reinterpret American corporate finance in these terms. In the 1930s, the Depression put many financial structures into upheaval. What was best suited to survive the Depression was a relatively fragmented financial system of federally-guaranteed commercial banks with local branching systems, disconnected from investment banks. For fifty years, this system broke down along the edges, but did not "evolve" into a new system.[36]

On to take a bigger picture: On an overall basis liberal capitalism has thus far beaten all alternatives. But the efficiency of any single *embedded* institution is not proven by survival and resort to the evolutionary metaphors, because it's the overall system - not its parts - that was selected for success. Liberal capitalism is a blend of economics (private property and competitive markets) and politics (some quantum of social programs). Private property and competitive markets provide wealth; social programs provide political stability. From a punctuated equilibrium perspective, analyzing the efficiency of any single subset of economic institutions is misleading, because it's the *overall* blended structure that provides stability and wealth. American corporate finance had to adapt to the rules best fit for a Depression economy, and it did. It did not need to adapt any further.[37]

---

35 See GOULD (supra note 8) at 119; S.J. GOULD, Wonderful Life: The Burgess Shale and the Nature of History (1989); N. ELDREDGE, Time Frames: The Rethinking of Darwinian Evolution and The Theory of Punctuated Equilibria 15 (1985) ("[O]nce a species evolves, it will usually not undergo great change ..."). E. MAYR, One Long Argument - Charles Darwin and the Genesis of Modern Evolutionary Thought (1991) 65, 160. To be sure, punctuated equilibrium is controversial.

36 D. LANGEVOORT, Statutory Obsolescence and the Judicial Process: The Revisionist Role of the Courts in Federal Banking Regulation, 85 Mich. L. Rev. 672 (1987).

37 There are proof problems in using path dependence, in that it yields refutable implications with great difficulty. I've elaborated on the proof problems, in the

Evolutionary metaphors can go only so far, because natural selection works without consciousness. It propels a species to the top of the local evolutionary mountain and there the species will remain stuck absent cataclysmic change or genetic drift, despite that the next much higher mountain is attainable if the species could back-track a bit down the current mountain. We human beings are, in contrast, conscious of our business and legal institutions and, if we believe we are stuck in a local equilibrium due to path dependence or original conditions that are now irrelevant, we can change our environment. We can move ourselves from one mountain to another. If we are mired in strong path dependence, we can consciously re-engineer our road system.[38]

Thinking about path dependence tempts us toward greater government direction. For many law and economics' advocates (and I include myself here), it is most satisfying to believe in evolution-toward-efficiency if we could believe that no path could be inefficient. Then we need not consider the possibility that a centralized administrator might get the information fastest and make a correct decision to change the path. A mistrust of governmental action is more persuasive (and more personally satisfying in helping construct a coherent belief system) if one could convincingly accord a strong presumption of efficiency to every economic institution we see. If we cannot, because too much depended on original conditions or path dependence, then the verbal space would widen in which to debate government action and directives for change.[39]

I do not believe that in the U.S., with our pattern of government, we should search widely for path dependent traps. Even if much of what we see may be path determined, government directives to change would be unwise. Loosening up evolutionary constraints from regulation is the wisest government task. But this is a belief, based on observation of the limits of American government; it is not a belief derived from a sense that evolution inevitably yields the most efficient results. It is not a matter deduced from thinking about path dependence.

---

section entitled "Two Risks in Thinking Too Much About Chaos, Evolution, and Path Dependency - Imprecision: The Absence of Refutable Implications," in Chaos and Evolution in Law and Economics.

38 For genetic drift giving the push off a genetic peak, see GOULD (supra note 8) at 126 n.*. Note that social institutions could replicate the detrimental effect of a genotype disappearing but becoming useful later. If we cannot adopt something that is non-existent, because, say, of the limits of human cognition, then an institution's disappearance could knock it off as an evolutionary possibility. Similarly, institutions are embedded in complex networks; once the arrayed network adapts to accommodate an institution of type X during a period of flux, type Y may disappear and not be available later when it would be useful, because the surrounding institutions at the later time accommodate X, not Y.

39 Path dependence analysis has another scar: it yields us, for now, little policy prescription and few refutable implications that would give it scientific rigor.

VII. Conclusion

I sought in this essay to refine the evolutionary model from law and economics, first by making it accommodate concepts from chaos theory, from path dependence, and from punctuated equilibrium theory, and then by applying path dependence analysis to a corporate structure problem.

Path dependence can be seen as either weak, semi-strong, or strong: If weak, if needn't have done much work and yet it still can explain why we have one of several efficient possibilities; if semi-strong, we didn't do as well as we could have done but the costs of change make further adaptation unwise; if strong, change is recommended but a society is stuck due to lock-in effects arising from public choice or information problems.

The evolution-toward-efficiency paradigm has an America-centered origin. We - American corporate and business law scholars in general - sought to explain American business institutions. Many of us have an underlying policy preference for limiting government directives. With the U.S. for years as the world's leading economy, American institutions could not be grossly inefficient, and we tended to find efficiency explanations for much of what we saw. As European and Asian economies caught up, we saw them sometimes adopting the same institutions (either because they were finally becoming efficient or because they were imitating the presumptive leader in efficiency). This trend toward convergence confirmed the evolution-toward-efficiency explanations. But foreign evolution sometimes did not lead to the same institutions we had, institutions that we thought best explicable in the U.S. by efficiency. If they didn't adopt our institutions and if their economies were roughly at the same level as ours, we needed further explanation.

Although economic institutions cannot be *too* inefficient if they survived, evolution toward efficiency only *constrains* within possibly broad parameters; it does not fully determine the institutions we observe. What survives depends not just on efficiency but on the initial, often accidental conditions (chaos theory), depends on the history of what problems had to be solved in the past - problems that may be irrelevant today (path dependence), and depends on evolutionary accidents - what might do best today could have been selected out for extinction in the past when a feature, which might survive if competing today, met its evolutionary demise.

Trends in Japanese Corporate Governance

Hideki Kanda

Contents

I. Introduction

In this article, I will describe the recent trends in corporate governance in Japan.[1] I will focus on three points. First, in Japan, it is often said that banks are powerful and important in corporate governance, and that there is an indication today that the power of banks is decreasing. While these statements are true, in discussing corporate governance, one must distinguish two notions: giving influence to the company and monitoring management of the company. I think that banks are strong in giving influence, but it is difficult to show that banks are strong monitors in Japanese corporate governance. Second, in Japan, employees are important. Indeed, despite the premise of the Japanese company law that shareholders are the owners of the company, it is commonly believed that Japanese companies are in fact owned by employees and Japanese companies are run for the best interest of employees, not the best interest of shareholders. I am not sure what implications this has for Japanese corporate governance. There is no evidence to show that shareholders are victimized. But anyway it is true that executives and directors in Japanese companies are, in almost all cases, former employees of those companies. Third, in Japan, the role of shareholders in corporate governance is not entirely clear. As in other

---

1 This article is based on my oral presentation at the conference "Comparative Corporate Governance" held on 14 June 1995. In describing the Japanese law and practice, I take the risk of oversimplification, rather than attempt to describe the details of law and practice in Japan. I thank Erik Berglöf for his insightful suggestions.

countries, shareholders are highly institutionalized in Japan. The key question then is whether institutional shareholders play any active role in Japanese corporate governance. Traditionally, they serve as "stable" shareholders, that is, they do not sell shares, or more accurately, they do not reduce their shareholdings in the company of which they are "friends".[2] They do not exercise voting rights against the management. But there is an indication today that institutional shareholders have begun to reduce their shareholdings.

I will elaborate these three points. I will begin with shareholders, and then look at employees and banks. But at the outset, I will give a brief note on the basic legal framework and some data about Japanese companies and practice.

II. Public companies in Japan

All publicly held business corporations in Japan take a legal form called "kabushikigaisha", translated into English as a stock company. This is the Japanese counterpart of a U.S. business corporation, a U.K. public company, German Aktiengesellschaft, and the Belgian and French société par action. Today, there are about 1.3 million stock companies in Japan, but most of them are closely held companies, and the number of large publicly held companies is roughly 7,000.[3] Among them, about 2,200 are listed on stock exchanges. Japan has eight stock exchanges, of which the largest is the Tokyo Stock Exchange. As of March 31 1995, there are about 1,600 listed companies on the Tokyo Stock Exchange. Canon, Sony, Toyota, and other well-known Japanese firms are all listed on the Tokyo Stock Exchange.

These companies (namely publicly held stock companies in Japan) are all incorporated under, and governed by, a set of legal rules known as the "company law," which is codified in the statute called the Japanese Commercial Code (Law No. 48 of 1899, as amended). The Japanese company law has its origin in late-19th century Germany, but it did not import the board of auditors system, or Aufsichtsrat. More importantly, after World War II, Japan imported many U.S. rules, and most importantly, the board of directors system was adopted in 1950. So today, the Japanese system is a one-tier board system. Employee participation in the board, or codetermination, is not adopted in Japan. That is to say, all directors are elected at the shareholders meeting, and directors constitute the board. The board elects representative directors (the

---

2 Japanese corporate investors often sell and buy the same stock to realize capital gain (for accounting and tax purposes) and maintain the ownership relationship with the firm.

3 By "large publicly held companies" I mean "large stock companies" defined under the statute. A large stock company is a stock company having either capital in the amount of 500 million yen or more, or total debt (on its balance sheet) in the amount of 20 billion yen or more.

Japanese counterpart of U.S. officers or executives). They are the management, and run the company. In Japan, the highest rank among representative directors is a president.

There are two unique systems required by the Japanese company law. First, a stock company must have *kansayaku*, often (somewhat misleadingly) translated into English as statutory auditor, and this auditor's job is to "monitor" the management (that is what the law says, and there is no way of knowing whether this system is functioning well). Statutory auditors are elected at the shareholders' meeting, and do not have to be accountants or other professionals. As a result of the statutory amendments in 1993, a "large" company (defined in the statute)[4] must have at least three statutory auditors, and at least one of them must be an "outside" statutory auditor. An auditor is "outside" when he did not serve as a director or employee of the company or its subsidiary for at least five years preceding his appointment as auditor. In practice, most outside auditors are former non-outside auditors, and they are all former employees of the company.

Second, a "large" stock company must have an accounting auditor, who must be a certified public accountant. This accounting auditor's primary job is to audit the company's annual financial statements. The law expects collaboration between accounting auditors and statutory auditors, so in theory, if there is something wrong, it must be discovered by these two auditors. Historical experiences, however, show almost no occasion that some wrongs were uncovered by these two auditors.

Now a few words about practice. I will oversimplify in order to highlight the actual Japanese situation. Boards of directors in Japan are homogeneous. The board of directors in a typical large Japanese company consists of about twenty five men, most of whom are at least fifty years old. They are all former employees of the company. There are almost no executives of other firms, no women, no academics and no outsiders of any kind. These directors elect managers. Managers, with the top position being a president, are the highest rank in the life of "salary man", the word which describes a typical university graduate under the lifetime employment system in Japan. Japanese company law does not require outside directors. It instead requires outside statutory auditors. And again, it is difficult to know whether this outside statutory auditor system is functioning well.

A number of firms recently announced that they will reduce the number of directors and statutory auditors. Their explanation is that this is necessary and appropriate because they began cutting the number of employees to cope with current unfavorable economic conditions. My prediction is that the number of

---

4 See supra note 3.

directors and statutory auditors will decrease, but the homogeneity in the Japanese boards will not change in the near future.

III. Shareholders

Who owns Japanese public companies? As of 31 March 1995, the ownership structure of listed companies on the eight stock exchanges is the following. Individuals own 23% of the total shares listed on the eight stock exchanges, financial institutions own 45%, and non-financial companies own 24%. Among financial institutions, banks own 21%, life insurance companies own 13% and investment trusts own 3%. I might add that in Japan pensions are managed by trust banks and insurance companies, and there are no independent statistics available with respect to stock ownership by pensions.

Unlike in the U.S., banks may hold shares of other companies for investment purposes (under Article 65 of the Japanese Securities and Exchange Law, the Japanese version of Glass-Steagall), but they cannot own more than five percent of a single company under the Anti-Monopoly Law. This five percent limitation also applies to securities firms, and ten percent rather than five applies to insurance companies.

What does the ownership structure of a typical manufacturing company look like, for instance? Such company typically has ten bank shareholders, each owning two to three percent, as well as twenty other major corporate shareholders.

I must add that in Japan, what we call "mutual stockholding" by companies is common, and known as "*keiretsu*". This means that Company A owns Company B's shares and Company B owns Company A's shares. But a high percentage of two-way holdings is unpopular. That is, Company A's holding of Company B's shares may range from 1% to 100%, but Company B typically owns 1% to 2% of Company A's shares. Again, for banks and insurance companies, the antitrust limitations apply.

What are the recent trends about shareholders? First, a number of institutional shareholders recently announced that they may not be able to keep their stable shareholdings, and they may start selling their shares. The reason, they say, is that in the past they owned shares to maintain their long-term relationship with the company but today it is costly to do so. Also, the life insurance industry recently announced that they are unsatisfied about low-

level dividends in most companies in which they have stable shareholdings. I must note that institutional shareholders have not announced that they will exercise voting rights to satisfy their need. Instead, they are speaking to the public.

Second, in recent years, several shareholders' derivative actions were brought in Japan seeking large-amount damages against directors of several public companies. In my view, most of the claims in these actions are unwarranted on merit, but the recent increase in these actions is perceived by directors in most companies as a threat, which may mean something good at the margin in corporate governance, in the sense that directors today tend to act more carefully in running their companies.

Finally, a few words about takeovers in Japan. The system of stock tender offer was first introduced under the Japanese Securities and Exchange Law in 1971. The regulation was modernized in 1990, and today the rule is similar to that in the U.S. In actual practice, only three tender offers were consummated between 1971 and 1990. After the amendments in 1990, nine tender offers took place by the end of 1993, all of which were friendly takeovers.

Despite the large number of mergers and asset sales in Japan, the number of stock tender offers is very limited. There have been no (successful) hostile takeovers in Japan. One might ask why. In light of the fact that hostile takeovers, economists say, helped to discipline inefficient management in the U.S. in the 1980s, a question may be asked whether Japan lacks effective mechanisms to discipline management in public corporations. A somewhat more difficult question is whether the law, particularly the regulation of tender offers, has something to do with the unpopularity of tender offers, and the non-existence of hostile takeovers in Japan. In theory, there probably are a variety of mechanisms, other than hostile takeovers, by which managers of public companies in Japan are monitored and disciplined.[5]

IV. Employees

Among non-stockholder constituencies of Japanese companies, employees and banks are important. While employees are not the owners of their company under the Japanese legal system, a traditional oft-made statement is that Japanese companies are run for the best interest of employees and not the best interest of shareholders. Thus, a common phenomenon is that when a Japanese company faces financial distress, management cuts dividends before it starts firing employees. Under Japanese practice, most directors and statutory auditors are elected from former employees of the company. Lifetime employment, compensation tied to seniority, and company-by-company labor unions are often pointed out as three distinctive characteristics of Japanese companies and have functioned to keep employee supremacy alive in the past decades.

---

5 See J.M. RAMSEYER, Takeovers in Japan: Opportunism, Ideology and Corporate Control, 35 UCLA Law Review 1 (1987).

However, even if Japanese companies are run for the benefit of employees, it does not necessarily mean that shareholders are victimized. A proposition that Japanese companies are not run for the best interest of shareholders lacks empirical support.[6]

V. Banks

Banks are another important player in corporate Japan. Japanese companies rely more on banks than on capital markets for debt finance. The relative underdevelopment of the Japanese bond markets might be the result of a political victory by the banking industry. Banks thus are important. But how they operate is far from clear.

The bank-customer relationship in Japan has several distinct characteristics. Some of them are common in other business relationships in Japan, and others are unique to banking transactions. Banking transactions between banks and their customer firms in Japan show three unique characteristics. First, banks and their customer firms engage in a very wide range of transactions, from straightforward lending to a new type of transaction, such as swap transactions, and even to a bank's stockholding in their customer firms. Second, a company usually establishes a long-term contractual relationship with more than one, and typically several, banks. One of these banks typically serves as the "main bank". Third, banks obtain a strong legal position under a standard form contract known as the Banking Transactions Agreement, but they sometimes show behavior that looks quite inconsistent with their strong legal position. To take a familiar situation where a firm is in a financial trouble, the traditional behavior of the main bank (which usually has a first mortgage over the firm's property securing its loans) often pay off other debts (debts which are legally subordinated to the bank's claim) and pay off outstanding debentures or bonds.

All of these characteristics, however, have begun to evaporate in recent years. In particular, because of the development of capital markets and deregulation in the capital markets, large Japanese companies today can obtain cheaper capital from capital markets, and so, the presence of banks as lenders is inevitably reduced. And in fact, bank borrowing by large Japanese companies has been decreasing. On the bank's side, today, banks say that they will not

---

6 Recent empirical studies suggest that Japanese companies are run for the best interest of shareholders. See S. KAPLAN, Top Executive Rewards and Firm Performance: A Comparison of Japan and the U.S., Journal of Political Economy 102 (1994); S. KAPLAN and B. MINTON, Appointments of Outsiders to Japanese Boards: Determinants and Implications for Managers, 36 Journal of Financial Economics 225 (1994). See also E. BERGLÖF and E. PEROTTI, The Governance Structure of the Japanese Financial Keiretsu, 36 Journal of Financial Economics 259 (1994).

rescue their customer firm as often as in the past and they also say that they will not buy defaulted bonds from public bondholders. I am not sure the truth about these recent statements made by several banks, but it is probably true that banks' power is decreasing. Japanese economists say that in the past banks were the most powerful monitor in Japanese corporate governance, and today, there is no single powerful monitor, so that monitoring is spread out.

VI. Theoretical Note

There is a vast amount of literature on the Japanese firm.[7] Most articles, however, do not discuss the interaction between law and practice. They usually do not consider the existence of legal rules that appear to encourage different behavior from what they think they observe about public companies in Japan. The interaction between law and practice is sometimes difficult to identify, but once it is properly identified, one can better tell how legal rules affect corporate behavior in Japan and thus obtain a better understanding of how firms operate in Japan.

Take as an example the main bank concept. While past research is divided as to whether the main bank is the most powerful monitor of its customer firm, such research does not show how legal rules affect the main bank's (and others') behavior.[8] Focus on the main bank's behavior when the costumer firm is in financial distress.[9] The conventionally observed behavior of the main bank in such situation is to "rescue" the firm. One question is how. Another question is under what legal rules. And the most important question is why. Past literature tried to answer the first and third questions. But failure to consider the second question would easily lead to wrong answers to the other questions.

Economists recently developed an interesting theory that the main bank is a delegated monitor of other creditors.[10] That is, other creditors delegate their

---

7 Recent studies by economists about Japanese firms have been numerous. The key question is whether Japanese and Western firms are different. See M. AOKI and R. DORE (eds.), The Japanese Firm (1994) and Y. MIWA, Firms and Industrial Organization in Japan (1996). Also, the comparative study of corporate governance among major countries, including Japan, has attracted researchers in Japan and elsewhere. English language works by Japanese researchers include M. FUKAO, Financial Integration, Corporate Governance, and the Performance of Multinational Companies (Brookings Institute, 1995) and K. KOJIMA, Corporate Governance: An International Comparison (A Discussion Paper, May 1995).

8 A notable exception is J.M. RAMSEYER's work. See Explicit Reasons for Implicit Contracts: The Legal Logic to the Japanese Main Bank System, in: M. AOKI and H. PATRICK (eds.), The Japanese Main Bank System 231 (1994).

9 See P. SHEARD, Main Banks and the Governance of Financial Distress, in: AOKI and PATRICK (supra note 8) at 188.

10 P. SHEARD, The Main Bank System and Corporate Monitoring and Control in Japan, 11 Journal of Economic Behavior and Organization 399 (1989).

monitoring task to the main bank. The problem is that this theory does not explain what we observe. In theory, two sets of questions must be answered. First, why do other creditors delegate monitoring to the main bank? And how can they freeride on the main bank's monitoring efforts (or otherwise contract with the main bank)? Second, why does the main bank do such "excessive" monitoring? And why does it agree to that? The explanation offered by the delegated monitoring theory centers upon hypothetical (or implicit) contracting between the main bank and other creditors.[11] It seems, however, that this ex ante approach is the source of a problem. In my view, the main bank's rescue behavior is better explicable when one focuses on the bank's behavior after the customer firm gets into financial trouble. In such a situation, the bank (which usually is the first mortgage holder) has a choice: to foreclose the mortgage or to rescue (often by employing a legal reorganization procedure). When the bank chooses the latter, that is rescuing, it is beneficial for the bank to take control of the whole reorganization process (assuming that the bank --and the debtor-- have better information than other creditors). In the past, the main bank often paid off other debts (which were legally subordinated to its claim), and always paid off outstanding bonds. By doing so, the bank could get control of the restructuring process. Other creditors could have disagreed, but the bank were armed with the threat of enforcing its first mortgage right.

VII. Conclusion

I predict that shareholders will become somewhat more important players in the future of Japanese corporate governance. Rapid developments in capital markets will also be important. It is interesting to see how banks will change in the future. We still know little, and much remains to be researched on about Japanese corporate governance.

---

11 Id.

Table 1: The Number of Corporations in Japan

Type	Amount of Capital	Number
Kabushikigaisha (stock company)	10 million yen or less	739,000
	above 10 million and less than 100 million yen	523,000
	10 million yen or more	32,000
	TOTAL	1,295,000
Gomeigaisha (incorporated partnership)		19,000
Goshigaisha (incorporated limited partnership)		78,000
Yugengaisha (limited liability company)		1,633,000
TOTAL		3,024,000

As of June, 1992
Source: Ministry of Justice

Table 2: Stock Ownership by Type of Investors (All Listed Companies)

(%)

	Government and local government	Financial institutions (excluding investment trusts)	Investment trusts	Securities companies	Business corporations	Indivduals and others	Foreigners
1960	0.2	21.7	7.6	3.7	17.5	47.8	1.5
1965	0.2	21.6	7.9	4.4	18.4	45.6	1.9
1970	0.3	30.7	1.2	1.4	22.0	41.1	3.3
1975	0.2	33.9	1.6	1.3	27.1	33.4	2.5
1980	0.2	36.9	1.9	2.0	26.1	30.4	2.5
1985	0.2	38.5	1.1	1.9	25.9	26.3	6.1
1990	0.7	42.3	3.7	2.0	24.8	22.6	3.9
1994	0.6	40.8	3.0	1.3	23.9	23.7	6.7

Source: Ministry of Finance, The National Conference of Stock Exchanges

Corporate Governance and Corporate Performance: A Comparison of Germany, Japan and the U.S.

*Steven N. Kaplan**

Contents

This paper compares aspects of corporate governance in Germany, Japan, and the U.S. First, the paper summarizes my work on top executive turnover and compensation, and their relation to firm performance in the largest companies in the three countries. Executive turnover in all three countries increases significantly with poor stock performance and earnings losses. Executive compensation in Japan and the U.S. is also related to stock returns and earnings losses. The effects in all three countries are generally economically and statistically similar. The fortunes of German and Japanese top executives, therefore, like those in the U.S., are strongly affected by stock performance and current cash flows. Sales growth, a measure of market share, plays a smaller role. There is no evidence, therefore, that U.S. managers are more short-term oriented than their German and Japanese counterparts. Managers in all three countries are affected by similar forces to roughly the same extent. The paper concludes with an explanation for the similarities and with some conjectures on the relative advantages and disadvantages of the three governance systems.

---

* Graduate School of Business, University of Chicago and NBER. This paper forms the basis for a talk presented at the conference on "Corporate Governance - Structural Reforms in the American and German Corporation Law," in Heidelberg, July 1, 1995. This research was supported by the Lynde and Harry Bradley Foundation, the Olin Foundation and the Center for Research in Security Prices. Address correspondence to Steven Kaplan at Graduate School of Business, University of Chicago, 1101 East 58th St., Chicago, IL 60637.

I. Introduction

Corporate governance systems have received an increasing amount of attention - from academics, government, the popular press, and businesses themselves. Much of this attention has focused on differences between the U.S. system and those of its strongest industrial competitors - Germany and Japan. The U.S. corporate governance system is generally characterized as a market-based system. U.S. capital markets are liquid and company ownership is relatively unconcentrated. Managers are supposedly monitored by an external market for corporate control and by boards of directors usually dominated by outsiders. The German and Japanese governance systems, in contrast, are characterized as relationship-oriented systems. Ownership in Germany and Japan is concentrated and capital markets are relatively illiquid. Managers there are allegedly monitored by a combination of banks, large corporate shareholders, and other intercorporate relationships that are maintained over long periods. An external market for corporate control is small, if not absent. Chart 1 summarizes these differences.

The differences in governance systems, in turn, are usually associated with differences in managerial behavior and firm objectives. One view, probably the majority view, argues that the close financial ties and relationships in Germany and Japan "reduce agency costs and allow investors to monitor managers more effectively than in the U.S."[1] According to this view, there are lower costs to changing poorly performing management because banks and large shareholders have the power to make needed changes. Costly hostile takeovers or proxy fights are avoided.

This view is also associated with claims that German and Japanese firms are less concerned with or affected by short-term earnings, and, therefore, better able than U.S. firms to manage for the long-term - i.e., invest in projects with long-term payoffs. This view assumes that current stock prices can diverge

1 See M. AOKI, H. PATRICK and P. SHEARD, The Japanese main bank system: An introductory overview, in: M. AOKI and H. PATRICK (eds.) (1994); T. HOSHI, A. KASHYAP and D. SCHARFSTEIN, The role of banks in reducing the costs of financial distress in Japan. Journal of Financial Economics 27 (1990) 67-88; T. HOSHI, A. KASHYAP and D. SCHARFSTEIN, Corporate Structure Liquidity and Investment: Evidence from Japanese Panel Data. Ouarterly Journal of Economics 106 (1991) 33-60; M. LIPTON and S. ROSENBLUM, A new system of corporate governance: The quinquiennial election of directors. University of Chicago Law Review 58 (1991) 187-253; M. PORTER, Capital disadvantage: America's failing capital investment system. Harvard Business Review (1992) 65-83; S. PROWSE, Institutional Investment Patterns and Corporate Financial Behavior in the U.S. and Japan. Journal of Financial Economics 27 (1990) 43-66; M. AOKI, Towards an Economic Model of the Japanese Firm, Journal of Economic Literature 28 (1990) 1-27; W.C. KESTER, Japanese Takeovers: The Global Contest for Corporate Control (1991).

from long-term shareholder values. Because banks and large shareholders have both better information and more power to use that information than the widely dispersed shareholders of the typical U.S. company, financing is more readily available for value-increasing long-term projects in Germany and Japan. The supposed monitoring and information advantages have led some to call for the U.S. corporate governance system to imitate aspects of the German and Japanese systems.[2]

Some, however, argue the alternative view that the German and Japanese systems entrench managers and employees at the expense of shareholders. Banks, allied with incumbent managers, may receive abnormally high fees or interest rates in exchange for agreeing to bail out managers (and their companies) in cases of poor performance and financial distress even if not efficient to do so.[3]

As suggested above, many observers have been quick to distinguish the U.S. system from its Germany and Japanese counterparts, and to draw conclusions about the nature of those differences. Most of these distinctions, however, are based on anecdotes, cases, and surveys. In contrast, my work[4] provides some of the first systematic evidence on how the German and Japanese systems operate and how they differ from the U.S. system. The results are not always in agreement with the anecdotes.

In this essay, I summarize and discuss the implications of the results in those three papers. Executive turnover in all three countries increases significantly with poor stock performance and earnings losses. Executive compensation in Japan and the U.S. is also related to stock returns and earnings losses. The effects in all three countries are generally economically and statistically similar. The fortunes of German and Japanese top executives, therefore, like those in

---

2 In particular, see PORTER (supra note 1) who argues that the U.S. system leads to underinvestment.

3 See J. ABEGGLEN and G. STALK, Kaisha: the Japanese Corporation (1985); TH. BAUMS, Corporate governance in Germany: The role of the banks, American Journal of Comparative Law 40 (1992) 503-526; TH. BAUMS, The German banking system and its impacts on corporate finance and governance, Working paper, Institut für Handels- und Wirtschaftsrecht (1993), and J.C. COFFEE, Liquidity versus control: The institutional investor as corporate monitor, 6 Columbia Law Review (1991) 1277-1368; for a discussion of these views. P. MILGROM and J. ROBERTS, Economics: Organizations and Management (1992), and M.J. ROE, Some differences in corporate structure in Germany, Japan, and the United States, Yale Law Journal 102 (1993) are also sympathetic to this conclusion.

4 S.N. KAPLAN, Top Executives, Turnover, and Firm Performance in Germany, 10 Journal of Law Economics & Organization (1994), 142-159; S.N. KAPLAN, Top Executive Rewards and Firm Performance: A Comparison of Japan and the U.S., Journal of Political Economy (1994); S.N. KAPLAN and B. MINTON, Appointments of Outsiders to Japanese Boards: Determinants and Implications for Managers, Journal of Financial Economics (1994).

the U.S., are strongly affected by stock performance and current cash flows. Sales growth, a measure of market share, plays a smaller role. There is no evidence, therefore, that U.S. managers have any more incentive to be short-term oriented than their German and Japanese counterparts. To first order, managers in all three countries are affected by similar forces to roughly the same extent. I conclude the paper with an explanation for the similarities and with some conjectures on the relative advantages and disadvantages of the three governance systems.

II. What incentives do corporate governance systems provide?

As I noted above, most discussions of managerial motivations in Germany, Japan, and the U.S. are based on anecdotes or surveys. In my research, I decided to test the anecdotes by asking one simple question: What incentives do the different corporate governance systems really provide to top managers? Specifically, by understanding why top managers are fired and why they are paid more, one can infer what incentives they actually have.

1. The relation of managerial rewards and punishments to firm performance

Kaplan studies corporate governance in the largest companies in the three countries - 42 in Germany, 119 in Japan, and 146 in the U.S. - from 1980 to 1988. The analyses focus on the top group of managers or operating executives in each firm in these countries. These executives are management board members in Germany; representative directors in Japan; and executive directors in the U.S. In the next several paragraphs, I describe the management and board structures in the three countries in more detail.

In Germany, the management board - the Vorstand - is comprised of the 7 or 8 top managers. They include the Chairman who is the equivalent of the CEO. German firms also have a supervisory board - the Aufsichtsrat - which is the equivalent of an outside board in the United States. Under the German co-determination system, the supervisory board includes both shareholder and labor representatives. In larger public companies, the supervisory board will typically have 19 members.

In Japan, the typical board has 21 members almost all of whom are insiders. The president is the chief executive officer or CEO. In each company, three or four directors, including the president, are given special rights to represent the company. These are known as the representative directors.

Finally, in the U.S., the firm is governed by a board of directors of typically 13 or 14 members. Approximately 1/3 are insiders and 2/3 are outsiders. The CEO is the most powerful of the managers and directors. In my research, I study executive directors - the operating managers who also are on the board of directors. This group typically includes 4 or 5 members and always includes the CEO.

The first question I asked is what kind of performance causes the top operating managers in these firms to lose their jobs? In technical terms, this involved estimating the following regression:

$$\text{Probability of losing job} = a + \beta \times \text{Performance} + e$$

I use four measures of firm performance: (1) company stock returns; (2) sales growth; (3) change in pre-tax income as a fraction of total assets; (4) and a dummy variable equal to one if pre-tax income is negative. Sales growth is meant to be a measure of market share, and, presumably a measure of "long-term" management. The dummy variable for negative pre-tax income, in contrast, which indicates that accounting earnings are less than operating and financial expenses, is perhaps the most short-term measure of performance.

The turnover results are presented in graphs 1 - 3. In all three countries, managers are more likely to lose their jobs when their company's stock performs poorly (Graph 1). In all three countries, managers are more likely to lose their jobs when their company experiences an earnings loss (Graph 2). In fact, Japanese and German managers are approximately twice as likely to lose their jobs in a year with a loss than in a year with positive earnings. Interestingly, the sensitivities or relations in the three countries are not different from one another in a statistical sense. Finally, managers are more likely to lose their jobs in Japan and the U.S. when sales growth is poor (Graph 3). Surprisingly, German managers are unaffected by poor sales performance. Furthermore, sales growth is less important in Japan than earnings and stock performance.

The second set of tests considers top management compensation and its relation to firm performance in Japan and the U.S.[5] It is true, as is commonly believed, that Japanese executives do earn lower levels of cash compensation than U.S. executives. The important question for incentives, however, is when are the top managers in those two countries paid more? To answer this, as with turnover, I estimate a simple regression:

$$\text{Percentage change in compensation} = a + \beta \times \text{Performance} + e$$ using the same four measures of performance.

The results are presented in graphs 4 and 5. Just as is the case with top executive turnover, Japanese management compensation is strongly related to earnings, stock, and sales performance. And again, the sensitivities in Japan and the U.S. are virtually identical. A two standard deviation change in stock returns leads to roughly an 8% increase in compensation in both Japan and the

5 These data were unavailable for German executives.

U.S. An earnings loss leads to a 13% pay cut in Japan and a (statistically indistinguishable) pay cut of 18% in the U.S.

What do these results for turnover and compensation mean? Three very different systems generate very similar outcomes. The fortunes of German and Japanese managers (and U.S. managers) are tied to stock performance and current cash flows - measures that some would refer to as "short-term." Furthermore, the punishments and rewards for German and Japanese managers are not more sensitive to sales growth - a measure some would refer to as "long-term" - than those of the U.S. If anything, they are less sensitive. It is difficult, therefore, to reconcile these findings with the view that German and Japanese managers are more patient - i.e., can ignore current cash flows to pursue increases in market share or sales growth. Finally, it is also difficult to reconcile these results with the view that the U.S. system is more short-term.

These results, in turn, suggest two broader conclusions. First, successful corporate governance systems respond to current measures of performance - earnings and stock prices. Second, the current stock price reflects a firm's current and future health.

2. *The impact of banks, corporate shareholders and relationships*

The results for top executive punishments and rewards relative to stock and earnings performance in Germany and Japan cannot be driven by an external market for corporate control because such a market does not exist in either country. This section considers possible explanations for or sources of the turnover-performance and compensation-performance results. As noted earlier, the most likely forces behind those results are banks, large corporate shareholders, and other intercorporate relationships. Kaplan[6] and Kaplan and Minton[7] present evidence on the importance of those forces in Germany and Japan, respectively.

The first question the two papers ask is when do banks or large shareholders take an active interest in the sample companies. The papers measure such an interest as particular types of board appointments. In Germany, I study new appointments to the supervisory board. In Japan, Bernadette Minton and I study appointments of "outsiders" to the board, where outsiders are individuals who are not lifetime firm employees, but have previous work experience at a bank or large shareholder. Both supervisory board appointments in Germany and outside appointments in Japan are increasingly likely as stock performance deteriorates. These results are consistent with the governance relationships in Germany and Japan playing a monitoring and disciplinary role.

---

6 Op. cit. (supra note 4).
7 Op. cit. (supra note 4).

Kaplan and Minton (1994) continue with a more detailed comparison of outside appointments in Japan. Appointments of bank directors in Japan - outsiders affiliated with banks - increase with earnings losses, as well as with poor stock performance. Appointments of outsiders in Japan also increase with measures of the intensity of the relationships: appointments of bank directors increase with a firm's borrowings from banks; appointments of corporate directors increase with shareholder concentration and with corporate group affiliation.

While these results are consistent with the governance relationships in Germany and Japan playing a monitoring and disciplinary role, they are also consistent with an insurance interpretation in which the presence of an outsider signals to suppliers, customers or others that the bank or the affiliated corporation will support - i.e, bail out, and, therefore, insure - the appointing firm. Kaplan and Minton (1994) distinguish between the two interpretations by considering the relation between outside director appointments and top executive turnover. Turnover increases substantially in periods when outsiders are appointed, even when controlling for firm performance. We interpret this results as saying that banks and corporate shareholders play an important monitoring and disciplinary role in Japan.

Overall, therefore, the results indicate that the bank and intercorporate relationships in Germany and Japan play a monitoring and disciplinary role. In this sense, the relationships do appear to substitute (at least partially) for the more market-oriented U.S. control mechanisms.

III. Why are the results so similar?

The bottom line of my three papers is that very different corporate governance systems in Germany, Japan, and the U.S. generate very similar outcomes. The key similarity is that all three countries have successful market economies. In this section, I discuss why I think the results have to be similar.

To understand this, it helps to look at two dimensions (see Chart 2). First, governance differences should be less important when firms cannot survive if they don't maximize. That will be true when product markets are competitive, government subsidies are small, and few (economic) rents are lying around. In those circumstances, managers face two basic choices: maximize or fail. Managers who do not maximize, and often their firms, will not survive.

Second, governance differences become less important as firms require more capital. When industries are growing or changing and firms need capital, it is difficult to obtain financing to pursue excessive or unprofitable growth. In other words, if a firm's corporate governance structure allows its managers to waste resources, that firm will not be able to obtain financing. Given that competitive product markets and competitive capital markets dominate most capitalist economies, the great similarity in the German, Japanese, and U.S. results should not be particularly surprising.

Governance, in a real sense, takes care of itself when industries are growing and changing, and when industries are competitive.

Governance differences will matter most in mature industries or in non-competitive industries where firms can survive for substantial periods without maximizing, and waste substantial resources in the process. Jensen (1986) describes such firms and industries as being susceptible to large agency costs of free cash-flow. Oil companies in the U.S. in the 1980s and many Japanese firms in the late 1 980s fit this description.

IV. Which system is best?

The final and most interesting question to be addressed is which governance system, if any, is best?

On the dimensions I studied in my research, the three systems are similar. There is no clear difference between the three governance systems in responding to poor stock and earnings performance. That result has been confirmed by the recent responses of German companies to competitive difficulties and exchange rate movements. Japanese companies also have responded in "American" ways to its recession and strong yen. There also do not appear to be clear differences in incentives to manage for the "short-term" or for the "long-term."

As I argued in the previous section, there are good reasons to believe that the similarities are the inevitable product of successful market economics. In other words, as long as an economy is competitive or market-based, governance systems will be pushed by the market to become relatively efficient. Different systems, then, will generate satisfactory outcomes.

While the three systems are similar in many respects, there are two dimensions in which the U.S. system has important advantages particularly over the Japanese system. First, the U.S. system provides better incentives to firms that are already performing well. Such firms will include firms in mature industries or in industries that are not perfectly competitive. The better incentives come form the fact that U.S. managers hold much larger equity positions that managers in Japan (see graph 6) and, probably, managers in Germany. Because they own more shares, it is arguably less tempting for U.S. managers to overinvest or waste the extra cash that a successful firm generates. If anything, these incentives have become stronger since 1992 when the U.S. Securities and Exchange Commission (SEC) both imposed stricter reporting 10 requirements on executive compensation and gave shareholders greater ability to communicate with each other and, ultimately, with management.

Second, it is relatively easier for companies to return cash to shareholders in the U.S. (and German) systems. U.S. companies pay dividends and are allowed to repurchase stock (which are tax advantaged). Furthermore, U.S. companies also pay out large amounts of cash when they purchase other companies (for cash). In Germany, although share repurchases are illegal, dividend payments are tax advantaged.

In contrast, it is very difficult for companies to return cash to shareholders in Japan. Until last year, it was illegal for a Japanese company to repurchase its stock. Such repurchases are still greatly restricted. Dividend payments in Japan are also problematic because so many shares are held by other companies. Under the Japanese tax code, dividend payments to other corporations are tax disadvantaged. Furthermore, the substantial cross-holdings mean that only a fraction of dividend payments will actually leave the corporate sector and go to non-corporate investors.

Overall, then, the three governance systems generate similar outcomes for companies that perform poorly. The U.S. system, however, arguably has some advantages over the other two in restricting successful companies from overinvesting.

Appendices

A Comparison of German, Japanese, and U.S. Corporate Governance Systems:

	Germany	**Japan**	**U.S.**
Executive Compensation	Moderate	Low	High
Board of Directors	Management / Supervisory	Primarily insiders	Primarily outsiders
Ownership	Concentrated: High family / corp. / bank	Less Conc.: High bank / High corp. / low mgmt.	Diffuse: Non-corporate High magmt.
Capital Markets	Relatively illiquid	Somewhat liquid	Very liquid
Takeover / Control Mkt.	Minor	Minor	Major
Banking System	Universal Banking	Mini Bank System	

When do governance differences matter?

	Competive Markets	*Uncompetive Markets*
Growing / changes	Least	Somewhat
Mature	Somewhat	Most

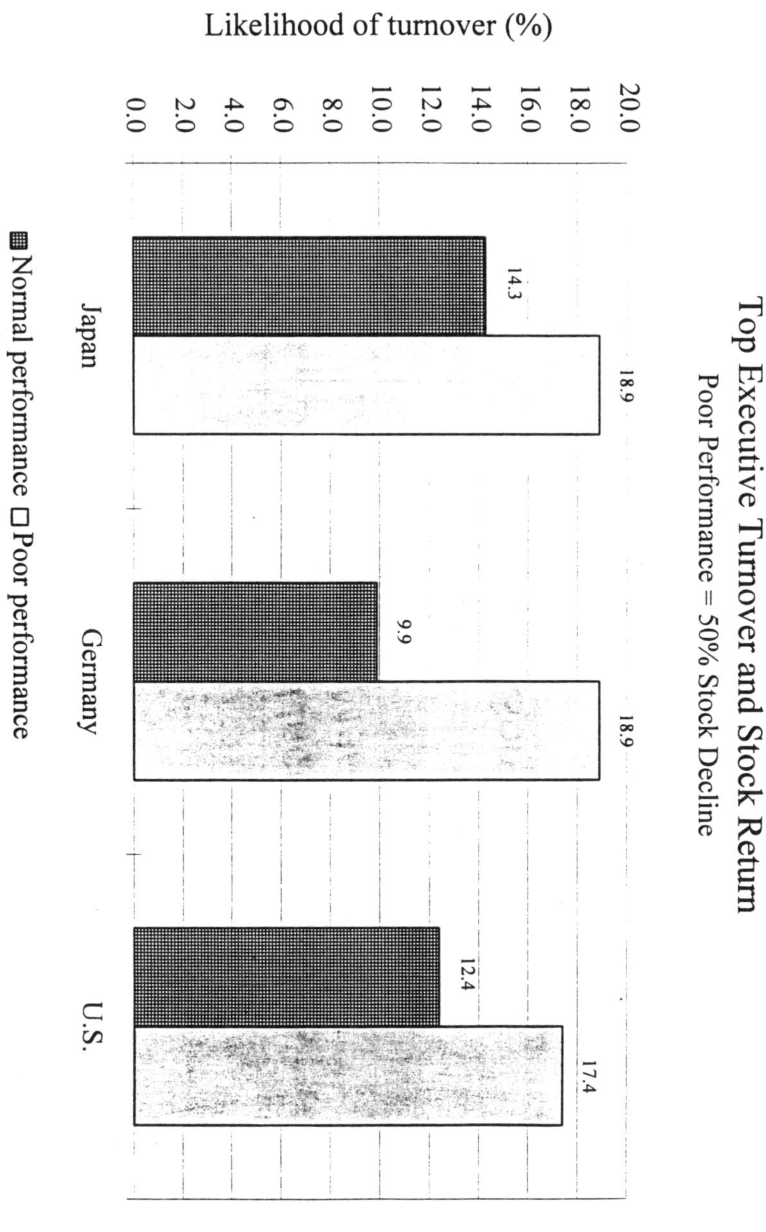
Top Executive Turnover and Stock Return
Poor Performance = 50% Stock Decline
Likelihood of turnover (%)
20.0
18.0
16.0
14.0
12.0
10.0
8.0
6.0
4.0
2.0
0.0
14.3
18.9
9.9
18.9
12.4
17.4
Japan
Germany
U.S.
Normal performance
Poor performance

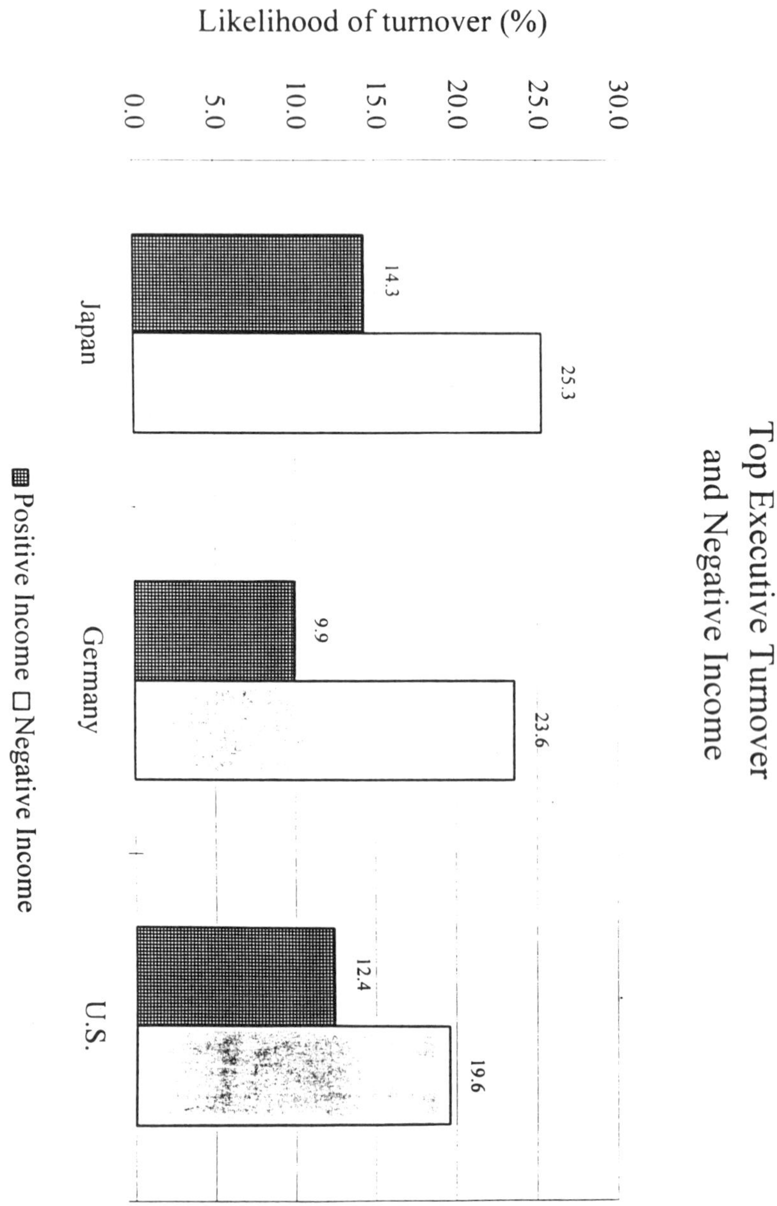
Top Executive Turnover
and Negative Income
Likelihood of turnover (%)
0.0
5.0
10.0
15.0
20.0
25.0
30.0
14.3
25.3
9.9
23.6
12.4
19.6
Japan
Germany
U.S.
Positive Income
Negative Income

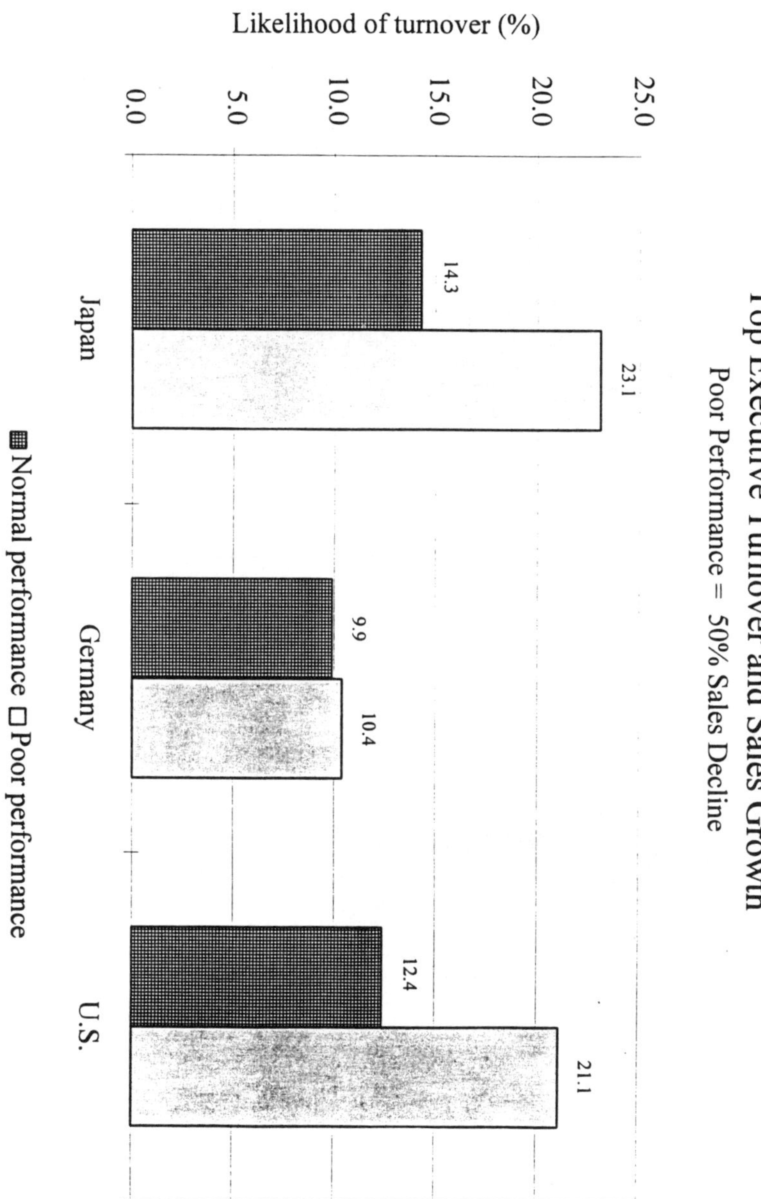
Top Executive Turnover and Sales Growth
Poor Performance = 50% Sales Decline
Likelihood of turnover (%)
0.0
5.0
10.0
15.0
20.0
25.0
14.3
23.1
9.9
10.4
12.4
21.1
Japan
Germany
U.S.
Normal performance
Poor performance

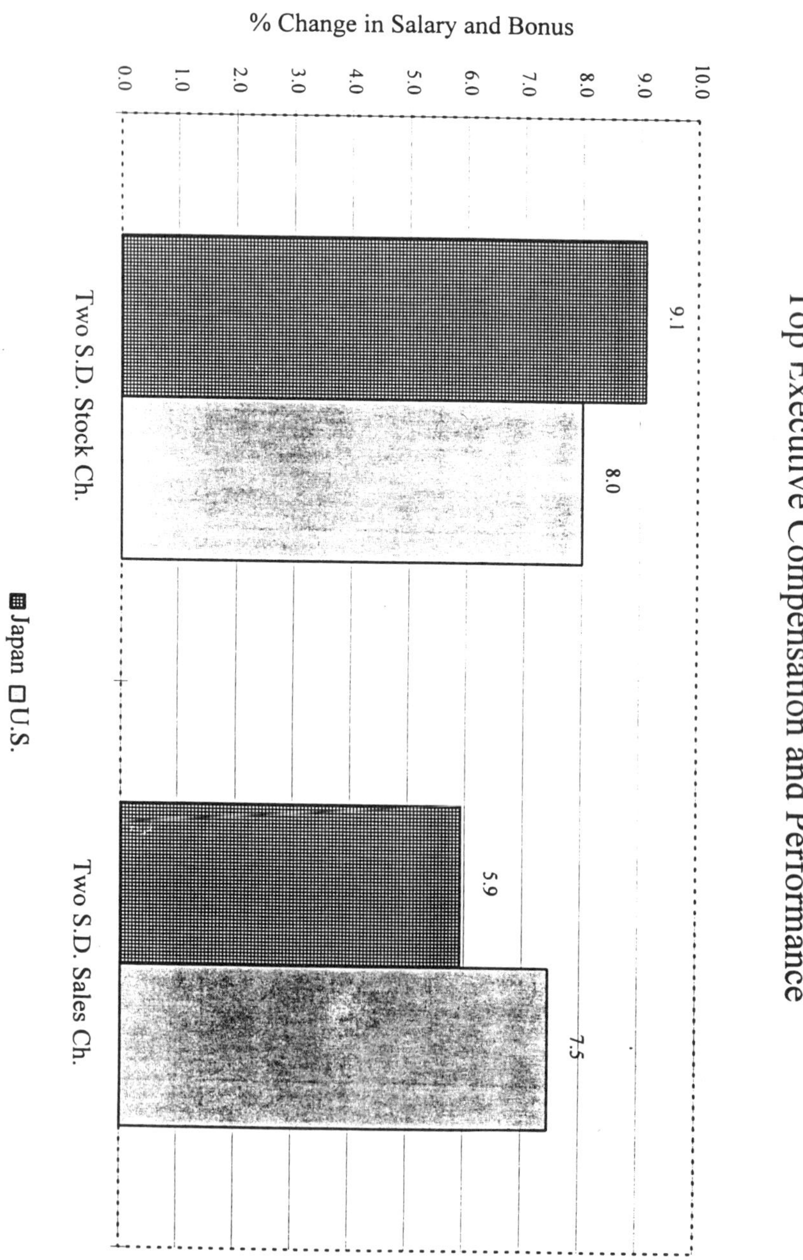
Top Executive Compensation and Performance
% Change in Salary and Bonus
0.0
1.0
2.0
3.0
4.0
5.0
6.0
7.0
8.0
9.0
10.0
9.1
8.0
5.9
7.5
Two S.D. Stock Ch.
Two S.D. Sales Ch.
Japan
U.S.

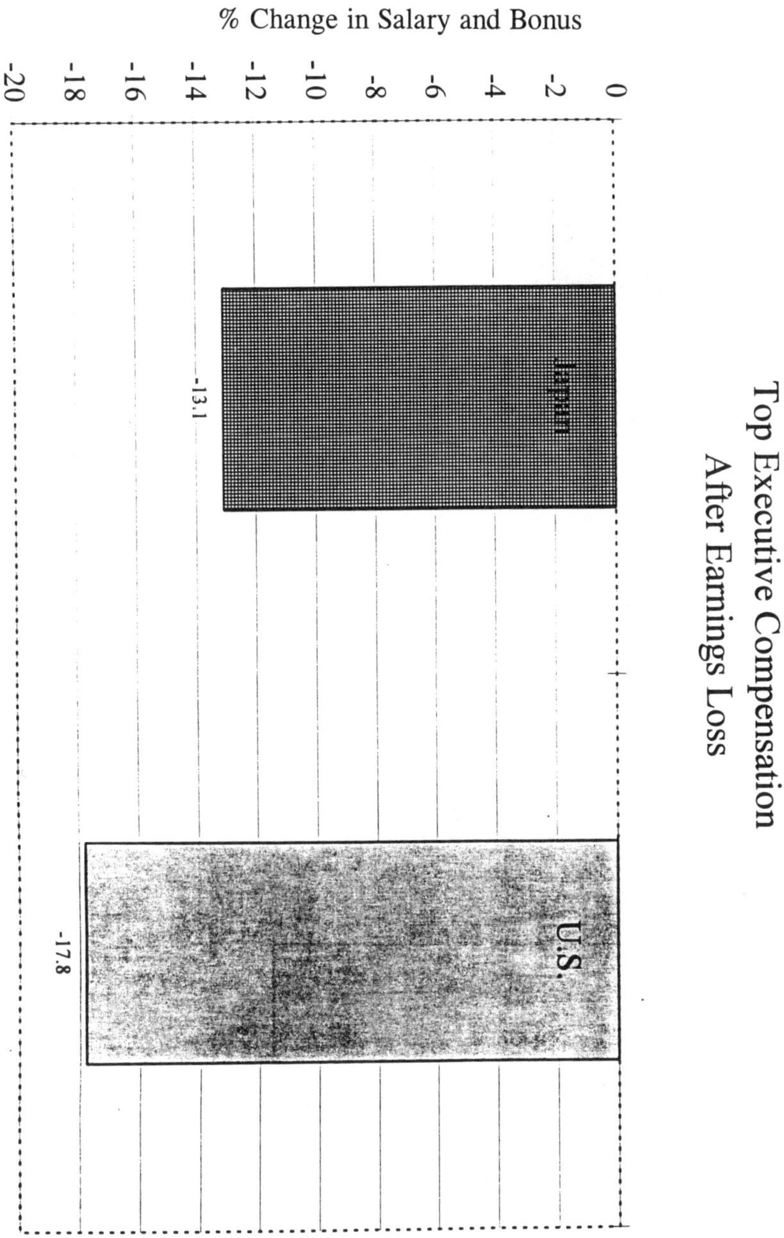
Top Executive Compensation
After Earnings Loss
% Change in Salary and Bonus
0
-2
-4
-6
-8
-10
-12
-14
-16
-18
-20
Japan
-13.1
U.S.
-17.8

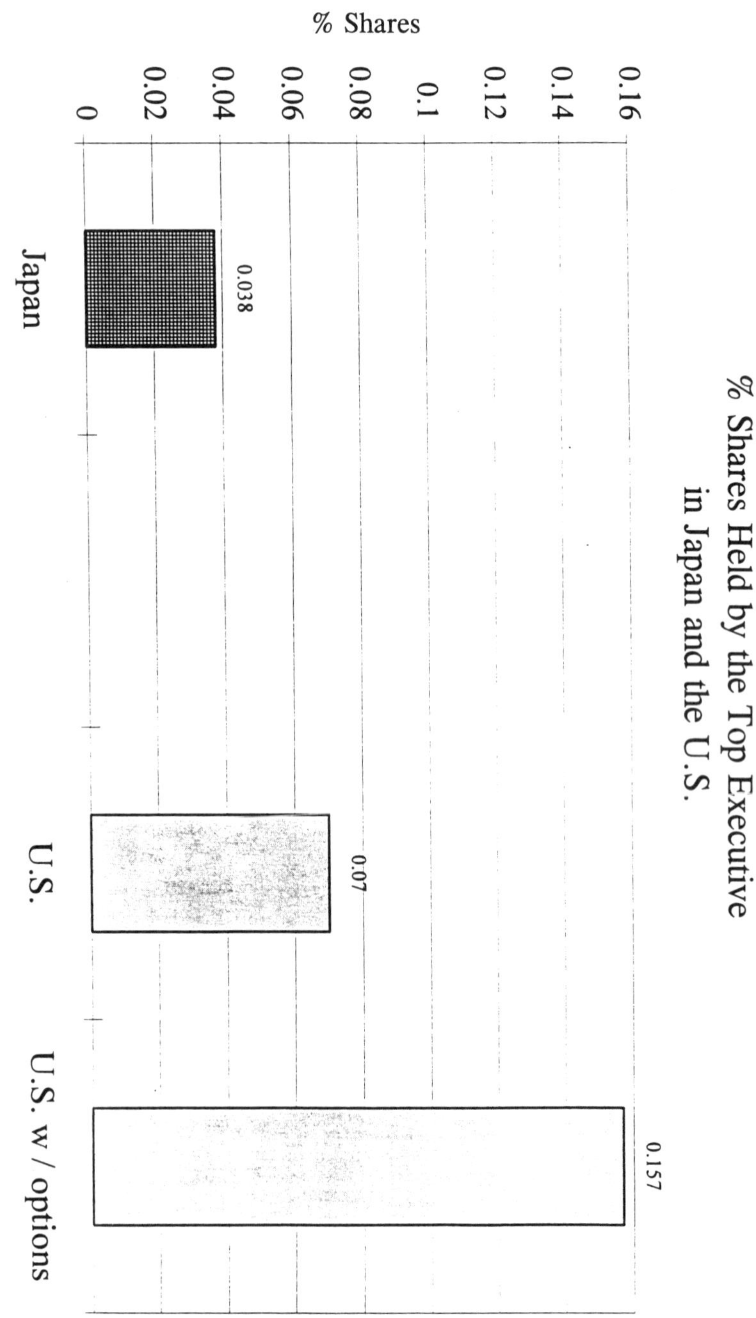
% Shares Held by the Top Executive
in Japan and the U.S.
% Shares
0.16
0.14
0.12
0.1
0.08
0.06
0.04
0.02
0
0.038
0.07
0.157
Japan
U.S.
U.S. w / options

Part Two: Materials

● ● REPORT OF THE COMMITTEE ON ● ●

THE FINANCIAL ASPECTS OF CORPORATE GOVERNANCE

THE CODE OF BEST PRACTICE

GEE

Additional copies of The Code of Best Practice are available from the Publishers, price £10.00 per pack of ten. Multiple copies may be purchased at a rate competitive with current photocopying charges.

Gee (a division of Professional Publishing Ltd)
South Quay Plaza
183 Marsh Wall
London E14 9FS
Freephone: (0800) 289520
Fax: (071) 537-2557

The full report of the Committee on the Financial Aspects of Corporate Governance may also be purchased from the Publishers, price £10.00 per copy (including a copy of the Code of Best Practice).

First published December 1992

ISBN 0 85258 914 X (Code of Best Practice)
ISBN 0 85258 915 8 (Report with Code of Best Practice)

Printed in Great Britain by Burgess Science Press.

INTRODUCTION

1 The Committee was set up in May 1991 by the Financial Reporting Council, the London Stock Exchange, and the accountancy profession to address the financial aspects of corporate governance.

2 The Committee issued a draft report for public comment on 27 May 1992. Its final report, taking account of submissions made during the consultation period and incorporating a Code of Best Practice, was published on 1 December 1992. This extract from the report sets out the text of the Code on pages 6 and 7 below. It also sets out, as Notes on pages 9 to 12, a number of further recommendations on good practice drawn from the body of the report.

3 The Committee's central recommendation is that the boards of all listed companies registered in the United Kingdom should comply with the Code. The Committee encourages as many other companies as possible to aim at meeting its requirements.

4 The Committee also recommends:

(a) that listed companies reporting in respect of years ending after 30 June 1993 should make a statement in their report and accounts about their compliance with the Code and identify and give reasons for any areas of non-compliance;

(b) that companies' statements of compliance should be reviewed by the auditors before publication. The review by the auditors should cover only those parts of the compliance statement which relate to provisions of the Code where compliance can be objectively verified (see note 14 on page 12).

5 The publication of a statement of compliance, reviewed by the auditors, is to be made a continuing obligation of listing by the London Stock Exchange.

6 The Committee recommends that its sponsors, convened by the Financial Reporting Council, should appoint a new Committee by the end of June 1995 to examine how far compliance with the Code has progressed, how far its

INTRODUCTION

other recommendations have been implemented, and whether the Code needs updating. In the meantime the present Committee will remain responsible for reviewing the implementation of its proposals.

7 The Committee has made clear that the Code is to be followed by individuals and boards in the light of their own particular circumstances. They are responsible for ensuring that their actions meet the spirit of the Code and in interpreting it they should give precedence to substance over form.

8 The Committee recognises that smaller listed companies may initially have difficulty in complying with some aspects of the Code. The boards of smaller listed companies who cannot, for the time being, comply with parts of the Code should note that they may instead give their reasons for non-compliance. The Committee believes, however, that full compliance will bring benefits to the boards of such companies and that it should be their objective to ensure that the benefits are achieved. In particular, the appointment of appropriate non-executive directors should make a positive contribution to the development of their businesses.

THE CODE OF BEST PRACTICE

1 The Board of Directors

1.1 The board should meet regularly, retain full and effective control over the company and monitor the executive management.

1.2 There should be a clearly accepted division of responsibilities at the head of a company, which will ensure a balance of power and authority, such that no one individual has unfettered powers of decision. Where the chairman is also the chief executive, it is essential that there should be a strong and independent element on the board, with a recognised senior member.

1.3 The board should include non-executive directors of sufficient calibre and number for their views to carry significant weight in the board's decisions. (Note 1)

1.4 The board should have a formal schedule of matters specifically reserved to it for decision to ensure that the direction and control of the company is firmly in its hands. (Note 2)

1.5 There should be an agreed procedure for directors in the furtherance of their duties to take independent professional advice if necessary, at the company's expense. (Note 3)

1.6 All directors should have access to the advice and services of the company secretary, who is responsible to the board for ensuring that board procedures are followed and that applicable rules and regulations are complied with. Any question of the removal of the company secretary should be a matter for the board as a whole.

2 Non-Executive Directors

2.1 Non-executive directors should bring an independent judgement to bear on issues of strategy, performance, resources, including key appointments, and standards of conduct.

2.2 The majority should be independent of management and free from any business or other relationship which could materially interfere with the exercise of their independent judgement, apart from their fees and shareholding. Their fees should reflect the time which they commit to the company. (Notes 4 and 5)

2.3 Non-executive directors should be appointed for specified terms and reappointment should not be automatic. (Note 6)

2.4 Non-executive directors should be selected through a formal process and both this process and their appointment should be a matter for the board as a whole. (Note 7)

3 Executive Directors

3.1 Directors' service contracts should not exceed three years without shareholders' approval. (Note 8)

3.2 There should be full and clear disclosure of directors' total emoluments and those of the chairman and highest-paid UK director, including pension contributions and stock options. Separate figures should be given for salary and performance-related elements and the basis on which performance is measured should be explained.

3.3 Executive directors' pay should be subject to the recommendations of a remuneration committee made up wholly or mainly of non-executive directors. (Note 9)

4 Reporting and Controls

4.1 It is the board's duty to present a balanced and understandable assessment of the company's position. (Note 10)

4.2 The board should ensure that an objective and professional relationship is maintained with the auditors.

4.3 The board should establish an audit committee of at least 3 non-executive directors with written terms of reference which deal clearly with its authority and duties. (Note 11)

4.4 The directors should explain their responsibility for preparing the accounts next to a statement by the auditors about their reporting responsibilities. (Note 12)

4.5 The directors should report on the effectiveness of the company's system of internal control. (Note 13)

4.6 The directors should report that the business is a going concern, with supporting assumptions or qualifications as necessary. (Note 13)

NOTES

These notes include further recommendations on good practice. They do not form part of the Code.

1 To meet the Committee's recommendations on the composition of sub-committees of the board, boards will require a minimum of three non-executive directors, one of whom may be the chairman of the company provided he or she is not also its executive head. Additionally, two of the three non-executive directors should be independent in the terms set out in paragraph 2.2 of the Code.

2 A schedule of matters specifically reserved for decision by the full board should be given to directors on appointment and should be kept up to date. The Committee envisages that the schedule would at least include:

(a) acquisition and disposal of assets of the company or its subsidiaries that are material to the company;

(b) investments, capital projects, authority levels, treasury policies and risk management policies.

The board should lay down rules to determine materiality for any transaction, and should establish clearly which transactions require multiple board signatures. The board should also agree the procedures to be followed when, exceptionally, decisions are required between board meetings.

3 The agreed procedure should be laid down formally, for example in a Board Resolution, in the Articles, or in the Letter of Appointment.

4 It is for the board to decide in particular cases whether this definition of independence is met. Information about the relevant interests of directors should be disclosed in the Directors' Report.

5 The Committee regards it as good practice for non-executive directors not to participate in share option schemes and for their service as non-executive directors not to be pensionable by the company, in order to safeguard their independent position.

6 The Letter of Appointment for non-executive directors should set out their duties, term of office, remuneration, and its review.

NOTES

7 The Committee regards it as good practice for a nomination committee to carry out the selection process and to make proposals to the board. A nomination committee should have a majority of non-executive directors on it and be chaired either by the chairman or a non-executive director.

8 The Committee does not intend that this provision should apply to existing contracts before they become due for renewal.

9 Membership of the remuneration committee should be set out in the Directors' Report and its chairman should be available to answer questions on remuneration principles and practice at the Annual General Meeting. Best practice is set out in PRO NED's Remuneration Committee guidelines, published in 1992. (Available at the price of £5 from PRO NED, 1 Kingsway, London WC2B 6XF, telephone 071-240 8305.)

10 The report and accounts should contain a coherent narrative, supported by the figures, of the company's performance and prospects. Balance requires that setbacks should be dealt with as well as successes. The need for the report to be readily understood emphasises that words are as important as figures.

11 The Committee's recommendations on audit committees are as follows:

(a) They should be formally constituted as sub-committees of the main board to whom they are answerable and to whom they should report regularly; they should be given written terms of reference which deal adequately with their membership, authority and duties; and they should normally meet at least twice a year.

(b) There should be a minimum of three members. Membership should be confined to the non-executive directors of the company and a majority of the non-executives serving on the committee should be independent of the company, as defined in paragraph 2.2 of the Code.

(c) The external auditor and, where an internal audit function exists, the head of internal audit should normally attend committee meetings, as should the finance director. Other board members should also have the right to attend.

(d) The audit committee should have a discussion with the auditors at least once a year, without executive board members present, to ensure that there are no unresolved issues of concern.

(e) The audit committee should have explicit authority to investigate any matters within its terms of reference, the resources which it needs to do so, and full access to information. The committee should be able to obtain outside professional advice and if necessary to invite outsiders with relevant experience to attend meetings.

(f) Membership of the committee should be disclosed in the annual report and the chairman of the committee should be available to answer questions about its work at the Annual General Meeting.

Specimen terms of reference for an audit committee, including a list of the most commonly performed duties, are set out in the Committee's full report.

12 The statement of directors' responsibilities should cover the following points:

- the legal requirement for directors to prepare financial statements for each financial year which give a true and fair view of the state of affairs of the company (or group) as at the end of the financial year and of the profit and loss for that period;
- the responsibility of the directors for maintaining adequate accounting records, for safeguarding the assets of the company (or group), and for preventing and detecting fraud and other irregularities;
- confirmation that suitable accounting policies, consistently applied and supported by reasonable and prudent judgements and estimates, have been used in the preparation of the financial statements;
- confirmation that applicable accounting standards have been followed, subject to any material departures disclosed and explained in the notes to the accounts. (This does not obviate the need for a formal statement in the notes to the accounts disclosing whether the accounts have been prepared in accordance with applicable accounting standards.)

NOTES

The statement should be placed immediately before the auditors' report which in future will include a separate statement (currently being developed by the Auditing Practices Board) on the responsibility of the auditors for expressing an opinion on the accounts.

13 The Committee notes that companies will not be able to comply with paragraphs 4.5 and 4.6 of the Code until the necessary guidance for companies has been developed as recommended in the Committee's report.

14 The company's statement of compliance should be reviewed by the auditors in so far as it relates to paragraphs 1.4, 1.5, 2.3, 2.4, 3.1 to 3.3, and 4.3 to 4.6 of the Code.

● ● REPORT OF THE COMMITTEE ON ● ●

THE

FINANCIAL ASPECTS

OF

CORPORATE GOVERNANCE

GEE

First published December 1992

ISBN 0 85258 913 1 (Report)
ISBN 0 85258 915 8 (Report with Code of Best Practice)

Gee (a division of Professional Publishing Ltd)
South Quay Plaza
183 Marsh Wall
London E14 9FS
Freephone: (0800) 289520
Fax: (071) 537-2557

Printed in Great Britain by Burgess Science Press.

STATEMENT OF DIRECTORS' RESPONSIBILITY FOR PREPARING THE ACCOUNTS

APPENDIX 3

1 In paragraph 4.28 of the report, and in the Code of Best Practice, the Committee recommends that a brief statement of directors' responsibility for preparing the accounts should appear in the report and accounts. The purpose of such a statement is to make clear that responsibility for preparing the accounts rests with the board of directors, and to remove any misconception that the auditors are responsible for the accounts. The directors' statement should be placed immediately before the auditors' report which in future will include a separate statement (currently being developed by the Auditing Practices Board) on the responsibility of the auditors for expressing an opinion on the accounts. Positioning the two statements alongside each other in this way will achieve maximum clarity about respective responsibilities.

2 The explanation of directors' responsibilities will require a relatively formal statement, which should cover the following points:

(a) the legal requirement for directors to prepare financial statements for each financial year which give a true and fair view of the state of affairs of the company (or group) as at the end of the financial year and of the profit and loss for that period;

(b) the responsibility of the directors for maintaining adequate accounting records, for safeguarding the assets of the company (or group), and for preventing and detecting fraud and other irregularities;

(c) confirmation that suitable accounting policies, consistently applied and supported by reasonable and prudent judgements and estimates, have been used in the preparation of the financial statements;

(d) confirmation that applicable accounting standards have been followed, subject to any material departures disclosed and explained in the notes to the accounts.

3 Boards may also wish to use the above statement as a vehicle for reporting that they have maintained an effective system of internal control, and that the business is a going concern, with supporting assumptions or qualifications as necessary, once the necessary guidance on these subjects has been developed (see paragraphs 5.16 and 5.22 of the main report).

4 The above statement does not obviate the need for a formal statement in the notes to the accounts disclosing whether the accounts have been prepared in accordance with applicable accounting standards.

AUDIT COMMITTEES

APPENDIX 4

1 In the main body of the report the Committee recommends that all listed companies which have not already done so should establish an audit committee, and places great emphasis on the importance of properly constituted audit committees in raising standards of corporate governance.

2 Many UK companies already have an audit committee, and a recent research study ('Audit Committees in the United Kingdom', published by the ICAEW, April 1992) has found a steady growth in their number. Audit Committees are now established in 53% of the top 250 industrial firms in the Times 1000, and the figure rises to 66% if unlisted companies and foreign subsidiaries are excluded from the calculation. Most major UK listed financial institutions have also formed an audit committee.

3 Audit Committees are well established in the United States, where they have been a listing requirement of the New York Stock Exchange since 1978. A 1989 study revealed that 97% of major corporations had them. In Canada, they are a legal requirement.

4 If they operate effectively, audit committees can bring significant benefits. In particular, they have the potential to:

(a) improve the quality of financial reporting, by reviewing the financial statements on behalf of the Board;

(b) create a climate of discipline and control which will reduce the opportunity for fraud;

(c) enable the non-executive directors to contribute an independent judgement and play a positive role;

(d) help the finance director, by providing a forum in which he can raise issues of concern, and which he can use to get things done which might otherwise be difficult;

(e) strengthen the position of the external auditor, by providing a channel of communication and forum for issues of concern;

(f) provide a framework within which the external auditor can assert his independence in the event of a dispute with management;

(g) strengthen the position of the internal audit function, by providing a greater degree of independence from management;

(h) increase public confidence in the credibility and objectivity of financial statements.

5 The effectiveness of audit committees will be reduced, however, if they act as a barrier between the auditors and the executive directors on the main board, or if they encourage the main board to abdicate its responsibilities in the audit area, so weakening the board's collective responsibility for reviewing and approving the financial statements. They will also fall short of their potential if they lack the understanding to deal adequately with the auditing or accounting matters that they are likely to face, if they remain under the influence of any dominant personality on the main board, or if they simply get in the way and obstruct executive management, and stifle entrepreneurial skills.

6 Audit committees will be as good as the people on them: effectiveness depends crucially on a strong, independent chairman who has the confidence of the board and of the auditors, and on the quality of the non-executive directors. Structure is also important, however, and adherence to the following recommendations, repeated here from the main part of the report, will ensure that audit committees are soundly based.

(a) Audit committees should be formally constituted as sub-committees of the main board to whom they are answerable and to whom they should report regularly; they should be given written terms of reference which deal adequately with their membership, authority and duties; and they should normally meet at least twice a year.

(b) There should be a minimum of three members. Membership should be confined to the non-executive directors of the company and a majority of the non-executives serving on the committee should be independent of the company. This means that apart from their directors' fees and shareholdings, they should be independent of management and free from any business or other relationship which could materially interfere with the exercise of their independent judgement as a committee member. It is for the board to decide in individual cases whether this definition is met.

(c) The external auditor and, where an internal audit function exists, the head of internal audit should normally attend audit committee meetings, as should the finance director. Other board members should also have the right to attend.

(d) The committee should have a discussion with the auditors, at least once a year, without executive board members present, to ensure that there are no unresolved issues of concern.

(e) The audit committee should have explicit authority to investigate any matters within its terms of reference, the resources which it needs to do so, and full access to information. The committee should be able to obtain outside professional advice and if necessary to invite outsiders with relevant experience to attend meetings.

(f) Membership of the committee should be disclosed in the annual report and the chairman of the committee should be available to answer questions about its work at the Annual General Meeting.

7 Specimen terms of reference for an audit committee, compiled from the many examples that are available, are annexed. They are intended simply as a guide for companies who will wish to adapt and build on them to suit their own circumstances. They will particularly need tailoring for group rather than single company audit committees. The list of duties in the annex reflects the most commonly performed duties in the UK and the US but no single set of duties has emerged as standard practice.

8 There are many excellent publications on audit committees. The Committee's objective is not to rewrite them but to secure the widespread adoption of best practice. For further discussion of the duties and functioning of audit committees, readers are referred in particular to:

- Chapter 3 of the Report by the Institute of Chartered Accountants of Scotland entitled 'Corporate Governance – Directors' Responsibilities for Financial Statements', February 1992
- Guidance booklets produced by individual firms of accountants
- Chapter 2, section IV of the Report of the National Commission on Fraudulent Financial Reporting (the Treadway Commission), USA, October 1987
- 'Audit Committees in the United Kingdom' by P. Collier, published by the Institute of Chartered Accountants of England and Wales, April 1992.

ANNEX

Specimen Terms of Reference for an Audit Committee

FOR GUIDANCE ONLY

Constitution

1 The Board hereby resolves to establish a Committee of the Board to be known as the Audit Committee.

Membership

2 The Committee shall be appointed by the Board from amongst the Non-Executive Directors of the Company and shall consist of not less than three members. A quorum shall be two members.

3 The Chairman of the Committee shall be appointed by the Board.

Attendance at meetings

4 The Finance Director, the Head of Internal Audit, and a representative of the external auditors shall normally attend meetings. Other Board members shall also have the right of attendance. However, at least once a year the Committee shall meet with the external auditors without executive Board members present.

5 The Company Secretary shall be the Secretary of the Committee.

Frequency of meetings

6 Meetings shall be held not less than twice a year. The external auditors may request a meeting if they consider that one is necessary.

Authority

7 The Committee is authorised by the Board to investigate any activity within its terms of reference. It is authorised to seek any information it requires from any employee and all employees are directed to co-operate with any request made by the Committee.

8 The Committee is authorised by the Board to obtain outside legal or other independent professional advice and to secure the attendance of outsiders with relevant experience and expertise if it considers this necessary.

Duties

9 The duties of the Committee shall be:

(a) to consider the appointment of the external auditor, the audit fee, and any questions of resignation or dismissal;

(b) to discuss with the external auditor before the audit commences the nature and scope of the audit, and ensure co-ordination where more than one audit firm is involved;

(c) to review the half-year and annual financial statements before submission to the Board, focusing particularly on:

(i) any changes in accounting policies and practices

(ii) major judgemental areas

(iii) significant adjustments resulting from the audit

(iv) the going concern assumption

(v) compliance with accounting standards

(vi) compliance with stock exchange and legal requirements.

(d) to discuss problems and reservations arising from the interim and final audits, and any matters the auditor may wish to discuss (in the absence of management where necessary);

(e) to review the external auditor's management letter and management's response;

(f) to review the Company's statement on internal control systems prior to endorsement by the Board;

(g) (where an internal audit function exists) to review the internal audit programme, ensure co-ordination between the internal and external auditors, and ensure that the internal audit function is adequately resourced and has appropriate standing within the Company;

(h) to consider the major findings of internal investigations and management's response;

(i) to consider other topics, as defined by the board.

Reporting procedures

10 The Secretary shall circulate the minutes of meetings of the Committee to all members of the Board.

● ● REPORT OF THE COMMITTEE ON ● ●

THE FINANCIAL ASPECTS OF CORPORATE GOVERNANCE

COMPLIANCE WITH THE CODE OF BEST PRACTICE

24 MAY 1995

First published May 1995

ISBN 1 86089 006 7
(Report on Compliance with the Code of Best Practice)

Gee Publishing Ltd
South Quay Plaza
183 Marsh Wall
London E14 9FS
Freephone: 0800 289520
Fax: 0171 538 8623

Printed in Great Britain by Burgess Science Press

Summary of Main Conclusions

15 All listed companies whose accounts have been examined are complying with the London Stock Exchange listing requirement to make a statement in their report and accounts on the extent of their compliance with the Code of Best Practice. Statements of full compliance are most likely to be made by companies in the top 500, whilst the smaller the company the higher the percentage of statements disclosing limited compliance.

16 Although not a requirement of the Code, the majority of companies have split the roles of Chairman and Chief Executive, and where the roles are combined, there is more often than not an independent element of non-executive directors on the board, as recommended in the Report. There is a relationship between the size of a company and the number of non-executives on the board, with the larger companies most likely to have three or more. There has been a marked increase in the disclosure of Audit, Nomination and Remuneration Committees since the publication of the Code. The larger the company, the more likely it is to have three or more non-executive directors on the Audit Committee, but there has also been an increase in the disclosure of Audit Committees comprising two non-executives, particularly in smaller companies.

17 The majority of companies of all sizes have boards on which all or the majority of non-executive directors are independent. The larger the company, the more likely it is to have three or more independent non-executives on the board.

18 While larger companies have disclosed compliance with the requirement to have formal terms of appointment for non-executive directors, such disclosure decreases in relation to company size. However, high levels of compliance with both the requirement to have a schedule of matters reserved to the board and to have an agreed procedure for independent advice were found in companies of all sizes. There is a higher incidence in all the sample groups of rolling as opposed to fixed-term three-year contracts. The incidence of contracts in excess of three years (either rolling or fixed-term) is very low.

INSTITUTIONAL SHAREHOLDERS' COMMITTEE

Constituent Members:

Association of British Insurers
Association of Investment Trust Companies
British Merchant Banking and Securities Houses Association
The National Association of Pension Funds Ltd
Unit Trust Association

Institutional Shareholders' Committee, 10-15 Queen Street, London EC4N ITT

INSTITUTIONAL SHAREHOLDERS'COMMITTEE

The Role and Duties of Directors - A Statement of Best Practice

General Introduction

Institutional investors are increasingly being approached by companies and their advisers with requests to indicate what in their view would be the reasonable expectation of shareholders in such matters as the provisions governing the appointment and removal of directors, the duties of non-executive directors, directors' service contracts and emoluments, their borrowing powers etc.

The Companies Act imposes certain fundamental obligations in respect of disclosure of emoluments, service contracts etc. Beyond this and any obligations imposed on listed companies by the Listiner Agreement of The International Stock Exchange, however, there is a rich variety of practice in the composition of Boards of Directors of UK companies and in the approach to remuneration of directors, which reflects the widely different circumstances of companies across the whole spectrum of size and catecory.

The Institutional Shareholders' Committee (ISC) feels that a Statement of Best Practice such as this which summarises the views of institutional shareholders will enable these shareholders to give a more coherent and consistent response when their views and votes are solicited by companies. The ISC feels also that its publication will be helpful to companies and other interested bodies when considering, structure and practice in these areas.

The Statement of Best Practice clearly cannot be exhaustive. It is hoped that companies wl ill accept the general thrust of the Statement and that, in the absence of special circumstances, its sucraested provisions will be observed in company practice.

The ISC supports the United Kincrdom system of unitary boards. All directors have an equal responsibility in helpincr to provide their company with effective u'dance and leadership and it is recognised that they must, and in almost all cases do, act at all times entirely in the best interests of the company. In this context the Companies Act, The International Stock Exchancre book "Admission of Securities to Listinex" (i.e. the Listincy Acyreement or "Yellow Book") and the Takeover Code all contain provisions which are relevant to the contents of this Statement, to which reference should be made where appropriate.

Appointment and Removal of Directors

A director must be elected by the Company in General Meeting unless provision is made otherwise. The directors may appoint additional directors if the Articles so provide and any chance in the directorate must be notified to the International Stock Exchange immediately. Such an appointment terminates automatically at the next Annual General Meetin(y when the director would normally be ell(ylble for election at that meeting..

It is suggested that, as a matter of good practice, these further provisions should be observed:-

(a) The Articles should provide for a maximum as well as a minimum number of directors. One-third of the directors should be subject to retirement by rotation each year. They can stand for re-election if they so choose.

(b) The combination of the roles of Chairman and Chief Executive constitutes a concentration of power and can give rise to conflicts. The Board has the power to appoint, monitor the performance of and, if necessary, dismiss the Chief Executive. This may be difficult if the Chief Executive is also the Chairman. The roles of Chairman and Chief Executive should not, therefore, normally be combined. In circumstances where they are combined it is unlikely that institutional shareholders will be satisfied unless there is a strong body of independent non-executive directors who are aware of their overall responsibilities to shareholders (outlined below).

(c) Where companies feel that they must provide for divisional or assistant directors or some other category whose title includes the word director, such persons must be clearly seen not to have any statutory authority or ability to act on behalf of the company in the capacity of a director.

(d) The Articles should provide that a director may be dismissed from his or her office by written resolution of all co-directors (or at the very least a majority of 75% of co-directors) who should obtain shareholder approval at the next general meeting for their course of action.

(e) The Articles should provide that a director may be dismissed from office by his or her fellow directors for failure to attend a specified number of meetings of the Board "or Board Meetings held in a specific period".

(f) Brief biographical details of each director should be set out in the Annual Report showing the director's relevant experience and suitability. In particular, the Annual Report should disclose the ages of all directors and in the cases of those aged over 70, on the occasion when they stand for election or re-election, an explanation of why it is felt appropriate that such directors be retained.

Non-Executive Directors

Institutional shareholders stronaly support the presence of independent directors on Boards of companies. There has been a growing awareness of the value of audit committees and the importance of non-executive directors has become evident, particularly in matters concerninc top manaaement succession, remuneration of the senior management and in circumstances where there is potential for conflict of interest such as management buy-outs. They have a primary function to comment on corporate strategy where they can brine an objectivity and independence of view borne by their outside experience. While it is recognised that in some instances professional advisers bring their own particular expertise to this role, the value of the independent non-executive director is the independence, personality and experience which he or she can contribute to the deliberations of the Board.

A detailed Code of Recommended Practice on non-executive directors published by ProNed, which institutional shareholders fully endorse, includes the following main tasks of non-executive directors:

i) to contribute an independent view to the Board's deliberations;
ii) to help the Board provide the company with effective leadership;
iii) to ensure the continuing effectiveness of the executive directors and management;
iv) to ensure high standards of financial probity on the part of the company.

It is suggested that, as a matter of good practice, these further provisions should be observed:

(a) The non-executive directors should be sufficient in number and calibre for their views to carry significant weight on the Board. This is particularly necessary if the roles of Chairman and Chief Executive are combined.

(b) While all directors have a duty to monitor the performance of a company, the nonexecutive directors should acknowledge a particular duty to monitor the performance of the Board as a whole, and to report to the shareholders if they are not satisfied after reasonable efforts have been made by them to remedy the causes of their dissatisfaction.

(c) Non-executive directors should be independent, i.e. free from bias, involvement or partiality. It is recognised that professional advisers such as merchant bankers and solicitors may well fulfil a specialist role but they should not be regarded as a substitute for the independent non-executive director. Independence is more likely to be assured inter alia when the director:

(i) Has not been employed in any executive capacity by the company concerned within the last few years.

(ii) Is not retained as a professional adviser by the company (either personally or through his or her firm) and

(iii) Is not a significant supplier or customer of the company.

(d) In order not to impair their impartiality, non-executive directors should not, under normal circumstances, be offered participation in share option schemes, nor in performance related or other incentivised remuneration schemes, nor in any company pension schemes. They should not be entitled to any compensation for loss of office.

(e) Non-executive directors should hold other directorships in the same industry only with the approval of the board.

Service Contracts

As a matter of law and Stock Exchange requirements, copies of all directors' service contracts with an unexpired term of 12 months or more must be made available in an accessible place for inspection by shareholders. Service contracts may not be entered into for a period in excess of five years without the consent of the company in general meetings. The unexpired period of any service contract must be disclosed where a director is being proposed for re-election.

It is suggested that, as a matter of good practice, these further provisions should be observed:-

(a) All service contracts should be approved by a Compensation Committee.

(b) Despite the legislative provisions, contracts should not run for a period of more than three years and there may be circumstances where a rolling contract should be limited to a period of no more than one year.

(c) Service contracts should not permit the executive directors to engage in, or have an interest in, any business similar to that carried on by any group company except with approval of the Board (thoucrh the ability to hold shares in listed companies carryiner on such business is accepted).

Emoluments

The disclosure required in the Annual Report of directors' emoluments and of any compensation payments in respect of loss of office made to directors is considered by institutional shareholders to be an important feature of company legislation.

The Companies Act and The International Stock Exchange impose certain requirements governing such payments includina the issue of shares and grant of loans, guarantees etc.

It is suagested that, as a matter of good practice, these further provisions should be observed:-

(a) A Compensation Committee should be appointed by the Board, consisting solely or mainly of non-executive directors (and in the latter case chaired by a non-executive director). The Committee's function is to determine the salaries and emoluments packaaes of the executive directors. This would include salaries and also participation in share options, profit sharing and incentive remuneration schemes and all other bonuses and benefits receivable by the executive directors. Executive directors should not play any part in deciding their own compensation packages. The composition of the Compensation Committee should be disclosed in the Annual Report.

(b) Those companies which do not have a sufficient body of non-executive directors to form a Compensation Committee should take steps to remedy the situation. In the interim their Annual Report should state the method by which all directors' compensation is determined.

(c) A summary of the details of any performance-linked remuneration schemes and of all types of share option and other incentive and profit sharing and bonus schemes should be disclosed in the Annual Report.

(d) Details of any ex gratia payments or payments by way of compensation should be disclosed to shareholders in the Annual Report and Accounts.

(e) It is in general undesirable that details of any compensation payments or ex gratia payments should be subject to confidentiality agreements or similar arrangements.

Duty to Employees

The Companies Act 1985 states inter-alia that "the matters to which the directors of a company are to have regard in the performance of their functions include the interests of the company's employees in general, as well as the interests of its' members".

The ISC considers it important that this onus placed on directors by the Companies Act should not be overlooked. Directors should appreciate the significance of the role played in a company's progress by its workforce and should always consider the interests of all those involved in working together to improve their company's performance.

Borrowing Powers

There is no requirement either under the Statutes or under the Listing Agreement that the powers of directors to borrow on behalf of a company should be limited.

It is suggested that, as a matter of good practice, there should be a reasonable limit under the Articles of Association on the power of the directors to borrow, which should relate to the borrowings of the group as a whole. It is desirable that the amount permitted under the Borrowing Powers Article should be stated in the Annual Report and Accounts.

Director of Companies in Difficulties

The Insolvency Act 1986 impose obligations on a director once he knows that the company is unlikely to avoid insolvent liquidation.

Management Buy-Outs

Considerable concern has been expressed at the inadequacy of information given to shareholders, particularly when compared with the knowledge of the business held by the management buy-out team, and also of the need to have competent independent advice. The advent of a takeover or a management buy-out imposes obligations on management to make all. relevant information available and the Takeover Code imposes quite stringent obligations in bid situations. Given the potential for conflicts of interest, however, where the buy-out consortium comprises or includes management, the need for full disclosure and independent advice becomes more acute.

It is suggested that, as a matter of good practice, these further provisions should be observed:-

(a) The directors must use their best endeavours to ensure that there is made available to shareholders sufficient information to enable them properly to assess the value of the company or other assets which it is proposed to sell.

(b) Ideally, the Board should appoint a separate committee consistlncr wholly or mainly of non-executive directors with direct access to independent advisers. The independent advisers should have access to all information necessary to enable them to give a fully informed opinion as to the merits of the offer. The committee should be responsible for a separate statement to shareholders, giving the views both of itself and of the independent advisers on the bid.

(c) The consortium should not have access to the company's usual professional advisers, since this would agaravate the conflict of interest.

In December 1989 the Institutional Shareholders' Committee issued a more detailed Guidance Note to those involved in management buy-outs, to which the reader is also referred.

18th April 1991

INSTITUTIONAL SHAREHOLDERS'COMMITTEE

Constituent Members:

Association of British Insurers
Association of Investment Trust Companies
British Merchant Banking and Securities Houses Association
The National Association of Pension Funds Ltd
Unit Trust Association

Institutional Shareholders' Committee, 51 Gresham Street, London EC2V 7HQ

INSTITUTIONAL SHAREHOLDERS' COMMITTEE

The Responsibilities of Institutional Shareholders in the UK

1. Introduction

The IS C's Statement of Best Practice on the Role and Duties of Directors was published in April 199 1. Implicit in that document was the understanding that shareholders are the true proprietors of a company. This ownership gives rise to responsibilities which have, for many years, been acknowledged by a large number of institutional shareholders. This document considers the nature of those responsibilities against the background of the overriding obligations of @titutional investors, which must be to those on whose behalf they invest.

2. Communication

Because of the size of their shareholdings, institutional investors, as part proprietors of a company, are under a strong obligation to exercise their influence in a responsible manner. Many institutions already have effective channels of communication with the Boards of companies in which they invest, both directly and through advisers. Such channels need to be developed more widely if the conununication process is to be made more effective.

Shareholders receive Reports and Accounts and other explanatory circulars from companies which are required by statute or for example by the Stock Exchange. They also have the right to attend company meetings where they can raise questions about the affairs of the company. These are formal methods of communication, but in themselves they may not be sufficient to establish the type of direct relationship which enables directors and shareholders to obtain a deeper understanding of each other's aims and requirements.

It is felt, therefore, that institutional shareholders have a responsibility actively to encourage contact with companies which will include contact at senior executive level on both sides. Such dialogue will enable shareholders to gain a better appreciation of the management's objectives, the problems confronting it and the quality of those involved, while also focusing the attention of management more sharply on the expectations and requirements of shareholders.

Institutions do not wish to be made insiders, and such contacts should not include the transmission of price-sensitive infomiation. Where, exceptionally, there are compelling reasons for a Board to consult institutional shareholders on issues which are price-sensitive, those shareholders may have to accept that such consultation would involve the receipt of confidences which will require that they suspend their ability to deal in the company's shares. It is important that such confidences are not disclosed to investors by companies or their advisers inadvertently or without the investors' prior consent.

A meaningful and established conununications process will assume a special importance when
there is a bid, whether the company concemed is the recipient of a bid or is itself the offeror.

3. Voting

Shareholders' ability to influence management depends on the proportion of the votes which they can exercise and the use they make of these votes.

It is considered important that institutional shareholders support Boards by a positive use of their voting rights unless they have good reasons for doing otherwise. Such shareholders should register their votes wherever possible on a regular basis. Where a Board has received steady support over a period of time, it should become a matter of concem to the Board if that support is not forthcoming on a particular matter.

There will be occasions when an institutional investor will feel it appropriate to vote against a proposal which it considers undesirable. In such circumstances it is important that, wherever possible, representations are made in time for the problem to be considered and for consultation to take place witli a view to achievina a satisfactory solution. Where a satisfactory outcome cannot be achieved on an important issue, it may be desirable for a spokesperson to attend the relevant meeting of the company and explain why the particular proposal is being opposed. In such cases a poll should be demanded to ensure that the vote is duly recorded.

In view of the foregoing, institutional shareholders have for many years been opposed to the creation of equity shares which do not carry full voting rights and have sought the enfranchisement of existing restricted voting or non-voting shares.

4. Composition of the Board

The composition of a company's Board must be a matter of legitimate concern to shareholders. They have the opportunity to confirm all appointments to the Board which are initiated by the existing directors, and there is a growina acceptance that a properly balanced Board is essential to the wellbeing of a company. Institutions individually, or where appropriate collectively, are increasingly prepared to suggest chanae to remedy perceived weaknesses and where necessary to encourage Boards to appoint an adequate number of independent non-executive directors. Institutional shareholders seek to identify serious deficiencies at an early stage, and to initiate appropriate action. The most effective action is taken quickly, and without publicity. It is exceptional for such initiatives to be taken collectively, because of the need for speed of action, and confidentiality. It is also undesirable for more than the minimum number of individuals to receive information or knowledge of events which at times may be highly price-sensitive.

Institutional shareholders have urged, and should fully support, the appointment of Compensation and Audit Committees, whose value is becoming widely recognised.

5. Emoluments of Directors and Senior Managers

As a matter of general principle the emoluments of Executive Directors and Senior Management are a matter for the Board, and this should be dealt with by an independent Compensation Committee. Adequate disclosure of the principles upon which directors' emoluments are determined is essential, however, so that shareholders are made aware of performance-linked contracts and so as to ensure that in the event of a contract beina terminated prematurely, any compensation for loss of office will not become a matter of contention between shareholders and remaining directors.

6. Takeover Bids

The greatest potential for tension between management and shareholders arises when a company becomes the object of a takeover bid wliich is launched without prior agreement of the incumbent Board. There may be added tension when a bid emanates from overseas, where the offeror may not be vulnerable to the same market pressures.

Institutional shareholders have a primary duty to those on whose behalf they invest and they should, therefore, consider all offers objectively. They should listen carefully to the arguments of both offeror and offeree before coming to a decision on their merits. They should not, and generally do not, conunit themselves to a particular course of action until they have taken the opportunity to consider the best information available.

When a bid is in the fonn of cash or shares with an underwritten cash alternative, additional considerations will apply because the future value of income stream or capital growth is crystallised. This value is certain and may well be at such a high level that the institutions' fiduciary responsibilities cannot be ignored.

Where a company has kept its shareholders infon-ned of its long tenn plans, confidence and understanding will have developed between management and shareholders, making it less likely that a hostile bid will succeed. Where good relations have been established and shareholders understand the lona term objectives of management they are more likely to support the incumbent Board in its resistance to an unwelcome bid.

Some considerations, such as the impact of a takeover on competition or on the ptiblic or national interests, must be the direct concem of government. The professional and fiduciary obligations of institutional shareholders must override such considerations, in the absence of goverm-nent action.

SUMMARY

The foregoing may be summarised in the following principles of good practice:

(a) Institutional investors should encourage regular, systematic contact at senior executive level to exchange views and information on strategy, performance, Board membership and quality of management.

(b) Institutional investors will not wish to receive price sensitive information as a result of such dialogue but may agree to accept it on an exceptional basis as the price of a long-term relationship, although this would require that they suspend their ability to deal in the shares.

(c) Institutional investors are opposed to the creation of equity shares which do not carry full voting rights.

(d) Institutional investors should support Boards by a positive use of voting ricrhts, unless they have good reasons for doing otherwise. Reasons for votincer against a motion should be made known to the Board beforehand.

e) Institutional investors should take a positive interest in the composition of Boards of Directors, with particular reference to:

(i) Concentrations of decision-making power not formally constrained by checks and balances appropriate to the particular company.

(ii) The appointment of a core of non-executives of appropriate calibre, experience and independence.

(f) Institutional investors support the appointment of Compensation and Audit Committees.

(g) Institutional investors encourage disclosure of the principles upon which directors' emoluments are determined.

(h) In takeover situations institutional investors will consider all offers on their merits and will not commit themselves to a particular course of action until they have reviewed the best and most up-to-date information available.

(i) In all investment decision-making institutional investors have a fiduciary responsibility to those on whose behalf they are investin or, which must override other considerations.

December 1991

DIRECTORS' REMUNERATION

Report of a

Study Group

chaired by

Sir Richard Greenbury

17 July 1995

First published July 1995

ISBN 1 86089 012 1

Additional copies of the report, at £10.00 per copy, may be obtained from:

Gee Publishing Ltd
(a division of Professional Publishing Ltd)
South Quay Plaza
183 Marsh Wall
London E14 9FS
Freephone: (0800) 289520
Fax: (0171) 537-2557

Designed by Design Directive.
Printed in Great Britain by Burgess Science Press.

2 CODE OF BEST PRACTICE

Introduction

2.1 The purpose of the accompanying Code is to set out best practice in determining and accounting for Director's remuneration. The references at the end of each provision of the Code are to the fuller discussion in sections 4 to 7.

2.2 The detailed provisions have been prepared with large companies mainly in mind, but the principles apply equally to smaller companies.

2.3 We recommend that all listed companies registred in the UK should comply with the Code to the fullest extent practicable and include a statement about their compliance in the annual reports to shareholders by their remuneration committees or elsewhere in their annual reports and accounts. Any areas of non-compliance should be explained and justified.

2.4 We further recommend that the London Stock Exchange should introduce the following continuing obligations for listed companies:

- an obligation to include in their annual remuneration committee reports to shareholders or their annual reports a general statement about their compliance with section A of the Code which should explain and justify any areas of non-compliance;

- a specific obligation to comply with the provisions in section B of the Code which are not already covered by existing obligations, and with provision C10 of the Code, subject to any changes of wording which may be desirable for legal or technical reasons.

2.5 Within section B, provision B3 requires remuneration committees to confirm that full consideration has been given to sections C and D of the Code.

The Code

A The remuneration commmittee

A1 To avoid potential conflicts of interest, Boards of Directors should set up remuneration committees of Non-Executive Directors to determine on their behalf, and on behalf of the shareholders, within agreed terms of reference, the company's policy on executive remuneration and specific remuneration packages for each of the Executive Directors, including pension rights and any compensation payments (paragraphs 4.3 - 4.7).

A2 Remuneration committee Chairmen should account directly to the shareholders through the means specified in this Code for the decisions their committees reach (paragraph 4.4).

A3 Where necessary, companies' Articles of Association should be amended to enable remuneration committees to discharge these functions on behalf of the Board (paragraph 4.3).

A4 Remuneration committees should consist exclusively of Non-Executive Directors with no personal financial interest other than as shareholders in the matters to be decided, no potential conflicts of interest arising from cross-directorships and no day-to-day involvement in running the business (paragraphs 4.8 and 4.11).

A5 The members of the remuneration committee should be listed each year in the committee's report to shareholders (B1 below). When they stand for re-election, the proxy cards should indicate their membership) of the committee (paragraphs 4.12 and 5.25).

A6 The Board itself should determine the remuneration of the Non-Executive Directors, including members of the remuneration committee, within the limits set in the Articles of Association (paragraph 4.13).

A7 Remuneration committees should consult the company Chairman and/or Chief Executive about their proposals and have access to professional advice inside and outside the company (paragraphs 4.14 - 4.17).

A8 The remuneration committee Chairman should attend the company's Annual General Meeting (AGM) to answer shareholders' questions about Director's remuneration and should ensure that the company maintains contact as required with its principal shareholders about remuneration in the same way as for other matters (paragraph 5.27)

A9 The committee's annual report to shareholders (B1 below) should not be a standard item of agenda for AGMs. But the committee should consider each year whether the circumstances are such that the AGM should be invited to approve the policy set out in their report and should minute their conclusions (paragraphs 5.28 - 5.32).

B Disclosure and approval provisions

B1 The remuneration committee should make a report each year to the shareholders on behalf of the Board. The report should form part of, or be annexed to, the conoany's Annual Report and Accounts. It should be the main vehicle through which the Company accounts to shareholders for Directors' remuneration (paragraph 5.4).

B2 The report should set out the Company's policy on executive Directors' remuneration, including levels, comparator groups of companies, individual components, performance criteria and measurement, pension provision, contracts of service and compensation commitments on early termination (paragraphs 5.5 - 5.7).

B3 The report should state that, in fraiming its remuneration policy, the committee has given full consideration to the best practice provisions set out in sections C and D below (paragraph 5.25).

B4 The report should also include full details of all elements in the remuneration package of each individual Director by name, such as basic salary, benefits in kind, annual bonuses and long-term incentive schemes including share options (paragraphs 5.8 - 5.12).

B5 Information on share options, including SAYE options, should be given for each Director in accordance with the recommendations of the Accounting Standards Board's Urgent Issues Task Force Abstract 10 and its successors (paragraphs 5.13 - 5.16).

B6 If grants under executive share option or other long-term incentive schemes are awarded in one large block rather than phased, the report should explain and justify paragraph 6.29).

B7 Also included in the report should be pension entitlements earned by each individual Director during the year, calculated on a basis to be recommended by the Faculty of Actuaries and the Institute of Actuaries (paragraphs 5.17-5.23).

B8 If annual bonuses or benefits in kind; are pensionable the report should explain and justify (paragraph 6.44).

B9 The amounts received by, and commitments made to, each Director uinder B4, B5 and B7 should be subject to audit (paragraph 5.4).

B10 Any service contracts which provide for, or imply, notice periods in excess of one year (or any provisions for predetermined compensation on termination which exceed one year's salary and benefits) should be disclosed and the reasons for the longer notice Periods explained (paragraph 7.13).

B11 Shareholdings and other relevant business interests and activities of the Directors should continue to be disclosed as required in the Companies Acts and London Stock Exchange Listing Rules (paragraph 5.24).

B12 Shareholders should be invited specifically to approve all new long-term incentive schemes (including share option schemes) whether payable in cash or shares in which Directors and senior executives will participate which potentially commit shareholders' funds over more than one year or dilute the equity (paragraph 5.33).

C Remuneration policy

C1 Remuneration committees must provide the packages needed to attract, retain and motivate Directors of quality required but should avoid paying more than is necessary, for this purpose (paragraphs 6.5 - 6.7).

C2 Remuneration committees should judge where to position their company relative to other companies. They should be aware what other comparable companies are paying and should take account of relative performance (paragraphs 6.11-6.12).

C3 Remuneration committees should be sensitive to the wider scene, including pay and employment conditions elsewhere in the company, especially when determining annual salary increases (paragraph 6.13).

Code of Best Practice

C4 The performance-related elements of remuneration should be designed to align the interests of Directors and shareholders and to give Directors keen incentives to perform at the highest levels (paragraph 6.16).

C5 Remuneration committees should consider whether their Directors should be eligible for annual bonuses. If so, performance conditions should be relevant, stretching and designed to enhance the business. Upper limits should always be considered. There may be a case for part-payment in shares to be held for a significant period (paragraphs 6.19 - 6.22).

C6 Remuneration committees should consider whether their Directors should be eligible for benefits under long-term incentive schemes. Traditional share option schemes should be weighed against other kinds of long-term incentive scheme. In normal circumstances, shares granted should not vest, and options should not be exercisable in under three years. Directors should be encouraged to hold their shares for a further period after vesting or exercise subject to the need to finance any costs of acquisition and associated tax liability (paragraphs 6.23 - 6.34).

C7 Any new long-term incentive schemes which are proposed should preferably replace existing schemes or at least form part of a well-considered overall plan incorporating existing schemes, which should be approved as a whole by shareholders. The total rewards potentially available should not be excessive (paragraph) 6.35). (*See* also B12.)

C8 Grants under all incentive schemes, including new grants under existing share options schemes, should be subject to challenging performance criteria reflecting the company's objectives. Consideration should he given to criteria which reflect the company's performance relative to a group of comparator companies in some key variables such as total shareholder return (paragraphs 6.38 - 6.40).

C9 Grants under executive share option and other long-term incentive schemes should be phased rather than awarded in one large block (paragraph 6.29). (*See* B6.)

C10 Executive share options should never, be issued at a discount (paragraph 6.29).

C11 Remuneration committees should consider the pension consequences and associated costs to the company of basic salary increases, especially for Directors close to retirement (paragraphs 6.42 - 6.45).

C12 In general, neither annual, bonuses nor benefits in kind should he pensionable (paragraph 6.44) (*See* B8).

D Service contracts and compensation

D1 Remuneration committees should consider, what compensation commitments their Directors' contracts of service, if any, would entail in the event of early termination, particularly for unsatisfactory performance (paragraph 7.10).

D2 There is a strong case for setting notice or contract periods, at, or reducing them to one year or less (*see* B10). Remuneration committees should, however, be sensitive and flexible, especially over timing. In some cases notice or contract periods of up to two years may be acceptable. Longer periods should be avoided wherever possible (paragraphs 7.11 - 7.15).

D3 If it is necessary to offer longer notice or contract periods, such as three years, to new Directors recruited from outside, such periods should reduce after the initial period (paragraph 7.16).

D4 Within the legal constraints remuneration committees should tailor their approach in individual early termination cases to the wide variety of circumstances. The broad aim should be to avoid rewarding poor Performance while dealing fairly with cases where departure is not due to poor performance (paragraphs 7.17 - 7.18).

D5 Remuneration committees should take a robust line on payment of compensation where performance has been unsatisfactory and on reducing compensation to reflect departing Directors' obligations to mitigate damages by earning money elsewhere (paragraphs 7.19 - 7.20).

D6 Where appropriate, and in particular where notice or contract periods exceed one year, companies should consider paying all or part of compensation in instalments rather than one lump sum and reducing or stopping payment when the former Director takes on new employment (paragraph 7.20).

General Motors, Washington 1995

GUIDELINES ON SIGNIFICANT CORPORATE GOVERNANCE ISSUES

Selection and Composition of the Board

1) Board Membership Criteria

The Committee on Director Affairs is responsible for reviewing with the Board, on an annual basis, the appropriate skills and characteristics required of Board members in the context of the current make-up of the Board. This assessment should include issues of diversity, age, skills such as understanding of manufacturing technologies, international background, etc. -- all in a context of an assessment of the perceived needs of the Board at that point in time.

2) Selection and Orientation of New Directors

The Board itself should be responsible, in fact as well as procedure, for selecting its own members and in recommending them for election by the stockholders. The Board delegates the screening process involved to the Committee on Director Affairs with the direct input from the Chairman of the Board, as well as the Chief Executive Officer. The Board and the Company have a complete orientation process for new Directors that includes background material, meetings with senior management and visits to Company facilities.

3) Extending the Invitation to a Potential Director to Join the Board

The invitation to join the Board should be extended by the Board itself, by the Chairman of the Committee on Director Affairs (if the Chairman and CEO hold the same position), the Chairman of the Board, and the Chief Executive Officer of the Company.

Board Leadership

4) Selection of Chairman and CEO

The Board should be free to make this choice any way that seems best for the Company at a given point in time.

Therefore, the Board does not have a policy, one way or the other, on whether or not the role of the Chief Executive and Chairman should be separate and, if it is to be separate, whether the Chairman should be selected from the non-employee Directors or be an employee.

5) Lead Director Concept

The Board adopted a policy that it will have a Director selected by the outside Directors who will assume the responsibility of chairing the regularly scheduled meetings of outside Directors or other responsibilities which the outside Directors as a whole might designate from time to time.

Currently, this role is filled by the non-executive Chairman of the Board. Should the Company be organized in such a way that the Chairman is an employee of the Company, another director would be selected for this responsibility.

Board Composition and Performance

6) Size of the Board

The Board presently has 14 members. It is the sense of the Board that a size of 15 is about right.

However, the Board would be willing to go to a somewhat larger size in order to accommodate the availability of an outstanding candidate(s).

7) Mix of Inside and Outside Directors

The Board believes that as a matter of policy there should be a majority of independent Directors on the GM Board (as stipulated in By-law 2.12). The Board is willing to have members of Management, in addition to the Chief Executive Officer, as Directors. But the Board believes that Management should encourage senior managers to understand that Board membership is not necessary or a prerequisite to any higher management position in the Company. Managers other than the Chief Executive Officer currently attend Board meetings on a regular basis even though they are not members of the Board.

On matters of corporate governance, the Board assumes decisions will be made by the outside directors.

8) Board Definition of What Constitutes Independence for Outside Directors

GM's By-law defining independent directors was approved by the Board in January 1991. The Board believes there is no current relationship between any outside director and GM that would be construed in any way to compromise any Board member being designated independent. Compliance with the By-law is reviewed annually by the Committee on Director Affairs.

9) Former Chief Executive Officer's Board Membership

The Board believes this is a matter to be decided in an individual instance. It is assumed that when the Chief Executive Officer resigns from that position, he/she should offer his/her resignation from the Board at the same time. Whether the individual continues to serve on the Board is a matter for discussion at that time with the new Chief Executive Officer and the Board.

A former Chief Executive Officer serving on the Board will be considered an inside director forpurposes of corporate governance.

10) Directors Who Change their Present Job Responsibility

It is the sense of the Board that individual directors who change the responsibility they held when they were elected to the Board should submit a letter of resignation to the Board.

It is not the sense of the Board that in every instance the Directors who retire or change from the position they held when they came on the Board should necessarily leave the Board. There should, however, be an opportunity for the Board, via the Committee of Director Affairs, to review the continued appropriateness of Board membership under these circumstances.

11) Term Limits

The Board does not believe it should establish term limits. While term limits could help insure that there are fresh ideas and viewpoints available to the Board, they hold the disadvantage of losing the contribution of directors who have been able to develop, over a period of time, increasing insight into the Company and its operations and, therefore, provide an increasing contribution to the Board as a whole.

As an alternative to term limits, the Committee on Director Affairs, in consultation with the Chief Executive Officer and the Chairman of the Board, will review each director's continuation on the Board every five years. This will also allow each director the opportunity to conveniently confirm his/her desire to continue as a member of the Board.

12) Retirement Age

It is the sense of the Board that the current retirement age of 70 is appropriate.

13) Board Compensation Review

It is appropriate for the staff of the Company to report once a year to the Committee on Director Affairs the status of GM Board compensation in relation to other large US companies. As part of a Director's total compensation and to create a direct linkage with corporate performance, the Board believes that a meaningful portion of a Director's compensation should be provided in common stock units.

Change in Board compensation, if any, should come at the suggestion of the Committee on Director Affairs, but with full discussion and concurrence by the Board.

14) Executive Sessions of Outside Directors

These outside Directors of the Board will meet in Executive Session three times each year. The format of these meetings will include a discussion with the Chief Executive Officer on each occasion.

15) Assessing the Board's Performance

The Committee on Director Affairs is responsible to report annually to the Board an assessment of the Board's performance. This will be discussed with the full Board. This should be done following the end of each fiscal year and at the same time as the report on Board membership criteria.

This assessment should be of the Board's contribution as a whole and specifically review areas in which the Board and/or the Management believes a better contribution could be made. Its purpose is to increase the effectiveness of the Board, not to target individual Board members.

16) Board Interaction with Institutional Investors, the Press, Customers, etc.

The Board believes that the Management speaks for General Motors. Individual Board members may, from time to time at the request of the Management, meet or otherwise communicate with various constituencies that are involved with General Motors. If comments from the Board are appropriate, they should, in most circumstances, come from the Chairman.

Board Relationship to Senior Management

17) Regular Attendance of Non-Directors at Board Meetings

The Board is comfortable with the regular attendance at each Board meeting of non-Board members who are members of the President's Council.

Should the Chief Executive Officer want to add additional people as attendees on a regular basis, it is expected that this suggestion would be made to the Board for its concurrence.

18) Board Access to Senior Management

Board members have complete access to GM's Management.

It is assumed that Board members will use judgment to be sure that this contact is not distracting to the business operation of the Company and that such contact, if in writing, be copied to the Chief Executive and the Chairman.

Furthermore, the Board encourages the Management to, from time to time, bring managers into Board meetings who: (a) can provide additional insight into the items being discussed because of personal involvement in these areas; and/or (b) represent managers with future potential that the senior management believes should be given exposure to the Board.

Meeting Procedures

19) Selection of Agenda Items for Board Meetings

The Chairman of the Board and the Chief Executive Officer (if the Chairman is not Chief Executive Officer) will establish the agenda for each Board meeting.

Each Board member is free to suggest the inclusion of item(s) on the agenda.

20) Board Materials Distributed in Advance

It is the sense of the Board that information and data that are important to the Board's understanding of the business be distributed in writing to the Board before the Board meets. The Management will make every attempt to see that this material is as brief as possible while still providing the desired information.

21) Board Presentations

As a general rule, presentations on specific subjects should be sent to the Board members in advance so that Board meeting time may be conserved and discussion time focused on questions that the Board has about the material. On those occasions in which the subject matter is too sensitive to put on paper, the presentation will be discussed at the meeting.

Committee Matters

22) Number, Structure and Independence of Committees

The current Committee structure of the Company seems appropriate. There will, from time to time, be occasions in which the Board may want to form a new Committee or disband a current Committee depending upon the circumstances. The current six Committees are Audit, Capital Stock, Director Affairs, Finance, Incentive and Compensation, and Public Policy. The Committee membership, with the exception of the Finance Committee, will consist only of independent Directors as stipulated in By-law 2.12.

23) Assignment and Rotation of Committee Members

The Committee on Director Affairs is responsible, after consultation with the Chief Executive Officer and with consideration of the desires of individual Board members, for the assignment of Board members to various Committees.

It is the sense of the Board that consideration should be given to rotating Committee members periodically at about a five-year interval, but the Board does not feel that such a rotation should be mandated as a policy since there may be reasons at a given point in time to maintain an individual Director's Committee membership for a longer period.

24) Frequency and Length of Committee Meetings

The Committee Chairman, in consultation with Committee members, will determine the frequency and length of the meetings of the Committee.

25) Committee Agenda

The Chairman of the Committee, in consultation with the appropriate members of management and staff, will develop the Committee's agenda.

Each Committee will issue a schedule of agenda subjects to be discussed for the ensuing year at the beginning of each year (to the degree these can be set). This forward agenda will also be shared with the Board.

Leadership Development

26) Formal Evaluation of the Chief Executive Officer

The full Board (outside Directors) should make this evaluation annually, and it should be communicated to the Chief Executive Officer by the (non-executive) Chairman of the Board or the Lead Director.

The evaluation should be based on objective criteria including performance of the business, accomplishment of long-term strategic objectives, development of Management, etc.

The evaluation will be used by the Executive Compensation Committee in the course of its deliberations when considering the compensation of the Chief Executive Officer.

27) Succession Planning

There should be an annual report by the Chief Executive Officer to the Board on succession planning.

There should also be available, on a continuing basis, the Chief Executive Officer's recommendation as to his successor should he/she be unexpectedly disabled.

28) Management Development

There should be an annual report to the Board by the Chief Executive Officer on the Company's program for Management development.

This report should be given to the Board at the same time as the succession planning report, noted previously.

ARCO (Atlantic Richfield Company, Los Angeles)

CORPORATE GOVERNANCE PRINCIPLES

Note: ARCO's Board of Directors adopted the following set of principles in December 1995. They are reprinted here for the information of all stockholders.

ROLE AND COMPOSITION OF THE BOARD OF DIRECTORS

1. Except for those matters reserved for decision by the Company's stockholders, the Board of Directors is the ultimate decision-making body of the Company. The Board's primary responsibility is to oversee the affairs of the Company for the benefit of its stockholders. It elects the senior management team, which is charged with the conduct of the Company's business, acts as an advisor and counselor to this team and monitors its performance. It is the general policy of the Board that all major decisions be considered by the Board as a whole.

2. It is the policy of the Board that the majority of its members be Outside Directors and that the number of directors not exceed a number that can function efficiently as a body. The Company's By-laws provide that the number of directors shall be fixed from time to time by resolution of the Board. "Outside Director" means a director who:

   - a. Is not a member of management and has not been a member of management for a minimum of 5 years;
   - b. Has no close family relationship with any member of executive management;
   - c. Is not a significant advisor, consultant, or supplier to the Company; and
   - d. Does not have any other relationship with the Company that, in the opinion of the Board, could be considered to affect the director's ability to exercise his/her independent judgment as a director.

3. In furtherance of its policy of having major decisions made by the Board as a whole, the Company has a broad orientation process for new Board members that includes extensive materials, meetings with key management, and visits to Company facilities.

4. It is the policy of the Board that the positions of Chairman of the Board and Chief Executive Officer be held by the same person, except in unusual circumstances. This combination has served the Company well over many years. It is also the policy of the Board that an employee director shall resign from the Board coincident with his/her retirement as an employee of the Company. However, upon such employee director's retirement, the Board may invite the employee director to remain on the Board in order for the Company to profit from continued access to

such former employee director's expertise. This option will be reviewed by the Corporate Governance Committee at the time of an employee director's retirement, and decided by the full Board.

5. The Chairman and Chief Executive Officer is responsible for establishing effective communications with the Company's stakeholder groups, i.e., stockholders, customers, Company associates, communities, suppliers, creditors, governments, and corporate partners. It is the policy of the Board that management speaks for the Company.

COMMITTEE STRUCTURE, COMPOSITION AND PRACTICES

1. Committee Structure

   In furtherance of its policy of having all major decisions made by the Board as a whole, the committee structure of the Board is limited to those committees required for the operation of a publicly-owned company and to balance the need for Board input or oversight and the efficient use of available director time. Currently those committees are: the Audit Committee; Corporate Governance Committee; Environment, Health and Safety (EH&S) Committee; Executive Committee; Management Development and Compensation Committee; and Public Policy Committee. The members and chairs of these committees are recommended to the Board annually by the Corporate Governance Committee in consultation with the Chairman of the Board and Chief Executive Officer. The Audit Committee and the Corporate Governance Committee are made up of only Outside Directors, and the Management Development and Compensation Committee is composed of all non-employee directors.

2. Corporate Governance Committee

   - 2.1 The Corporate Governance Committee, in consultation with the Chairman of the Board and Chief Executive Officer, considers and makes recommendations to the Board concerning the appropriate size and needs of the Board. The Corporate Governance Committee considers candidates to fill vacant Board positions. Candidates are selected for their character, judgment, business experience, and acumen. Final approval of a candidate is determined by the full Board.
   - 2.2 The Corporate Governance Committee annually reviews the compensation of directors and considers other policies relating to the Board and directors, including committee structure and size, share ownership, and retirement and resignation.

3. Management Development and Compensation Committee

- 3.1 The Board plans for succession to the position of Chairman of the Board and Chief Executive Officer as well as certain other senior management positions. The Management Development and Compensation Committee is responsible for this planning. To assist the Management Development and Compensation Committee, the Chairman of the Board and Chief Executive Officer annually provides the Committee with an assessment of senior managers and their potential to succeed him/her. He/she also provides the Committee with an assessment of persons considered potential successors to certain senior management positions.
- 3.2 The Management Development and Compensation Committee also is responsible for setting annual and long-term performance goals for the Chairman of the Board and Chief Executive Officer and for evaluating his/her performance against such goals. The Committee meets annually with the Chairman of the Board and Chief Executive Officer to receive his or her recommendations concerning such goals. The Committee, or its chairperson, meets at least once a year with the Chairman of the Board and Chief Executive Officer to evaluate his/her performance.
- 3.3 A Compensation Subcommittee of the Management Development and Compensation Committee is responsible for reviewing and approving or recommending modifications to the Company's executive compensation and benefit plans and criteria for awards to be issued under such plans. The Subcommittee is composed of only Outside Directors who are not beneficiaries of any of the employee benefit plans administered by the Subcommittee and who have never been officers of the Company. The Subcommittee shall review and administer all executive compensation and benefit plans and shall recommend annual executive compensation levels and awards under such plans to the full Management Development and Compensation Committee. The Management Development and Compensation Committee meets at least once a year to review and approve executive compensation and awards under the Company's executive compensation and benefit plans.

4. Executive Committee

- 4.1 The Executive Committee, composed of both employee directors and Outside Directors, may exercise all powers and authority of the Board if Board action is necessary between meetings of the Board. Such actions are reported to the full Board at its next meeting.

5. General Committee Practices

- 5.1 It is the policy of the Board that the chairpersons of the Audit, Corporate Governance, EH&S, Management Development and Compensation, and Public Policy committees of the Board each act as the chairperson at meetings or executive sessions of the directors at which the principal items to be considered are within the scope of the authority of his/her committee. Experience has indicated that this practice provides for leadership at all of the meetings or executive sessions of directors without the need to designate a "lead director".
- 5.2 The frequency, length, and agenda of meetings of each of the committees are determined by the chairperson of the committee in consultation with appropriate members of management. Sufficient time to consider the agenda items is provided. Materials related to agenda items are provided to the committee members sufficiently in advance of the meeting to allow the members to prepare for discussion of the items at the meeting.
- 5.3 The responsibilities of each of the committees are determined by the Board from time to time based upon recommendations of the Corporate Governance Committee. Each committee may recommend changes to its charter for consideration by the Corporate Governance Committee and the Board.
- 5.4 It is the policy of the Board to rotate committee assignments and chairmanships from time to time, subject to the need for continuity in committee

membership necessary for effective functioning and oversight.

BOARD PRACTICES AND PROCEDURES

1. The Chairman of the Board and Chief Executive Officer sets the agenda for Board meetings with the understanding that certain items necessary for appropriate Board oversight, such as annual budgets and long range plans, must appear periodically on the agenda. Board members may request that particular items be placed on the agenda. Agenda items that fall within the scope of responsibilities of a Board committee are reviewed with the chairperson of that committee prior to being presented to the full Board.

2. Board materials related to agenda items are provided to Board members sufficiently in advance of Board meetings to allow the directors to prepare for discussion of the items at the meeting.

3. At the invitation of the Board, members of senior management recommended by the Chairman of the Board and Chief Executive Officer attend Board meetings or

portions thereof for the purpose of participating in discussions. Generally, presentations of matters to be considered by the Board are made by the manager responsible for that area of the Company's operations. In addition, Board members have free access to all other members of management and employees of the Company.

4. Meetings of Outside Directors without management present are held several times a year in connection with the management development process. Outside Directors may hold additional executive sessions from time to time, with or without the Chairman of the Board and Chief Executive Officer present, as is desired.

PERIODIC REVIEW

The Corporate Governance Committee is responsible for periodic review of these principles, as well as consideration of other corporate governance issues that may, from time to time, merit consideration by the entire Board.

CalPERS: STATEMENT OF GOVERNANCE PRINCIPLES

To ensure that the accountability and authority for governance and management of CalPERS is clearly stated, the Board sets forth herein governing principles to identify and distinguish between the roles of the Board, the Board President, the Board Vice President, Committees, Committee Chairs, Vice Chairs, and the Chief Executive Officer.

I. The Board's Role

All authority granted by the Constitution and statutes to the Board of Administration is retained, except as delegated by specific resolution. Consistent with its fiduciary role as
Trustee of the Fund, the Board's principal role is to ensure that CalPERS is appropriately governed and managed. With the overriding goal of protecting Fund assets, the Board's role is to:

A. Adopt and Monitor Policies

- Set the long-term strategic direction and annual business plan for CalPERS, focusing on the goals of CalPERS against which its performance is measured and monitored.
- Set policies for CalPERS focusing on:
- Select, regularly evaluate, and, if necessary, take disciplinary action against the Chief Executive Officer.
- Delegate execution of established Board policy and strategic objectives to the Chief Executive Officer and through him redelegation to the employees of CalPERS.

B. Review and Evaluate Performance

- Monitor performance and regularly review results as compared to:
- Benchmarking, incorporating measures that, if realized, clearly position CalPERS within the top quartile of comparable funds with which it is compared.
- Assure plans are in place that provide for senior management succession.
- Review, approve, and monitor actuarial data and assumptions.

C. Review and Evaluate Financial and Administrative Operations

- Review and approve the annual budget, including budget change proposals (BCPs), financial standards and policies, material capital allocations and material transactions not in the ordinary course of business as set forth in the Finance Committee Charter.

- Ensure the integrity of the financial control and reporting system.
- Oversee all audits, including approve the outside auditor, the annual internal audit plan, and provide that financial controls and reporting systems are as set forth in the Finance Committee Charter.

D. Executive Sessions

The Board will meet in Executive session where authorized by law, and when needed, at least annually to review reports of the Executive Performance and Compensation Committee with respect to the performance and compensation of the Chief Executive Officer. It may also meet with the Chief Executive Officer with respect to the performance appraisal and salary recommendations of non-delegated executive staff, and such other employees as the Chief Executive Officer may wish to discuss and include, based on their salaries and responsibilities.

E. Other Board Responsibilities

- Have in place Board policies and guidelines regarding proposed legislation (state and federal), corporate governance, shareholder voting, and the adoption/amendment of administrative code, rules and regulations.
- At all times meet high ethical standards that exceed legal minimums.
- Organize the board of trustees; organize its Committees; and approve charters and delegations to Committees and the Chief Executive Officer.
- Periodically evaluate the Board, its performance and take any steps necessary to improve Board operations.
- Set the Board agenda, by identifying, articulating, prioritizing and scheduling matters the Board will regularly address.
- Be responsible and accountable to members, beneficiaries, their representative organizations, and participating public employers and others with oversight interests in the Retirement System including the Legislature and taxpayer organizations.

The Board is responsible for creating and maintaining an atmosphere that encourages frank and collegial discussions both at the Board and Committee level and as between the Board and management. The Board strives to achieve a governing style that emphasizes:

- Strategic leadership
- Outward vision
- Focus on the future
- Proactivity

- Encouragement of collegiality
- Respect for diversity in viewpoints
- Governance by consensus
- A partnership with PERS management
- Ethical conduct of Board business to avoid even the appearance of impropriety

The Board establishes and communicates Board policies and priorities and then monitors performance in light of its established policies and priorities. The Board recognizes that the achievement of its goals requires self-discipline by the Board as a whole and by individual Board members to live by the policies articulated herein and to govern with excellence.

II. Board/Chief Executive Officer Relationship

The Board has delegated to the Chief Executive Officer the responsibility for the administration and management of the System. Policy and direction set by the Board is implemented through the Chief Executive Officer so that a strong relationship between the Board and Chief Executive Officer and clear delineation of authority is critical to the accomplishment of the Board's objectives.

III. Individual Board Member Responsibilities

A. Board members have no obligation to meet with or communicate with advisors, managers, consultants, contractors or vendors. Any contacts and communications between individual Board members and advisors, managers, consultants, contractors and vendors to CalPERS shall be at the option, discretion, and judgment of each Board member. Individual Board members shall avoid favoritism, conflicts and disclosure of privileged information and at all times individual Board members shall act in the best interest of CalPERS consistent with his/her fiduciary duty.

B. Individual Board members are not to become involved in operational management, except as requested by the Chief Executive Officer.

C. Individual Board members shall refer proposals or other communications regarding potential or existing investments or other contracts directly to the Chief Executive Officer.
D. Whenever the Board or the Chief Executive Officer is involved in the selection or employment of advisors, managers, consultants, contractors and vendors, individual Board members shall not communicate with regard to that contract with any person who may be under consideration in such a selection or hiring process prior to the actual selection or hiring.

IV. Chief Executive Officer Authority

The Board has delegated to the Chief Executive Officer, responsibility for the administration and management of the System consistent with Board delegation of authority. This includes broad responsibility for: (1) investment decisions and the hiring of outside advisors and asset managers, as delegated; (2) hiring, supervising, monitoring, evaluating, and, when necessary, taking disciplinary action or terminating senior managers and staff as delegated; (3) services to beneficiaries; (4) budgeting; (5) governmental affairs/media relations; (6) employee training and development; (7) succession planning; (8) actuarial valuations; and (9) legal representation.

The Chief Executive Officer's duties are defined by the Board and include the following:

- With advice and counsel from the Board, achieve the long-term policies and strategic objectives established for the System by the Board, including as necessary:
- Represent CalPERS, or designate other staff representatives, to outside parties and organizations.
- Participate with the Board in the hiring, evaluating for compensation purposes, disciplining, and terminating all non delegated executive staff.
- Provide leadership to CalPERS employees in terms of collegiality and ethical conduct.
- Act as the liaison for communication and information flow between the Board and CalPERS employees.

V. Board President Authority

The Board President's principal role is to lead the Board in the conduct of Board business by managing the affairs of the Board and ensuring the integrity of the Board's process. The President's specific duties, delegated by the Board, are to:

- Provide leadership to the Board in terms of collegiality and ethical conduct. Ensure that Board operations are consistent with its own policies and those legally imposed upon it from outside CalPERS:
- Set the Board agenda with input from Board members and the Chief Executive Officer, articulating, prioritizing and scheduling agenda items as appropriate.
- Conduct Board meetings, controlling the process of Board deliberations pursuant to rules adopted by the Board.
- Ensure information flow to the Board is comprehensive and timely without being over-detailed.

nd Committee Chairs, determine the frequency, subjects and format of information to be provided to Board members and Committees prior to meeting.

- Make decisions in those areas for which the Board has expressly delegated the President decision-making authority.
- Represent CalPERS, or designate other Board representatives, to outside parties and organizations.
- Act as the liaison for communications between the Board and Chief Executive Officer.
- Recommend Board and Committee meeting calendars, with the advice of the Chief Executive Officer and Committee Chairs.
- Lead the Board's ongoing assessment of Board performance, process and organization, recognizing that continuing improvement will require periodic change to meet future needs and conditions.
- Implement the Board's Conflict of Interest, Incompatible Activities, Insider Trading, Reporting and Travel Policies.
- The Board President and Vice President will be elected by members of the Board in open session at the January meeting of the Board for the term of one calendar year.

While it is the Board to whom the Chief Executive Officer is accountable, it is expected that the Board President will have the most frequent contact with the Chief Executive Officer.

VI. Board Vice President Authority

In the absence or incapacity of the Board President, the Vice President shall have the duties and responsibilities delegated and established by Board policy and in general conformance with the authority of the President.

VII. Committees, Committee Chairs and Committee Vice Chairs

A. Standing Board Committees have an important role in assisting the Board to carry out its responsibilities. In fulfilling this role they:

- Assist the Board by considering policy alternatives and implications for Board deliberations and actions.
- Act for the Board when formally delegated such authority for specific purposes. Committee authority is limited to areas explicitly delegated by the Committee's Charter, with care to avoid conflict with authority delegated to the Chief Executive Officer.
- Perform a monitoring role as to Chief Executive Officer performance in areas specifically delegated in the Committee's Charter.

B. All Board members shall be advised of the meetings of each Committee, and may choose to attend any Committee meeting, regardless of whether or not they are a member of the Committee. Board members may participate in Committee discussions, but may only vote in Committees in which they are members.

C. Committee Chairs will be selected by the members of each Committee, with consideration given by members to the periodic rotation of Committee Chairs.

D. Committee Chairs are responsible for organizing the work of the Committees. In fulfilling this function they:

- In consultation with the President, set the Committee agenda in accordance with the Committee Charter.
- Convene and chair meetings of the Committee.

Ensure that the Committee operates to assist the Board consistent with its charter and Board rules including:

- Work directly with the staff person(s) assigned by the Chief Executive Officer on matters within the Committee Charters.
- Act as a liaison between the Committee, the Board President, and the Board.

E. Committee Vice Chairs
In the absence or incapacity of the Committee Chair, the Vice Chair shall have the duties and responsibilities delegated and established by the Committee's Charter. Committee Vice Chairs will be selected by the members of each Committee. Consideration will be given to the rotation of Committee Vice Chairs so that members of the Committee can gain added experience and can assume added future responsibilities based on demonstrated interest and ability.

TIAA
CREF

Important Elements of Good Corporate Governance

INTRODUCTION

Teachers Insurance and Annuity Association-College Retirement Equities Fund, as responsible long term investors, recognize the overriding interest that our economy and our society have in the long-term development and vitality of our public corporations. We acknowled that even an ideal system of corporate governance does not guarantee superior performance. Conversely, superior performance can be achieved despite a governance system that is less than perfect. Nevertheless, TIAA-CREF believes that certain principles are the hallmark of an equitable and efficient corporate governance structure. Good corporate governance must be expected to maintain an appropriate balance between the rights of shareholders - the owners of the corporation - and the need of management and the board to direct the corporation's affairs free from distracting short-term pressures. TIAA-CREF acknowledges a responsibility to be an advocate for improved corporate governance and performance discipline. This statement, based on a process of our boards' Corporate Governance and Social Responsibility Committees, is offered as a basis for dialogue with senior corporate management and boards of directors with the objective of improving corporate governance practices. It represents the TIAA-CREF perspective on what we believe are important elements of good corporate governance, and it identifies our voting guidelines on certain proxy issues.

Board of Directors

It is recognized that the primary responsibility of the board of directors is to foster the long-term success of the corporation consistent with its fiduciary responsibility to the shareholders. TIAA-CREF supports the primary authority of the board in such areas as the selection of the chief executive officer, review of the corporadon's long-term strategy, and selection of nominees for election to the board. However, in order to sharpen the accountability of directors to shareholders, we believe:

The board should be composed of a ma.jority of independent directors. The board committee structure should include audit, compensation and nominating committees consisting entirely of independent directors. For this purpose independence means no present or former employment by the company or any significant financial or personal tie to the company or its management which could interfere with the director's loyalty to the shareholders. We concur in principle with the New York Stock Exchange (NYSE) definition of independence which excludes persons who act on a regular basis either individually or as a representative of an organization serving as a professional adviser, consultant or legal counsel to the company if the relationship is considered material. The NYSE definition would not disqualify a director from independent status due to customary conunercial transactions carried on at arm's length in the ordinary course of business if, in the board's discretion, the relationship would not interfere with the individual's ability to exercise independent judgment.

The board should establish a fixed retirement policy for directors, and a requirement that all directors should own common shares in the company. A reasonable minimum ownership interest could be defined as stock holdings equal to approximately one-half of the amount of the director's annual retainer fee.

The board should be composed of qualified individuals who reflect diversity of experience, gender, race and age. Each director should represent all shareholders; therefore, TIAA-CREF opposes the nomination of specific representational directors, and the practice of cumulative votina in the election of directors.

TIAA-CREF recognizes the responsibility of the board to organize its functions and conduct its business in the manner it deems most efficient, consistent with these or similar good guidelines. Therefore, in the absence of special circumstances, ordinarily we would not support shareholder resolutions concerning separation of the positions of CEO and Chairman, the formation of shareholder advisory committees, the requirement that candidates for the board be nominated by shareholders, shareholder mandated election of directors on an annual basis, or a requirement that directors must attend @ specific percenta,ac of board meetings, unless the board supports such measures. We are also against restricting the date of the annual meeting since it is management's prerogative to set the meeting date. The corporation should be free to indemnify directors for legal expenses and judgments in connection with their service as directors and eliminate the directors'liability for ordinary negliaence. Directors should be held liable to the corporation for violations of their fiduciary duty involving gross or sustained and repeated negligence.

The board should have a mechanism to evaluate its performance and that of individual directors. At a minimum, there should be an annual review of performance by the board that measures results against appropriate criteria defined by the board.

While TIAA-CREF normally votes for the board's nominees, we vote for alternative candidates when our analysis indicates that those candidates will better represent shareholder interests. We may also decline to vote for unopposed candidates when their record indicates that their election to the board would not be in the interest of shareholders, or when we have requested a meedna with independent directors and have been refused.

Shareholders Rights and Proxy Voting

Unlike other groups that have dealings with the corporation - customers, suppliers, lenders and labor - common shareholders do not have contractual protection of their interests. They must rely on the board of directors - whom they elect - and on their right to vote on proposals the corporation is required to submit for shareholder approval. The proxy vote is thus the key mechanism by which shareholders play a role in the governance of the corporation. In exercising its votes, TIAA-CREF believes:

In order to protect the importance of the proxy vote, and to eliminate the appearance of any impropriety or unfairness, the corporation should adopt confidential votincr for the election of directors and all other matters voted on by shareholders.

The board should adhere to the principle of each share of common stock having one vote and should not create multiple classes of common' stock with disparate voting rights.

Any authorized but unissued shares with voting rights to be determined by the directors should not be issued without prior shareholder approval.

Equal financial treatment for all shareholders is a principle the board should adopt. TIAA-CREF supports "fair price" provisions and measures to limit the corporation's ability to buy back shares from a particular shareholder at higher-than-market prices. TIAA-CREF supports proposals that eliminate preemptive rights, except where our analysis indicates that such rights have value to shareholders.

Any action which alters the fundamental relationship between shareholders and the board - such as an "anti-takeover"measure - should be submitted for prior shareholder approval even,when it is not required by law.

Any action to adopt "super-majority" requirements which interfere with a shareholder's ricrht to elect directors and ratify corporate actions will be opposed.

Changes in a corporation's domicile should only be proposed for valid business reasons, and not to obtain protection against unfriendly takeovers.

Corporations should opt out of coverage under state laws mandadng anti-takeover protection.

TIAA-CREF opposes elimination or reduction (through a change in by-laws or state of incorporation) of the shareholders'right to demand independent appraisal of the value of the holdings.

Disparate issues should not be combined and presented for a single vote. TIAA-CREF normally will vote against a package if we oppose any of its constituent parts.

Any substantial increases in the authorized number of common or preferred shares without adequate reason will be opposed.

TIAA-CREF supports equal access for large shareholders to a company's proxy statements to comment on management proposals, unless such access would impose undue costs or other burdens on the corporation.

TIAA-CREF believes that, unless state law already so provides, a corporation's charter or by-laws should provide that abstentions will not be counted as votes present when tallying shareholder votes. Abstentions, however, should still be counted for purposes of establishing a quorum.

Executive Compensation

TIAA-CREF believes a board and its compensation committee should set executive compensation levels adequate to attract and retain qualified executives. These executives should be rewarded in direct relationship to the contribution they make in maximizing shareholder wealth. A "pay for performance" system is needed to ensure equitable treatment between the shareholders and corporate management. TIAA-CREF is not equipped to evaluate thoroughly the specific issues surrounding executive compensation at each of its portfolio companies.

The three key issues are:

Determining what constitutes "excessive" executive compensation.

Evaluating the soundness and reasonableness of the policies, standards, and processes for setting compensation levels.

Deciding what constitutes adequate disclosure of executive compensation to shareholders and the public. With the number of firms in a large institutional investor's portfolio, it is difficult for an investor to determine what constitutes excessive" compensation without thoroughly evaluating a whole ranae of topics and data, to which the investor does not have ready access. Therefore, it seems more prudent for an investor to recommend policies, standards and processes for setting executive compensation levels. These include:

Compensation should include salary and performance components.

Salary should have a defined relationship to salaries in industry peer groups.

Total compensation should be adequate to attract, motivate and retain quality talent.

Performance measures should relate to key characteristics accepted within the particular industry to measure success.

Performance should be measured over time periods adequate to assess and link actual performance with responsibilities.

Compensation should be appropriate in liaht of the current financial rewards to shareholders and employees.

Compensation should be determined by the compensation committee of a board and care should be taken to avoid interlocking compensation committee memberships with other boards.

Stock options and '.restricted stock awards should be integrated with other elements of compensation to formulate a competitive package.

The board should set forth annually in the proxy statement the criteria used to evaluate performance of the chief executive officer and other senior management. TIAA-CREF supports the spirit of the SEC rules on enhanced executive compensation disclosure and compensation committee reports to shareholders.

TIAA-CREF opposes any ban on "golden parachute" severance agreements. We abstain on resolutions calling for prior shareholder ratification of golden parachute severance agreements, but TIAA-CREF supports resolutions that call for shareholder approval of golden parachutes which exceed IRS guidelines.

Stock option, stock purchase, stock appreciation rierhts, savinas, pensions, bonus and management incentive award proposals are scrutinized closely by TIAA-CREF. Consideration should be given to the need of the company to attract, motivate and reward people. This must be balanced against the concerns of shareholders. TIAA-CREF guidelines for voting proxies on these issues are in the appendix to this statement.

CEO Performance Evaluation

The evaluation of a corporation's chief executive officer is a critical board responsibility. A clear understanding between the board and the CEO regarding the corporation's expected performance and how that performance will be measured is very important. We believe:

A high standard of performance accountability and ethical behavior should be set at the top of the corporation.

The board should establish a specific set of performance objectives for the CEO annually. These should include concerns of shareholders, other investors, employees, customers and the community in which the company is located.

Performance objectives should include both annual and multi-year time periods.

The board should establish an annual review process that would permit it to evaluate CEO performance in executive session. A subsequent dialogue with the CEO is encouraged.

Strategic Planning

Every company needs a strategic plan to ensure future economic success. The strategic allocation of corporate resources to each of the company's businesses is critical to its future success and to increased shareholder value needed for efficient capital formation. The board should discuss the strategic plan of each of the company's businesses at least annually. The strategic plan can be expected to include many of the following components, though TIAA-CREF recognizes that each company will need to fashion its own specific blend:

An assessment of customers, markets and products for each business seament.

A review of the competitive strengths of the business and its position in the marketplace.

A review of human resource management issues.

A review of the technological leadership, product attributes and costs of production and/or providing the service necessary to maintain a competitive advantage.

An evaluation of the marketina and distribution channels for price and competitive superiority.

A review of the information processing technology required to provide competitive leadership.

A projection of the capital formation and financial implications of the plan.

Fiduciary Oversight

The board has a primary duty to exercise its fiduciary responsibility in the best interests of the corporation and its shareholders. This would include periodic reviews to ensure that corporate resources are used only for appropriate business purposes. To address some of the most important areas of fiduciary responsibility, the board should:

Foster and encourage a corporate environment of strong internal controls, fiscal accountability, high ethical standards and compliance with applicable laws and regulations. Develop appropriate procedures to assure the board is advised of alleged or suspected violations of corporate standards or of non-compliance and manacrement's resolution thereof, on a timely basis. (For example, by regular reports from the general counsel to the full board or a committee thereof.)

Appoint an audit committee composed exclusively of outside independent directors.

Appoint an independent audit firm to conduct an annual audit of the company's books and records.

Install a mechanism to review corporate policies and practices (e.g., travel and entertainment policy, executive perquisites, etc.) to ensure proper use of corporate resources.

Provide an explicit mechanism for major shareholders to communicate directly with the board (e.g., designating a non-executive chairman, a lead director, or a committee of independent directors).

Social Responsibility Issues

TIAA-CREF believes buildina long-term shareholder value is consistent with directors giving careful consideration to social responsibility issues and the common good of the community. The board should develop policies and practices to address the following issues:

The environmental impact of the corporation's operations and products.

Equal employment opportunities for all segments of our population.

Open channels of communication permitting employees, customers, suppliers and the community to freely express their concerns.

Effective employee trainina and development.

Evaluation of corporate actions that can negatively affect the common good of the conununity and its residents.

To prohibit deliberate and knowin(y exploitation of any of the non- shareholder constituencies.

Dialogue Between TIAA-CREF and Companies

TIAA-CREF believes that its policies on corporate governance should be shaped and allowed to evolve in collaboration with the companies in which it invests. Accordinaly, we will take the following steps:

Provide copies of these guidelines and their updates to all domestic companies in which we invest. We will suggest that the companies distribute the guidelines to all officers and directors.

Periodically seek suggestions from these companies for ways to improve the guidelines.

Arrange for occasional informal forums for company managers, directors, and TIAA-CREF managers to review the guidelines.

Send copies of the guidelines to other large institutional investors, make them available to anybody or any organization upon request, send them to appropriate information clearinghouses, and publish them for TIAA-CREF participants and participating institutions to review and offer suggestions for change.

Conclusion

TIAA-CREF promulgates this statement to encouracremore widespread adoption of effective corporate governance practices. We would encourage dialogue to create a better understanding of corporate governance issues with the hope these issues can be addressed and resolved in a spirit of cooperation. While this statement is intended primarily for domestic corporations, we will endeavor to apply comparable principles, as appropriate, in voting proxies on the foreign corporations in our portfolio.

Appendix

TIAA-CREF Guidelines for Voting Proxies on Executive Compensation

Introduction

In view of the fact that the issues involved in executive compensation are technical and complex, these guidelines for voting proxies on executive compensation are designed with the following principles in mind:

1. Focus on good practice (e.g., a board compensation committee composed entirely of independent directors; and a clear and convincing statement by the compensation committee in the proxy statement of the principles followed in developing the company's compensation package);

2. Recognize that we are only called upon to vote on compensation plans, not on the way a particular plan will actually be administered;

3. Recognize the difficulty of obtaining valid company-specific data (e.g., the true economic value of a company's total compensation package and its relation to packa(yes at comparable firms);

4. Seek to affirm mainstream practice while focusing on extreme cases (i.e., where compensation plans violate TIAA-CREF's proxy voting guidelines and where further investigation shows a current failure to follow good practice, or a history of actual abuse including a lack of a reasonable relation between a company's financial performance and the compensation of its executives).

The following voting guidelines identify what TIAA-CREF believes are key issues, and "red flags" which call for further research on a particular portfolio company. If that research indicates procedural faults in the development of a compensation plan (such as lack of independence by the compensation committee), or a history of abusive practices, TIAA-CREF will vote against the plan. We will also vote against a plan that does not raise a "red flag" if the company's current practices or history of awards are such as to cause serious concerns about the way the plan would be administered.

VOTING GUIDELINES

Issue: Dilution from Stock-Based Plans

Red Flag: Total potential dilution from existing and proposed compensation plans (apart from restricted stock which is treated separately) exceeds 15% over duration of plan(s) or 1.5% per year.

Override: Increase threshold to 25% for plans proposed by companies in high technology industries in which coveraae extends through at least middle management levels. Increase threshold to 20% for firms whose market equity capitalizadons are under $100 million.

Comment: The two override conditions are each designed to address a specific consideration. The first addresses the needs of human-capital- intensive industries where generous stock-based grants are necessary to retain personnel and where significant contributions are made by individuals outside the ranks of senior management. The second override addresses the need to provide packages with sufficient value at lower capitalization firms, since a given level of dilution has a lower economic value the lower the market capitalization of the firm.

Issue: Reload Options

Red Flag: Proposal provides for granting reload options.

Override: Plan (i) limits the frequency with which options can be reloaded; (ii) provides for a reload only if market price increases a specified percent; and (iii) prohibits resale of shares purchased for which options were reloaded.

Comment: Reload options are automatically "reloaded" after exercise at the then-current market price. This creates an option that can be exercised several times over its full tenn. For this reason, reload options convey higher value to their recipients because they are, in effect, families of options. In addition, they enable the individual receiving them to reap the maximum potential benefit from options awards, by allowina him or her to take advantage of all increases in stock price that occur over the duration of the option with no attendant risk. This advantage is at odds with the payout structure of common stock, and thus can create a divergence between the interests of outside shareholders and the option recipient.

Issue: Option pricing

Red Flag: Unspecified exercise price or exercise price below 85% of fair market value on the date of the grant.

Override: Equivalent value transfer percentage from the proposed plan plus all other stock-based plans (apart from restricted stock which is treated separately) does not exceed the recommended maximum percentage of 2.25% over a ten-year period. For small capitalization firms, maximum value transfer percentage is 3.00%, and for firms in high technology industries, the maximum percentage is 3.75%.

Comment: Options that are at-the-money or out-of-the-money afford the recipient with no downside risk, and thus may encourage a "bet the bank" psycholooy that is not in the best interests of common stockholders. Granting options at a discount can overcome this shortcoming to some degree. However, the discretion to make in-the-money option grants can also lead to redundancy with other cash-based compensation plans. The override provides additional flexibility while concurrently guarding aerainst potential abuses. It is based on the concept that there is a maximum permissible value transfer over the life of the plan. Therefore the override offers companies with less dilutive plans more flexibility with respect to the pricina of options.

The maximum permissible value transfer percentage of 2.25% is arrived at by multiplying the 15% recommended dilution level by the 15% permissible discount (. 15

x 15=.0225) to fair market value. Note that for companies where TIAA-CREF's guidelines allow greater dilution tolerances, those tolerances are substituted for the 15% dilution in the aforementioned calculation.

To calculate the value transfer percentage from existing and proposed option plans, add the sum of dilution from existing and proposed options plan times their respective discount from fair market value.

Issue: Restricted Stock

Red Flag: The proposed plan plus existing restricted stock plans provide equivalent value transfer percentage that exceeds recommended maximum of 2.25%. Note the actual value transfer percentage is simply the dilution from existina plus proposed restricted stock plans.

Override: For small capitalization firms, increase the maximum value transfer percentage to 3.00%, and for firins in high technology industries, increase the maximum percentage to 3.75%, consistent with dilution recommendation described above.

Comment: At many companies restricted stock awards are viewed as a substitute for some portion of cash compensation. To the degree that the use of restricted stock in lieu of cash injects the compensation package with an incentive-based component, these awards are a more effective means of transferring cash value.

We have designed our recommendations on restricted stock awards so that they transfer no more in the way of cash value than would an option plan that passes the recommended tests.

Issue: Coverage

Red Flag: Plan is limited to a small number of senior employees.

Override: Pemiit awards to a small number of employees at small capitalization companies whose market equity

capitalizations are under $1 00 million.

Issue: Omnibus Plans/Redundancy

Red Flag: Proposed plan provides overlapping benefits either within the plan itself or with existing plans or with other proposed plans.

Override: Plans that give rise to redundancy to expire within two years or have remaining share authorizations that are less than 3% of outstanding stock.

Coniment: Rather than blanket rejection of omnibus plans, we recommend that they be approved if they do not create redundancy in the compensation structure. For example, a proposal that seeks authorization for a plan that provides for stock options with tandem SARS, restricted stock, and performance units would be accepted under our proposed criteria as long as the company did not have other active plans that also provided for similar awards. The basic notion is to vote FOR any proposal whose elements would be approved on a sequential basis. In such instances, the omnibus plan is no more than a consolidation of awards that otherwise are provided for under distinct plans.

Many omnibus plans, however, do create redundancies. They frequently provide for not only tbe usual stock-based awards, but also various phantom awards that accomplish the same thing. Under our guidelines, TIAA-CREF would reject plans structured in this manner. The redundancy issue also pertains to plans that are not omnibus plans. Proposals seeking approval for a single type of award that is already granted duough existing plans for which ample authorizations remain should be rejected.

Issue: Excess Discretion

Red Flag: Terms of awards, such as coverage, option price, or type of award provided for by the proposed plan, are not specified in the proposal.

Override: None.

Issue: Bundling

Red Flag: Vote on executive compensation plan is coupled with vote on one or more unrelated proposals.

Override: None.

Issue: Stock-Based Plans for Non-Employee Directors

Red Flag: Alone or in conjunction with either existing or proposed plans triggers any of the red flags discussed above.

Override: None.

PENSION INVESTMENT ASSOCIATION OF CANADA

INTRODUCTION:

The PIAC Board of Directors has approved General Principles for Corporate Governance and a Mandate for the Corporate Governance Committee. The Committee considered it advisable to interpret and enlarge on the General Principles in the form of Corporate Governance Standards, which were broken down into four sub-headings:

A. Obligations of Boards of Directors
B. Executive Compensation
C. Takeover Protection
D. Shareholder Rights

The principal avenue for PIAC members to advocate and support these standards is by means of their proxy votes. Meeting the standards will generally indicate which way a manager should vote a proxy. Nevertheless, the committee will go on to develop a rating system for distinguishing effective Boards of Directors from less effective Boards.

PIAC expects that adherence to these General Principles and Standards and rating Boards of Directors on their conformance will lead to improving corporate governance in Canada and increasing confidence in, and improving the efficiency of, Canadian capital markets. This will
ultimately enhance the competitiveness of the Canadian economy.

A. OBLIGATIONS OF BOARDS OF DIRECTORS

Preamble: A general principle for corporate governance adopted by the Pension Investment Association of Canada enunciated that:

"Corporate management is accountable to the Board of Directors. The Board of Directors is responsible for maximizing long term growth of shareholder values. The Board reports to the shareholders. The Board should reinforce these concepts in making its appointments and by appropriately defining the separate roles of boards members and management."

Additionally, PIAC holds that directors collectively represent all shareholders, not any special interest group; and that generally shareholders should not interfere with management, but should ensure that the Board is capable of independent thought and action, so that it can effectively discharge its responsibility (and oversee management performance).

Majority owners and other shareholders of closely-held companies ought to have the same interest in creating shareholder values as shareholders of widely-held companies.

Obligations: The following points are essential for Boards of Directors to function effectively:

1. The majority of the Board of Directors is independent of management and has no financial interest in the affairs of the property of the company, other than as a shareholder.

2. The role of Chairman of the Board is different from that of Chief Executive Officer, and it follows that one person cannot fulfill both roles without conflict. Therefore, the Chief Executive Officer runs the company with the Chairman ensuring that the Board effectively judges management's performance.

3. Committees have become accepted mechanisms of corporate governance. Corporations of sufficient size include at a minimum a Nominating Committee, an Audit Committee, and a Compensation Committee. The majority of members of each of these committees are independent of management, as is the committee Chairman.

4. The Board consists of fewer than 12 or at most 15 members, which is small enough to be cohesive and effective. Since directors have to take responsibility and be accountable, they need to be remunerated accordingly and they must limit the number of their other directorships in order to devote adequate time to each board.

B. EXECUTIVE COMPENSATION

Preamble: Executive pay is a cost that shareholders are willing to pay for having agents (corporate management) run the company for them. That is the essence of the corporate contract. One party puts up the capital, and another puts in the labor. Shareholders have to pay a price for having someone else do the work.

As long as corporate ownership is separated from corporate control, managers will be presented with conflicts of interest. Shareholders want compensation to be not excessive, but to be enough to encourage dedication and a profitable company. Management wants compensation to be largely guaranteed, whereas shareholders want it to be tied to company performance and market return. Mishandling this conflict can interfere with the common goal of increasing long term shareholder values.

Our role as institutional fiduciaries is to ensure long-term growth of shareholder values, and a properly rewarded management team that can perform that task is our principal interest.

Standards: The design of a compensation plan is more important than the size of the total remuneration. In this connection, shareholders have six main objectives:

1. Shareholders' principal interest is in building long-term shareholder values. Compensation packages should induce management to become owners of enough stock that their interests coincide with those of the shareholders.

2. Compensation must be high enough to attract qualified management; to be competitive within its industry, but not structured to reward failure or mediocrity.

3. Executive compensation should motivate management to achieve its goal of increasing long-term share values. This requires a positive and significant correlation over a reasonable time period between pay and the enhancement of shareholder values.

4. Loans to purchase stock or options that obligate the executive beyond his ability to pay and could impose severe financial hardship if share prices fall should be avoided.

5. Unrestricted stock options, options priced below current market value or low interest loans are anathema to PIAC. Reducing the exercise price of options when the stock has underperformed the market is not acceptable.

6. Shareholders do not want to design pay packages, but they want directors serving on the compensation committee to be independent from management and capable of overseeing thorough, simple disclosure of all significant sources of executive compensation.

C. TAKEOVER PROTECTION

Preamble: Some of the takeover protection measures devised in recent years are inimical to shareholder democracy and the growth of long-term shareholder values. These takeover protection measures usually (but not exclusively) come in one or more of the following forms:

1. Poison Pills. 2. "Crown Jewel Defense" and "Going Private" transactions. 3. Leveraged Buyouts and "Lock-Up" arrangements.

Each measure may undermine shareholders' rights to determine the future course of the company and may devalue the shares.

Standards: PIAC favors Boards of Directors that:

1. Submit major corporate changes to a committee of independent directors for review and approval.

2. Submit major corporate changes to a vote of shareholders not controlled by management (without impediment).

3. Give shareholders ample time for review and enough information (usually audited financial statements) to make informed judgments.

4. Do not allow management to :short track" a takeover bid by, for example: --using the company's retained earnings or borrowing power to buy up large blocks of stock, or --seeking out a friendly third party to buy large blocks of stock without extending the offer to other shareholders.

D. SHAREHOLDER RIGHTS

Preamble: Stock ownership rights, which include proxy votes and participation in corporate bankruptcy proceedings and shareholder litigation, are a financial asset. They must be managed with the same care, skill, prudence and diligence as any other financial asset. Such rights must be exercised by fiduciaries for the exclusive benefit of pension plan beneficiaries in such a way as to protect and enhance long-term shareholder value.

Managing stock ownership rights and the proxy vote includes questions about preserving the full integrity - and value - of the ownership characteristics of common stock. For example, the value of the vote may be diminished by a classified board or by dual class capitalization, and the right to transfer stock to a willing buyer at a mutually agreeable price may be abrogated by the adoption of a "poison pill."

Standards:

1. Effective shareholders will keep themselves informed about corporate governance issues, not shrink from an activist role and manage their proxy votes in order to protect stock ownership rights from erosion.

2. Effective shareholders will not allow a preoccupation with the short term to interfere with management's ability to concentrate on long-run returns, productivity and competitiveness.

3. The proxy voting system must ensure that neither management nor shareholders are able to dominate the system or exercise undue influence.

4. All shareholders should be treated equally, with the same rights per share, with the exception of stock purchased as part of a senior class with separate, explicitly defined rights. Any issuance of new stock with rights beyond those in the shares outstanding should be offered on a pro-rata basis to existing shareholders before it is sold to outsiders.

Pension Investment Association of Canada, 61 Shaw Street, Toronto, Ontario M6J 2W3, Tel. (416) 504-1116 Fax: (416) 504-1117

"WHERE WERE THE DIRECTORS?"

GUIDELINES FOR IMPROVED CORPORATE GOVERNANCE IN CANADA

REPORT OF
The Toronto Stock Exchange Committee on Corporate Governance in Canada

DECEMBER 1994

Guidelines for Improved Corporate Governance

The following are the proposed guidelines for effective corporate governance:

(1) The board of directors of every corporation should explicitly assume responsibility for the stewardship of the corporation and, as part of the overall stewardship responsibility, should assume responsibility for the following matters:

(i) adoption of a strategic planning process

(ii) the identification of the principal risks of the corporation's business and ensuring the implementation of appropriate systems to manage these risks;

(iii) succession planning, including appointing, training and monitoring senior management;

(iv) a communications policy for the corporation; and

(v) the integrity of the corporation's internal control and management information systems.

(paragraphs 4.2, 4.3 and 4.6)

(2) The board of directors of every corporation should be constituted with a majority of individuals who qualify as unrelated directors. An unrelated director is a director who is independent of management and is free from any interest and any business or other relationship which could, or could reasonably be perceived to, materially interfere with the director's ability to act with a view to the best interests of the corporation, other than interests and relationships arising from shareholding. A related director is a director who is not an unrelated director. If the corporation has a significant shareholder, in addition to a majority of unrelated directors, the board should include a number of directors who do not have interests in or relationships with either the corporation or the significant shareholder and which fairly reflects the investment in the corporation by shareholders other than the significant shareholder. A significant shareholder is a shareholder with the ability to exercise a majority of the votes for the election of the board of directors. (paragraphs 5.7 and 5.8)

(3) The application of the definition of "unrelated director" to the circumstances of each individual director should be the responsibility of the board which will be required to disclose on an annual basis whether the board has a majority of unrelated directors or, in the case of a corporation with a significant shareholder, whether the board is constituted with the appropriate number of directors which are not related to either the corporation or the significant shareholder. Management directors are related directors. The board will also be required to disclose on an annual basis the analysis of the application of the principles supporting this conclusion. (paragraph 5.18)

(4) The board of directors of every corporation should appoint a committee of directors composed exclusively of outside, i.e. non-management, directors, a majority of whom are unrelated directors, with the responsibility for proposing to the full board new nominees to the board and for assessing directors on an ongoing basis. (paragraph 5.25)

(5) Every board of directors should implement a process to be carried out by the nominating committee or other appropriate committee for assessing the effectiveness of the board as a whole, the committees of the board and the contribution of individual directors. (paragraph 5.27)

(6) Every corporation, as an integral element of the process for appointing new directors, should provide an orientation and education program for new recruits to the board. (paragraph 5.36)

(7) Every board of directors should examine its size and, with a view to determining the impact of the number upon effectiveness, undertake where appropriate, a program to reduce the number of directors to a number which facilitates more effective decision-making. (paragraph 5.42)

(8) The board of directors should review the adequacy and form of the compensation of directors and ensure the compensation realistically reflects the responsibilities and risk involved in being an effective director. (paragraph 5.50)

(9) Committees of the board of directors should generally be composed of outside directors, a majority of whom are unrelated directors, although some board committees, such as the executive committee, may include one or more inside directors. An inside director is a director who is an officer or employee of the corporation or of any of its affiliates. (paragraph 6.3)

(10) Every board of directors should expressly assume responsibility for, or assign to a committee of directors the general responsibility for, developing the corporation's approach to governance issues. This committee would, amongst other things, be responsible for the corporation's response to these governance guidelines. (paragraph 6.4)

(11) The board of directors, together with the CEO, should develop position descriptions for the board and for the CEO, involving the definition of the limits to management's responsibilities. In addition, the board should approve or develop the corporate objectives which the CEO is responsible for meeting. (paragraph 6.12)

(12) Every board of directors should have in place appropriate structures and procedures to ensure that the board can function independently of management. An appropriate structure would be to (i) appoint a chair of the board who is not a member of management with responsibility to ensure the board discharges its responsibilities or (ii) adopt alternate means such as assigning this responsibility to a committee of the board or to a director, sometimes referred to as the "lead director". Appropriate procedures may involve the board meeting on a regular basis without management present or may involve expressly assigning the responsibility for administering the board's relationship to management to a committee of the board. (paragraph 6.15)

(13) The audit committee of every board of directors should be composed only of outside directors. The roles and responsibilities of the audit committee should be specifically defined so as to provide appropriate guidance to audit committee members as to their duties. The audit committee should have direct communication channels with the internal and external auditors to discuss and review specific issues as appropriate. The audit committee duties should include oversight responsibility for management reporting on internal control. While it is management's responsibility to design and implement an effective system of internal control, it is the responsibility of the audit committee to ensure that management has done so. (paragraphs 6.20 and 6.21)

(14) The board of directors should implement a system which enables an individual director to engage an outside adviser at the expense of the corporation in appropriate circumstances. The engagement of the outside adviser should be subject to the approval of an appropriate committee of the board. (paragraph 6.29)

Other Recommendations

The implementation of our proposals is based upon our recommendation to The Toronto Stock Exchange that the Exchange adopt, as a listing requirement, the disclosure by each listed corporation incorporated in Canada or a province of Canada of its approach to corporate governance, on an annual basis commencing with companies with June 30, 1995 year ends. (paragraphs 8.1 and 8.2)

In addition, the Report contains recommendations for legislative reform which are summarized as follows:

(1) We recommend that the governing corporate statutes be revised to eliminate any possible interpretation of the directors' responsibility as being to manage the business day-to-day. Rather, the statutes should describe the responsibility as being to supervise the management of the business. (paragraph 4.10)

(2) The government departments responsible for the administration of the corporate laws in each of the federal and provincial jurisdictions should undertake a review of all legislation enacted in their particular jurisdiction imposing personal liability upon directors. Following the review, all legislatures should repeal or modify legislation imposing personal liability on directors which no longer serves the purpose for which it was enacted and legislation not so repealed should be amended if necessary, to ensure directors are provided with an effective due diligence defence. (paragraphs 5.60 and 5.62)

(3) We recommend that the issue of legislated civil liability upon directors in respect of timely and continuous disclosure by corporations should be examined by Canada's securities administrators and any proposal should afford the business and financial community with an opportunity to comment. We would not support any recommendations to legislate civil liability of directors for timely and continuous disclosure, unless our general recommendation concerning civil liability of directors is also accepted and implemented. (paragraphs 7.16 and 7.17)

CNPF

AFEP

Le Conseil d'Administration des Sociétés Cotées

Juillet 1995

ETP

éditions techniques professionnelles

31, avenue Pierre 1er de Serbie - 75116 Paris

Dépôt Légal : juillet 1995 - ISBN 2-86658-069-9- Imprimerie CIRNOV - 75116 PARIS

SOMMAIRE

INTRODUCTION

I - MISSION ET ATTRIBUTIONS DU CONSEIL D'ADMINISTRATION

II - LA COMPOSITION DU CONSEIL D'ADMINISTRATION

III - LE FONCTIONNEMENT DU CONSEIL D'ADMINISTRATION

Les privatisations et l'ouverture du marché de Paris aux investisseurs étrangers ont favorisé le rapide développement d'un nouvel actionnariat, souvent peu familier des règles et des pratiques de fonctionnement des conseils d'administration des sociétés cotées françaises et qui est naturellement demandeur d'éclaircissements.

Un véritable débat est ainsi né, nourri d'ailleurs par les réflexions qui ont été antérieurement conduites Outre Atlantique et Outre Manche sur le " gouvernement " des entreprises.

Le Conseil National du Patronat Français (CNPF) et l'Association Française des Entreprises Privées (AFEP) ont confié à un Comité spécialement constitué pour ce faire (1) le soin d'examiner les principaux problèmes relatifs à la composition, aux attributions et aux modes de fonctionnement des conseils d'administration des sociétés cotées.

Le Comité a passé en revue ces problèmes et les différentes solutions qui ont pu y être proposées. Les conclusions de cet examen détaillé sont exposées ci-après.

Plus fondamentalement, le Comité s'est interrogé sur l'adaptation aux attentes du marché et aux besoins des entreprises des dispositions de la loi du 24 juillet 1966 relatives aux conseils d'administration ainsi que sur les principes qui doivent constamment inspirer tant les conseils eux-mêmes que chacun des administrateurs des sociétés cotées.

Les recommandations qu'il formule à cet égard lui paraissent s'imposer pour raffermir la confiance des souscripteurs dans les organes sociaux des entreprises dans lesquelles ils sont invités à investir.

Faut-il modifier les textes légaux relatifs au conseil d'administration ?

Le Comité constate que les règles applicables aux conseils d'administration des sociétés cotées permettent, sans modifications majeures, de résoudre les problèmes posés.

Sur ce point, qui était au centre de sa mission, le Comité relève que la loi française est très détaillée, qu'elle est à la fois précise et souple, qu'elle règle déjà les principaux problèmes qui ont pu être soulevés dans d'autres pays et qu'elle ne fait en tout état de cause pas obstacle à une évolution de la composition des conseils ou à une plus grande formalisation de leurs travaux qui sont souvent évoquées par les participants au débat sur le " gouvernement " des entreprises.

(1) voir en annexe : la lettre de mission du Comité et sa composition.

Deux exemples illustrent ce constat.

A la différence de certains droits étrangers, la législation française limite déjà de façon très stricte la participation au conseil d'administration de la " technostructure " de l'entreprise, puisque le nombre des directeurs généraux ou des salariés pouvant être administrateurs est plafonné (2). Il est clair que ces dispositions ne s'opposent pas à la nomination d'administrateurs indépendants et qu'elles la favorisent plutôt.

De même, chaque conseil peut constituer en son sein tel ou tel comité d'étude. Bien des sociétés se sont ainsi dotées de " comités des rémunérations ", de " comités d'audit " ou de " comités stratégiques " qui fonctionnent depuis plusieurs années de manière satisfaisante sous l'empire des textes actuels.

Ceux-ci traduisent un principe que le Comité considère essentiel : **quelles que soient la composition ou les modalités d'organisation du conseil d'administration, ce dernier est et doit demeurer une instance collégiale qui représente collectivement l'ensemble des actionnaires et à qui s'impose l'obligation d'agir en toutes circonstances dans l'intérêt social de l'entreprise.**

La mission du conseil d'administration

En exerçant ses prérogatives légales, le conseil d'administration remplit selon le Comité une quadruple mission : **il définit la stratégie de l'entreprise, désigne les mandataires sociaux chargés de gérer celle-ci dans le cadre de cette stratégie, contrôle la gestion et veille à la qualité de l'information fournie aux actionnaires ainsi qu'aux marchés à travers les comptes ou à l'occasion d'opérations très importantes.**

La formalisation des travaux du conseil d'administration

Bien entendu, il appartient au conseil d'organiser ses travaux comme il l'estime nécessaire ; il peut se doter ou non de comités consultatifs spécialisés ou d'un règlement intérieur.

Traditionnellement les conseils d'administration français formalisent peu l'organisation de leurs travaux, encore qu'une tendance inverse se fasse jour depuis quelques années, tendance que le Comité estime devoir vivement encourager.

Ce caractère informel suscite en effet la perplexité d'une partie de l'actionnariat qui s'interroge sur la qualité du fonctionnement de conseils dont il ignore le déroulement.

---

(2) L'article L93 du Code des sociétés limite au tiers du conseil le nombre des administrateurs liés à la société par un contrat de travail et l'article L115 à cinq celui des directeurs généraux.

Pour répondre à cette interrogation légitime, faut-il imposer systématiquement des modes d'organisation et de fonctionnement, plus formalisés et identiques, à tous les conseils d'administration des sociétés cotées ?

Le Comité considère que cela n'est pas souhaitable : étant constatée l'extraordinaire diversité des sociétés cotées, l'organisation des travaux du conseil comme sa composition doivent être appropriées à la composition de l'actionnariat, à la dimension et à la nature de l'activité de chaque entreprise comme aux circonstances particulières qu'elle traverse. Chaque conseil en est le meilleur juge et sa première responsabilité est d'adopter le mode d'organisation et de fonctionnement qui lui permet d'accomplir au mieux sa mission. Si une évolution des pratiques dans le sens des recommandations du Comité est souhaitable, elle ne saurait donc pas être imposée de façon systématique et uniforme.

Le Comité estime en conséquence que **chaque conseil a la double obligation d'examiner périodiquement sa composition, son organisation et son fonctionnement et de faire part aux actionnaires des positions ou dispositions qu'il a alors prises.**

Cet examen périodique du conseil doit notamment porter sur les points suivants :

- Adéquation, à l'exercice des missions du conseil, de la fréquence et de la durée de ses réunions ainsi que de l'information dont il dispose pour délibérer utilement.

- Opportunité de la création en son sein de comités d'études et notamment d'un comité de sélection des administrateurs et des mandataires sociaux, d'un comité de la rémunération des mandataires sociaux et d'un comité d'audit des méthodes et procédures comptables.

  Si de tels comités sont créés, une réflexion particulière doit être consacrée à leur composition qui doit être de nature à garantir l'objectivité de l'instruction des affaires qu'ils examinent.

- Opportunité de réserver au conseil certaines catégories de décisions ainsi que de formaliser par des décisions ponctuelles du conseil ou dans un réglement intérieur la répartition des compétences ainsi définies.

- Adéquation de la composition du conseil à celle de l'actionnariat de la société ; opportunité de la participation d'un ou plusieurs administrateurs indépendants, c'est-à-dire de personnes dénuées de tout lien d'intérêt direct ou indirect avec la société ou les sociétés de son groupe.

  S'agissant des administrateurs réciproques, le conseil doit particulièrement veiller à ce que leur nombre excessif ou les fonctions particulières qui leur sont éventuellement dévolues, par exemple au sein de comités, ne puissent faire craindre une perte d'indépendance préjudiciable à l'exercice de leur mission ou au fonctionnement collégial du conseil.

- Caractère suffisant des dispositions prises pour assurer, le cas échéant, la succession du Président et des mandataires sociaux.

- Utilité d'imposer des obligations particulières aux administrateurs, telles que détention d'un nombre minimum d'actions fixé par le conseil ou sanctions en cas de manquement aux devoirs énumérés par la " charte de l'administrateur " formulée par le présent rapport.

  Le Comité a examiné de manière détaillée tous ces points et il a estimé devoir exprimer ci-après ses recommandations en invitant chaque conseil à délibérer de l'adaptation des principes qu'elles expriment aux particularités de sa société.

*

Ainsi sans prétendre se substituer à la réflexion propre qu'il convient à chaque conseil de conduire, le Comité s'est successivement attaché à étudier les diverses questions qui peuvent être soulevées et relatives aux attributions du conseil, à sa composition et à son fonctionnement. Il espère contribuer ainsi à accentuer l'évolution déjà entreprise vers une plus grande formalisation des travaux des conseils des sociétés cotées et vers l'amélioration de la transparence particulièrement nécessaire dont ils sont les garants à l'égard des actionnaires.

Le Comité estime qu'il est souhaitable qu'un nouvel examen de ces questions soit effectué dans trois ans pour mesurer alors cette évolution.

*

I
MISSION ET ATTRIBUTIONS DU CONSEIL D'ADMINISTRATION

1. La finalité de la mission du conseil

Dans les pays anglosaxons, l'accent sur ce point est principalement mis sur l'objectif de maximisation de la valeur de l'action, alors que, sur le continent européen et en particulier en France, il est plutôt mis sur l'intérêt social de l'entreprise.

Il s'agit là de nuances plutôt que de conceptions absolument différentes : l'intérêt social ne saurait bien entendu pas conduire à méconnaître le marché, régulateur de la vie économique, mais il est le pôle vers lequel les dirigeants sociaux et tous les administrateurs doivent orienter leur conduite et qui leur impose de respecter en toutes circonstances un intérêt plus large que les leurs propres.

L'intérêt social peut ainsi se définir comme l'intérêt supérieur de la personne morale elle-même, c'est-à-dire de l'entreprise considérée comme un agent économique autonome, poursuivant des fins propres, distinctes notamment de celles de ses actionnaires, de ses salariés, de ses créanciers dont le fisc, de ses fournisseurs et de ses clients, mais qui correspondent à leur intérêt général commun, qui est d'assurer la prospérité et la continuité de l'entreprise.

Le Comité considère que l'action des administrateurs doit être inspirée par le seul souci de l'intérêt de la société concernée.

2. Conseil d'administration et assemblée générale des actionnaires

Représentant l'ensemble des actionnaires, le conseil d'administration répond collectivement de l'exercice de ses missions devant leur assemblée générale envers laquelle il assume légalement les responsabilités essentielles : c'est lui qui convoque et fixe l'ordre du jour de l'assemblée, nomme et révoque le président et les directeurs généraux chargés de la direction de l'entreprise, contrôle leur gestion et en rend compte par le rapport annuel et les comptes qu'il a arrêtés.

Bien que la société soit instituée par un contrat, les compétences respectives des organes sociaux sont définies en France par la loi et ne peuvent être modifiées par le pacte social.
Le Comité a examiné la répartition légale des pouvoirs entre l'Assemblée générale

des actionnaires et le conseil d'administration et **n'a pas relevé l'existence de problèmes nécessitant une intervention législative ou de suggestions tendant à modifier significativement les rôles respectifs des deux organes.**

La seule question de compétence qui ait donné naissance à un contentieux, d'ailleurs limité à quelques affaires, est relative à la cession d'actifs ou d'activités très importants. La jurisprudence est à cet égard bien établie : les cessions d'actifs ou d'activités sont de la compétence du conseil d'administration ou de son Président sauf si elles portent atteinte à l'objet social que seule l'Assemblée générale extraordinaire a pouvoir de modifier.

Il appartient bien entendu au conseil de respecter la compétence propre des actionnaires si l'opération qu'il envisage est de nature à modifier en droit ou en fait l'objet social qui est la cause même du contrat instituant la société. Même si ce n'est pas le cas, **le Comité estime qu'il est souhaitable que le conseil recueille l'avis de l'assemblée générale si la cession concerne une part prépondérante des actifs ou activités du groupe.**

3. Le conseil d'administration et le marché

Au-delà même du strict respect de ses obligations légales à l'égard des actionnaires, **le conseil d'administration d'une société cotée est investi d'une responsabilité particulière à l'égard du marché.**

Sans doute est-ce au Président que revient la tâche d'assurer au jour le jour l'information du marché, mais c'est au conseil qu'il appartient d'assumer celle-ci à l'occasion des arrêtés des comptes semestriels et annuels ou de la réalisation d'opérations financières : il doit alors bien entendu veiller à la qualité de l'information, et notamment à sa fiabilité et à sa clarté, afin que les transactions puissent être effectuées de manière équitable.

Le Comité estime que, dans cet objectif de transparence, le conseil doit rendre public son avis sur les conditions des opérations concernant les titres de la société même quand la réglementation ne l'exige pas. Ainsi paraît-il normal que le conseil donne son avis sur le prix proposé dans le cadre, par exemple, d'une garantie de cours ou sur l'opportunité pour la société d'une offre publique de retrait portant sur ses actions. Le devoir de réserve de l'administrateur ne s'oppose pas à ce qu'il fasse connaître le cas échéant son opinion divergente s'il l'estime indispensable.

4. Le conseil d'administration et son président

Deux critiques sont souvent formulées à l'encontre de l'organisation des pouvoirs au sein des conseils d'administration français : la répartition des compétences entre le président et le conseil serait trop ambiguë et le cumul des fonctions de président du conseil et de directeur général assurerait au président une prépondérance excessive par rapport au conseil.

Les compétences respectives :

On sait que sous réserve des pouvoirs propres que la loi réserve au conseil dans son ensemble, le conseil et le président sont l'un et l'autre investis " des pouvoirs les plus étendus pour agir en toute circonstance au nom de la société ".

Si ses détracteurs critiquent la concurrence des compétences qui est ainsi organisée par la loi, ils ne précisent guère les inconvénients effectifs qui en résulteraient et que l'on ne constate guère en fait.

Pas plus d'ailleurs que dans les pays étrangers dotés d'organes sociaux similaires, le conseil d'administration n'a en réalité vocation à prendre collégialement les multiples décisions qu'implique la direction de l'entreprise et qui appartiennent par nature aux dirigeants qu'il nomme à cette fin et dont il contrôle la gestion.

Le Comité estime que, loin d'être source de confusion, la souplesse du droit français présente des avantages manifestes : chaque conseil peut adapter au mieux la répartition des compétences aux circonstances ainsi qu'aux caractéristiques et aux besoins propres de l'entreprise, restreindre le champ de ses interventions préalables pour ne pas risquer de gêner inutilement la gestion ou élargir celles qu'il entend se réserver en définissant des catégories d'opérations dont il entend être saisi et, s'il veut formaliser cette répartition, il lui est loisible d'adopter un réglement intérieur aussi précis qu'il le souhaite.

Ainsi, sans prétendre se substituer à l'organe exécutif, le conseil peut-il directement s'impliquer si nécessaire dans la prise des décisions qui lui paraissent les plus importantes.

Le Comité estime que la faculté très large laissée au conseil de répartir les compétences en son sein est indispensable au bon fonctionnement des organes sociaux des entreprises en raison même de leur diversité et de la variété des circonstances qu'elles traversent.

Il n'y a là pas matière à un débat " constitutionnel " théorique, qu'obscurcit d'ailleurs l'abus d'un vocabulaire emprunté à tort à la vie politique.

Bien entendu, cette large faculté dont dispose le conseil connait des limites et lui crée une obligation ; le conseil ne peut évidemment pas se dessaisir des pouvoirs propres que lui attribue la loi et il doit exercer pleinement ses missions, notamment contrôler la gestion comme l'information fournie au marché et définir la stratégie de l'entreprise.
La clarté de la stratégie n'est pas seulement le gage indispensable d'une bonne ges-

tion ; elle est aussi un élément fondamental de l'information due aux actionnaires et au marché.

Le Comité estime que s'il appartient au président d'élaborer et de proposer la stratégie de l'entreprise, celle-ci doit être arrêtée en conseil. Celui-ci doit, en conséquence, examiner et décider les opérations d'importance véritablement stratégique soit directement en formation plénière, soit, si celà paraît plus opportun, après étude au sein d'un comité ad hoc qui ne provoque la réunion du conseil que si nécessaire.

La dissociation des fonctions n'est pas une panacée :

Certains observateurs extérieurs à la vie des entreprises critiquent également le fait qu'une même personne assure à la fois la direction générale de l'entreprise et la présidence du conseil qui contrôle sa gestion : ils suggèrent de dissocier ces fonctions.

Le Comité observe qu'elles ont bien été dissociées en France jusqu'à la dernière guerre et que c'est précisément pour mettre fin aux dysfonctionnements en résultant qu'elles ont été réunies. La dissociation a sans doute des mérites là où les administrateurs exerçant des fonctions exécutives dans l'entreprise peuvent constituer une fraction importante voire prépondérante du conseil. Tel n'est pas le cas en France où la loi limite strictement leur nombre et où le nombre maximum autorisé des directeurs généraux est d'ailleurs rarement atteint en pratique.

En outre, à celles des sociétés qui souhaitent séparer rigoureusement les fonctions exécutives des fonctions de contrôle, la loi française offre la possibilité de choisir la structure duale du directoire et du conseil de surveillance.

Cette forme de société est, il est vrai, peu répandue en France. Il est possible que la rigidité de la répartition légale des rôles des organes sociaux fasse obstacle à une utilisation plus fréquente de ce mode d'organisation des pouvoirs au sein de l'entreprise (3) . Le Comité n'en a pas entrepris l'analyse qui était étrangère à sa mission.

Il considère pour sa part que si en France la plupart des sociétés cotées, comme d'ailleurs la plupart des sociétés anonymes, sont dotées d'un conseil d'administra tion, c'est que le plus souvent une très stricte séparation des fonctions ne paraît pas

(3) Plusieurs assouplissements sont souvent suggérés : la loi pourrait par exemple laisser aux statuts la faculté d'attribuer au conseil de surveillance le pouvoir de révoquer les directeurs, celle de désigner plus librement un directeur unique ou de prévoir que les directeurs ne soient nommés que sur proposition du président du directoire.

s'imposer et qu'elle ne constitue pas, dans la plupart des cas, la condition nécessaire d'une bonne direction générale ou d'un contrôle efficace de la gestion.

Le conseil d'administration répond d'ailleurs collectivement et simultanément de l'un et de l'autre devant l'assemblée générale des actionnaires. Le président et le conseil assument ainsi ensemble tant le succès ou l'échec de la direction générale que la qualité ou la défaillance du contrôle de la gestion et c'est ensemble qu'ils doivent prendre les dispositions propres à satisfaire les actionnaires à qui ils rendent compte.

Gestion et contrôle de la gestion forment un tout. Au conseil de se constituer et de s'organiser de manière à exercer avec diligence l'ensemble de ses missions.

II
LA COMPOSITION DU CONSEIL D'ADMINISTRATION

1. Principes directeurs

La composition des conseils d'administration fait l'objet de débats variés concernant la représentation en leur sein de catégories particulières d'intérêts ou de compétences et au travers desquels le public manifeste un certain doute à l'égard de l'indépendance et de l'objectivité des membres des conseils.

Le Comité a examiné les critiques et les diverses suggestions qui sont faites. Au terme de cet examen, il **croit devoir réaffirmer son attachement aux principes traditionnels du droit et de la pratique français : quelles que soient sa composition et l'origine de ses membres, le conseil d'administration représente collectivement l'ensemble des actionnaires ;** il n'est pas un agrégat disparate de représentants d'intérêts contradictoires ; sa mission doit s'exercer dans l'intérêt social commun et, s'il y manque, il engage la responsabilité solidaire de tous ses membres.

De même, **quelles que soient sa qualité ou sa compétence particulières, chaque administrateur doit se considérer comme le représentant de l'ensemble des actionnaires et se comporter comme tel dans l'exercice de ses fonctions sauf à engager sa responsabilité personnelle.**

Le conseil d'administration d'une société cotée doit tout particulièrement veiller à appliquer ces principes comme il doit consacrer une réflexion particulière à la confiance que doit inspirer sa propre composition au marché, en prenant en compte la composition et la nature de l'actionnariat de la société.

Le Comité estime qu'à cet effet **chaque conseil doit s'interroger sur l'équilibre souhaitable de sa composition ou de celle des comités qu'il constitue en son sein, en prenant des dispositions propres à assurer les actionnaires et le marché que ses missions sont accomplies avec l'indépendance et l'objectivité nécessaires.** Sans accroître excessivement le nombre de ses membres, au risque de compromettre la participation effective de chacun aux délibérations, le conseil doit ainsi s'interroger notamment sur l'opportunité de la nomination d'un ou plusieurs administrateurs indépendants et sur le nombre de mandats réciproques en son sein.

2. Les administrateurs " indépendants " face à la technostructure et à l'actionnariat.

Le débat sur la nécessaire présence dans les conseils d'administration d'administrateurs " indépendants " est né aux Etats Unis et en Grande Bretagne en réaction à la sur-représentation, au sein des conseils de ces pays, de dirigeants exerçant des fonctions exécutives dans l'entreprise.

Il s'est récemment développé en France où a priori il n'a pas lieu d'être, puisque le nombre des administrateurs participant à la " technostructure " de l'entreprise y est strictement plafonné, ce qui paraît d'ailleurs tout à fait normal au Comité.

C'est que la définition de l'administrateur " indépendant " ne l'oppose pas seulement aux directeurs généraux ou aux salariés de l'entreprise, mais également à tous ceux qui ont un intérêt particulier à leur relation avec celle-ci : actionnaires, fournisseurs, clients ...

L'administrateur indépendant peut en effet, en s'inspirant des standards anglo saxons, être défini comme une personne qui est dénuée de tout lien d'intérêt direct ou indirect avec la société ou les sociétés de son groupe et qui peut ainsi être réputée participer en toute objectivité aux travaux du conseil : il doit ainsi n'être ni salarié, ni président ou directeur général de la société ou d'une société de son groupe ni ne l'être plus depuis une période suffisante qui est d'au moins trois ans ; n'être pas un actionnaire important de la société ou d'une société de son groupe ni être lié de quelque manière que ce soit à un tel actionnaire ; n'être enfin pas lié de quelque manière que ce soit à un partenaire significatif et habituel, commercial ou financier, de la société ou des sociétés de son groupe.

Les conseils d'administration des principales sociétés cotées comportent déjà bien des personnes choisies exclusivement en fonction de leur compétence personnelle et qui sont des administrateurs indépendants au sens de cette définition.

Faut-il généraliser cette pratique et dans quelle mesure ?

Tout en considérant que le conseil, représentant collectif des actionnaires, doit d'abord comprendre des actionnaires, le Comité constate que la participation d'administrateurs indépendants répond à une attente du marché et qu'elle est de nature à améliorer la qualité des délibérations et à garantir le respect des principes traditionnels rappelés ci-dessus.

La composition du conseil implique un équilibre qui est à rechercher cas par cas entre les administrateurs liés aux actionnaires, les administrateurs indépendants et la technostructure dont les représentants doivent être en tout état de cause peu nombreux.

Le Comité estime en conséquence qu'il est souhaitable que chaque conseil d'une société cotée comporte au moins deux administrateurs indépendants, étant entendu qu'il appartient à chaque conseil de rechercher l'équilibre optimal de sa composition.

3. Les représentants de catégories spécifiques.

Faut-il, comme le suggèrent certains, multiplier au sein du conseil les représentants de telle ou telle catégorie d'intérêts spécifiques ?

Le Comité considère qu'il n'est pas souhaitable d'aller dans cette voie parce que le conseil risquerait d'être le champ clos d'affrontements d'intérêts particuliers au lieu de représenter collectivement l'ensemble des actionnaires et parce que la présence d'administrateurs indépendants est un gage suffisant de ce que tous les intérêts susceptibles d'être pris en compte l'auront été.

Ceci n'exclut pas, bien entendu, que, dans des cas particuliers, il soit utile de faire place à la représentation d'intérêts catégoriels : à chaque conseil de l'apprécier. En tout état de cause, une fois nommé, l'administrateur doit se conduire en représentant de l'ensemble des actionnaires et poursuivre le seul intérêt social de l'entreprise.

Salariés et salariés actionnaires :

La législation française offre la double particularité d'associer aux travaux du conseil des représentants du Comité d'Entreprise qui ont une voix consultative et en outre de prévoir la possibilité d'une pleine participation au conseil d'élus des salariés (ordonnance de 1986) ou de salariés-actionnaires (loi de 1994).

Le Comité s'étonne que l'ordonnance de 1986 maintienne une représentation spécifique du Comité d'Entreprise alors même que la société a choisi de faire siéger à son conseil des représentants élus des salariés en qualité d'administrateurs.

Actionnaires minoritaires dans les sociétés contrôlées :

Lorsqu'une société est contrôlée par un actionnaire majoritaire (ou un groupe d'actionnaires agissant de concert), l'actionnaire majoritaire assume une responsabilité propre à l'égard des autres actionnaires, directe et distincte de celle du conseil d'administration.

Celui-ci doit, dans une société contrôlée, veiller avec une particulière attention à prévenir les éventuels conflits d'intérêts, à tenir équitablement compte de tous les intérêts et à assurer la transparence de l'information fournie au marché.

Faute que puisse siéger au conseil un représentant de chaque minoritaire, les nombreux minoritaires non représentés d'une société cotée contesteront toujours les systèmes spécifiques de représentation qui leur seraient proposés.

Aussi le Comité estime-t-il que la meilleure formule consiste à nommer plusieurs administrateurs indépendants dans les sociétés contrôlées plutôt que de tenter d'assurer une représentation spécifique des minoritaires.

Ces administrateurs indépendants seront les garants de l'objectivité des délibérations du conseil.

Petits actionnaires dans les sociétés non contrôlées :

Dans les sociétés à actionnariat éclaté, apparaît de même une revendication de représentation spécifique des " petits actionnaires ".

Pour des raisons analogues à celles qui conduisent à écarter la suggestion d'une représentation spécifique des actionnaires minoritaires, le **Comité estime que la prise en compte de leurs intérêts doit être faite par la désignation d'administrateurs indépendants, qui peuvent d'ailleurs être bien entendu choisis parmi des personnes ayant leur sensibilité.**

4. Participations croisées et administrateurs réciproques :

La faiblesse relative du capitalisme français est à l'origine d'une multiplication des participations croisées.

L'indispensable création de fonds de pension, une incitation de l'épargne française à s'orienter plus vers la détention d'actions ainsi que l'afflux des capitaux étrangers, devraient, en favorisant le développement des fonds propres des entreprises, réduire naturellement ces croisements de capitaux.

Le croisement des participations apparaît ainsi comme un état transitoire du capitalisme français, dont la résorption aussi rapide que possible est au demeurant très souhaitable.

Ce croisement implique souvent, bien que de manière non inéluctable, la détention réciproque de mandats d'administrateurs, chacune des sociétés concernées ayant un représentant au conseil de l'autre société : cette situation suscite des interrogations du marché.

Aussi le Comité estime-t-il que **lorsque le conseil examine l'équilibre optimal de sa composition, il doit particulièrement veiller à ce que le nombre des mandats réciproques ne soit pas excessif en son sein.**

De même le Comité recommande-t-il que le **conseil d'une société A évite de nommer au sein de son comité des rémunérations comme de son comité d'audit des administrateurs venant d'une société B lorsque au comité analogue de la société B siège déjà un administrateur venant de la société A.**

Enfin, la recommandation faite plus loin sur la limitation du cumul des postes d'administrateurs dans les sociétés cotées devrait contribuer à réduire la réciprocité des mandats.

5. La sélection des administrateurs et des mandataires sociaux :

Si le pouvoir de nommer ou révoquer les administrateurs appartient à l'assemblée générale des actionnaires, le conseil d'administration joue un rôle déterminant dans sa propre composition puisqu'il peut coopter ses membres et qu'il propose leur désignation à l'assemblée.

Actuellement la recherche d'administrateurs et de mandataires sociaux se fait le plus souvent de manière très informelle, ce qui ne garantit pas qu'ont été délibérés et pris en compte tous les éléments qui concourent à l'équilibre souhaitable de la composition du conseil.

Enfin, à défaut d'une procédure formalisée, le marché tend à supposer que les présidents jouent un rôle excessif dans le choix des personnes appelées à siéger au conseil.

Aussi le Comité recommande-t-il à chaque conseil de constituer en son sein un comité de sélection des administrateurs et mandataires sociaux ; à défaut, les tâches évoquées ci-après peuvent être dévolues au comité des rémunérations.

Le comité de sélection :

Composé de trois à cinq membres, y compris le président ainsi qu'au moins un administrateur indépendant, ce comité aurait la charge de faire des propositions au conseil après avoir examiné de manière circonstanciée tous les éléments qu'il doit prendre en compte dans sa délibération : équilibre souhaitable de la composition du conseil au vu de la composition et de l'évolution de l'actionnariat de la société, notamment nombre souhaitable des administrateurs indépendants, représentation éventuelle d'intérêts catégoriels, recherche et appréciation des candidats possibles, opportunité des renouvellements de mandats ...

La succession des mandataires sociaux :

La désignation du président et, sur proposition du président, des autres mandataires sociaux, qu'ils soient membres ou non du conseil, relève de la responsabilité propre de celui-ci.

Le comité de sélection doit naturellement être chargé d'examiner les propositions du président et de formuler son avis au conseil.

A la différence des conseils étrangers, les conseils français passent pour ne pas se préoccuper d'organiser la succession du président. Cette situation inquiète le marché.

Le Comité recommande que le " comité de sélection " ait pour mission expresse d'être à tout moment en situation de proposer au conseil des solutions de succession en cas de vacance imprévisible, même si celles-ci doivent demeurer confidentielles.

III
LE FONCTIONNEMENT DU CONSEIL D'ADMINISTRATION

Le fonctionnement des conseil français est encore très informel. Même lorsque les conseils ont formalisé leurs procédures internes, ils le font peu connaître.

Il en résulte une certaine inquiétude de l'opinion qui se demande si les conseils des sociétés cotées remplissent effectivement et pleinement leurs missions.

Le Comité estime que chaque conseil doit rendre compte aux actionnaires des dispositions qu'il prend pour être en situation de remplir ses missions et qu'il a le devoir de s'interroger périodiquement sur l'adéquation à ses tâches de son organisation et de son fonctionnement. Il recommande l'adoption d'un plus grand formalisme dans la préparation des délibérations.

1. Les réunions du conseil

En général les conseils d'administration des sociétés cotées se réunissent trois à quatre fois par an et leurs réunions durent en pratique environ deux heures.

La périodicité et la durée des réunions ne se prêtent guère à la définition de normes ; à chaque conseil de les apprécier. Il est clair que les conseils doivent se réunir lorsque les circonstances l'exigent et, à défaut de circonstances particulières, quatre à six réunions sont suffisantes pour contrôler la marche du groupe et prendre les décisions essentielles surtout si celles-ci ont été préparées par les travaux de comités spécialisés ; la réunion doit être d'une durée suffisante pour débattre utilement de l'ordre du jour.

Le Comité a relevé deux obstacles particuliers à des consultations rapides du conseil :

En premier lieu, la loi semble exiger que toute délibération soit prise en une réunion effective : il serait souhaitable qu'elle soit modifiée pour permettre la tenue de conseils sous forme de conférences téléphoniques ou audiovisuelles qui permettent aujourd'hui une véritable délibération collégiale à distance.

En second lieu, le Président a l'exclusivité de la convocation du conseil sauf si celui-ci ne s'est pas réuni depuis plus de deux mois auquel cas le tiers des administrateurs peut procéder à la convocation : chaque conseil pourrait examiner l'opportunité d'une modification statutaire allégeant ces conditions.

Les délibérations doivent être claires.

Le procès-verbal de séance résume les débats et précise les décisions prises. Il revêt une importance particulière puisque c'est lui qui fournit, le cas échéant, la trace des diligences du conseil dans l'accomplissement de ses missions. Sans être inutilement détaillé, il doit succinctement mentionner les questions soulevées ou les réserves émises.

2. L'information du conseil et des administrateurs

Certains insinuent que les administrateurs ne disposent pas d'une information suffisante pour exercer leur mission.

Faut-il rappeler que le président a l'obligation de fournir aux administrateurs, dans un délai suffisant, les informations significatives qui leur sont nécessaires pour exercer pleinement leur mission de contrôle ? Il convient que les administrateurs reçoivent en temps utile un dossier sur les points de l'ordre du jour qui nécessitent une analyse particulière et une réflexion préalable (et chaque fois que le respect de la confidentialité ne l'interdit pas).

Le Comité estime que si un administrateur considère qu'il n'a pas été mis en situation de délibérer en toute connaissance de cause, il a le devoir de le dire au conseil et d'exiger l'information indispensable.

3. La création de comités spécialisés au sein du conseil

De nombreux conseils se sont dotés de comités permanents spécialisés qui instruisent les affaires dont ils ont la charge et formulent leurs propositions au conseil.

Le Comité est très favorable à une telle organisation des travaux du conseil qui permet d'approfondir les analyses sans mobiliser tous ses membres et garantit que l'aspect correspondant de sa mission est effectué avec une diligence suffisante.

Chaque conseil peut souhaiter se doter de comités spécialisés correspondant à telle ou telle préoccupation particulière : en aucun cas la création de comités ne doit dessaisir le conseil lui-même qui a seul le pouvoir légal de décision ni conduire à un démembrement de son collège qui est et doit demeurer collectivement responsable de l'accomplissement de ses missions.

Pour sa part, le Comité recommande que chaque conseil se dote au moins d'un comité de sélection des administrateurs, d'un comité des rémunérations et d'un comité des comptes et informe les actionnaires, lors de l'assemblée générale annuelle, de l'existence de ces comités ainsi que du nombre de réunions qu'ils ont tenues au cours de l'année.

Le comité de sélection des administrateurs a déjà été évoqué.

Le comité des rémunérations

La plupart des conseils sont déjà dotés d'un comité des rémunérations, chargé de proposer la rémunération des mandataires sociaux ainsi que parfois les plans de souscriptions ou d'achat d'actions (tâche parfois dévolue à un autre comité).

La composition de ces comités est souvent critiquée car ils comporteraient un nombre élevé d'administrateurs réciproques ; aussi faut-il y prêter une attention particulière.

Comme il a déjà été dit, **le Comité recommande d'éviter de nommer dans le comité des rémunérations d'une société A, un administrateur venant d'une société dans le comité analogue de laquelle siègerait réciproquement un administrateur venant de la société A.**

Le comité des comptes ou comité d'audit

C'est principalement à l'occasion de l'arrêté des comptes que le conseil doit assumer deux de ses missions essentielles : le contrôle de la gestion et la vérification de la fiabilité et de la clarté des informations qui seront fournies aux actionnaires et au marché.

La préparation de la délibération du conseil par un comité spécialisé, dont les attributions et la composition sont portées à la connaissance du public, est de nature à lui garantir la diligence et l'objectivité qu'impliquent ces missions.

Aussi **le Comité recommande-t-il que chaque conseil se dote d'un comité ayant pour tâche essentielle de s'assurer de la pertinence et de la permanence des méthodes comptables adoptées pour l'établissement des comptes consolidés et sociaux de l'entreprise et de vérifier que les procédures internes de collecte et de contrôle des informations garantissent celles-ci.**

Il s'agit moins d'entrer dans le détail des comptes que d'apprécier la fiabilité de l'appareil qui concourt à leur établissement ainsi que la validité des positions prises pour traiter les opérations significatives.

Il est également souhaitable qu'à l'occasion de l'examen des comptes le comité se penche sur les opérations importantes à l'occasion desquelles aurait pu se produire un conflit d'intérêt et qu'il soit appelé à donner son avis sur la nomination des commissaires aux comptes ainsi que sur la qualité de leurs travaux.

Enfin ce comité doit avoir la faculté de rencontrer, hors de la présence des mandataires sociaux ou plus généralement des administrateurs qui exercent des fonctions actives dans l'entreprise, les personnes qui, à un titre ou à un autre, participent à l'élaboration des comptes ou à leur contrôle : direction financière, direction de l'audit interne, commissaires aux comptes.

Il doit rendre compte au conseil de ses travaux et porter à sa connaissance tous les points qui lui paraissent poser problème ou appeler une décision, facilitant ainsi ses délibérations.

Aussi le Comité estime-t-il que cette pratique devrait se généraliser rapidement parmi les sociétés cotées.

Une attention particulière doit être apportée à la composition du comité, qui devrait comprendre trois administrateurs au moins, dont aucun exerçant des fonctions de direction générale ou salariale dans l'entreprise, et dont l'un au moins doit être un administrateur indépendant. La recommandation relative aux " croisements intercomités " faite pour le comité des rémunérations s'applique également au comité des comptes.

4. Les droits et obligations des administrateurs

La charte de l'administrateur

Qu'ils découlent des textes eux-mêmes ou résultent de l'usage, les devoirs de l'administrateur ne font guère l'objet d'exposés systématiques et demeurent souvent implicites.

Les administrateurs en ont une plus claire conscience que ne le suppose généralement l'opinion publique, mais il est préférable que toute ambiguïté soit levée par une formulation sans équivoque de la déontologie essentielle.

A ce titre, le Comité estime que **tout administrateur (4) d'une société cotée doit se considérer tenu aux obligations suivantes :**

- Avant d'accepter ses fonctions, **l'administrateur doit s'assurer qu'il a pris connaissance des obligations** générales ou particulières **de sa charge**. Il doit notamment prendre connaissance des textes légaux ou réglementaires, des statuts, de la présente charte et des compléments que chaque conseil peut lui avoir apporté ainsi que, le cas échéant, des règles de fonctionnement interne dont ce conseil s'est doté.
- **L'administrateur doit être actionnaire à titre personnel** et posséder -au-delà des seules exigences statutaires- un nombre relativement significatif d'actions : à défaut de les détenir lors de son entrée en fonction, il doit utiliser ses jetons de présence à leur acquisition.

(4) Les obligations sont bien entendu autant celles du représentant permanent d'une personne morale administrateur que celles des personnes physiques administrateurs.

- Bien qu'étant lui-même actionnaire, **l'administrateur représente l'ensemble des actionnaires** et doit agir en toutes circonstances dans l'intérêt social de l'entreprise.

- **L'administrateur a l'obligation de faire part au conseil de toute situation de conflit d'intérêt** même potentiel et doit s'abstenir de participer au vote de la délibération correspondante.

- **L'administrateur doit consacrer à ses fonctions le temps et l'attention nécessaires.** Lorsqu'il exerce des fonctions de président ou de directeur général, il ne devrait en principe pas accepter d'exercer plus de cinq mandats d'administrateur dans des sociétés cotées françaises ou étrangères extérieures à son groupe.

- **L'administrateur doit être assidu** et participer à toutes les réunions du conseil ou, le cas échéant, des comités auxquels il appartient.

- **L'administrateur a l'obligation de s'informer**. A cet effet, il doit réclamer dans les délais appropriés au président les informations indispensables à une intervention utile sur les sujets à l'ordre du jour du conseil.

- S'agissant des informations non publiques acquises dans le cadre de ses fonctions, **l'administrateur doit se considérer astreint à un véritable secret professionnel** qui dépasse la simple obligation de discrétion prévue par les textes.

- **L'administrateur** doit enfin bien entendu **s'abstenir d'effectuer des opérations sur les titres** des sociétés sur lesquelles (et dans la mesure où) il dispose de par ses fonctions d'informations non encore rendues publiques.

Enfin le Comité estime qu'il est très souhaitable que tous les administrateurs assistent aux réunions de l'Assemblée générale des actionnaires.

Il appartient à chaque conseil de compléter, le cas échéant, cette liste des obligations fondamentales de l'administrateur par les dispositions particulières que son fonctionnement lui paraît exiger.

Le conseil et ses membres

Le mandat de l'administrateur s'exerce au sein d'un collège dont il partage solidairement la responsabilité collective et à qui il a le devoir de faire part de ses préoccupations ou réserves.

Le Comité estime que le conseil d'administration doit collectivement s'interroger sur le statut de ses membres, s'assurer que ceux-ci sont en situation de remplir leur mission, notamment en disposant de l'information nécessaire, et ne pas hésiter à compléter la liste de leurs obligations fondamentales si la situation de l'entreprise lui paraît l'exiger. Ces tâches peuvent être dévolues au Comité de sélection des administrateurs.

Il doit notamment s'interroger sur l'opportunité d'instituer ou non un nombre minimum d'actions que chaque administrateur doit détenir au-delà même du seuil statutaire qui est souvent très bas. Pour éviter que cette exigence ne soit une contrainte excessive pour certains administrateurs, il peut envisager que le montant net d'impôt de leurs jetons de présence soit consacré à l'acquisition de titres de la société jusqu'à ce qu'ils détiennent le minimum d'actions souhaité.

Contrairement à ce que suppose l'opinion publique, l'absentéisme des administrateurs est rare. S'il se manifeste, le conseil a l'obligation de prendre des dispositions pour assurer une participation effective de ses membres à ses délibérations plénières ou aux réunions de ses comités spécialisés (par exemple : proportionnalité des jetons de présence à l'assiduité ; publication de la participation des administrateurs aux séances ; fixation dans le règlement intérieur d'un nombre d'absences à partir duquel l'administrateur serait invité à se démettre ou serait révoqué en assemblée générale).

Compte tenu des responsabilités encourues par les administrateurs et du temps qu'ils doivent consacrer à leurs fonctions, les jetons de présence ne doivent pas être symboliques. Il paraît naturel que la participation des administrateurs à des comités spécialisés soit encouragée par un montant supplémentaire de jetons de présence.

*

* *

Au terme de l'examen auquel il a procédé, le Comité tient à souligner à nouveau que les administrateurs des sociétés cotées assument personnellement et collectivement une responsabilité particulière à l'égard du marché.

Dès qu'elle s'adresse à celui-ci, une société change en quelque sorte de nature et son conseil doit répondre de ses diligences non seulement à ses actionnaires actuels mais aussi à tous les souscripteurs potentiels.

Ceci lui impose de répondre aux interrogations de l'opinion publique par une plus grande formalisation de l'organisation de ses travaux et par un plus grand souci de faire connaître les dispositions qu'il a prises pour ce faire.

Les règles actuelles permettent cette évolution qui est déjà commencée. Elles ne peuvent toutefois suppléer au respect d'une stricte déontologie qui est jusqu'ici demeurée trop implicite et que le Comité s'est efforcé de formuler en invitant tous les conseils d'administration des sociétés concernées à délibérer des conditions dans lesquelles chacun l'applique en son sein.

Un mouvement est en cours vers une meilleure organisation des travaux des conseils. Le Comité espère avoir contribué à son accélération et à son renforcement.

Collection des **rapport offciels**

Rapport au Premier ministre

La modernisation du droit des sociétés

Philippe Marini

La **documentation** Française

Résumé des propositions contenues dans le rapport

Favoriser la liberté d'entreprendre
Un droit plus neutre

Envisager la création d'un patrimoine fiscal d'affectation

1 Étudier l'opportunité de la création d'un patrimoine fiscal d'affectation permettant de calculer l'impôt sur le revenu et les charges sociales sur la seule fraction des résultats prélevée par l'exploitant.

Assurer la neutralité fiscale et sociale des différentes formes de sociétés

2 Aligner le statut fiscal des gérants de SARL, y compris des gérants associés uniques d'EURL qui ont opté pour l'impôt sur les sociétés. sur celui des dirigeants de sociétés anonymes, (l'option ouverte en faveur des SARL familiales pour le régime d'imposition des sociétés de personnes étant bien entendu maintenue).

3 Harmoniser les statuts sociaux des dirigeants de sociétés, sur la base d'une option entre régime général et régime des non-salariés.

4 Harmoniser le régime fiscal des cessions de droits sociaux en rendant applicable aux cessions de parts de SARL le régime fiscal des cessions d'actions.

Un droit plus souple

Préserver et conforter la diversité actuelle des formes sociales

Préserver les formes sociales existantes

5 Ouvrir à tout associé d'une société en nom collectif (SNC) la possibilité de demander en justice la révocation du gérant pour cause légitime.

6 Harmoniser la durée de la prescription de l'action en responsabilité contre les gérants de la SNC avec celle applicable aux dirigeants des autres sociétés commerciales.

7 Autoriser la création de sociétés par actions simplifiées unipersonelles.

Conforter la spécificité des formes sociales les plus utilisées

8 Relever le capital minimum de la SARL à 100 000 francs (50 000 francs pour l'EURL).

9 Relever le capital minimum de la SA à 500 000 francs (3 millions de francs en cas d'appel public à l'épargne).

Préciser les exigences légales en cas d'appel au marché

10 Donner une définition légale de l'appel public à l'épargne.

11 Prévoir une différenciation des assouplissements aux exigences légales relatives à l'organisation de la SA selon qu'il s'agit ou non de sociétés dont les titres sont négociés sur un marché réglementé (voir *infra*)

Suivre attentivement l'évolution du droit communautaire

12 Favoriser l'harmonisation des règles en matière d'opérations transfrontières.

13 Favoriser la création de formes sociales communautaires.

Introduire la fiducie en droit français

14 Introduire en droit français la fiducie-sûreté et la fiducie-transmission.

Simplifier et favoriser la liberté contractuelle

La société à responsabilité limitée

Constitution de la SARL

15 Donner la faculté aux associés de libérer leurs apports en numéraire par fractions.

16 Supprimer le nombre maximum d'associés.

17 Laisser les associés fixer eux-mêmes les conditions de restitution de leur apports en numéraire en cas de non-constitution.

Gestion de la SARL

18 Alligner le régime de la révocation du gérant sur celui de sa nomination, les statuts pouvant prévoir une majorité renforcée.

19 Permettre une gestion avec gérant (s) et conseil de surveillance qui pourrait devenir obligatoire au-delà de certains seuils en capital ou en nombre d'associés.

Les associés de la SARL

20 Donner un caractère supplétif aux dispositions de l'article 45 de la loi de 1966 imposant une double majorité dans le cas des cessions de parts à des tiers étrangers à la société.

La société anonyme

Constitution de la societé anonyme

21 Permettre la constitution de sociétés anonymes entre deux personnes.

22 Créer la société anonyme unipersonnelle, qui ne pourrait pas faire appel public à l'épargne.

23 Autoriser le rentrait des fonds sur simple demande des apporteurs munis du reçu attestant de leur souscription en cas de non constitution de la société.

24 Assouplir les conditions de nomination des premiers administrateurs, membres du conseil de surveillance et commissaires aux comptes qui pourraient être désignés dans les statuts, comme c'est le cas actuellement, mais aussi dans un acte séparé.

25 Unifier la durée maximale des fonctions des administrateurs et membres du conseil de surveillance quel que soit leur mode de désignation.

Gestion de la société anonyme

26 Introduire, pour les sociétés non cotées, en deçà de certains seuils, une faculté de gestion sans conseil d'administration.

27 Permettre la dissociation des fonctions de président du conseil d'administration et de directeur général.

Statut des dirigeants sociaux

28 Renvoyer aux statuts la question de savoir si les administrateurs ou membres du conseil de surveillance doivent posséder la qualité d'actionnaire, ainsi que l'éventuelle fixation d'un âge limite pour l'exercice de ces fonctions, de celles de président du conseil d'administration, de directeur général et de membre du directoire, que la société soit cotée ou non.

29 Laisser aux statuts le soin de fixer le nombre maximum d'administrateurs, de directeurs généraux, de membres du directoire et du conseil de surveillance.

30 Abandonner la règle selon laquelle certains directeurs généraux doivent être administrateurs au-delà d'un certain seuil de capital.

31 Autoriser la délégation d'un administrateur dans les fonctions de président en cas de démission ou de révocation de ce dernier.

32 Valider les conventions d'indemnisation du président et des autres membres du conseil d'administration, en cas de révocation sans faute de leur part, dès lors que l'indemnité prévue ne serait pas dis-

proportionnée aux services rendus à la société et qu'elle ne constituerait pas une charge telle qu'elle pourrait dissuader les actionnaires d'user de leur droit de révocation.

33 Autoriser un administrateur à conclure, postérieurement à sa désignation, un contrat de travail avec la société, sous réserve que ce contrat corresponde à un emploi effectif.

Actions et assemblées d'actionnaires

34 Admettre sans limitation la clause d'agrément dans les sociétés non cotées; la réputer non écrite dans les sociétés cotées.

35 Donner aux sociétés non cotées la possibilité de prévoir statutairement l'expression de la volonté des actionnaires par voie de consultation écrite, sauf en ce qui concerne les comptes annuels et, le cas échéant, les comptes consolidés.

36 Ouvrir aux statuts des sociétés non cotées la faculté de moduler à la hausse les conditions de quorum et de majorité dans les assemblées tant ordinaires qu'extraordinaires, sans toutefois pouvoir exiger l'unanimité.

37 Aligner le quorum prévu pour les assemblées spéciales sur celui des assemblées extraordinaires.

38 Ouvrir une possibilité de réduction des délais de convocation de l'assemblée extraordinaire, sur autorisation judiciaire.

39 Substituer à l'obligation de lecture du rapport du conseil d'administration ou du directoire, la simple présentation dudit rapport.

40 Attribuer la police de l'assemblée générale au bureau de celle-ci.

41 Permettre aux actionnaires de couvrir à l'unanimité, la nullité de délibérations prises par une assemblée sans qu'ait été atteint le quorum prévu par la loi, qu'il s'agisse d'une assemblée ordinaire, extraordinaire ou spéciale.

Permettre un meilleur fonctionnement des sociétés

Améliorer les modalités de gestion des entreprises

Les modalités de fonctionnement des organes sociaux

Le conseil d'administration

42 Renvoyer aux statuts le soin de fixer le nombre maximal des administrateurs salariés dans la limite de la moitié des postes, au lieu du tiers actuellement.

43 Étendre la limitation actuelle du cumul des mandats, qui ne s'applique qu'aux seuls mandats d'administrateurs personnes physiques, aux mandats exercés au nom d'une personne morale.

44 Prendre en compte dans cette limitation le nombre de mandats exécutifs, pour les très grandes entreprises.

45 Pour les mandats exercés dans des filiales. remplacer le critère du seuil de 20% de détention du capital, par celui du contrôle majoritaire.

46 Permettre, sous certaines conditions, la tenue de conseils sous forme de vidéoconférences.

Les comités spécialisés

47 Ouvrir aux statuts la faculté de déléguer certaines compétences propres du conseil d'administration à des comités spécialisés (sélection, rémunérations, audit), dans le cadre d'une liste limitative fixée par la loi.

48 Relever les commissaires aux comptes de leur obligation de secret à l'égard des membres des comités d'audit.

L'application des principes de la *corporate governance* aux entreprises publiques

49 Privilégier la forme sociale à directoire et conseil de surveillance pour les entreprises publiques.

50 Abandonner, lors des privatisations, la pratique dite des « noyaux durs ».

La modernisation du droit des valeurs mobilières

Simplifier et unifier le régime des valeurs mobilières

51 Donner une définition de la notion de valeurs mobilières.

52 Unifier le régime des titres donnant accès directement ou indirectement au capital.

53 Unifier le régime des titres de créance.

Aménager les procédures de délégation des émissions

Les titres donnant accès au capital

54 Améliorer le régime d'autorisation globale.

55 Prévoir un rapport annuel en assemblée générale sur l'utilisation qui a été faite des délégations données au conseil par l'assemblée et supprimer les rapports dits de carence qui font double emploi avec cette procédure.

56 Permettre les subdélégations aux directeurs généraux.

57 Modifier le régime des délégations en période d'OPA ou d'OPE.

Les titres de créance

58 Supprimer la compétence de l'assemblée générale pour autoriser les émissions d'obligations.

59 Permettre, sous certaines conditions et limites, la subdélégation à un directeur « technique », non-membre de la direction générale ou du conseil d'administration.

Assouplir les modalités techniques des émissions

Les titres de capital

Les émissions avec droit préférentiel de souscription (DPS)

60 Supprimer le délai de 6 jours entre la publication au BALO et l'ouverture de la souscription.

61 Fixer le délai d'exercice du DPS en jours calendaires pour les sociétés non cotées.

Les émissions sans DPS

62 Limiter l'augmentation de capital aux souscriptions recueillies.

63 Permettre l'émission réservée à une « catégorie de public ».

64 Légaliser la pratique dite de la « rallonge ».

65 Réduire le délai de fixation du prix d'émission.

66 Restreindre l'obligation du rapport du commissaire aux comptes aux seuls cas de suppression du DPS.

Les titres de créance

67 Supprimer le délai de deux ans avant qu'une société soit autorisée à émettre des obligations.

Assurer une meilleure protection des porteurs de valeurs mobilières composées et de certificats d'investissement

Les valeurs mobilières composées

68 Prévoir une représentation collective des titulaires de droits à l'attribution de titres de capital.

69 Prévoir un droit de communication au profit des titulaires de valeurs mobilières composées.

Les certificats d'investissement

70 Supprimer le quorum sur deuxième convocation pour les assemblées spéciales de porteurs de certificats d'investissement.

71 Permettre la suppression conjointe du DPS aux actions et aux certificats d'investissement.

72 Permettre l'exercice du droit préférentiel de souscription des porteurs de certificats d'investissement, lorsque celui-ci est maintenu, en actions plutôt qu'en certificats d'investissement.

Diverses mesures de simplification

73 Améliorer et compléter le régime du rachat par une société de ses propres actions.

74 Autoriser une société à émettre des valeurs mobilières donnant accès au capital de l'une de ses filiales.

75 Instituer un régime général des titres en déshérence.

76 Aménager le régime du compte joint de titres.

Mieux prendre en compte la réalité des entreprises

Les pactes d'actionnaires

77 Affirmer la validité des conventions de vote.

78 Renforcer l'efficacité des pactes relatifs aux cessions de droits sociaux, sous réserve de leur publicité.

Retrait et exclusion des actionnaires minoritaires

79 Étendre aux sociétés fermées les procédures de retrait des actionnaires minoritaires lorsque l'actionnaire majoritaire, ou les actionnaires majoritaires liés par une convention publiée, soit détient plus de 95% du capital, soit modifie substantiellement les statuts ou les activités de la société.

80 Étendre aux sociétés fermées contrôlées à 95% l'exclusion des minoritaires pour « justes motifs ».

Le droit des groupes

L'approbation des comptes consolidés

81 Prévoir l'approbation des comptes consolidés par l'assemblée générale la société mère.

82 Prévoir une levée réciproque du secret professionnel entre les commissaires aux comptes de la société mère et ceux des filiales.

De nouveaux régimes spécifiques aux groupes de sociétés

83 Étendre le régime des conventions réglementées aux conventions conclues entre sociétés liées en capital au-delà d'une participation de 10%.

84 Étendre aux actionnaires de la société mère. représentant au moins le dixième du capital social, la faculté de demander une expertise de minorité des filiales.

85 Prévoir un régime optionnel de contrôle renforcé pour les sociétés détenues à plus des deux tiers par un même actionnaire (libre circulation des actifs, consolidation des bénéfices, garantie des droits des créanciers et protection des minoritaires).

Promouvoir un meilleur équilibre des pouvoirs et des responsabilités au sein de l'entreprise

Améliorer les contrôles internes

Valoriser le rôle des actionnaires

Favoriser l'exercice direct par les actionnaires des pouvoirs qu'ils détiennent

86 Améliorer les conditions de fonctionnement et de vote des assemblées générales et favoriser la démocratie d'entreprise

87 Imposer la désignation d'un mandataire indépendant.

88 Restreindre les limitations statutaires à l'exercice des droits de vote.

Responsabiliser les organismes intermédiaires

89 Accorder aux associations d'actionnaires les plus représentatives les mêmes droits qu'aux associations d'investisseurs, en ce qui concerne la défense judiciaire des droits de leurs adhérents.

90 Assouplir les conditions de constitution des associations d'actionnaires et transférer leur agrément à la COB.

91 Prévoir dans la loi l'obligation d'exercice du droit de vote, conformément aux intérêts fiduciaires des porteurs de parts, tant pour les OPCVM existants que pour d'éventuels fonds de pension.

Mieux définir le rôle des commissaires aux comptes

Préciser la mission des commissaires aux comptes

92 Prévoir l'information systématique du conseil d'administration, le cas échéant par l'intermédiaire du comité d'audit, sur les investigations menées par les commissaires aux comptes.

93 Donner une base légale à l'avis du commissaire aux comptes sur la cohérence entre les informations financières de synthèse et l'activité de l'entreprise.

94 Préciser l'intervention des commissaires aux comptes au titre des conventions réglementées.

Accroître l'indépendance des commissaires aux comptes

95 Ouvrir une procédure d'avis sur tout cas d'espèce, avant l'approbation des comptes, pour les commissaires aux comptes devant le Comité d'urgence prévu au sein du Conseil National de la Comptabilité.

96 Réfléchir à l'opportunité de créer une procédure d'injonction de rétablir des comptes exacts, préalablement à l'approbation des comptes.

Rénover le droit pénal des sociétés

Dépénaliser les négligences formelles

97 Maintenir l'incrimination des seuls comportements intentionnels ou frauduleux.

98 Renvoyer pour certains comportements au droit pénal général.

99 Définir des actions civiles de substitution: injonction de faire sous astreinte, amende commerciale, nullités.

Mieux définir certaines infractions

Les célits comptables

100 Élargir aux comptes consolidés, en l'adaotant, le délit de publication ou de présentation de faux bilans.

L'abus de biens sociaux

101 Engager une réflexion globale sur le régime de la prescription en droit pénal des affaires.

102 Donner une définition plus précise de l'infraction faisant référence cumulativement l'atteinte aux intérêts patrimoniaux de la société et à la recherche d'un enrichissement personnel.

*

* *

Conclusion

103 Envisager une refonte de l'organisation des tribunaux de commerce, en vue:
- de renforcer leurs compétences tout en assurant le fonctionnement satisfaisant d'une justice proche du terrain.
- d'assurer des contacts organiques et croisés entre magistrats professionnels du siège et magistrats consulaires élus.

DIE BESCHLÜSSE DES 61. DEUTSCHEN JURISTENTAGES KARLSRUHE 1996

E. Abteilung Wirtschaftsrecht

Thema: Empfehlen sich gesetzliche Regelungen zur Einschränkung des Einflusses der Kreditinstitute auf Aktiengesellschaften?

I. Regelungsbedarf

1. Der Einfluß der Kreditinstitute auf Aktiengesellschaften beruht neben der bankgeschäftlichen Beziehung (insbes. dem Kreditgeschäft) auf den drei aktienrechtlichen Einflußfaktoren Beteiligungsbesitz, Vollmachtsstimmrecht und Aufsichtsratsmandate.
angenommen: 61:0:3

   Der Einfluß kann sich vorteilhaft wie nachteilig auswirken. Deshalb ist nicht zu empfehlen, ihn zu eliminieren oder undifferenziert zu beschränken.
angenommen: 60:3:2

2. Die Kumulierung der Einflußfaktoren gibt Anlaß zu der Frage, ob
   - aktienrechtliche
   - kapitalmarktrechtliche
   - kartellrechtliche

   Korrekturen des geltenden Rechts veranlaßt sind.
angenommen: 55:4:6

   Der Schwerpunkt der Reformüberlegungen sollte im Aktienrecht liegen. Allerdings sollte das Gesellschaftsrecht nicht mit Regelungsaufgaben der Bankenaufsicht oder der Sicherung des Wettbewerbs betrachtet werden.
angenommen: 55:4:6

3. Für verbreitete Mißstände beim Einfluß der Kreditinstitute auf Aktiengesellschaften und damit für einen breitflächigen Reformbedarf sind Anzeichen nicht ersichtlich.
angenommen: 60:9:7

4. Eine Reihe von Unternehmenskrisen und Zusammenbrüchen der jüngeren Vergangenheit legen den Schluß nahe, daß die Überwachungsfunktion des Aufsichtsrats nicht immer hinreichend wahrgenommen wird.
angenommen: 51:3:11

II. **Beteiligungsbesitz**

5. Der Beteiligungsbesitz von Kreditinstituten an Aktiengesellschaften sollte

a) über die Regelungen des KWG hinaus gesetzlich nicht beschränkt werden.
angenommen: 56:9:1

b) begrenzt werden
auf 25 %:
abgelehnt bei 3 Ja-Stimmen

auf 10 %:
abgelehnt bei 11 Ja-Stimmen

auf 5 %:
abgelehnt bei 1 Ja-Stimme

6. Soweit eine Beschränkung aus wettbewerbspolitischen Gründen veranlaßt sein sollte, bietet sich das GWB als Regelungsmaterie an (vgl. unter V).
angenommen: 67:1:9

7. Wechselseitige Beteiligungen und Ringverflechtungen, die

a) geeignet sind,
angenommen: 50:18:1

b) darauf abzielen, (Antrag: Hartenfels)
abgelehnt: 7:42:12

den Markt für Unternehmenskontrolle zu behindern, sind rechtlich zu mißbilligen. Sie sollten gegenüber dem geltenden Recht stärker beschränkt werden.
angenommen: 50:14:5

An der in der Praxis bewährten Schwelle des § 19 **Abs. 1** AktG ist festzuhalten (Antrag: Michel).
abgelehnt: 15:42:12

III. Vollmachtstimmrecht

8. Das geltende System des Vollmachtstimmrechts ist

a) für Depotbanken abzuschaffen (Antrag: Wozniewski)
abgelehnt bei 1 Ja-Stimme

b) auf die Ausübung des Stimmrechts aufgrund von Einzelvollmachten zu beschränken
abgelehnt bei 4 Ja-Stimmen

c) durch ein Modell gesetzlicher Stimmrechtsvertreter zu ersetzen.
abgelehnt (keine Ja-Stimme)

d) durch Wettbewerb unabhängiger Stimmrechtsvertreter (Aktionärsvereinigungen, unabhängiger institutioneller Investoren, Freiberufler) um die Stimmrechtsvertretung zu verbessern
abgelehnt bei 4 Ja-Stimmen

e) im Sinne eines Botenstimmrechts ohne Interessenbindung der Kreditinstitute gegenüber den Depotkunden zu modifizieren (Ausübung des Stimmrechts entsprechend den Verwaltungsvorschlägen bei fehlender Weisung).
abgelehnt bei 9 Ja-Stimmen

f) auf die Ausübung des Stimmrechts aufgrund von Einzelweisungen zu beschränken.
abgelehnt bei 13 Ja-Stimmen

g) trotz seiner grundsätzlichen Probleme mangels besserer Alternativen beizubehalten.
angenommen: 46:18:0

9. Zur Verbesserung der Transparenz im Zusammenhang mit der Ausübung des Vollmachtstimmrechts

a) sind die Abstimmungsvorschläge zu allen Beschlußvorschlägen der Tagesordnung mit einer schriftlichen Begründung zu versehen,

und zwar aa) durch die Verwaltung
angenommen: 34:24:10

bb) durch die Depotbanken
abgelehnt: 16:39:10

b) ist der Beteiligungsbesitz der Depotbanken, soweit er 5% des Grundkapitals übersteigt, offenzulegen;
angenommen: 55:1:6

c) sind personelle Verflechtungen zwischen der Depotbank und der betreffenden Aktiengesellschaft offenzulegen.
angenommen: 57:4:6

10. Kreditinstitute, die über einen Beteiligungsbesitz von mehr als

a) 5 %
abgelehnt: 16:45:2
b) 10 %
abgelehnt: 28:28:5
c) 25 %
angenommen: 39:22:3

an der Aktiengesellschaft verfügen, dürfen das Vollmachtstimmrecht in dieser Gesellschaft ohne Einzelweisung nur ausüben, wenn sie auf die Stimmrechtsausübung aus dem Beteiligungsbesitz verzichten.

11. Ein Kreditinstitut soll bei Fehlen von Einzelweisungen gehindert sein, das Vollmachtstimmrecht auszuüben, wenn

a) es um die Wahl von Organmitgliedern und Mitarbeitern von Kreditinstituten zum Aufsichtsrat geht;
angenommen: 33:31:3

b) sich das Kreditinstitut hinsichtlich eines Beschlußvorschlags in einem aktuellen Interessenkonflikt befindet.
angenommen: 54:3:11

12. Soweit Kreditinstitute nur aufgrund einer Aktionärsweisung das Vollmachtstimmrecht ausüben

dürfen, sollte Schriftform der Aktionärsweisung verlangt werden.
angenommen: 57:5:6

IV. Aufsichtsrat

13. Aufsichtsratsmitglieder von Aktiengesellschaften schulden diesen

a) ihre volle Aufmerksamkeit und den sachlich erforderlichen Zeiteinsatz

b) vollen Einsatz und die erforderliche Zeit (Antrag: Lutter)

und müssen dies bei der Übernahme von Mandaten beachten.

Abstimmung über Alternativformulierung (Antrag Lutter):
abgelehnt: 18:49:0

Abstimmung über Formulierung a)
angenommen: 66:2:1

Gesetzlicher Regelungsbedarf besteht jedoch nicht (Antrag: Kallmeyer)
angenommen: 36:22:9

14. Die Höchstzahl der Aufsichtsratsmandate - außer Konzernmandaten - sollte

a) unverändert bleiben
angenommen: 40:25:2

b) auf 5 Mandate begrenzt werden.
abgelehnt: 25:40:2

Dabei sollte der Aufsichtsratsvorsitz zählen:

aa) dreifach
abgelehnt bei 14 Ja-Stin=en

bb) doppelt,
angenommen mit 45 Ja-Stimmen

cc) einfach
abgelehnt bei 9 Ja-Stimmen

dd) Enthaltungen
2 Stimmen

Der stellvertretende Vorsitz sollte zählen:

aa) doppelt
abgelehnt bei 12 Ja-Stimmen

bb) einfach
angenommen mit 53 Ja-Stimmen

cc) Enthaltungen
2 Stimmen

Dabei sollen auch Mitgliedschaften in Beiräten oder sonstigen dem Aufsichtsrat vergleichbaren Gremien berücksichtigt werden (Antrag: Blenske).
abgelehnt: 21:39:10

15. Bei mitbestimmten Aufsichtsräten sollte die Möglichkeit geschaffen werden, abweichend § 7, Abs. 1 Ziff. 2 und 3 MitbestG durch die Satzung die Zahl der Aufsichtsratssitze auf 12 oder 16 zu beschränken.
angenommen: 57:6:5

Aufsichtsräte mit mehr als 12 Mitgliedern haben mindestens einen Personal-, einen Planungs- und einen Bilanzausschuß zu bilden; andere gesetzliche Vorschriften bleiben unberührt (Antrag: Lutter).
angenommen: 32:27:8

16. Für den Wahlvorschlag zum Aufsichtsrat sollte § 124 Abs. 3 S. 3 AktG dahin gehend ergänzt werden, daß auch die Organfunktionen (Vorstand/Aufsichtsrat) der Kandidaten bei anderen Gesellschaften angegeben werden.
angenommen: 62:1:6

17. Eine Regelung über die Unvereinbarkeit von Aufsichtsratsmandaten mit Vorstands- und Aufsichts-

ratsmandaten in konkurrierenden Unternehmen sollte gesetzlich getroffen werden.
angenommen: 35:30:3

18. Zur Verbesserung der Überwachungsfunktion des Aufsichtsrats sollte

a) § 318 Abs. 1 S. 4 HGB dahin geändert werden, daß bei Aktiengesellschaften der Prüfungsauftrag nicht vom Vorstand, sondern vom Aufsichtsrat erteilt wird;
angenommen: 61:4:4

die Erteilung von Beratungsaufträgen an den Abschlußprüfer der Zustimmung des Aufsichtsrats bedürfen (Antrag: Schüppen);
angenommen: 43:17:5

b) § 170 Abs, 3 AktG dahin geändert werden, daß der Prüfungsbericht des Abschlußprüfers allen Aufsichtsratsmitgliedern ausgehändigt wird;
angenommen: 59:1:7

c) § 171 Abs. 1 S. 2 AktG dahin geändert werden, daß der Abschlußprüfer an den Verhandlungen des Aufsichtsrats über den Jahresabschluß teilzunehmen hat;
angenommen: 65:0:2

Der Abschlußprüfer sollte verpflichtet werden, über Verlauf und Ergebnisse der Prüfung an die Mitglieder des Aufsichtsrats zu berichten (Antrag: Schüppen);
angenommen: 62:0:4

d) § 110 Abs. 3 AktG dahin geändert werden, daß die gesetzliche Mindestzahl von Sitzungen für börsennotierte Aktiengesellschaften auf 4 pro Jahr erhöht wird.
angenommen: 35:25:7

19. Der Grundsatz der höchstpersönlichen weisungsfreien Amtsausübung sollte

a) beibehalten werden.
angenommen: 62:0:4

b) gegen Umgehungen durch gesetzliche Sanktionen abgesichert werden.
abgelehnt: 16:39:10

20. a) Die Kosten für die Aufsichtsratstätigkeit (back office) dürfen nicht von der Gesellschaft getragen werden, der das Aufsichtsratsmitglied im Hauptamt angehörte
abgelehnt: 15:40:10

b) Die Aktiengesellschaft hat ihren Aufsichtsratsmitgliedern die erforderlichen sachlichen und personellen Mittel für die Erfüllung ihrer Aufgaben zur Verfügung zu stellen
(Antrag: Lutter),
angenommen: 42:13:11

21. Zur verbesserten Durchsetzung von Schadensersatzansprüchen gegen Aufsichtsratsmitglieder wegen Überwachungsmängeln

a) sollten die quantitativen Anforderungen an die Geltendmachung solcher Ansprüche (§ 147 Abs. 1 AktG) herabgesetzt werden;
angenommen: 53:7:6

b) sollte der Streitwert im Rahmen von § 147 Abs. 1 AktG begrenzt werden (Antrag: Engelke);
angenommen: 41:16:9

der Kläger sollte verpflichtet werden, für die Prozeßkosten bei Klageeinreichung angemessene Sicherheit zu leisten (Antrag: Engelke)
abgelehnt: 13:35:17

c) sollte die Aktionärsklage nach dem Vorbild des § 309 Abs. 4 AktG zugelassen werden.
angenommen: 32:29:5

sollte der Streitwert im Rahmen der Aktionärsklage begrenzt werden. (Antrag: Staubach)
angenommen: 33:23:8

22. Die steuerliche Benachteiligung der Aufsichtsratsvergütung ist zu beseitigen.
angenommen: 52:0:10

V. Sonstiges

23. a) Kreditinstituten ist eine Beteiligung an Kapitalanlagegesellschaften nicht gestattet (Antrag: Adams).
abgelehnt: 5:50:7

b) Kapitalanlagegesellschaften sollte die Stimmrechtsausübung aus fondszugehörigen Aktien auf der Hauptversammlung einer Aktiengesellschaft untersagt werden, soweit diese Gesellschaft ihrerseits an der Kapitalanlagegesellschaft beteiligt ist.
abgelehnt: 34:27:4

24. Die Regelungen über die Fusionskontrolle in § 23 Abs. 2 GWB sollten dahin geändert werden, daß

a) dem Kreditinstitut die Vollmachtsstimmen im Rahmen von § 23 Abs. 2 Nr. 2 S. 4 GWB zugerechnet werden, die es auf der letzten Hauptversammlung ohne Vorliegen von Aktionärsweisungen vertreten hat;
abgelehnt: 13:40:13

b) die Anteilsquoten von 25 und 50 % nicht nach dem nominellen, sondern nach der durchschnittlichen Hauptversammlungspräsenz der letzten drei Jahre berechnet werden.
abgelehnt: 20:35:10

Committee on Corporate Governance

Recommendations for Corporate Governance

Recommendations for sound governance, supervision and effective accountability.

28 October 1996

Secretariat Committee on Corporate Governance
c/o Beursplein 5
3012 JW Amsterdam
The Netherlands
tel. + 31 20 - 5234004
fax. + 31 20 - 5234960

Appendix 1
Summary of the recommendations of the Committee on Corporate Governance[5]

1. The Supervisory Board[6] should draw up a public profile which is periodically amended (2.2).

2. The composition of the Supervisory Board should be such that board members are able to operate independently of one another and of the Executive Board and to judge critically (2.3).

3. The annual report should contain the information on supervisory board members indicated by the Committee (2.4).

4. No more than one former executive board member of the company should occupy a seat on the Supervisory Board. Special consideration should be given to the appointment of a former chairman of the Executive Board, especially when he has been put forward as a prospective chairman of the Supervisory Board (2.5).

5. All supervisory board members who are appointed on the basis of a nomination should perform their duties without a mandate from those who nominated them and independently of subsidiary interests associated with the company (2.6).

6. The re-appointment of supervisory board members should not be automatic and will be given careful consideration (2.7).

7. Supervisory board members should resign before the end of their allotted term if a failure to complete their tasks adequately, a fundamental difference of insight, an

5 These summaries have been formulated as briefly and pithily as possible with a view to giving a practical overview. The recommendations should be read and applied within the context of the full report of the Committee.

6 The Committee's recommendations with regard to supervisory board (members) will also apply as far as possible in cases where the supervision of a (bourse-listed) company is structured along different lines.

irreconcilable conflict of interests or other circumstances so dictate (2.8).

8. A supervisory board member facing a conflict of interests must inform the chairman of the Board immediately (2.9).

9. The number of supervisory board seats at listed companies held by a single indivicual should be limited in such a way as to guarantee the satisfactory fulfilment of the allotted tasks. A company should allow employees in active service to take up supervisory posts in other companies (2.10).

10. Members of a company's Supervisory Board should not simultaneously hold a seat on the Supervisory Board of one of that company's operating companies (2.11).

11. A supervisory board member's shareholdings in the company where he has a seat on the Supervisory Board should serve as a long-term investment. The total shareholdings and options rights held jointly by the supervisory board members is published annually (2.12).

12. The remuneration of supervisory board members should not be linked to the financial results of the company concerned. Any business (commercial) links with the company should be published in the notes to the annual accounts (2.13).

13. Any appearance of a conflict of interests between the company and its supervisory board members is to be avoided (2.14).

14. The Chairman of the Supervisory Board has specific tasks which are laid down in a set of regulations (3.1).

15. The Supervisory Board should consider the appointment of a selections and appointments committee from among its members, as well as an audit committee and a remunerations committee (3.2).

16. The Board should meet according to a predetermined timetable. Individual members should be asked to explain in the event of frequent non-attendance (3.3).

17. At least once a year the Supervisory Board should discuss the composition of the Executive Board, the company's strategy and the associated risks and the results of the executive board's assessment of the company's internal system of control. This should be disclosed in the report of the Supervisory Board contained in the company's annual report (3.4).

18. At least once a year the Supervisory Board should hold a meeting from which the Executive Board is excluded to discuss the functioning of the Supervisory Board and its relationship with the Executive Board. Its discussions should further include an assessment of the Executive Board, referring also the questions of succession and salary (3.5).

19. The adoption (approval) of the annual accounts and the approval

of the policies pursued by the Executive Board and the supervision exercised by the Supervisory Board should be separate items on the agenda for the annual General Meeting of Shareholders (3.6).

20. A permanently delegated supervisory board member is considered not desirable (3.7).

21. The Supervisory Board operates under a protocol governing the relations with the Executive Baord, works council and capital investors (3.8).

22. The Executive Board should report in writing to the Supervisory Board on the corporate goals, strategy and associated risks and the mechanisms in place to manage risks of a financial nature. The main topics discussed in the report should be a permanent part of the annual accounts (4.2 and 4.3).

23. The total sum of the remunerations in the annual report should be separated into remunerations to sitting and former executives (4.4).

24. An executive board member's shareholdings in the company should serve as a long-term investment. The aggregate number of shares, depositary receipts and options held by the executive board members are published annually (4.5).

25. Any appearance of a conflict of interests between the company and its executive board members is to be avoided (4.6).

26. Based on the principle that finance and influence should be in line, companies and investors should be asked to reassess the part played by capital in their company (5.1).

27. For all companies the general meeting of shareholders should be the forum in which the Executive and Supervisory Boards report and to which they are accountable with regard to their performance (5.2).

28. The Executive Board and the Supervisory Board should have the confidence of the meeting of shareholders. This should be borne in mind when appointing board members (5.3).

29. The management of the company should assess the degree of influence exerted by investors and will report to a shareholders' metting in 1998 (5.4-5.6).

30. Requests made by the investors to place items on the Agenda of the General Meeing of Shareholders, should in principle be honoured (5.7).

31. The quality and specialisation of investment analysis in the Netherlands - particularly as regards industry sectors - should be enhanced (5.8).

32. An efficient system of proxy solicitation should be introduced (5.9).

33. Parties which have gained control over a quoted company by holding 50 percent or more of its shares must make a bid for the remainging shares and/or non-voting depositary receipts of share

within an acceptable period on realistic terms (5.10).

34. The company should explain and report on the extent of its compliance with the recommendations in its annual report (6.1).

35. The company should consider whether an accountant's investigation into the accuracy of the report is deemed necessary as regards compliance with relevant and verifiable recommendations (6.2).

36. The accountant's role within the framework of Corporate Governance is primarily to advise and to signal possible problems as regards the set-up (and functioning) of the internal control system for safeguarding the reliability of the provision of financial information. The accountant can further play a role as regards internal control systems designed to safeguard the effectiveness and efficiency of company procedures and legislative and regulatory compliance (6.3).

37. The supervisory Board or the audit committee should meet with the external accountant at least once a year (6.4).

38. Reports from rating agencies should be discussed in the Supervisory Board (6.5).

39. The Committee proposes that an organization equipped for this task be requested to monitor, evaluate and publish the implementation of and compliance with the Corporate Governance recommendations, and the deliberations within the general meeting of shareholders (7.1).

40. The results and the evaluation of this monitoring process will be of significance to the further debate on the subject of Corporate Governance in the Netherlands (7.2).

Fédérations des Entreprises de Belgique (FEB), Recommendations pour le bon fonctionnement du conseil d'administration d'une société, Bruxelles, décembre 1996

INTRODUCTION

Le conseil d'administration est un rouage majeur d'une société commerciale. Les décisions qui s'y prennent engagent souvent de manière fondamentale le devenir de la société. Par ailleurs, les administrateurs sont soumis à une responsabilité qui ne cesse de se renforcer.

Pour ces raisons, il est essentiel que le conseil d'administration fonctionne correctement ce qui implique en particulier que les administrateurs soient placés dans des conditions qui leur permettent de décider en connaissance de cause et qu'ils soient respectueux des obligations auxquelles ils souscrivent en acceptant de devenir membres du conseil d'administration.

La Feb en tant qu'organisation interprofessionnelle fédérale entend contribuer à cet objectif en formulant un certain nombre de recommandations. Ces recommandations relévent davantage de l'éthique que de la loi: elles n'appellent dès lors pas une intervention du législateur.

Pour ce faire, elle a tenu compte non seulement de la pratique de nombre de conseils d'administration mais aussi d'études publiées en Belgique et à l'étranger sur la question.

Trois limitations ont été prises en compte:

1. L'énoncé de certaines règles recommandables n'est pas exhaustif.

La Feb s'est attachée à certains aspects essentiels de la problématique tout en étant consciente que certains aspects particuliers mériteraient ultérieurement de faire également l'objet de recommandations.

2. Les recommandations sont formulées en des termes généraux.

En effet, les principes énoncés doivent permettre de rencontrer des situations variables au niveau tant de la taille des sociétés et de la configuration de leur actionnariat que des problèmes concrets qui peuvent se poser.

Il a dès lors paru préférable de rédiger ces recommandations en des termes suffisamment larges que pour couvrir ces réalités différentes.

3. Les recommandations n'entendent pas figer la situation.

La matière est évolutive. Aussi, la Feb se propose-t-elle de mettre en place un Observatoire composé de quelques dirigeants d'entreprise pour faire régulièrement le point et apprécier s'il y a lieu de proposer aux organes de décision de la Feb de compléter, d'adapter ou d'approfondir les recommandations.

La Feb en formulant ses recommandations s'adresse à toutes les sociétés, qu'elles fassent ou non appel public à l'épargne et qu'elles soient ou non cotées en bourse.

Elle exprime ainsi des exigences communes minimales qui devront le cas échéant être complétées en fonction des impératifs propres à certaines catégories de sociétés.

*

* *

1. Le conseil d'administration détient des compétences majeures pour le bon fonctionnement de la société.

En effet, outre des attributions particulières comme l'arrêt des comptes annuels, il définit la stratégie de la société, approuve les budgets d'investissement, de recherche et de développement, nomme les responsables de la gestion journalière de la société et exerce la surveillance de cette gestion.

2. Dans ses décisions, le conseil d'administration est guidé par l'intérêt de la société, celui-ci comprenant entre autres l'intérêt de l'ensemble des actionnaires.

3. Les administrateurs doivent être choisis en fonction de leur compétence propre et de leur disponibilité.

   Ils doivent consacrer à leur fonction le temps et l'attention nécessaires. Il en découle que dans certains cas, il peut être souhaitable que le nombre de mandats exercés par un même administrateur soit limité.

4. Le conseil d'administration constitue le plus souvent le reflet des rapports de force existant au niveau de l'assemblée générale.

   Des administrateurs non liés à l'actionnariat peuvent dans certains cas apporter une contribution importante aux délibérations du conseil.

5. Un fonctionnement efficace du conseil d'administration suppose dans le chef de ses membres une connaissance suffisante de l'entreprise. Il faut, dès lors, veiller à assurer une continuité dans la composition du conseil d'administration, par exemple, par un remplacement des administrateurs par roulement.

   Par ailleurs, le conseil d'administration doit bénéficier de dynamismes nouveaux. Il est, dès lors, souhaitable de fixer dans les statuts ou dans le règlement d'ordre intérieur une limite d'âge maximum pour l'octroi d'un mandat d'administrateur.

6. L'exercice du mandat d'administrateur peut être gratuit ou rémunéré. Dans le cas où le mandat est rémunéré, il doit l'être par la société. Afin qu'il soit exercé en

toute indépendance, il faut exclure qu'il soit rémunéré par un actionnaire ou un tiers autre que l'employeur de l'administrateur. Compte tenu du temps que les administrateurs doivent y consacrer, l'exercice de fonctions particulières, comme la présidence du conseil d'administration ou la participation à des comités internes peut être rétribué par le versement d'une rémunération supplémentaire.

7. Le conseil d'administration est un organe collégial.

Ceci implique que:

- l'ordre du jour des réunions parvienne à chaque administrateur en temps utile et que tout effet de surprise soit évité;

- le conseil d'administration doit en temps utile être mis en possession de toute l'information nécessaire pour délibérer en connaissance de cause.

  Cette information doit, si possible, être écrite et explicitée verbalement lors de la réunion.

- sauf exceptions légales, toutes les décisions soient prises après une délibération qui permette à chaque administrateur d'exposer de maniére circonstanciée son point de vue;

- une fois la décision prise, chaque administrateur en soit solidaire sauf s'il a expressément fait mentionner au procès-verbal de la réunion son désaccord.

8. Compte tenu de l'importance d'une délibération active préalable à la prise de décision, le conseil d'administration ne doit pas être pléthorique. Un nombre limité d'administrateurs constitue un facteur qui favorise la discussion et la collégialité.

Par ailleurs, il n'est pas souhaitable que le conseil d'administration comprenne trop de personnes ayant une fonction exécutive dans la société.

9. La fonction du Président du conseil d'administration, avec son rôle de surveillance, et la fonction de Chef de l'exécutif, avec son rôle d'exécutif, sont des fonctions différentes qui sont normalement confiées à des personnes différentes. Si le conseil désire néanmoins les confier à une seule et même personne, il devrait en tout cas en avoir débattu clairement et en avoir tiré les conséquences pour la surveillance du responsable de l'exécutif.

10. Lors de la prise de décision, l'administrateur arrête sa position en toute indépendance, au vu des informations qu'il a reçues et/ou de ce qui s'est dit lors de la délibération. Il peut ainsi justifier son vote.

11. L'administrateur peut demander que le conseil entende le commissaire, l'expert comptable et/ou toute personne qualifiée du management. Le conseil d'administration se prononce sur cette demande.

12. En cas de doute sur l'attitude à adopter et/ou sur la portée de ses engagements, l'administrateur peut demander que le conseil sollicite l'avis du conseiller juridique de la société. Le conseil d'administration se prononce sur cette demande.

13. Le conseil d'administration se réunit à une fréquence telle qu'il puisse effectivement assumer les compétences telles que définies sous le point 1.

14. Compte tenu de la responsabilité que les administrateurs peuvent encourir, les procès-verbaux reflètent fidèlement et de manière circonstanciée les décisions du conseil d'administration et les raisons essentielles de leur adoption. Tout administrateur qui le demande a le droit de faire acter ses réserves ou son opposition à la décision prise.

Les procès-verbaux sont envoyés à tous les membres du conseil d'administration. Ils doivent être soumis pour approbation au plus tard lors de la réunion suivante et après approbation signés par les administrateurs qui ont pris part à la délibération et à la décision et par ceux qui en font la demande.

15. Le conseil d'administration peut créer un comité de direction, des comités d'audit et d'autres comités internes pour mettre en oeuvre ses décisions ou pour préparer la prise de décisions, étant entendu que celle-ci appartient en dernier ressort au conseil plénier. Il arrête la mission, la composition et les modalités de fonctionnement de ces comités.

16. L'administrateur respecte la confidentialité de l'information qu'il reçoit et des délibérations.

    En tout état de cause, il ne peut utiliser cette information que dans l'intérêt de la société, ce qui peut impliquer qu'il n'en fasse pas état vis à vis des actionnaires ou de tiers.

    La nature de l'information à donner à propos des décisions du conseil d'administration et ses destinataires est décidée, en-dehors de ce qui est légalement ou réglementairement obligatoire, par le conseil d'administration ou les personnes déléguées à cet effet.

17. Le conseil d'administration veille à ce que le comportement des collaborateurs de la société soit conforme à la loi, à la morale des affaires et, en particulier, à l'éventuel code éthique propre à l'entreprise.